The English of Quebec

From Majority to Minority Status

Collection «Identité et changements culturels» no 2

THE ENGLISH OF QUEBEC

FROM MAJORITY TO MINORITY STATUS

Gary Caldwell

Eric Waddell

1982

INSTITUT QUÉBÉCOIS DE
RECHERCHE SUR LA CULTURE

ISBN 2-89224-019-0
ISSN 0714-5608
Dépôt légal — Bibliothèque nationale
du Québec

4ᵉ trimestre 1982

Institut québécois de recherche sur la culture,
93, rue Saint-Pierre,
Québec, G1K 4A3

Gary Caldwell is a researcher at the Institut québécois de recherche sur la culture (IQRC) and Eric Waddell is an associate professor of geography at Laval University. Both are members of Anglo Quebec En Mutation (AQEM).

The maps and diagrams in this volume were prepared by Isabelle DIAZ, Andrée G.-LAVOIE and Serge DUCHESNEAU, under the direction of Louise MARCOTTE, of the Laboratoire de cartographie, Département de géographie, Université Laval. Clément NOLETTE of the Centre de traitement de l'information constructed the cartograms using the computer programme ANAM that he developed for this purpose.

Table of contents

Preface 11

Introduction — The Editors
Taking Stock and Confronting the Future 15

Part I — The Background to English Quebec 25

    Eric Waddell
    Place and People 27

    Gary Caldwell
    People and Society 57

    Robert Sweeny
    A Brief Sketch of the Economic History of English Quebec 73

    Alan W. Jones
    Education for English-Speaking People until 1964 91

Part II — Consciousness of self, other, and of Quebec 103

    Michael Stein
    Changing Anglo-Quebecer Self Counciousness 107

    Edouard Cloutier
    What's in a Name? Problems of Group Identity in Quebec 127

    Sheila McLeod Arnopoulos
    Anglophones Who Are Integrating Into Quebec Society 143

Part III — The Many Faces of English Quebec 155

    David Rome
    Jews in Anglophone Quebec 159

    Carla Lipsig-Mummé
    The English Working Class of Quebec: Fragmentation and Silence 177

Stuart Richards
Development Plans, Salt Mines and the English Community
of Grosse Isle, Magdalen Islands 189

Part IV — Institutional Experiences and Crises 205

Nathan H. Mair
The Protestant Churches 211

David Allnut
The Quebec Public Service 225

Eric Kierans, Irving Brecher and Thomas Naylor
The «Sun Life» Issue 237

Part V — The Educational Establishment 253

Wallace Lambert and Richard G. Tucker
Graduates of Early French Immersion 259

Lise Bissonnette
School Restructuration on the Island of Montreal: A Missed
Opportunity for the Anglophones 279

Jean-Louis Roy
Quebec's English Universities Revisited 293

Part VI — The Media 303

David Waters
The English Media and the New Quebec 307

Arthur Siegel
The Quebec Media and Canadian Unity 325

David Thomas
The Anglo Press in the Seventies: Conspiracy or Just Plain
Incompetence? 347

Part VII — The Political Realm 357

John D. Jackson
The Language Question in Quebec: On Collective and Individual
Rights 363

William Tetley
The English and Language Legislation: A Personal History 379

Henry Milner
The Anglophone Left in Quebec and National Self-Determination 399

Conclusion — The Editors
Looking to the Future 415

Bibliography. 451

Preface

The gestation of this volume was particularly difficult, even painful: the kind of experience one would never want to undertake again. Conception took place in the minds of AQEM (Anglo Quebec En Mutation) committee members in 1978. By the fall of 1979, the texts were written and the manuscripts submitted to the Carleton Library which had indicated interest in the project. By the spring of 1980 — after a number of revisions and prunings — the editorial board of the Carleton Library had decided to proceed with publication, only to have its decision nullified by Gage. The latter had just acquired MacMillan, the company that had previously published and distributed the Carleton Library.

Subsequent to this miscarriage, in itself symptomatic of publishing in Canada, the manuscript lay dormant while the fall of 1980 and the spring 1981 referendum and election passed into history. However, in the fall of 1981, the Institut québécois de recherche sur la culture (IQRC), to which one of the editors is attached, expressed interest in publishing the manuscript, and we, the editors, proceeded to consult our very patient contributors as to the pertinence of publishing articles originally drafted in 1979.

We, ourselves were of the conviction that publication of updated articles was worthwhile, and our reasons were threefold. Firstly, the issues raised by our authors are still very much with us, witness the debate on the proposed reform of the educational system. Secondly, the Referendum settled very little: it did not mark the end of one era and usher in another at least as far as the fate of English- speaking Quebec is concerned. Finally, a record of the state of English-speaking Quebec in the post-war period is an essential condition of the emergence of an historical consciousness in English Quebec — too many times the same issues have been taken up in an historical vacuum, and the texts in our collection are a substantial contribution to this record. As it happened, our contributors agreed with us, and moreover, they agreed (with one justifiable exception) to up-date their contributions in the light of what had transpired between 1979 and 1981.

At this point, we should add that all concerned are particularly gratified that the texts, given the nature of the subject matter, are being published in English and in French by the IQRC. Indeed, the resolve of the editors to make the texts written in English available in English to English-speaking Quebecers, as opposed to first bringing them out in French, finds itself accomplished in the simultaneous appearance of the English and French versions. Yet, the will to do so is one thing and the capacity to see it through is another: the production of generaly more than adequate French translations (two contributions were written in French) is the outcome of the remarkable job done by Francine Paradis and her able team. The IQRC's policy of publishing, in the language of the population concerned, studies which have as their object segments of the Quebec population whose mother tongue is not French is to be applauded.

We pass now to more technical considerations. References to items which are specific to one article appear with full bibliographical information in footnotes;

references of more general interest are listed in abbreviated form in footnotes, with the complete citations given in a general bibliography at the end of the volume. There are, however, amongst the references a certain number that are to unpublished texts, notably those written for our collection and subsequently dropped owing to persistent and irresistible pressure to reduce the length of the manuscript. Such references can be traced either through the authors of the chapters in question, or if need be, through the editors via the IQRC.

As the reader initiated to the trials and complexities of publishing will know, dealing with twenty-five authors, arranging for translation, imposing uniform spelling and stylistic convention, proof-reading, etc. is a herculean task beyond the capacity of one, even two, editors. In our case, we were blessed with the efficient and rigorous collaboration of two treasured colleagues: Paule Obermeir who served as production co-ordinator with a critical eye, and Jocelyne Mullin who did the mechanical work of typing, photocopying, mailing, etc.; in fact they both were present over the entire four-year protracted gestation period.

Finally, we also wish to thank the Principal and Vice- Principal Administration of Bishop's University who made available office-space and other facilities of University during much of the time work on this volume was proceeding.

Introduction

TAKING STOCK AND CONFRONTING THE FUTURE

The editors

Until recently, the concept of «English Quebecer» scarcely existed in the consciousness of anyone in this country. One was either English or French Canadian (or, more realistically, Canadian or French Canadian), a harsh duality that left no basis for legitimizing the particular status and identity of those English speakers that happened to live among the French in the province of Quebec. Indeed, such recognition was scarcely necessary for, in the eyes of the English-Canadian majority, the terms alluded to two nations defined strictly in terms of language: the territory of one spanning the whole of Canada and the presence of the other being tolerated in part of the country. It was only with the demise in the sixties and seventies of the term «French Canadian», and its replacement by «Québécois» as the dominant expression of collective identity, that the problem of Anglo-Quebecer identity was posed.

By redefining their identity to reflect a demographic and geopolitical consolidation within Quebec, the French had conferred for the first time an unequivocal minority status on their English *concitoyens*. At the same time, the English, in continuing to characterize themselves as «English Canadians», found themselves deprived of a culturally prescribed strategy to facilitate their political and social insertion in the new Quebec.

Given the circumstances, for them the choices were clear: they could either actively contest francophone affirmation of their national identity or come to terms with it. The former meant an essentially reactionary stance acceptable only to those die-hard anglophones opposed to any modification of French-English relations within Quebec or elsewhere in Canada. The latter meant either leaving Quebec (handing over the territory by default to the majority) or reformulating one's presence within it. All three courses of action are evident in contemporary English Quebec, but it is the last which is the most uncertain and hazardous because it involves putting the collective ethnic identity up for scrutiny. It involves seeking answers to a multitude of questions: whether one is an English Canadian, English Quebecer, or a *Québécois*; whether it is possible to be all three at the same time; what role anglophones can reasonably expect to assume in the new Quebec; whether English Quebec can survive and come to terms with the change in political equilibrium between Quebec and the rest of Canada; what form this survival is likely to take, etc. Significantly, these questions, and the many others that they invoke, are novel ones, and no ready-made answers to them are forthcoming, this in spite of twenty years of modernization and nationalist fervour in Quebec plus almost six years of Parti Québécois rule.

The above are some of the preoccupations that inspire this book — a concern to undertake a fundamental stock-taking with respect to the socio-cultural identity and political allegiance of Anglo-Quebecers in the hope of thereby facilitating their reinsertion into the continuing history of the province. For a multitude of reasons, the task is no easy one. Apart from the constantly changing larger political reality, English Quebec, even in 1982, is still largely lacking the internal resources to facilitate the exercise. Certainly, in Alliance Quebec, it now possesses a province-wide umbrella organization that is handsomely funded by the Federal government and that is devoted to the defence of the minority group interests. However, the alliance is, as yet, a fragile one that scarcely conceals the real divisions between those that accept many of the recent transformations in Quebec and search for accommodation with the francophone majority, and those desiring confrontation with a view to returning to the *statu quo ante*. Certainly, English Quebec possesses large and powerful educational institutions, but those institutions are staffed to a very large extent by outsiders and by individuals who espouse a continental if not indeed a universalistic scholarly tradition. In consequence, there is no real tradition of study of English Quebec, little academic or analytical material on it and no intelligentsia formed by it. Certainly, there are a few theses, articles and monographs[1] Sellar's classic, *The Tragedy of Quebec* and, more recently, Clift and McLeod-Arnopoulos, *The English Fact in Quebec*, but there exists no seminal work. Admittedly Anglo-Quebecers are now the focus of considerable attention, be it via investigative reporting in *The Gazette* or the efforts of the ill-fated Centre for English Quebec Studies at Concordia University «dedicated to giving back to the population the place that is due to it in history». But the real impact and significance of these innovations remain to be seen. Meanwhile, basic questions are left unresolved. Do the English constitute a community, or are they simply an aggregate of disparate communities, a population that shares little beyond a common language? Are they to be found in all levels of Quebec society? Do they all live west of St. Lawrence and north of Sherbrooke streets on the island of Montreal, or are English to be found throughout the province? Is the population a «rooted» one, with a strong sense of place, or footloose and with little attachment to Quebec?

The very fact that such questions are currently being raised and, in some cases, left unanswered is indicative both of a lack of information necessary for answering them and the apparent absence of an indigenous intelligentsia interested in these issues and committed to the idea of a Quebec *anglophonie* that is an integral part of, and hence helps define, the larger society.[2] It is this intellectual void which, without a doubt, explains the fragility of the collective memory of English Quebec and its inability to generate a serious and sustained debate over matters that affect it. This malaise was most noticeable in its inconsistent, ill-prepared and ill-informed opposition and reaction to successive language legislation (Laws 63, 22 and 101), something that is searingly revealed in Tetley's paper in this collection. Tetley has, of course, a strong Quebec and Canadian historical consciousness, whence his personal trauma as a politician «on the front line» prior to the demise of Bourassa's Liberal government. It is this intellectual void which also explains the essentially *reactive* nature of anglophone initiative and response to events of the past decade or so. Without a sense of itself and of its history Quebec *anglophonie* lacks a vision of the future and is consequently chronically incapable — although one must be careful not to preclude future developments — of helping create and define that future. A notable instance of this is to be found in Bissonnette's description of the Montreal Island School Council. The Montreal English educational establishment is now obliged to accept, from a position of weakness and with a sense of defeat, what it might before have conceded with generosity from a position of strength in the interest of the larger society. Little wonder, then, that Albert Brie (*Le Devoir*, June 4, 1979) could make the quip «what the anglophones of Quebec are unaware of is not so much what is going on as what is beyond them.»

Certainly, public debate on issues that directly concern anglophones is on the increase, facilitated by the birth of a variety of pressure groups — Positive Action, Participation Quebec, The Quebec Council of Minorities. . . — that have lately merged to form Alliance Quebec. There is even a vocal and militant air about much of the debate, and yet neither time nor the re-election of the Parti Québécois in 1981 have modified what remain essentially reactive strategies. Beneath the political posturing there remains the widespread conviction that, in the not too distant future, there will be a return to «free choice» and a bilingual Quebec. In this respect, for us, the editors, little has changed since 1978 when the collection of essays was first conceived. Although the Referendum may have come and gone, we remain convinced of the need for a deep-rooted and radical reflection on the place of the English in Quebec that will go beyond criticisms of and preoccupations with the larger society and with the government. Such is the spirit in which this book was prepared. Although making no claim to representativity, it is sincerely hoped that the various contributions will furnish some of the bearings and also some of the instruments for the reformulation of collective identity and aspirations. At the same time, the book provides a vehicle for a number of anglophones who, at different levels and in different ways, have played important roles in Quebec over the past decade or so. Yet, these authors distinguish themselves from a certain political leadership in that being less embroiled in the present, they have a certain temporal perspective on the recent history of the province. As such, they are, perhaps, well placed to challenge some of the myth-makers and counsel a population that still has a sense of being intellectually and politically decapitated.

Significantly, it is a sense of history that provides a common thread to the writing of most of these contributors. Contributors like Rome, Tetley and Waters are in no sense disembodied from the past; they evoke a sense of participating in history, and the future they envisage are defined in terms of the past. Like the other contributors to this book, they provide an authentic statement of contemporary English Quebec in the sense that they are statements made by individuals who have worked for many years to articulate some kind of relationship between their own language group and the larger Quebec society. Indeed, as participants in that larger society, they have sought to be at once anglophones and Quebecers. The book that results is far from being a clinical statement by disembodied intellectuals.

A serious attempt has been made in the following pages to cover all domains of anglophone interest; notably education, politics, religion and all matters pertaining to ethnic identity and relations. In only one crucial area have we failed to solicit response to our invitation to chart the spirit and experiences of the language group, and that is in the realm of business. Whereas the response was enthusiastic from other quarters, here our repeated requests only met with silence, procrastination and refusal. Although initially perplexed and frustrated by the situation, we have come, inexorably, to the conclusion that the silence accurately reflects the condition of this part of Quebec *anglophonie*. It is just possible that the world of anglophone business and finance distinguishes itself by its singular failure to reflect on and accommodate to the new Quebec of the 1960's and 1970's, hence its spokesmen have nothing to say to us. Reaction, confrontation and reference to a *statu quo ante* remain the continuing rules of the game for them. Certainly, we have little basis for disproving this hypothesis. [3]

If the collection seeks to offer a comprehensive image of contemporary English Quebec, that image is in no sense monolithic. A diversity of perspectives and visions are offered with a view to provoking *among* anglophones a debate in which the several parameters are defined *by* anglophones. We are concerned to adventure further along this trajectory, being painfully aware of the fact that Quebec *anglophonie* lacks the kind of radical tradition necessary to promote debate, controversy and reflection. Yet, to discuss such matters as collective identity and aspirations in the public arena, to have recourse to the results of academic research in the process, and even influence the course of such research, is to bear witness to a particular intellectual tradition that has for long prevailed in the larger Quebec society. It is a tradition that gave birth to a newspaper like *Le Devoir*, that fills its centre pages with «libres opinions», «documents» and «commentaires», that accounts for the prestige of the accomplished journalist and scholar in the larger society, and that explains the great public interest in sophisticated academic research and hard data dealing with demographic and linguistic issues, income differentials and so forth. Such a tradition is largely alien to English Canada as a whole, this in spite of the fact that Lester Pearson evoked something of it. *Canadian Forum* has always struggled to survive, George Grant's *Lament for a Nation*, in spite of its searing message, has always remained irrelevant to the public realm, and such far-ranging discussions as Herschel Hardin's *A Nation Unaware* and W.L. Morton's *The Canadian Identity* have remained unnoticed and unheeded. [4]

Over the past decade or so, English Quebecers have been slowly learning to share this French-Canadian intellectual tradition. This collection is but one manifestation of a new practice, and one that is both necessary for the survival of English Quebec and a reflection of its growing distinctiveness vis-à-vis the rest of English Canada. English Canadians, in reading what follows, must grasp this particularity in order to appreciate the content and «thrust» of the book. Hopefully, also, they will learn something from it.

In our concern to offer a diversity of authentic statements that may help define a healthy English Quebec of the future, and thereby a healthier Quebec society, we are also guided by the motivations of the larger group that initiated the original project which has been brought to completion by the Institut québécois de recherche sur la culture. While Caldwell and Waddell are the editors, the book has been very much an AQEM as well as an IQRC enterprise, and several members of the AQEM group have contributed chapters to the collection. Anglo Quebec En Mutation (whose research and animation activities were partially funded by the Secretary of State) is essentially a citizens' group or «think-tank» of a dozen individuals[5] from different parts of Quebec and from different backgrounds. They started meeting in mid-1976 out of a shared conviction that if English Quebec was to escape from its present impasse, it had to start asking questions of itself, engage in a process of self-criticism and self-discovery and begin to admit that, perhaps, some of its problems were of its own fabrication. One can play a creative role in the larger society, rather than being constantly threatened by, and threatening for, that same society once one knows oneself. Although of a diversity of political affiliations, members of AQEM share a participatory and integrationist philosophy born of various educative and social-action experiences (the Eastern Townships Social Action Groupe ETSAG, the Better French Committee of the PSBGM, etc.). In order to articulate such a position, AQEM generated information on English Quebec and then used that information for animation purposes. The first venture in this sense lay in a longitudinal three-stage study of the out-migration of young anglophones, the results of which were presented to representatives of the English Quebec educational establishment and to parents' committees and to which considerable attention was given in the media. The present collection, published by the IQRC, is the outcome of a much more considerable effort in the same direction.

That Caldwell and Waddell should be editors of the collection is no simple accident either. Apart from having both been involved directly or indirectly in the social animation field (Caldwell as one of the initiators of ETSAG, Waddell as an evaluator of certain aid projects of the Secretary of State Department's Programme for Official Language Minority Groups), both became involved in undertaking or directing research on English Quebec in the early seventies when the anglophone academic establishment considered such work to be trivial and inconsequential. More recently, Caldwell was named to an ad hoc committee formed to investigate and advise the Minister of Education of Quebec as to the future of the English college-level education in the Ottawa Valley, and Waddell was appointed to an advisory committee of the Department of the Secretary of State of Canada concerned to assist in reformulating its policy of aid to official language minority groups. Both editors are, finally, like a number of contributors to the collection and along with many of the «marginal anglophones» described by McLeod Arnopoulos, new to Quebec — 1963 and 1961 respectively — and therefore, unburdened by the historic English-French dialectic (although very much aware of it). At the same time, it must be admitted that we are both motivated by a certain vision of Quebec society which, for Caldwell, is perceived as the last hope for an independent Canada — a Canada different and separated from the United States — and which, for Waddell, has a prospect for a collectivity of human dimensions such as is envisaged by Denis de Rougemont and Claude Julien in Europe and a multitude of other proponents of the new regionalisms.

To admit to all these things is also to admit, of course, to the possibility that critics of this collection will cry «foul», accusing us of failing to provide a «representative» picture of contemporary Quebec *anglophonie*. Our answer to this is that all those who have contributed *think* about English Quebec, and English Quebec as an integral part of the larger Quebec. They know, freely admit to, and respect the differences of perspective and opinion among themselves. The book offers no «blueprint for the future», no simple recipes or strategies, but it does hopefully provide some guidelines, offer a *point de repère* that will help stimulate a larger debate, encourage those who disagree with the analysis to respond, help us address the future with enthusiasm and responsibility, help take us forward rather than back to some jingoistic past, in order that the new Quebec will be created, at least in part, in our image and hence, be home for future generations of English. We firmly believe that in the pages that follow, the reader will find abundant evidence that all this is possible. He will find moving testimonials from individuals and groups who have continued, often terribly alone, to work for a better Quebec society; he will discover aspects of English Quebec that he never knew existed and that no one spoke of or for; he will acquire a better understanding of his language group. Above all, he will, we hope, learn of the ultimate folly of viewing the world in terms of English and French, of «us» and «them».

NOTES

(1) See, for instance, G. Caldwell, 1974, S. Schachter 1982, R. Clarke 1972, A. Ross 1943 and 1954, and M. Stein 1977.

(2) The situation is, of course, complicated by the fact that the larger society remains equivocal as to the place it wishes to accord to the minority. This is most striking in the case of language legislation which renders largely invisible an English presence in Quebec in the sense that French is the only *langue d'affichage* permitted by law for business and commercial purposes and for public institutions. Quite evidently both language groups have a crucial role to play in determining the nature and degree of English integration into Quebec society.

(3) In this regard, one need only point to the continued and silent shift of head offices out of Quebec, as exemplified by the Prudential Insurance Company, or the continued indifference of such a major enterprise as Pratt and Whitney to the French language. On the other hand, there are signs of accomodation, exemplified by Steinberg and by the converging interests of the Montreal Board of Trade and the Chambre de Commerce de Montréal. Perhaps, in the business world, it is simply a question of being more cautious in commenting on one's actions!

(4) While in Western Canada in 1980, Caldwell made a point of visiting Morton to discuss the second edition of *The Canadian Identity* with its author. The latter was delighted, Caldwell being the very first person to seek such an opportunity in the eight years since the augmented second edition of his book had been published. Morton died shortly after.

(5) Present membership of AQEM includes, in addition to Caldwell and Waddell: Alan Jones, John Jackson, Paule Obermeir, David Rome, Anne Usher and Aline Visser. Alan Hatton, Anne MacLaren, Stuart Richards and Andrée Turgeon are former members.

(6) See G. Caldwell 1978, 1980, *Out-Migration...*, and 1981.

Part I

THE BACKGROUND TO ENGLISH QUEBEC

Place and People

Eric Waddell

ERIC WADDELL teaches cultural geography at Laval University in Quebec City. Prior to taking up this appointment in 1978, he taught for ten years at McGill University. A founding member of AQEM (Anglo Quebec En Mutation), he has a long-standing interest in French-English relations within Quebec and Canada, in French America, and in ethnicity and regional movements in general. He has, on occasion, acted as a consultant to the Official Language Minority Groups Programme of the Department of the Secretary of State in Ottawa.

It's only a popular song...

> Ça prend des racines
> Pour être moins flottant dans ses bottines
> Ça prend des amers
> Quand tu navigues plus su' l' sein d' ta mère
> Ça prend des points d' repère
> Pour pas faire les mêmes erreurs que son père...

Such is the theme of a recent popular song written and sung by the *chansonnier* Claude Gauthier. It is addressed to «my friend», that friend evidently being his Anglo-Quebecer compatriot. It is a piece of advice, well meaning and, as we shall see, well placed. It comes, not surprisingly, from one of the artisans of the Quiet Revolution in the domaine of the *chanson québécoise*. Gauthier's creativity was in fact heralded by no other than Hugh MacClellan who wrote an appreciation on the sleeve of his first L.P. back in the early 1960's.

Within the space of two short decades, however, there has been a remarkable shift in emphasis, initiative and authority — from an English-Canadian cultural elite that was firmly rooted in Quebec and that heralded the promise of the poets and song-writers of French Canada, to these very same craftsmen of language and music who counsel, authoritatively, as *Québécois* their anglophone *concitoyens* on how to survive and flourish in a province that has been profoundly transformed. And this same anglophone intelligentsia, no longer assured spokesmen for all Quebecers, grasps and shudders at the advice, appearing for all the world as if it lacks a yardstick to judge and measure against it.

Unbeknown to that elite, artistic creativity in French Quebec had, by the early 1960s, ceased to be something strictly to be admired, an end in itself, and had become an instrument of social change and of the creation of a modern collective consciousness. No such transformation has occurred in English Quebec. Hence the emergence of a situation today where «Léon Dion counsels Anglo-Quebecers on their future, Positive Action and the anglophone press responds in angry disarray, and Lise Bissonnette settles the question in a *Le Devoir* editorial».[1] The scene has an almost apocalyptic character about it: «Humpty-Dumpty fell off the wall, and all the king's horses and all the king's men couldn't put humpty-dumpty together again»...

«Comment ça se fait que nous sommes rendus là?»

Until a few years ago (dare I say November 15, 1976?) the English of Quebec scarcely existed as a separate reality. Although statistically speaking a minority, their leaders played a decisive role in the exercise of power in the province, while the group as a whole, as an extension of English Canada, was omnipresent. The ethnic boundaries of a French Quebec were poorly defined and only partially respected, hence the ability of the English to assume the role of a *minorité-majoritaire*.

This role was, of course, consistent with the logic and geopolitics of a British North America. Its roots were profound. In the circumstances, it was the others, the French, that existed — to be circumscribed, analyzed and objectified. During the nineteenth and early twentieth centuries, the *habitant*, and before him the *voyageur* and the *coureur de bois* intrigued and amused the English aristocracy. Notman's clients masqueraded in his clothes, British officers stationed in Lower Canada eagerly bought Krieghoff's joyous renditions of peasant life, and the «franglais» poems of William Henry Drummond were often recited at concerts and after-dinner speeches in the private clubs of Montreal. For sure, it was a fascination tinged with paternalism, of an urban, mercantile class towards its rural peasantry, of colonials towards the local inhabitants, of *seigneurs* towards *habitants*. Thus, the Countess of Aberdeen, in relating her travels through Canada in the late nineteenth century, describes the French Canadians as «... a thrifty, contented, law-abiding, religious people... the same simple Norman and Breton peasants who came out some hundreds of years ago» and she was struck by their «...universal civility and gentle courtesy»![2]

Nevertheless, Drummond's poems sold by the tens of thousands. Louis Fréchette called him «the pathfinder of a new land of song», and this romantic view of French Canada was slowly transformed into a more enduring scholarly interest. McCord painstakingly gathered the art and artefacts of a people, ultimately endowing the collectivity with perhaps the most vivid and dramatic portrayal of social life of anywhere in Canada. American sociologists, working out of Chicago, undertook a series of community studies in Quebec that led to the formulation of a major school of thought.[3] One of the scholars[4] came to McGill and initiated a long tradition of empirical sociological research in Quebec.

Notably, the English were absent, or appeared only tangentially, in most of these studies. The overriding concern was to produce a profile, through ethnographic research, of what essentially appeared to be an idiosyncratic North American minority, the French Canadians, a Catholic peasantry caught in the vortex of the twentieth century.

While the first half of the century saw a flourishing of scholarly interest in French Canada among Anglo-Americans, it also witnessed a souring of the romantic vision. «Suddenly» transformed from a proud rural peasantry to an oppressed urban proletariat in the «shops» of Montreal, the company towns of the province, and the cotton mills of New England, the elite came to acquire a marked distaste for the mass — a mass that spoke badly, ate poorly, drank excessively, was not particularly industrious, and that clung to a social order that was scarcely compatible with the interests and aspirations of an aggressive North American form of capitalism.

One eventually influenced the other, and the decline of a romantic appeal for French Canada led to an erosion of scholarly work within Quebec by anglophones. By the early 1970s we had quite clearly come to the end of an epoch: the Drummond vogue was long dead, the McCord Museum only open four days a week and operating on a shoe-string budget, and the local research conducted by and from anglophone institutions was, according to the parameters of international social science, mostly considered to be insignificant.[5]

There was, of course, a very considerable scholarly and intellectual activity *within* the anglophone community from the early nineteenth century on. Witness the creation of schools, universities, museums, libraries, literary and historical societies, orchestras, opera houses and the like. But the preoccupations were invariably continental and international (i.e., non-local), and the gestures of the intellectual and cultural elite were above all the reflection of a powerful and benevolent leadership of a dominant language group towards the citizenry at large. If one were so evidently successful in the accumulation of wealth and the exercise of power, what need had one to know or to ask questions of oneself?

All the while the francophone intelligentsia was asking questions of its own collectivity, initially motivated by a concern for group survival and subsequently by a desire to affirm identity and political strength as a majority within the province of Quebec.

The emergence of a powerful secular state in the 1960s, managed by a massively francophone bureaucracy, and the acquisition of political power by the nationalists in 1976 modified in a fundamental way the forces in play. Francophones, with a clear understanding of their own collectivity, and no longer preoccupied with issues of survival, now started increasingly to address themselves to the question of *their* minorities and the incorporation of those minorities within a francophone state. The English, of course, posed particular problems as a *minorité historique* and a minority until very recently *majoritaire*, hence a sudden and real interest in them manifested by the majority: an adult education course entitled «Le Québec anglophone» at the Université de Montréal, detailed consideration in the government's *Livre Blanc sur la Culture* (Ministre d'État au Développement culturel, 1978), and a multitude of conferences, newspaper articles and editorials. Yet, many of these are little more than programmatic statements.

In this shift in the focus of power, the English themselves were caught unaware and unprepared. Faced with an urgent need to know themselves in order to define their collective future as a *minority within Quebec* and no longer (or not simply) a *majority within Canada*, they found themselves without the tools to undertake the task. Hence the gravity of the present crisis. Many urgent and important decisions must be made in the future about, and above all by, the English, but these very same people are confronted by an intellectual void and are at a loss to know who they may be and what they represent. Indeed, the birth of a variety of organizations and movements representing anglophone interests, such as the Council of Quebec Minorities (subsequently transformed into Alliance Quebec), Quebec for All, etc. only serves to highlight the fundamental malaise.

Some basic facts... and sentiments

Conventional wisdom has it that anglophones constitute 20 per cent of the population of Quebec (over one million people), livre principally in the Montreal area (notably west of St. Lawrence Boulevard and north of Sherbrooke Street, reaching out to Ontario at Ste-Anne de Bellevue and Hudson), are rich, unilingual, Protestant, of British ethnic origin, and extremely well-endowed in terms of institutions and media. In other words, the group is numerically and economically powerful, and its strength is further ensured by a tight internal cohesion and geographical localisation.

As with all caricatures, there is a certain basic truth in the image. However, the impression it gives of a highly organized, articulate and ethnically homogeneous *community* is open to serious question. Furthermore, the image fails to take into account the constant mutations that have characterized the language group since the Second World War, mutations that are so profound in nature as to render Quebec «anglophonie» increasingly unrecognizable to itself.

In 1971, some 19,3 per cent of the population of Quebec, or 1 160 515 individuals, claimed a mother tongue other than French. However, only 13,1 per cent, or 789 185, recognized English to be that language. The «others», mostly first or second generation immigrants of European origin, are frequently «claimed» by anglophones as belonging to an enlarged minority community on the grounds that their children typically frequent English schools, that they place an enormous premium on the acquisition of the English language and are hence constantly exposed to anglophone media and moulded by anglophone opinion. Nevertheless such a claim is essentially ideological in nature, is disputed by the francophone majority, disregards the kinds of accommodation allophones seek to make to the Quebec situation and, above all, does not take into account the relative recency of this shift in allegiance for a large segment of the «other» group. For all these reasons, attention here is restricted to the English mother-tongue population.

The vast majority of anglophones, 595 395 or 75 per cent, live in the Montreal metropolitan area, the balance being divided more or less equally between: 1) other urban centres, defined here as municipalities with a total population in excess of 7 500, and 2) rural Quebec, including all the population living outside these municipalities (see Figures I and II). In other words, Quebec's anglophones are massively metropolitan, the percentage rising to over 80 per cent if one extends the definition to include the whole area lying within the sphere of influence of Montreal (defined in terms of employment, services, media etc.), this extending from Rigaud in the west to Rawdon in the north, Cowansville in the east, and

Huntingdon in the south. Within the metropolitan area, anglophones are also proportionally strong, constituting 21,7 per cent of the total population. Elsewhere, they are few in number, scattered and proportionally weak. Thus, what are increasingly referred to as the «off-island English» constitute, on average, only 5,4 per cent of the population of the smaller urban centres and 6,5 per cent of the rural population.

A closer examination of the distribution pattern of this non-metropolitan population in 1971 reveals a certain number of distinctive features (see figures III and IV). Urban anglophones are proportionally well represented in areas historically settled by them, notably the Eastern Townships (Sherbrooke, Magog, Cowansville and Granby), the Gaspé (Gaspé Town) and Argenteuil County (Lachute), and in single-industry towns that more or less owe their existence to large multinational corporations such as CIL, Noranda Mines and the various pulp and paper and textile companies operating in the province (Baie Comeau, Chibougamau, Val d'Or, Rouyn and Valleyfield). Both considerations contribute to the strength of the anglophone population in some centres (notably Lachute), while a significant federal presence, in terms of the Civil Service and Armed Forces, accounts for sizeable anglophone minorities elsewhere (Hull and St-Jean). In absolute terms, the second largest concentration of anglophones outside Montreal is to be found in the Quebec City metropolitan area (18 035) but here they are proportionally insignificant (3,5% of the total population), dispersed geographically and not associated with any particular large institutions. Hence, they are more or less invisible, a feature which extends to their behaviour as an ethnic group.

With respect to the «rural» population, seven major concentrations are to be identified, separated by considerable areas where anglophones are either more or less absent or not proportionally significant enough to contribute in an active way to defining the personality of the region (see Figures IV, V and VI). These concentrations are, in order of importance, the Eastern Townships (defined as Missisquoi, Brome, Shefford, Richmond, Sherbrooke, Stanstead and Compton counties) — 31 815 anglophones; Ottawa Valley-Temiscamingue (Temiscamingue, Pontiac, Gatineau, Hull and Papineau counties) — 20 175; Argenteuil-Terrebonne (Argenteuil, Terrebonne and Vaudreuil) — 10 425; The Chateauguay Valley (Huntingdon, Chateauguay and St-Jean) 10 090; the Lower North Shore (Saguenay) — 6 285; and the Québec City Laurentians (Québec) — 280.

In only two counties do anglophones actually constitute a majority, and a fragile one at that, namely Pontiac (57 per cent) and Brome (50,2 per cent). However, in all seven areas the proportion exceeds 10 per cent of the total population, rising to 20,9 per cent in the case of the Eastern Townships, 21,5 per cent in the Ottawa Valley-Temiscamingue, and 21,7 per cent in the Chateauguay Valley.

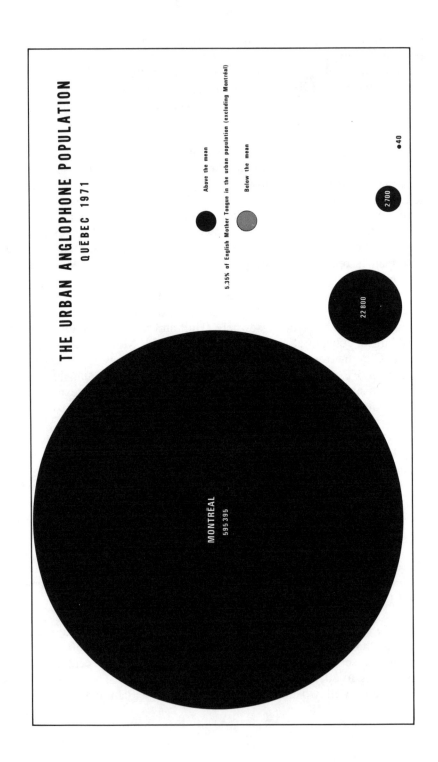

THE URBAN ANGLOPHONE POPULATION

QUÉBEC 1971

Above the mean

5.35% of English Mother Tongue in the urban population (excluding Montréal)

Below the mean

• 40

2 700

22 800

MONTRÉAL
595 395

34

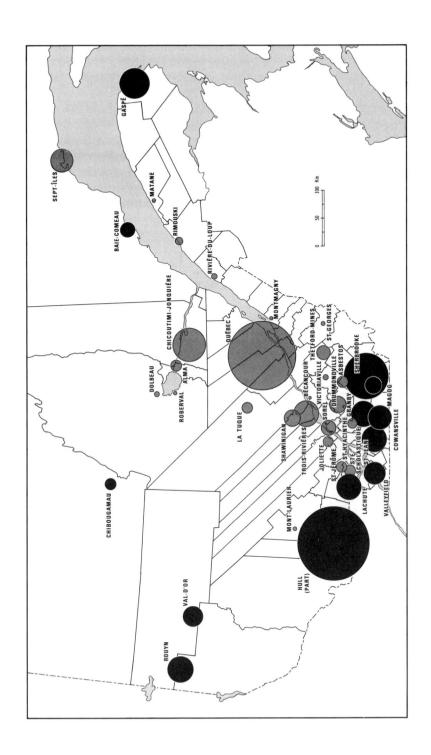

GASPÉ

SEPT-ÎLES

MATANE

RIMOUSKI

BAIE-COMEAU

RIVIÈRE-DU-LOUP

CHICOUTIMI-JONQUIÈRE

QUÉBEC

MONTMAGNY

THETFORD-MINES

ST-GEORGES

DOLBEAU

ALMA

SHERBROOKE

ASBESTOS

ROBERVAL

BÉCANCOUR

VICTORIAVILLE

DRUMMONDVILLE

GRANBY

MAGOG

LA TUQUE

SHAWINIGAN

SOREL

ST-HYACINTHE

COWANSVILLE

TROIS-RIVIÈRES

JOLIETTE

STE-
SCHOLASTIQUE

ST-JEAN

CHIBOUGAMAU

ST-JÉRÔME

LACHUTE

VALLEYFIELD

MONT-LAURIER

HULL
(PART)

VAL-D'OR

ROUYN

100 Km

50

0

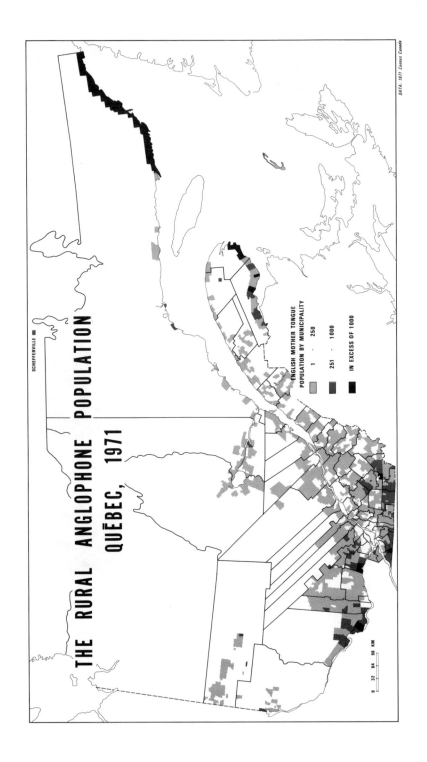

THE RURAL ANGLOPHONE POPULATION
QUÉBEC, 1971

SCHEFFERVILLE ■

ENGLISH MOTHER TONGUE
POPULATION BY MUNICIPALITY

1 - 250
251 - 1000
IN EXCESS OF 1000

0 32 64 96 KM

DATA: 1971 Census Canada

Even though, in strictly quantitative terms, the distribution of anglophones within Quebec is highly discontinuous, their presence pervades most of the province, the gaps being straddled by a filigree of small communities and memories to a past that has been effaced from the minds of all but a very few. That this diffusion was assured by the greater political and economic clout of a Quebec-based anglophone elite and the geo-political aspirations of a Lord Durham is immaterial. It is now simply part of the *patrimoine* of a radically transformed population, a *patrimoine* that has yet to be evoked.

Notable among such scattered English communities are *Grosse Ile* and *Entry Island* in the Iles-de-la- Madeleine, the former confronted by virtual annihilation in the past few years, first at the possibility of the island being turned into a park devoid of people (like Forillon in the Gaspé and Gros Morne in Newfoundland to name only two), and now with the imminent opening of a major salt mine that risks destroying the social fabric of the community and endangering the inshore fishery that provides the livelihood of these people and the Entry islanders.[6] Then there is *St-Malachie*, perched on the hills of Dorchester County, overlooking the Beauce, with, until the summer of 1981, its single classroom in the French school for the half-a-dozen or so English children at the primary level, its Irish Catholic mayor, and its sixteen families that reputedly still pay seigneurial dues to the «laird» — a Henderson, now living in Ontario! Or the Irish community of *Shannon* in Portneuf County that successfully negotiated its separation from Ste-Catherine back in 1948 in order to restore the anglophones to majority status and preserve its distinctive ethnic and linguistic character. Or *Otterburn Park*, on the Richelieu river initially conceived by Bruce Campbell, the son of the Scottish seigneur of Rouville (St-Hilaire), as an amusement park for the working classes of Montreal and subsequently settled largely by anglophones from Pointe-St-Charles, employees of the CN railway that served the locality. Although this little town has now assumed the aspesct of a dormitory suburb for Montreal, it continues to boast the finest athletics and boating clubs in the region. Or the few surviving English apple-growers of *Rougemont*. Or the stately resort communities of *Murray Bay* (Pointe-au-Pic) and *Cap-à-l'Aigle* in Charlevoix County and *Métis Beach* (Métis-sur-Mer) on the Lower St. Lawrence that drew the anglophone *haute bourgeoisie* of Montreal for more than a century, but also many Americans — President Taft is reputed to have governed the United States from Pointe-au-Pic each summer for the duration of his mandate! And one could go on and on...

THE URBAN POPULATION BY MOTHER TONGUE
QUÉBEC, 1971

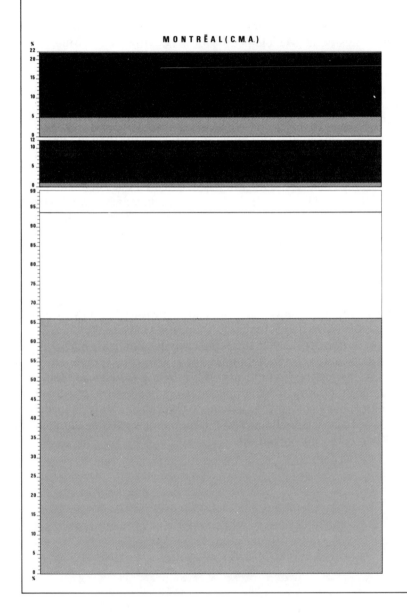

MONTRÉAL(C.M.A.)

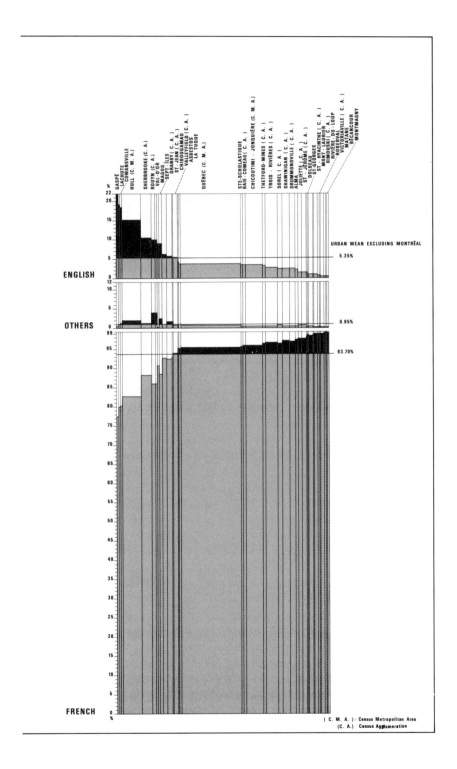

ENGLISH

OTHERS

FRENCH

GASPÉ
LACHUTE
COWANSVILLE
HULL (C. M. A.)
SHERBROOKE (C. A.)
ROUYN (C. A.)
VAL-D'OR
MAGOG
SEPT - ÎLES
GRANBY (C. A.)
ST - JEAN (C. A.)
CHIBOUGAMAU
VALLEYFIELD (C. A.)
ASBESTOS
LA TUQUE
QUÉBEC (C. M. A.)
STE-SCHOLASTIQUE
BAIE - COMEAU (C. A.)
CHICOUTIMI - JONQUIÈRE (C. M. A.)
THETFORD - MINES (C. A.)
TROIS - RIVIÈRES (C. A.)
SOREL (C. A.)
SHAWINIGAN (C. A.)
DRUMMONDVILLE (C. A.)
ALMA (C. A.)
JOLIETTE (C. A.)
ST - JÉRÔME (C. A.)
DOLBEAU
ST - GEORGES
ST - HYACINTHE (C. A.)
MONT - LAURIER
RIMOUSKI (C. A.)
RIVIÈRE - DU - LOUP
MONTRÉAL
VICTORIAVILLE (C. A.)
MATANE
BÉCANCOUR
MONTMAGNY

URBAN MEAN EXCLUDING MONTRÉAL

5.35%

0.95%

93.70%

(C. M. A.): Census Metropolitan Area
(C. A.) Census Agglomeration

39

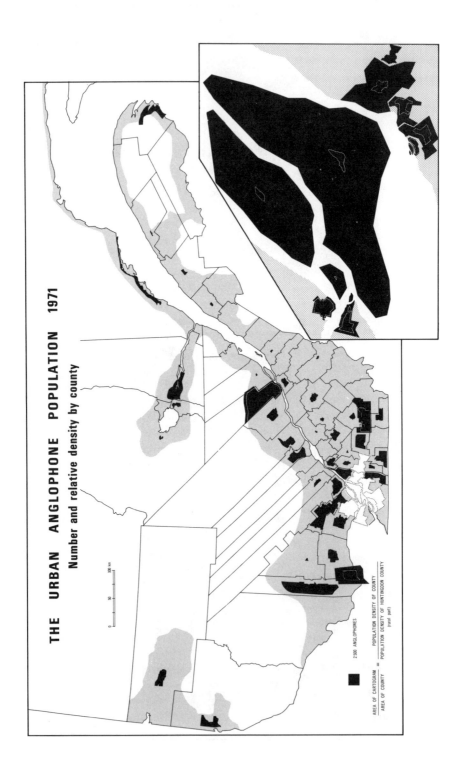

THE URBAN ANGLOPHONE POPULATION 1971

Number and relative density by county

0   50   100 km

2 500 ANGLOPHONES

$$\frac{AREA\ OF\ CARTOGRAM}{AREA\ OF\ COUNTY} = \frac{POPULATION\ DENSITY\ OF\ COUNTY}{POPULATION\ DENSITY\ OF\ HUNTINGDON\ COUNTY\ (rural\ part)}$$

40

Elsewhere, the memories of an English presence abound — *Cumberland*, near St-Georges-de-Beauce — «there's only one family left there now». Or the little Anglican church (Christ Church) in *Sorel*, witness to the fact that the town once bore the name William-Henry and was destined to be an English town settled by Loyalists. Or *Grosse Isle* in the St. Lawrence, just below the Ile d'Orléans, quarantine station for immigrants in the nineteenth century where between 5000 and 12000 Irish, fleeing the Potato Famine in 1847, died of typhoid. All that symbolises this tragedy today are the abandoned Catholic and Anglican churches and a Celtic cross, carved in Stanstead granite, erected in 1909 and clearly visible to passing ships. Or the fountain in the market-place at *St-Hyacinthe* erected in the memory of the Jones family, last seigneurs of Dessaulles — a casual reminder of the fact that in the 1840s two-thirds of the seigneuries of Quebec belonged to anglophones.

What these images evoke, implicitly at least, is of an Anglo-Quebec that is exclusively of British ethnic origin (English, Irish and Scottish). In fact, only 66,9 per cent of anglophones now claim British ethnic origin and, stated more cogently, 54,4 per cent of all non-francophones in Quebec are of «other ethnic origin» (i.e., neither British nor French). Furthermore, the *off-island* English are massively British in origin while Montrealers are of very diverse backgrounds. Such a distinction with respect to origin reinforces the spatial duality and creates a cleavage that is born as much of a sense of *past* as of *place*, the former being a rooted population and the latter having many of the characteristics of transients where the stock is renewed through immigration and assimilation at each generation.

Insofar as language is concerned, only one in three anglophones is bilingual, a surprising figure given the small size of the minority. Indeed in the Montreal area a higher proportion of francophones are bilingual than anglophones.[7] There are a number of reasons for this which transcend the issue of the capacity of the English language educational system to produce functionally bilingual graduates. Firstly, anglophones tend to be highly localized such as to constitute local majorities, and in these situations, they have readily imposed their language on the francophone minority. This applies as much to the West Island of Montreal as to the village of Shannon in Portneuf county, the child from this latter community being unlikely to be exposed to French in any real way until he goes to secondary school in Quebec City. English gains in strength by virtue of it being the majority and dominant language at the national and continental levels and by it continuing to be the language of much large scale business and commerce, hence, at least until very recently, the language of economic power and prestige.

Under the circumstances, the majority readily accepted the use of English in the public arena (by law in federal institutions and by volition elsewhere) such that, irrespective of the language skills of anglophones, institutional bilingualism prevailed throughout most of Quebec, and it was only in Quebec City and a few of the more isolated communities that French was generally accepted and used as the common language in interlinguistic contacts.

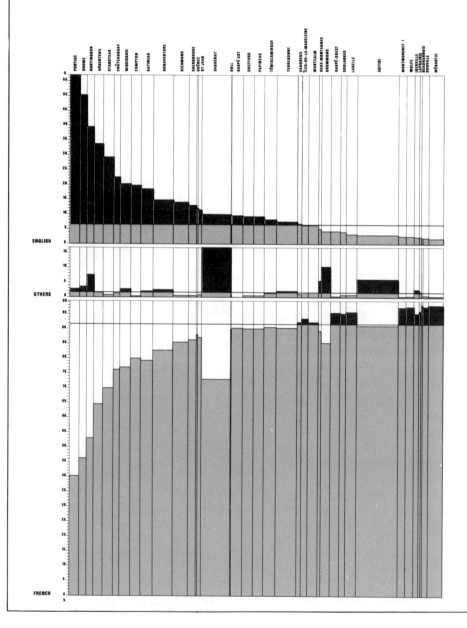

THE RURAL POPULATION BY MOTHER TONGUE, QUÉBEC 1971

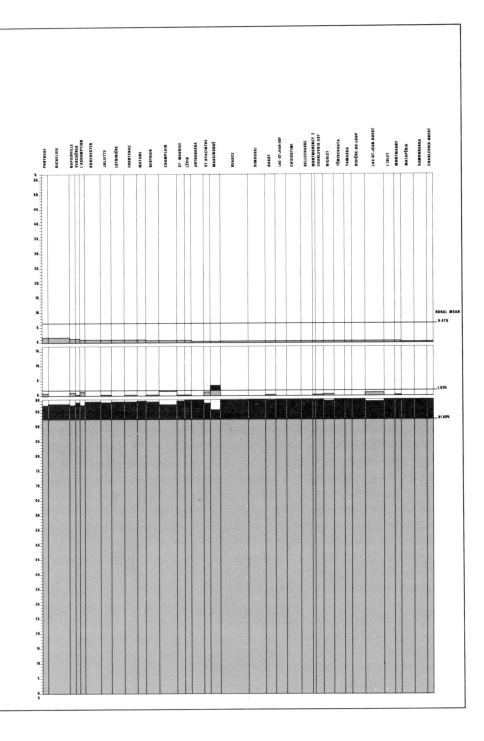

43

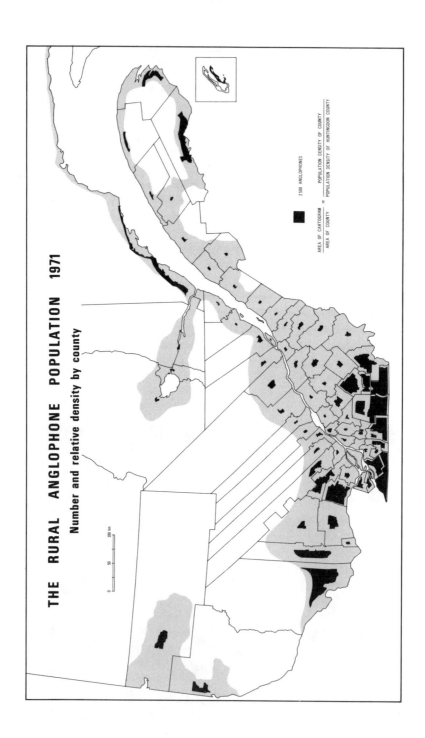

THE RURAL ANGLOPHONE POPULATION 1971

Number and relative density by county

2500 ANGLOPHONES

$$\frac{\text{AREA OF CARTOGRAM}}{\text{AREA OF COUNTY}} = \frac{\text{POPULATION DENSITY OF COUNTY}}{\text{POPULATION DENSITY OF HUNTINGDON COUNTY}}$$

0   50   100 km

With respect to religious affiliation, less than 45 per cent of Anglo-Quebecers profess to be Protestants, while approximately 39 per cent are Catholics, and 16 per cent fall under the rubric «other». Any semblance of Protestant strength is also belied by the plurality of «little churches». The United Church of Canada has as many members in Quebec as the Anglican Church, while most areas of English settlement also boast Baptist, Pentecostal and Presbyterian churches, not to mention Churches of Christ.

Perhaps the most sensitive piece of hard data regarding anglophones is that pertaining to their relative affluence within Quebec society. Gabrielle Roy's vivid and symbolic juxtaposition of a rich, English Westmount and a poor, French St-Henri in *Bonheur d'occasion* (Beauchemin, 1947) was confirmed in no uncertain manner by the Royal Commission on Bilingualism and Biculturalism in the late 1960s. An analysis of the 1961 census data for Quebec revealed that the mean income of male wage-earners of British ethnic origin was superior to that of all other ethnic groups. In fact, it exceeded the mean for all male wage-earners by 42 per cent, and then there followed in descending order various other groups (Scandinavian, Dutch, etc.) with the French and Italians ranked in twelfth and thirteenth positions with incomes 8,2 per cent and 15,4 per cent respectively below the mean. The Commission also established that anglophone unilinguals, on average, earned more than francophone unilinguals — a clear indication of the privileged status of the minority and the power of attraction of the English language.

These revelations stimulated an avalanche of research during the 1970s on the subject of income disparities as related to ethnicity, mother tongue and language skills.[8] This subsequent research points to a constantly narrowing gap over the past two decades in mean income levels for the two major linguistic groups. Thus, Boulet reveals that, insofar as male workers in the Montreal metropolitan zone are concerned:

> In 1961, there was a 51 per cent divergence between the average earnings of francophones... and those of anglophones. By 1970, this was reduced to 32 per cent, and had further decreased to 15 per cent by 1977.[9]

Likewise, Lacroix and Vaillancourt in their review of income levels for the Quebec labour force as a whole, conclude:

> ...in 1978, as a general rule, unilingual anglophones, all else being equal, do not have a higher income than unilingual francophones although this was the case in 1970. In 1978, as a general rule, the second-language knowledge of [...] anglophones [...], all else being equal, increases their income in a similar manner.[10]

In closing a major income gap between francophones and anglophones over a short period of two decades, a major bone of contention has been removed. Irrespective of this fact, it must be stressed that the initial observation about English «wealth» had a certain caricatural quality about it in the sense that the generalizations proffered in the literature failed to highlight the range of incomes within the language group. In reality, anglophones have always been represented in all social classes in Quebec and it is quite likely that the generalized pattern evident in the sixties and early seventies was skewed as a result of their massive presence in the highest income brackets within the private sector in Quebec — professionals, company directors, etc., who are notably highly mobile individuals. Certainly at the other end of the scale there is an anglophone working class, in the sugar refineries and aircraft industry of Montreal for example. Seven to 10 per cent of Quebec farmers are anglophones, and there are indications that these and other rural Quebecers are becoming a relatively disadvantaged group, they being ofter unilingual and their language not being at a premium in the region. Unequipped to obtain employment in the public and para-public sectors, Gaspé anglophones now probably experience higher than average unemployment levels and, there and elsewhere, poverty pockets coincide with certain anglophone communities.

From patterns to processes

If the stereotype of a certain English Quebec suffers from close scrutiny, the explanation lies as much in the changes to which that population is constantly subject as in a basic ignorance of it.

Right from the very beginnings of British colonization, a situation of flux has prevailed — Loyalists who moved into the Eastern Townships at the end of the eithteenth century to claim land granted them by the Crown and who immediately returned across the border to sell it to land-hungry Yankees from the New England states; a generation of English, Scottish and Irish settlement along the Laurentian front (notably between Montreal and Trois-Rivières and behind Quebec City) followed by virtual abandonment in mid-century; the transition from English to French dominance in the Eastern Townships beginning in the mid-nineteenth century and now virtually complete; the displacement of French Canadians by English-speaking Newfoundlanders on the Lower North Shore between 1860 and 1890; the existence of a powerful Channel Island mercantile empire in the Gaspé during the nineteenth century that brought settlers from Jersey and Guernsey; and the presence of an important community of whalers, shipbuilders and master mariners in Gaspé Bay during the same period.

The most striking mutation of all occurred in Montreal and Quebec City. In the mid-nineteenth century, both were essentially English cities. The majority of Montrealers were actually English-speaking between 1831 and 1861, while in 1861, 40 per cent of the inhabitants of Quebec City were of British ethnic origin (principally Irish). Late nineteenth and twentieth century English Quebec saw a shift in the focus of immigration from rural to urban areas, massive out-migration to other parts of North America, the dislocations of two World Wars, and a progressive change in the composition of the population towards increasing ethnic heterogeniety with a shift to continental Europe (first eastern and northern, and then the Mediterranean nations) as a major source of migrants.

These changes were dictated by a variety of considerations, economic and political, some specific to Quebec and some related to developments elsewhere in North America or Europe. The British government established planned settlements in Douglastown and New Carlisle in the Gaspé, and land grants in the Eastern Townships to Loyalists in recognition of their services to the Crown during the American War of Independence. The same government, from 1815 on, offered free passage across the Atlantic to prospective settlers, plus tracts of land, tools, seeds and rations. The reason: over-population and social unrest, particularly in Scotland and Ireland. Unemployed British soldiers, veterans of the wars of 1759-60, 1775-76 and 1812-14 were also offered land grants. The objectives were also geopolitical — to encircle the French-settled seigneurial lands by a zone of loyal British settlement.

However, almost from the start, the poverty of the Laurentian and Appalachian soils, the attraction of urban employment opportunities, the tendency to send children to be educated in these same centres, and the opening of Upper Canada and then the West encouraged the settlers to move. The rise and fall of an Irish Quebec City was closely related to the flourishing of the timber and particularly wooden shipbuilding industry.

Elsewhere, the shift from a French to an English Lower North Shore was associated with the transition from a salmon and sealing economy to one based on the cod fishery. If the Channel Island presence on «La Côte» (as the Gaspé was called in those islands) was also associated with the cod fishery, its viability could only be explained in terms of the articulation of a complex mercantile empire that linked the region with the Channel Islands, Europe, the Mediterranean, the West Indies and Latin America. The demise of a Channel Island presence in Gaspé became inevitable with the collapse of that empire in the late nineteenth century, the final blow being the Depression of the thirties.

Because of their identification with «the old country» and their participation in two European wars, many English communities saw their strength sapped. Residents of St-Malachie trace the origins of the real decline of their community to the First World War when virtually all anglophone males signed up to fight. After the war, instead of returning, most went to Western Canada. As in the case of the French Canadians, the mill towns of New England attracted many Irish families, particularly following the construction of the railways and the demise of shipbuilding in Quebec City. Nothing has changed — Ontario, the West and the United States still serve as powerful poles of attraction for young English Quebecers!

What emerges from these changes in English Quebec as a whole is a picture of a generalized decline, from 20 per cent of the total population in 1871 to 13 per cent in 1971, and of an increasingly localised distribution pattern. Certain rural centres survive as regional focii; thus, back in the mid-nineteenth century, Irish from the smaller communities of Chertsey, Chilton and Wexford, etc. relocated in Rawdon, attracted by the small industries. Similarly, in this century, Lennoxville has maintained, and even increased, its relative importance as an English town while surrounding communities wither, the elderly migrating in, drawn by an English milieu and services, and outsiders being recruited to staff the flourishing educational sector.

If the proportion of English in Montreal has declined[11], its relative dominance within English Quebec has increased significantly. The physical growth of the city has led to a major overspill of anglophones into the surrounding rural areas, such counties as Vaudreuil, Chateauguayy, Deux-Montagnes and Laprairie having experienced a significant increase in the proportion of anglophones within the total population over the past 50 years. Again, the dichotomy between Montrealers and the other English is emphasized; the former a massive, metropolitan, heterogeneous population characterized by a high turnover in membership, mobile therefore, and with relatively little sense of place or past with respect to Quebec; the latter, an aging, residual population with a strong sense of community, but a community that is increasingly removed from present-day Quebec society. McIntosh offers a rather poignant image of one such community — that of his grandparents — Bourg-Louis in Portneuf County, which has a population of 45 anglophones with an average age of 52,3 years and no children under 10 years:

> One interesting but sad circumstance is evident in the old church. There is but a single couple sitting on the left hand side of the church, the rest sit on the right. The present population still maintains the same seating arrangements in the church as that of their forefathers. What was once a full congregation with young and old alike, has become a place of worship for the aged few that remain.
>
> The church is usually cold in winter because the furnace is not turned on until the minister arrives, which is usually only a short time before the service. The minister does not have the time to go from farm to farm. . . «[12]

There is little organic relationship between the two realms of metropolitan and rural Quebec. The one possesses the major institutions and media, but largely neglects the other, if it is not indeed totally ignorant of it. And yet, ironically, the latter is patently necessary for the maturing of the former as a rooted population. The cleavage creates and reinforces profound cultural differences with respect to language and to behaviour. While in rural Quebec English is the language of a civilisation, a cultural tradition, and serves as a definer of identity, in Montreal it is increasingly a mere vehicle of communication between people of different cultures. It has, therefore, no real affective dimension to it and does not serve to create or maintain a distinctive cultural tradition. It is perceived rather as a continental, or universal, language, that facilitates mobility, and it has no particular meaning for those that, increasingly, use it in the context of Quebec society. In cultural terms, this creates the kind of harsh dualism unwittingly pinpointed by an anglophone student at Laval University in commenting, on a CBC radio programme in April 1979, about the departure of four English teachers from the English language CEGEP in Quebec City:

> QUESTION: Why are they leaving?
>
> ANSWER: [. . .]A change. They're the kind of people
> that move a lot[. . .] They're not Canadians.

It also accounts for the enormous difficulties inherent in current efforts to mobilize «anglophones» around «common» grievances and goals.

Some ethnic considerations

The survival of any minority group is closely bound up with the strength and diversity of its institutions, the contacts it maintains with its hearth population (or reference group), and the manner in which its relations with the majority in which it is in continuous contact are managed. A consideration of these variables, with respect to English Quebec, helps account for its basic vitality and, at the same time, for the more fundamental nature of the crisis presently confronting it.

In terms of institutions, Quebec «anglophonie» is generously served. It has a network of schools that span the province, four CEGEPs in the Montreal area, two elsewhere in the province, and English sections in Gaspé Town and Hull, plus three universities. It has its own hospitals and welfare agencies, enterprises where English is the language of work, and a wide range of professional services. Insofar as the media is concerned, there are two English language daily newspapers and a multitude of weekly and monthly newspapers scattered through rural Quebec from Val d'Or to the Gaspé coast. Over half the radio stations and two of the five television stations in Montreal broadcast in English. English T.V. is available in such obscure places as Fermont (as a part of CBC's policy of «Bringing Canadians Together»), while the isolated English communities across Quebec are expressly served by CBC Radio's Quebec Community Network which, in addition to furnishing national and regional programming, aims at providing local news.

Outside the realm of politics and government, then, anglophones were not often obliged to have recourse to the institutions of the majority. In addition, these many anglophone institutions have long served to form and employ a local elite — they have furnished a natural avenue for its aspirations — and in turn, that indigenous elite provided the intellectual leadership for the population at large.

Quebec society is, however, defined as much in terms of religious as linguistic affiliation and while, in the educational realm, Anglo-Protestants control their institutions, Anglo-Catholics do not. The latter are simply a minority within basically francophone institutional arrangements. As the proportion of Catholics within the anglophone population continues to increase, one can readily envisage the emergence of a situation in which a variety of educational (and religious) institutions will continue to serve English Quebec, but these same institutions will be under the control of the francophone majority and will exist by its grace. A similar shift has occurred in the sixties and seventies as a result of the increasing omnipresence of the state. In the realm of health, social welfare and education — to name only the most important — minority institutions have been progressively integrated networks controlled by the state, and hence, managed and financed by the latter. Such a loss of control to «others», to be explained by very different circumstances, is already evident in the work world and the media. The twentieth century has seen a shift from locally owned to nationally and continentally owned enterprise. Decisions affecting the world of English information are now increasingly made in Toronto, and this affects not only content but also staffing and survival. What were once English controlled local enterprises are now, more and more, branch plants of operations run from Toronto, Detroit, Chicago, or wherever. Consequently, while the world of anglophone institutions remains a diverse and comprehensive one, it is increasingly fragile in nature with Quebec anglophones exercising less and less control over it. The decision to transfer the head office of Sun Life was made in Toronto, so was the one to close *The Montreal Star*. English language programming for CBC radio and television is also largely determined in Toronto.

This loss of control has led to a profound modification in the behaviour of the anglophone elite over the past two decades. If Montreal was once the capital of a continent for an anglophone bourgeoisie and if Van Horne could «see the Pacific Ocean» from his office window in the tower of the Windsor Station, such is no longer the case. It is now a back-water that harbours branch plants of corporations whose headquarters are located elsewhere. Since the historic anglophone elite was grounded in the private sector, it is quite «natural» that that elite should respond to the geographic shift in economic power, and if it hasn't relocated itself, its children, as heirs to that tradition, have. Often the process is abetted by the parents so that while their children may still frequent the major private schools of the province (Lower Canada College, Bishop's College School, Stanstead College, etc.), they have forsaken McGill and Bishop's universities for Queen's, Toronto, the University of Western Ontario and, for the sporting kind, the University of New Brunswick. Few return.

While anglophone graduates within Quebec still typically direct themselves to the private sector, as employees of what are increasingly national and trans-national enterprises, they are perforce much more mobile than the preceding generations. Further, these same enterprises frequently delegate, as managers and professionals attached to local operations, people from outside the province with little knowledge of the place, history or language of the majority. Ironically, this same «ethic» now increasingly pervades the churches, schools and universities, such that a new generation of English Quebecers (an increasing proportion of whom are first or second generation immigrants) are being formed by what is a more or less disembodied elite. In the circumstances, it is scarcely possible to be socialized to Quebec — its past, its place, its symbols and traditions — or to form an intellectual and cultural elite to replace an earlier one that had taken root in the province.

The geographical distribution of the English, likewise, makes difficult a coming to terms with the new Quebec. The vast majority live on the margins of Anglo-America, either within Montreal itself or scattered along the border with Vermont, New York and Ontario. While the former are too numerous to be readily confronted by their minority status, the latter deal with it by crossing the border to shop, see films, bowl, play hockey and, increasingly, to be educated and to work. Even for the Magdalen Islanders, Prince Edward Island is just a ferry trip away, as is Newfoundland for the residents of the Lower North Shore.

Only a few English Quebecers experience the kind of isolation that char-acterizes the daily lives of most francophone minorities in Canada, these being principally located along the Gaspé coast, north of Quebec City, around Lachute and in the Bois-Francs (Inverness, etc.) and the northern parts of the Eastern Townships (around Richmond for example). For them, there is a certain sense of being a minority, of having to accommodate to the majority on a day-to-day basis. For the rest, such a notion makes little sense for it is imposed by the arbitrariness of political boundaries — a resident of Shawville told me that his English teacher used to say «the Ottawa River should have gone around the other side of Pontiac County!» — it disregards the fact that English is the language of the continent, and it is an affront to the profound Canadianness of English Quebecers who responded in a far greater proportion than French Quebecers to the call to fight in two World Wars. In this respect, the sense of being a *minorité majoritaire* is born as much of geography and self-ascribed ethnic identity as of the prestige and power historically attached to the English language in Quebec and in Canada.

Because of the constant geographical shifts in population through time and because of the basic duality of Quebec society, cultural brokers have assumed an important mediating role in inter-ethnic relations. Although everything is con-ceived today in terms of a simple dichotomy between anglophone and francophone, the terms only entered common usage in the sixties. For an older generation of Quebecers, a distinction based on religious affiliation was at least, if not more, important as one based on language. Thus, even today in parts of rural Quebec, the more common referents are Catholic and Protestant. The strength of the boundary was guaranteed by a certain religious discourse that actively discouraged intermarriage until the early sixties. For a long time it was this criterion that determined assimilation patterns in Quebec leading to the majority of Italians, prior to the Second World War, assimilating to French and the majority of Channel Islanders who, in the nineteenth century, were mostly French-speaking Anglicans to English.

However, while «Protestant» became synonymous with «English» the contrary was not the case. From the early nineteenth century the French Catholic Church acknowledged an Irish, and therefore English-speaking, presence in its midst. The creation of schools, churches and a clergy assured the emergence of an ethnic group that straddled the boundary between the two reference groups, sharing the language of one and the faith of the other. Contacts were maintained and, inevitably, family ties were established in both directions. The Irish, and to a lesser extent the Scots, made a profound mark on French-Canadian civilization. Assimilation occurred creating the Ryans, O'Neills and Burns that we know today. The debt in terms of popular culture is clearly recognized by the fiddler Jean Carignan and indicated in some of the research of the folklorist Schmitz.[13]

More important than any cultural borrowing or hybridization, however, was the fact that individuals drawn from this milieu repeatedly played an important role as brokers, particularly in the political process. Possessing the confidence and linguistic skills of both communities, it was often that they oversaw the transition from English to French in the Eastern Townships as described in the classic work of Aileen Ross.[14] Uncertain whether they were English or French, or both, and certainly equipped to play both roles, such individuals have become not only rectors at Laval University (Larkin Kerwin), presidents of the Montreal Urban Community (Lawrence Hannigan), and «French-Canadian» prime ministers of Canada (Louis Stephen Saint Laurent, Pierre Elliot Trudeau), but also policemen and mayors, or persons occupying a multitude of other mediating positions.

The secularization of Quebec society has led to the demise of the Anglo-Catholics as a broker group. Other considerations have, in all probability, resulted in declining levels of bilingualism among English and French. Certainly the French in the Gaspé, at St-Malachie, or in the Eastern Townships, are not as bilingual as they were earlier in the century; neither are the English. According to some reports, the opportunities for French immersion in the logging camps (shanties), and the small Catholic schools where English and French shared the same playground and the same teachers, have disappeared.

Deprived of arbiters to manage their inter-ethnic relations, anglophones tend increasingly to withdraw into their separate communities abandoning the political arena once they lose control of their institutions. The basic preoccupations become those of survival (but what survival if all the children are gone?) or a vision of the neighbourhood as a place of passage, a suburb of Toronto. Thus, the citizens of Mal Bay opt out of municipal politics with their incorporation in the Town of Percé, Grosse Islers and Entry Islanders fail to find the formula for participating in regional level institutions, while William Shaw, the former independent deputy representing the West Island in provincial politics, proposes the creation of an eleventh province.

For some, the marginal people that McLeod-Arnopoulos describes elsewhere in this collection will constitute the new generation of brokers. However, it is unclear whether such individuals have any constituency. They are perceived by many anglophones as having simply crossed the ethnic boundary rather than sitting astride it, and this crossing is dictated by choice rather than history. Hence, they are not perceived as loyal individuals. Further, the fact that many are academics and few are involved in the political arena would confirm the view that we are dealing with individual actions which respect the rigidity of the ethnic boundary; and the implications for the collectivity are likely to be few.

Nevertheless, the increasing number of anglophones placing their children in French schools or in immersion programmes within the English system points to a widespread recognition of the rigidity of the ethnic boundary and a desire, at the individual level, to transcend it. The implications of this massive acquisition of French language skills by young anglophones remain to be assessed. It could, ironically, lead to the reappropriation of the almost forgotten geography and history of an English Quebec.

...And what of the future?

The picture that emerges from this discussion of Quebec «anglophonie» is one of not a single but of a multitude of communities sharing a common vehicle of communication, the English language. Within the language group, one can discern powerful internal divisions founded on geography, class and culture. Although the group is extremely well-endowed in terms of institutions, there is abundant evidence to suggest that these are now over-extended (their strength having been assured by their powerful assimilating role vis-à-vis immigrants, particularly since the Second World War). Hence, the institutions are now extremely vulnerable, this vulnerability being intensified by the fact that many have fallen under the control of the state or of interests located outside Quebec. Because of this, decisions regarding them are not necessarily based on the interests of Anglo-Quebecers.

Furthermore, the historic elite that created and staffed these institutions has now more or less abandoned Quebec (or is actively counselling its children to do just that) so that they are now largely staffed by strangers who are often simply transients and who typically possess limited knowledge and understanding of Quebec «anglophonie» or, indeed, of Quebec in general. Alternatively, they are not staffed at all. Hence, one is constantly confronted by the kind of information that «x is the last English notary in Quebec City», «y is the only English *agronome* in the Eastern Townships», or that «the minister in x parish is a South African who had never seen a fisherman in his life before he came to the (fishing) community». Or that «there are no English professionals left on the Gaspé Coast», or that «Quebec High School recruited all its new teachers in Nova Scotia last year».

True or false, such statements are symptomatic of a profound malaise. They point to the intellectual weakening of the language group (in terms of leadership, creativity etc.), a weakening that becomes generalized with the rapid turn-over and almost total dominance of the Montreal-based population. Who is to socialize whom to what? The degree of disembodiment is profound. There is no one formulating or reformulating «la mémoire collective» (though thank God we've found David Fennario!).

In this sense, the crisis is structural, much more than demographic, where the umbilical cord linking a population with its immediate environment has been seriously weakened if not severed. Although by no means unique to Quebec, it takes on a particular configuration here because almost its entire elite is caught up in the continentalization process and the mobility that such implies.

Yet through it all there persists a certain awareness of a rich English past in Quebec, an appreciation of the contribution it has made to defining Quebec's specificity, be it in terms of a legal code, a sense of civism or a sporting tradition. Individuals, in considerable number, are now seeking to come to terms with a new, assertive French Quebec, through the acquisition of the appropriate language skills. Once that has been achieved, a new Quebec-based and Quebec-committed intellectual leadership can emerge, one which may well be capable of recuperating its past, of recovering a sense of place, and thereby directing itself into a future that it helps define. But in order to realise this, the contribution of a demographically weak and geographically fragmented rural Quebec «anglophonie» is likely to be critical.

NOTES

(1) There is nothing caricatural about this sequence of events. It actually occurred in April 1979.

(2) Countess of Aberdeen, *Through Canada with a Kodak* (Edinburgh, White, 1893):19-20.

(3) See especially Oscar Junek, *Isolated Communities: A Study of a Labrador Fishing Village*, New-York, American Book Co., 1937, as well as Horace Miner, *St Denis: A French-Canadian Parish*, Chicago, University of Chicago Press, 1939.

(4) We are thinking of Everett G. Hughes whose *French Canada in Transition* is recognized as a classical piece of work by all students of Quebec society.

(5) An important exception was the realm of bilingual instruction and French language immersion programmes. This research was carried out principally under the direction of Wallace Lambert of the Department of Psychology, McGill University (see Lambert and Tucker in this collection).

(6) See Stuart Richards in this collection.

(7) The situation is, undoubtedly, changing rapidly with regard to the level of bilingualism among anglophones, and the 1981 census figures are likely to reveal significantly increased percentages.

(8) See C. Veltman, «Les incidences du revenu sur...».

(9) Jac-André Boulet, *L'évolution des disparités linguistiques et revenus de travail...*, p. I.

(10) Robert Lacroix and François Vaillancourt, *Les revenus et la langue au Québec (1970-1978)*, p. 85.

(11) In 1971, the proportion of British ethnic origin in the Montreal region had fallen to 14,8 per cent of the total population, as compared with 21 per cent in 1941. By contrast, that of the other ethnic groups (excluding French) had risen from 10,6 to 17,8 per cent over the same period. (See J.-C. Marsan, «Montréal, de la domination au pluralisme»).

(12) C. McIntosh, *Devolution and Survival of the Rural English-Speaking Population...*, p. 43.

(13) N. Schmitz, «Éléments gaéliques...».

(14) Aileen Ross, «French and English Canadian...».

People and Society

Gary Caldwell

GARY CALDWELL. A resident of the Eastern Townships and former AQEM (Anglo Quebec En Mutation) research director, Gary Caldwell developed an interest and involvement in rural English-speaking Quebec while teaching sociology at Bishop's Univerity from 1971 to 1979. He is presently a researcher with the Institut québécois de recherche sur la culture.

If ever there was a virgin territory to be mapped in the social history of Anglo-Celtic Canada, it is the demographic and social history of English-speaking Quebec. Hence, the hazardous nature of such an undertaking: a sociological literature on English-speaking Quebec is just now emerging! In terms of book-length studies of the subject, there is nothing between Sellar's *The Tragedy of Quebec: the Expulsion of its Protestant Farmers*,[1] first published in 1907 at his own expense, and *The English Eact in Quebec* by Arnopoulos and Clift,[2] first published in French in 1979. There has, needless to say, been a rather extraordinary interest in the subject of late — since November 1976.

However, the subject had begun to attract the attention of one or two academics in the early seventies. Michael Stein wrote a comprehensive synthesis and commentary of existing materials in 1977.[3] He has, for the purpose of this book, been good enough to reconsider the subject in the light of more recent events. It is, then, in this rather dim light that we venture here to reconstruct the basic demographic and social-structural outlines of the evolution of English-speaking Quebec.[4] Before setting foot in this rather virgin territory, a certain time-period delimitation and a number of conceptual distinctions are in order.

For the purposes of the present discussion, we will distinguish three periods: everything which preceded World War II; the post-war period until Law 22 (1974); and finally, the «language laws» era. Obviously, it is the last quarter-century which has been privileged, a fact which we unabashedly admit is a direct result of the author's ignorance of the as of yet un-collated socio-economic history of the population concerned. Without wishing to qualify the above admission of ignorance, we would, however, suggest that it is in the last quarter-century of its existence that this population as a distinct entity has been thrust on to the stage of history for the first — and perhaps the last — time.

We will speak in terms of an English-speaking or anglophone population, rather than of one or several ethnic populations (as others have done), because we are of the opinion that the analytical framework which captures best the social mechanism at work in Quebec — in as much as the «English» population in concerned — is that of the dynamic majority/minority.

Our analytical point of departure is, consequently, the relationship of a power disequilibrium between two entities which distinguish themselves, one from another, linguistically. Each of the two entities mobilizes itself in order to promote its interest in the face of the threat of the other. The subsequent dynamic results, in the long term, is territorial consolidation of the minority and the creation and maintenance of social barriers between it and the majority, as well as a tradition of resistance which serves to reinforce the very same majority/minority dynamic. Thus, the term majority denotes, in this context, a supremacy of political power, rooted in economic, military or other advantage, but not necessarily implying a numerical majority.

Consequently, the social barrier which is the most acutely felt is that of language. The French-speaking population of Quebec has evolved from the self-perceived status of being a minority within Canada to that of a majority within Quebec... the basis of its territorial consolidation. For precisely the reason that the relationship majority/minority is, by definition, one of political power, and because French-speaking Quebec is in the process of legitimizing its political base, English-speaking Quebec becomes, by definition, a minority.

TABLE I — Ethnic Origin* Composition of the Population of Quebec: 1844-1911

	1 Total population	2** English	3 French	4 English born outside of Quebec	5 English % of total 2/1	6 English born outside of Quebec % of Eng. 4/2	7 % increase in the total population	8 % increase in the Eng. population
Year								
1844	697 084	166 876	524 244	81,216	24%	49%	—	—
1851	890 261	216 712	669 887	79,602	24%	37%	28%	30%
1861	1 111 566	260 564	850 564	93,240	23%	36%	25%	20%
1871	1 199 684	259 599	929 817	N/A	22%	—	8%	0%
1881	1 359 898	285 207	1 073 820	N/A	21%	—	13%	10%
1901	1 648 898	324 825	1 322 115	73,653	20%	23%	—	—
1911	1 986 387	445 559	1 605 347	N/A	22%	—	20%	37%

  * There do not exist statistics on language as such before 1931.
 ** For the years 1844, 1851 and 1861, all those born in Canada are classified as English or French. The limitations of the data published in the censuses in question impose such a construction. Consequently, column two includes all those of Anglo-celtic ethnic origin and those who would to-day be designated as being of "Other" ethnic origin, that is, neither English nor French.

Historic English Quebec: a Constant Presence

The anglophone population of Quebec presently represents approximately one fifth of the total population — although the 1981 census results, not yet available at the time this article was written, may indicate otherwise — and that proportion has remained relatively stable for over a century and a half (see column 5 in Table 1). Table 1 distinguishes the population of Quebec according to ethnic origin for the period 1844 to 1911. As those of other than Anglo-Celtic or French ethnic origin did not constitute a significant proportion of the Quebec population before 1911, and as there did not exist census data on language before 1931, we have assimilated non-French to anglophone.

Over a period of a century and a quarter, 1844 to 1971, the anglophone proportion — loosely defined — maintained itself at between one quarter and one fifth of the population of Quebec. Admittedly, the same figures point to a slow but persistent long-term decline over the same period, while they conceal certain short-term variations, as for instance, the buoyancy of the anglophone population over the period 1967-1971, and a predictable slump since.

Thus, recent developments aside, the anglophone proportion of the Quebec population has remained remarkably stable. In terms of absolute numbers, there was already a quarter of a million anglophones in Quebec by the mid-nineteenth century. In 1971, almost 900 000 persons in Quebec declared that the language they most often used in the home was English. At the time of the 1976 partial census, the mother tongue composition of the population of Quebec was as follows: English 797 425, French 4 988 540 and Other 330 885.[5]

Historic Demographic Instability

The stability of the English-speaking population as a *proportion of the total population* is, however, in stark constrast to its internal demographic instability. Unlike its French-speaking counterpart, the English-speaking population of Quebec has traditionally been subjected to a high degree of what might be called «demographic turn-over».

Even in the middle of the nineteenth century, as apparent in column 6 of Table 1, the proportion of anglophones who were not natives of Quebec oscillated around 40 per cent. To be expected in a period of settler colonization, this high degree of demographic turn-over did attenuate somewhat by the turn of the century. Yet, in the post-World War II period, English-speaking Quebec found itself again with a rate of turn-over similar to that which prevailed in the middle of the nineteenth century. The massive ASOPE study carried out during the school year 1971-1972 established that only 44 per cent of the parents of English high school students were born in Quebec.[6] Indeed, a special census tabulation drawn from the 1971 census has allowed us to determine that only 60 per cent of elementary-aged children who speak English had, in 1971, at least *one* parent who was both English mother tongue and born in Quebec.[7]

The factors responsible for such a state of affairs, in as much as the post-war period is concerned, have been examined;[8] however, our knowledge of the pre-war period is extremely limited. Writ large, it has been the out-migration of the most established elements of the population towards the other Canadian provinces and the U.S.A., and their replacement by newer elements, which has resulted in this state of constant turn-over. Sellar, writing at the very end of the nineteenth century, provides us with a rare recognition of this process. Speaking of the six counties of Stanstead, Sherbrooke, Waterloo, Missisquoi, Brome, and Huntingdon, he notes the presence of 56 000 Protestants in 1867 and he remarks that «appearances pointed to its he number of Protestants increase, for each summer saw the number enlarged by immigrants from Britain»; however, in 1911, almost a half-century later, there were, he admits, only 57 926 Protestants in the same six counties.[9] Much of the native population had, of course, like Donald Morrison, «the Megantic Outlaw», left for the West*. His parents had, before him, immigrated from Scotland to Quebec.

The structural particularity which this state of demographic instability represents is thrown into relief by the very different situation prevailing in the French-speaking population inhabiting the same territory. The almost total absence (up to very recently) of French- speaking immigration since the beginning of the eighteenth century has made French-speaking Quebec one of the most demographically homogenous populations in the modern world. The ASOPE study revealed that 88 per cent of the parents of French-speaking high school students (as opposed to less than half in the case of English-speaking students) were native Quebecers. Among anglophones, those persons who have a genealogy going back four generations in Quebec are sufficiently rare to be of note; whereas, among francophones, those who do not have seven generations behind them in Quebec are rarities.

Two English-Speaking Quebecs

Owing largely to the role played by Montreal in the demography of English-speaking Quebec, there are now essentially two English-speaking universes: the metropolitan Montreal area and the rest of the province. The combined result of the out-migration of anglophones from all of Quebec and the insertion of new immigrants via the institutional and economic complex of Montreal has, over time, led to an increasing demographic concentration of the anglophone population in the Montreal area. In 1921, the proportion of Anglo-Quebecers living in the Montreal area was approximately 70 per cent, in 1971 the proportion was moving towards 85 per cent.[10]

A direct manifestation of this process is the fact that all the large ethnic populations who are now English-speaking but not of Anglo-Celtic origin are established almost exclusively in Montreal. The Italian and the Jewish communities are the two most notable cases. More recent arrivals than the earlier Anglo-Celtic (American, English, Irish and Scots) settlers of the nineteenth century, their presence is now almost non-existent outside the Montreal metropolitan area. Hence, non-Montreal English-speaking Quebec is largely Anglo-Celtic in origin (except for assimilated French Canadians); whereas such is distinctly not the case in Montreal. Those non-Anglo-Celtic communities which once existed outside Mon-

---

(*) He returned however, and died in prison.

treal, the Jewish communities in Quebec City and Sherbrooke for instance, have largely disappeared.

Well equipped with an institutional structure laid down by the original Anglo-Celtic population, the Montreal English-speaking population has become, largely as a result of out-migration of the Anglo-Celts and of the lack of ethnic affinity in the case of the rest, cut-off from non-Montreal English Quebec. Indeed, non-Montreal English Quebec functions largely on a regional basis, with only periodic recourse to the English Montreal institutional world with which it formerly had a much closer relationship. However, the recent mobilization of English Quebec spearheaded by Alliance Quebec will, il all probability, lead to a consolidation of an «on-island/off-island» contact.

Of the almost 800 000 Quebecers who declared themselves to be of English mother tongue[11] in 1976, approximately 175 000 live outside the Montreal metropolitan area. Of this number, close to one-third are in the Ottawa Valley and another third in the area known historically (as opposed to the present administrative region) as the Eastern Townships. The remaining third are divided, principally, among the Gaspé, the Lower North Shore and the Quebec City area.

The English population in all of these regions shrank between 1971 and 1976, with the exception of the Ottawa Valley. However, growth in the Ottawa Valley was the result of inter-provincial migration which has now come to an abrupt halt.

The stablest English-speaking areas, although not the largest, are the Gaspé and the Lower North Shore. It is here, as well as in the upper Ottawa Valley, that one finds the most homogenous communities. In the old urban areas, Quebec City, Sherbrooke and even Hull, English-speaking Quebec is withering fast.

But rural English Quebec, largely unknown to outsiders, contains many communities which are, from a socio-demographic point of view, rather extraordinary. In the Magdalen Islands, for instance, there exists one island community which is 98 per cent English and Protestant. Around Shawville, in the Ottawa Valley, one finds a community of over five thousand which is 90 per cent English-speaking and composed largely of Irish Protestants! Up and down the Valley, one finds solid little communities which are also over 90 per cent English-speaking but entirely Catholic. A case in point is Low, in the Gatineau Valley, where a community of less than five hundred has been able to hold on to its own high school. In the middle of Quebec, one finds Inverness where the descendants of Scottish settlers who cleared the land are still very much present in a municipality, the visage of which still clearly reflects the cultural personality of their ancestors. Going towards the American border, directly south of Montreal, one comes upon the municipalities of Potton and the village of Mansonville where a very economically marginal English- Protestant population is still the local majority, and hanging on doggedly to the only part of the world that it considers home.

All these communities are long on local identity and short on young people equipped to deal with the fast-changing society around them. The schools and cultural institutions have yet to rise to the challenge of preparing a generation of young people who will be capable of carrying forward the social capital represented by these rather extraordinary communities. With little but limited local human and spiritual resources to depend upon, largely abandoned by a Montreal which is now barely aware of their existence, their survival hangs in the balance so long as their youth continues to be educated to leave.

Cultural and Social Fragmentation

It is now commonplace to point out that the English language is all that Anglo-Quebec has in common. Ethnically and culturally, there is no homogeneity which is why the Quebec government has been able to formulate its cultural development policy in terms of «the minorities», as opposed to «the minority», and make it stick.

On ethnic and cultural terms, it is impossible to contest the government's stance. It is only in linguistic terms that there is, effectively, «a minority». However, as we argued earlier, in political terms the linguistic demarcation is more real than the culture and ethnic frontiers. The many ethnic identities are, nevertheless, real, with the result that Anglo-Quebec is fragmented culturally. Quebecers of Anglo-Celtic origin represent scarcely half the population. Jews and Italians in Montreal are major cultural constituents of an English-speaking Quebec which harbours, in addition, a wealth of cultural tradition ranging from the Amerindians to the recently constituted black Jamaican community.

Furthermore, many of these cultural communities are fragmented from within. Thus, among the Anglo-Celts, there are Irish, Scottish and English elements, while among the European ethnic groups, social and historical differences separate the pre and post-World War II immigrants.

In some cases these cultural cleavages are compounded by religious differences, particularly the Catholic-Protestant split. English-speaking Quebec is now almost equally divided between the two . . . a long cry from the day when «anglais» and «Protestant» where considered to be synonymous. Although in the eye of the non-Quebec observer such a fact might not be thought to be of great relevance in the modernized, secularized world to which Quebec now appears to belong, the social-psychological security and the structural position of minorities in Quebec is closely tied up with whether they are officially Catholic or Protestant. The Irish Protestants of Shawville control their own schools, whereas the English- speaking Catholics of Low, many of them Irish in origin, do not. The Greeks of Montreal are officially Protestant, whereas the Italians are Catholic. Consequently, the Italians found themselves embroiled in the St. Leonard affair a decade ago, whereas the Greeks have been spared such a trial.

English-speaking Quebec is, of course, also fragmented along class lines. In the past, the most notorious feature of the socio-economic character of English Quebec is its privileged position with respect to the rest of the population. In the early sixties, a unilingual English Quebecer's annual income was very close to double that of a unilingual French Quebecer. Since this time, the gap has narrowed dramatically[12] if one disregards age and education. Yet, if one looks closer it becomes apparent that although the educated anglophones are still doing quite well, the working class and rural anglophone has suffered. In fact, the unilingual anglophone worker in Montreal now earns less than his unilingual French compatriot[13], and the rural unilingual anglophone is becoming increasingly marginal to the mainstream labour market.

Finally, in addition to the ethnic, religious and class cleavages, there is, for the non-Montreal metropolitan area English, the harsh fact of geographic dispersion and the consequent isolation from the rest of the language group. Indication of this is the fact that many of them have closer and more frequent media contact with a neighbouring non-Quebec jurisdiction: i.e., with New Brunswick in the Gaspé, with the U.S.A. in part of the Eastern Townships and with Ontario in the Ottawa Valley. When one wants to get to the Gaspé in a hurry, one flies via New Brunswick, and to the Ottawa Valley, via Ontario!

In the post-war period, increasing cultural and social fragmentation has, in combination with the high degree of demographic instability discussed earlier, taken its societal toll. Its effects are manifest in a lack of the cultural homogeneity, tradition and leadership necessary to produce what is generally understood to be a community, that is, a collectivity, the members of which have enough in common to want to, and to be capable of, entering into communication with one another with a view to reflecting upon and acting upon their shared destiny. With no such thrust, they are reduced to a reactive stance. It is for this reason that post-war English-speaking Quebec is more properly designated in terms of a *population*, rather than in terms of a *community*.

Institutional Change in the Post-War Period

Perhaps the most important institutional change in the post-war period has been the nationalization of the educational sector: a Quebec-wide phenomenon involving the integration of local boards into a highly centralized state-centered network. This centralization resulted, unintentionally perhaps, in the emergence of an English school «system» in the province. This «system» included, in addition to the schools, a whole series of para-educational organizations such as associations of parents, teachers and administrators.

Locally, one of the consequences of the rationalization process was an acceleration of school consolidation: local high schools were closed and students bussed to regional schools. Leaving home quite early in the morning and returning late in the afternoon, a whole generation lost contact with their local, French-speaking neighbours. Consequently, most of the youngsters of the regional school era are less bilingual and less integrated locally than their parents. However, school «rationalization» did produce an educational sector elite capable of operating on a province-wide scale, which elite became probably the most influential English elite in the sixties. They rightly sense that the re-structuring of public elementary and secondary education, as proposed by the present Minister of Education, would undercut the organizational basis of their power.

School centralization and rationalizaton is, of course, only one manifestation of increasing government financing of, and participation in, social services generally. Locally, this process — contrary to what happened in education — did not result in the creation of an English system. Instead, it put English institutions in the position of having to integrate into a single provincial network. This process, which is still going on, has tended to weaken, as opposed to consolidate, the Englishness of many of the institutions in question. Nonetheless, some of them have succeeded admirably in «integrating» while maintaining English services for the English. But we are speaking of changes which are very much in process and the outcome is still uncertain.

A less obvious, but probably more influential, change was the demise of local English capitalism in the face of the continentalization of economic activity. No longer do you find influential English families with a significant local economic base, be it in lumbering, construction, trade, finance or industry: their contemporary English-speaking counterparts work for large continental enterprises which bring in their wake continental cultural affinities and career patterns. There is no longer an English economic clan as such, in the sense that there was in the nineteenth century, in Quebec.

A culturally oriented institutional realm which has been touched, and hence distinctively altered by the continentalization of economic activity, has been the English media. The Montreal English media is now all owned or directed by organizations which are based outside Quebec.

Finally, a change which has been the subject of little commentary is the decline and loss-of-heart in the English churches, largely as a result of a failure to produce and retain an indigenous clergy. The English churches are in a distinct holding pattern, more concerned with the prudent management of remaining assets than with defining and actualizing their role with regard to the long-term future of those they serve. The English churches, Catholic or Protestant, have not produced any significant spokesmen in the current crisis, and they appear to be having great difficulty in providing even a minimal ministry to a population which gave much of its wealth and energy to build an impressive physical establishment.

There have been other institutional changes, notably in the political realm, but they are discussed elsewhere in this volume.

In the Eye of Quebec's Demographic Crisis

Falling between the post-war developments and the post 1974 language law era we now are living in, is the Quebec «demographic crisis» of the late sixties and early seventies. The very fact that this crisis hit the English-speaking Quebec as a bolt out of the blue and, at the same time, cast it as the chief villain, dramatizes the continued existence of the two solitudes down to the end of the seventies. Current acceptance of the reality of this crisis, as well as English Quebec's role in it, is equally indicative of the emergence of a leadership which has overcome its solitude.

To return to the crisis itself and a brief description of its mechanics, it arose when French-speaking Canada, having admitted defeat by assimilation outside of Quebec and in the process of consolidating itself culturally and politically within Quebec, discovered, in the late sixties, that even there it was threatened. The internal threat was an anglophone population which was on the verge of increasing its proportional strength in Quebec. Had the situation which prevailed in the Montreal in the late sixties continued, there would now be more young Montrealers in English schools than in French schools. And once the metropolis was anglicized, the rest of Quebec would eventually fall in line; or so the francophone definers of the situation would have us believe.

The apparent suddenness and the dramatic nature of the crisis was incomprehensible to an English Quebec which was carrying on, the way it has always been since the War: accepting into its ranks anglophone immigrants, assimilating the overwhelming majority of allophone immigrants and a good number of native francophones, and sending its most established elements off to the West or to Ontario.

The new factors which rather abruptly cast the assimilating function of English Quebec into relief were the fall in the French birth-rate and the French-speaking out-migration provoked by the long-term provincial economic decline which began in 1967. Many francophones went, as their ancestors before them, to Ontario and the U.S.A. to find jobs. Those who stayed behind were not having enough children to compensate for the loss by emigration and the massive assimilation to English.

Quebec, first during the Bourassa regime and subsequently under Lévesque, felt itself obliged to resort, in the short term, to the expedient of denying English schools their traditional assimilation function and, in the long term, the more far-reaching measure of making French the language of work.

When all this came crashing down on the anglophones, the pre-eminent elite — those manning the educational establishment — was also, unfortunately, the most immediately threatened. This elite reacted, as is entirely normal, with vehemence. Their organizational interest in maintaining a clientele was transposed as the rightful cause of all of English-speaking Quebec... if not of all those desirous of «defending natural right and human liberty»!

The Language Law Era and the Out-Migration Issue

Thus, Law 22 was a direct manifestation of francophone public consciousness of the demographic crisis. It provoked, as Michael Stein relates in his article in this collection, an immediate reactive posture among anglophones such that they were to become one of the major forces responsible for bringing down the Bourassa government.

But the wrath of English Quebec was in vain: Law 22 which restricted English schools to those who could *speak* English was replaced by Law 101 which further restricted English schools to those who *are* English; and after a transitional period, to *Quebec* English at that. In retrospect, Law 22 was very «liberal», in both senses of the word — it was less restrictive and it based entry to English schools on *acquired* as opposed to *ascribed* characteristics.

In the interval, between 1974 and 1977, anglophones learned about and accepted, generally, the fact of the «demographic crisis». As a consequence, the most responsible leadership consented to abandon the campaign for «free choice»; that is, entry to English schools for whoever wished to attend. This leadership has recognized the political imperative which makes free choice impossible in the forseeable future. Hence, such an objective has ceased to be an issue inside Quebec except for a rather marginal fringe. Nevertheless, the resurgence of English militancy provoked by the imposition of unilingualism on signs and the impending school re-organization may reveal that the free choice issue was dormant rather than dead.

Notwithstanding, the language legislation is a reality and English Quebec is now confronted with its consequences. Of these, the most crucial is the closing of the demographic in-flow which characterized English Quebec, while the outlet remains wide open. Since little can be done about the inlet — no future government is likely to return to free choice — concern has shifted to the out-flow. Out-migration of anglophones, its extent and what to do about it has become one of, if not the central, issue in English Quebec. Obviously, if people continue to leave at the customary rate — or even faster, as might be expected in the circumstances — and if there are no new-comers to fill the missing places or new recruits via assimilation, then English Quebec will be faced with a major contraction in its numbers.

We know, for instance, that in the period 1961 to 1971 a full half of the annual addition to the English population were immigrants or language transfers (assimilation) as opposed to natural increase. In other words, English Quebec is, ironically, faced with a situation whereby its demographic future depends largely upon its own internal resources. . . the situation which French Quebec has known since the beginning of the eighteenth century.

As to the extent of out-migration, the verdict — owing to the fact that its measurement in terms of linguistic characteristics is a relatively recent enterprise — is not clear. Estimates produced by anglophones have been questioned by Quebec government demographers and have, to date, remained unconfirmed by subsequent census data, although the information will be available soon with the impending publication of 1981 census language statistics.

There are two obstacles mitigating against an unequivocal measure of anglophone out-migration in the short term: one is the fact that we possess very imperfect means of determining how many people leave Quebec for points outside of Canada; the other is that it is becoming increasingly evident that Canadian mother-tongue statistics are not reliable, individuals changing their mother-tongue declaration from one census to another. This last difficulty is particularly acute in Quebec where a certain language polarization induces individuals to line up, linguistically, on the French or English side. Comparative examination of the 1971 and the 1976 censuses by selected age-groups reveals that an important contingent of Quebecers most certainly did not declare for themselves and their children the same mother tongue in 1976 as they did in 1971.[14] In fact, this phenomenon may lead to a serious over-representation of the English mother-tongue population in census figures.[15]

Yet, as more research effort is channelled into delimiting the nature and extent of migratory movements in Quebec, new types of data are being found or produced. At the moment, however, despite the fact that there is no conclusive statistical documentation, informed commentators believe that there has been, over the seventies, an acceleration in the number of young English-speaking adults leaving Quebec. Moreover, there is most certainly a selective process at work. The better educated and the wealthier, as well as the most solidly anglicized elements, are leaving in greater numbers than the anglophone population at large. Inversely, the economically marginal and those lacking transportable educational skills are less likely to leave. Such a process, most evident in the non-metropolitan areas will, if it continues for long, produce an English Quebec quite different from that of the traditional stereotype.

From a Population to a Community

One very apparent demographic consequence of the changes we have reviewed briefly here will be a shake-down and consolidation of the English-speaking population of Quebec. Without a doubt, the absolute number has or will decline (in the short-term at least), but this population will enjoy a demographic stability it has never before known. Out of the present «crisis» situation and the resulting demographic stability may well emerge an elite capable of more than the simple reactive posture that has characterized it until very recently.

A willingness to search for understanding and assume responsibility is, in fact, emerging. It is apparent in the difference between the way in which Law 101 is being dealt with and the way the Law 22 issue was handled just a few years earlier. A crisis, demographic stability, and a new leadership. . . elements which may yet make of this population aggregate an historical community.

NOTES

(1) It was reprinted by the University of Toronto Press in 1974.

(2) Sheila McLeod Arnopoulos and Dominique Clift, *The English Fact in Quebec*.

(3) Michael Stein, «Le rôle des Québécois non-francophones...».

(4) The present author first made such an attempt in «l'histoire des possédants anglophones au Québec».

(5) Source: census data 1976 — Volume I, pages 1 and 2.

(6) The study was carried out by the Faculté de l'éducation of the Université Laval and by the Département de sociologie of the Université de Montréal.

(7) Special tabulation requested by the author.

(8) See Hubert Charbonneau et Robert Maheu, *Les aspects démographiques de la question linguistique*; also Gary Caldwell, *A Demographic Profile of the English-Speaking Population of Quebec* and *Out-Migration of English Mother-Tongue High-School Leavers from Quebec, 1971-1976*.

(9) Robert Sellar, *The Tragedy of Quebec...*, p. 197-198.

(10) Gary Caldwell, *A Demographic Profile of the English-Speaking Population of Quebec*, p. 29.

(11) As opposed to English as the language most often used in the home, question not asked in 1976.

(12) See for instance the work of F. Vaillancourt of the Département des sciences économiques of the Université de Montréal, *Revenus et langues, Québec 1961-1971*, 1977; also: Jac-André Boulet, *L'évolution des disparités linguistiques et revenus de travail dans la zone métropolitaine de Montréal de 1961 à 1977*.

(13) See the writings of Calvin Veltman, particularly: «Les incidences du revenu sur les transferts linguistiques...».

(14) See Gary Caldwell, *Le Québec anglophone hors de la région de Montréal dans les années soixante-dix...*, chapter 11.

(15) See Robert Maheu, *La partie cachée de la mobilité linguistique*.

A Brief Sketch of the Economic History of English Quebec [1]

Robert Sweeny

ROBERT SWEENY. A native Montrealer, Robert Sweeny has studied at Bishop's, Sir George Williams, UQAM and McGill. He is presently teaching history at UQAM and is co-director of the Montreal Business History Project at McGill.

I once had a great aunt, who was born in Point St. Charles and died on the slopes of Westmount eighty-five years later. She loved to visit churches. On her eighty-first birthday, my uncle asked her if she would like to visit Eglise St. Jacques on St. Denis Street at the corner of St. Catherine. Oh no, she couldn't do that. After appropriate probing, my uncle discovered that it was because it was too far east. In fact, she had never gone past Bleury. Of such stuff myths are made.

Myths die hard, and the traditional ethnic approach to Canadian history is no exception. The simplistic drama of Lord Durham's two nations warring in the bosom of a single state still pervades much, too much, of English Canadian historiography. For it is a description that befits a man who saw little of the country and knew even less. It does poor justice to the complexity of our past. Perhaps this brief and all too superficial essay will do little better, but at least my myths — I naturally prefer to call them assumptions — are different. After all, I've gone past Bleury!

By placing the conquest of New France in a larger context, one can better understand the subsequent development of anglophones in Quebec. England had reconquered Ireland seventy years before, and two decades had almost passed since the suppression of the last major Scottish revolt. Foreign trade would soon account for a third of all of English commerce. On the eve of the first industrial revolution, the government of England had already shown itself to be responsive to the interests of manufacturing as well. In short, it was the leading bourgeois state of the mid-eighteenth century. Little surprise therefore, that four out of the five reasons William Pitt the elder gave for conquering Canada were purely economic.[2]

The initial impact of the conquest was minimal. Few Englishmen emigrated to Canada, most of the discharged British soldiers settled in sparsely populated regions to the west of Montreal,[3] and a *modus vivendi* was worked out with the Church and those seigneurs who elected to stay on. Nevertheless, the loss of the thirteen colonies in 1783 brought with it significant changes in the social composition, economic structure and military importance of Quebec. Of the approximately 40 000 United Empire Loyalists, roughly half settled in Quebec as it then was (Upper Canada was not created as a separate entity until 1791). By 1785, over 1 800 families had been settled in the eight new townships above Longueuil seigneury and in the area of the Bay of Quinte. A deliberate attempt was made by the British military authorities to maintain ethnic and religious uniformity in each of the townships, so, for example, the Anglicans were settled in one township, the Catholic Highlanders in another.

One of the prominent features of the British Empire in the late eighteenth and early nineteenth centuries were the extended mercantile partnerships. These firms were composed of a number of individual merchants, each of whom invested capital in the partnership, which was used to finance the export of manufactured products from Britain and the import of raw materials, or semi-manufactured products from the colonies. The partnership would operate under different names in different places, generally using the names of those partners resident in the city. Marital and familial ties were frequent among partners. The largest of these firms had their principal offices in London, Liverpool or Glasgow. With the loss of the American colonies and the significant increase in the size of the British garrisons in Quebec City and Montreal, a number of these mercantile firms moved their American offices to Lower Canada. Typical of this was the firm of Forsyth & Richardson, part of Phynn, Ellice, Inglis & Company of London, which, after moving to Montreal from Schenectady in the mid-1780s, quickly rose to be the most important firm in Montreal.

The period leading up to the end of the Napoleonic Wars saw the development of two important export industries in Lower Canada, both controlled by anglophone merchants. The fur trade had been an important component in the economy of New France, and it was to be further developed by a very small group of Anglo-Scottish merchants operating out of Montreal. The three-way rivalry between the Hudson's Bay Company, John Jacob Astor's American Fur Company of New York, and the variety of Montreal firms which merged to form the Northwest Company[4] pushed the systematic pillage of the Indian lands to as far north as Great Slave Lake by 1812. The Bourgeois of the Northwest, James McGill, Simon McTavish, William McGillivray, Joseph and Benjamin Frobisher, and Forsyth & Richardson accumulated large fortunes in the trade.

The second important export trade, squared timber, developed as a result of the strategic interests of Great Britain. In order to ensure an adequate supply of timber for her naval yards, from within the Empire, a series of preferential duties were established by Britain, starting in 1796 and peaking in 1814. At the port of Quebec, the principal trans-shipment point for the Canadas, there arose an influential group of merchants who owned the wharfs where the loading took place and advanced the capital necessary for the establishment of the *chantiers* on the tributaries of the St. Lawrence. The largest of these merchants were members of British mercantile houses such as Pollock & Gilmour, but the majority were Anglo-Scottish merchants operating on their own account.

The rapid integration of the economy of Lower Canada into the Imperial network, in the last decades of the eighteenth century, brought with it significant changes in the political structure of the province. By the Constitutional Act of 1791, an elected Legislative Assembly and an appointed Legislative Council, with the possibility of hereditary membership, were created. Much has been written about the constitutional conflicts between the elected, predominately francophone, Assembly, and the appointed Council, composed principally of leading English and Scottish merchants from Montreal and Quebec City. But as recent studies have shown,[5] these conflicts were limited, almost exclusively, to constitutional questions: the right of the Assembly to adopt a permanent Civil List, limitations on the prerogatives of the Governor in Council, etc. The overwhelming majority of Bills relating to public works, economic development and subsidies to hospitals and schools were adopted without division.

Nevertheless, these constitutional debates did reflect divergent interests concerning the future of the colony. The earliest anglophone political group was formed in the first decade of the nineteenth century, and was called the Scot Party. Its leading members were the merchants involved in the fur, timber and import trades, and they favoured a further integration of the colony into the Empire. Their position was accurately stated in the following editorial from the *Quebec Mercury* of 1806:

> This province is far too French for a British colony. It is absolutely necessary that we exert all our efforts, by every available means, to oppose the increase of the French and the augmentation of their influence. After 47 years' possession it is now fitting that the Province become truly British.

The policies advanced by the Scot Party were well received by the leading colonial officials in Quebec, due to the communality of class as well as ethnic interests:

> It seems to me truly absurd, milord, that the interests of an important colony, as well as those of a considerable part of the commercial class of the British Empire, should be placed in the hands of six unimportant shop-keepers, a blacksmith, a carpenter and fifteen ignorant peasants. [. . .] There is not to be found in the Assembly a single person that one could consider a Canadian gentleman.[6]

That the Scot party spoke for only a small part of the anglophone electorate in the colony was indicated by the fact that the county of Bedford, the only rural county where the anglophones were in a majority, elected a French Canadian to represent them in the Assembly.

* * *

The diversity of the anglophone community in Lower Canada was accentuated by the massive emigration from the British Isles after the Napoleonic Wars. The capitalist rationalization of agriculture, symbolized by the enclosure movements, the introduction of new techniques in industry which caused widespread unemployment and drastic wage cuts (over 75 per cent in weaving) in the traditional industries, and the systematic destruction of the Irish economy after the failure of the '98 Rebellion, all contributed to the enormous social and demographic dislocation that historians call the Industrial Revolution. Millions of peasants, labourers and artisans were forced to emigrate from the British Isles. Many came to Canada. There were only six years between 1829 and 1859 when the number of emigrants from England, Scotland and Ireland, arriving at the port of Quebec in a single shipping season, was lower than 20 000.

TABLE I — **Evolution in the Occupational Structure of Quebec City (1795-1831) & Montreal (1819-1831) by Linguistic Group (Francophone — Anglophone)***

A- QUEBEC CITY

	1795		1831	
	Franco.	Anglo.	Franco.	Anglo.
Professionals	18 (50%)	18 (50%)	52 (46%)	60 (54%)
Business men	142 (51%)	136 (49%)	441 (45%)	520 (55%)
Artisans	505 (76%)	160 (24%)	1102 (61%)	686 (39%)
Day-Labourers	159 (90%)	19 (10%)	427 (49%)	433 (51%)

B- MONTREAL

	1819		1831	
	Franco.	Anglo.	Franco.	Anglo.
Professionals	31 (40%)	45 (60%)	55 (40%)	82 (60%)
Business men	224 (34%)	424 (66%)	392 (35%)	727 (65%)
Artisans	225 (38%)	364 (62%)	869 (45%)	1039 (55%)
Day-Labourers	157 (75%)	51 (25%)	411 (47%)	449 (53%)

Source: Fernand Ouellet, *Éléments d'histoire sociale au Bas-Canada*, Montréal, HMH, 1972.

* The figures are for heads of households.

Already by 1831, the occupational structure of the anglophone communities in Montreal and Quebec City had been transformed. In short, close to 40 per cent of the heads of households in Quebec City and over 50 per cent in Montreal belonging to the popular classes were anglophone by 1831.

It would appear that relatively few of the hundreds of thousands of British and Irish immigrants of this period remained in Lower Canada. A contemporary account (1826) estimated that a mere 5 per cent stayed, and 15 per cent went on to settle in Upper Canada. The rest emigrated to the United States.[7] Even by the standards of the day, the conditions both aboard the immigrant ships and in the temporary housing erected for them on shore were horrendous. The colonial officials responsible for the emigrants attempted to make light of the situation; in 1831, the agent at Quebec City, A.C. Buchanan, stated:

> The voyage from the United Kingdom to the St. Lawrence is one of perfect health. The majority of the emigrants are from Ireland and Scotland and principally live on the light food of potatoes or stirabout made from oatmeal, so that very rarely indeed does any serious sickness occur; besides, the fogs and cold weather generally experienced in crossing the Banks of Newfoundland, are a complete extinguisher to disease or contagion. [8]

A year later, in the summer of 1832, within the limits of Lower Canada only, over 17 000 people (overwhelmingly Irish) died from cholera brought over on the timber ships used to transport the immigrants. There was, perhaps, some poetic justice in the fact that Buchanan, himself a Quebec City timber merchant, was unable to file his annual report that year; he was sick with cholera.

Having survived the trip over, few of the emigrants could establish themselves in their new land. Roughly 75 per cent were without capital, [9] while most of the land open to freehold tenure, 850 000 acres in the Eastern Townships, had been granted to the British American Land Company. It was available only at a price, a price that the victims of the British government's policy of «shovelling out the paupers», to use the expression of the day, could ill afford.

There had been some settlement of the Townships by Americans in the early decades of the nineteenth century. By some leading members of the anglophone community, this was considered a «mad policy», creating «a frontier-line of settlements inhabited by colonists of the same blood and religion as those of the enemy». [10] Two border areas received the bulk of these immigrants: the Missisquoi Bay area of Stanbridge, Dunham and St. Armand, and the Stanstead area, east of Lake Memphremagog, consisting of Hatley, Stanstead and Barnston. By 1825, each of these townships had more than a thousand residents. [11] Immigration continued into the Townships and by 1831, there were 37 000 inhabitants in the area, of whom close to 90 per cent were anglophone. [12] But in the years following the establishment of the Land Company, 1833, relatively few immigrants, from the United States or the British Isles, settled here. According to the 1851 census, more than 70 per cent of each of the five major regions in the Townships were native-born. The significant difference, with the earlier settlement, was that in the fastest growing areas (St. Francis, Leeds and Milton) over a third of the population was francophone. [13]

Although the land policy adopted by the Colonial authorities did not aid in settling the mass of immigrants in the Townships, it indirectly furthered economic development. Profits made by the Company aided in the formation of a class of

Canadian industrialists. William Price reinvested his profits in the opening up of the Saguenay to timber and later sawn lumber production, A.T. Galt invested in one of the earliest cotton mills in the colony, before going on to be the Finance Minister who proposed Confederation; and Richard William Heneker became President of the Eastern Townships Bank, promoter of the International Railway and owner of the Paton Manufacturing Company. However, poor immigrants in the cities of Montreal and Quebec were left little alternative than to become wage earners.

As Lord Goderich had commented, a year after the granting of the monopoly to the British American Land Company:

> Has it, on the other hand, been sufficiently considered... whether it would conduce to the real prosperity of the province to encourage every man who can labour, to do so only on his own account, to obtain and cultivate his own allotment of land without giving or receiving assistance from others? Without some division of labour, without a class of persons willing to work for wages how can a society be prevented from falling into a state of almost primitive rudeness; and how are the comforts and refinements of life to be preserved?[16]

The major public works of the early period, the Lachine Canal and the Rideau Canal, were both built by Irish labourers.[14] The most important railway in the province, the St. Lawrence and Atlantic, which ran from Montreal to Portland, Maine, was also built by Irish workmen. In the six workcamps strung along the line between Montreal and Sherbrooke in 1851, 898 of the 1 004 employees were day labourers, of whom 75 per cent were Irish Catholics. Only 7 per cent were native born Canadians.[15]

Those emigrants who stayed on in the colony tended to settle in either Montreal or Quebec City. There were no other major towns in the colony.[17] As a result, by mid-century, both cities had large anglophone populations. Dickens' opening lines to *A Tale of Two Cities* could well have been applied to Montreal or Quebec. Life was one of striking contrasts: a well known study by P. Carpenter, *On the Vital Statistics of Montreal* (1869), was subtitled «The City of Wealth and Death». In the suburbs of Griffintown and St. Mary,[18] thousands of families paid up to six dollars* a month for the «right» to live in crowded tenement flats. The entrance way to these flats was by means of a small courtyard, that doubled as the

---

* One must remember that, at that time, a labourer receiving 0,75 $ for a day of work (when he actually worked), was «well paid».

latrine for the up to ten families living around the yard. In the heat of the summer, the courtyards were cesspools; disease was rampant. Increasingly, the merchants and manufacturers moved out of the old part of the city, as it was transformed by the opening of the port to ocean-going ships and the industrialization along the Lachine Canal.[19] On the slopes of Mont Royal, they built elegant mansions and town houses, the Golden Square Mile, eloquent testimony to the success of their business ventures.

* * *

The economy of Canada East was in the midst of an important transformation. During the first half of the century, a number of important commercial partnerships had grown up with the trade between the Canadas and Great Britain. Banks and insurance companies had been founded by the merchants in both Quebec City and Montreal. The earlier network of canals, having proved inadequate in the competition for the inland trade, was being supplemented by the railroads, while the techniques of modern industry were no longer limited to the agricultural based businesses of brewing and distilling. The complex historical process of evolving from artisanal production to modern factory production was nearing completion in the largest industries: shoe making, flour milling, and lumber.[20] Nor was this process limited to production. Many small proprietors in the traditional trades came under increasing pressure with the growth of large-scale business operations.[21]

The debasing of traditional skills and trades radically altered the lives of the popular classes. This transformation was not achieved without resistance, and anglophone working people played an active role in the formation of early trade unions and strikes. Actions against the introduction of new machinery, the reorganization of the division of labour, work speed-ups, and wage reductions pepper the history of the period. At a time when trade unions were illegal, anglophone artisans and labourers formed benevolent societies which provided mutual life and health insurance as well as serving as informal trade unions.[22] The largest benevolent society in the province was the Quebec Ship Labourers' Benevolent Society, which numbered some 2 000 members in 1888. In a testimony before the Royal Commission of Inquiry on the Relations between Capital and Labor, Thomas Cullen, a laborer, stated:

> Before the formation of the Society those were the days of oppression and poverty for the ship labourers. The men were victims of very hard usage. They were looked upon as nothing. . . It was absolutely necessary that they should organize.[23]

Health care and education had long been serious questions in the colony. With the triumph of industrialism over the traditional popular values of «a just wage» and «a just price»,[24] they were posed all the more acutely. A variety of charitable institutions had been formed by merchants, in both Montreal and Quebec City in the early decades of the nineteenth century. Certain of these institutions, such as the Montreal General Hospital and the Montreal Foundling Hospital, were open to all Protestants; the majority of these institutions were more narrowly defined for the members of a particular denomination or nationality. Throughout the century, these institutions and a variety of later, more specialized ones, such as the MacKay and the Weredale, were the only social services available to the Protestant anglophone community. There was no public system. Financing was done through government grants and fund-raising drives.

The largest of these institutions were run by boards of directors that included members of the principal families of the bourgeoisie. The rest were run by, and were often the creation of, the wives of the upper classes.[25] Such charitable work demanded free time, and at least five institutions in Montreal doubled as employment agencies for domestic servants. From the mid-1840s to 1881, an average of 6,25 per cent of the total female population of Montreal worked as domestic servants, the majority, it would appear, being unmarried Irish women.[26]

For the Irish community — forming half of the anglophones in Montreal until the Jewish immigration at the turn of the century — social services were the almost exclusive preserve of the Roman Catholic Church. In the early period of massive Irish immigration, the Church was reticent to establish separate institutions for the Irish.[27] But in the wake of the 1837 Rebellion, when the Irish had been the most consistent allies of the Patriotes among the anglophones in Lower Canada, and with the continuance of secret societies among the Irish, the Church authorities allowed the establishment of both separate parishes and social institutions.

The separate, but unequal, policy in social services was also the rule in education. The establishment of the Royal Institution for the Advancement of Learning (McGill University is all that is left of the Royal Institute), in 1801, placed the onus for schooling squarely on the private sector. Partial funding, from public revenues, would be available for schools created by local individuals or groups. The result was a hodge-podge of small institutions, private in nature, with uneven academic and financial requirements. The various Protestant denominations were very active in the field. The Anglican Church founded a private school and a university in the Eastern Townships (Bishop's College and University). The more evangelical denominations provided a modicum of education in their Sunday schools. The religious nature of the school system in the colony was reflected in the guarantee that A.T. Galt had incorporated in the B N A Act whereby funding for *Protestant*, rather than *English*, education was guaranteed by the Constitution. Certain of the schools founded in this period, notably those in Montreal (historically linked to McGill), continued well into the twentieth century.[28] But for the majority of the anglophone population in the nineteenth century, an education was gained at home, or on the job, or not at all.

* * *

In the last half of the nineteenth century, the anglophone population of Quebec grew slowly, significantly slower than the francophone population. Added to this relative decline was the tendency for anglophones to concentrate in certain areas. Quebec City declined as a major centre in the last half of the nineteenth century. Without a rail link to central Canada and with the significant decline in timber exports after 1864, the city was reduced to a regional, rather than national, centre. By 1901 it had only a quarter of the population of Montreal.[29] Also, the Eastern Townships, before the rise of the dairy industry, had still not succeeded in becoming a viable agricultural region. With the loss of local control over a number of important regional manufacturing and financial concerns to Montreal and Toronto, the economic situation was not all that favourable. In both areas, the relative importance of the anglophone population declined.

Montreal was in a different situation. In 1861, slightly more than half the city's 90 300 inhabitants were of Irish or British origin; by 1901 this had been reduced to 37 per cent and... of a city that had more than doubled in population! An important indication of the future trends could be seen in the shift of population within the city limits:

TABLE II — **British & Irish Residence by District 1861 & 1901**

	1861		1901	
	% of B. & I.	% of district total	% of B. & I.	% of district total
Old City	12	49	1,5	34
West wards	46	68	59	65
Centre wards	27	49	25	41
East wards	15	31	14,5	13,5

Source: see foot-note no 30.

In short only the western wards of the city maintained their English *cachet*, and this was achieved by a large-scale exodus from the old city. The significance of this was that the population of the older part of the city had traditionally been professionals and bourgeois, those very same people who supplied the leadership for the anglophone educational and social institutions of the city. As they moved westward, so did these institutions.

Before discussing the impact on the anglophone population of this relative geographical concentration in the western end of Montreal, it is necessary to place the upper classes of this community in perspective. Since the 1840s the city had played a key role in the economic life of the country. By the turn of the century, the largest transportation companies, the largest bank, the most important mining companies, and most of the leading industrial companies were headquartered in Montreal. The market they controlled was pan-Canadian. The financial capital of the country was St. James Street. As recent studies have shown, in particular that of Gilles Piédalue,[31] there was a coalescence of financial and industrial power in the first decades of the twentieth century. Two of the three financial groups that were formed during this period in Canada were based in Montreal. Considering the size of the economy, these concentrations of power were more significant than either the Morgan or the Rockefeller groups were in the United States.

It was this immense power and the wealth that it generated that enlarged the fundamental inequality between the francophone and the anglophone communities in Montreal.[32] In the later part of the nineteenth century, this inequality was visible in the statistics on mortality:

TABLE III — **Average 1876-96 Mortality Rates by 1 000 of Population**

Ethnic Origin	Total rate	Infant mortality rate (under 5 years)
French	34,56	60,4
Irish	23,50	39,4
British	17,60	40,9

Source: Data from Noël Bélanger et al., *Les travailleurs québécois, 1851-1896* (Montréal, Les Presses de l'Université du Québec, 1975): 51.

Throughout the century this disparity had been visible in literacy rates,[33] and, as Alan Metcalfe has shown, it became increasingly evident in recreational activities.[34]

The localization of the anglophones combined with the private and ethnic nature of the social services, in this type of economic context, resulted in a privileged system that was self-perpetuating. This is not to deny the class nature of the anglophone community; Point St. Charles was distant from Westmount in a way only money can measure. Nevertheless, the educational opportunities,[35] the health care facilities,[36] and the job opportunities[37] for an anglophone worker were better than for his francophone counterpart. And in the first half of the twentieth century, the gap grew greater.

* * *

The last decade of the nineteenth century saw the beginning of the immigration from central Europe that would significantly alter the ethnic composition of the city. By 1901, over 15 per cent of the eastern ward of the old city and the two central wards that were directly north of it, St. Lawrence and St. Louis, spoke neither French nor English as their mother tongue.[38] In the central core of the city, running north from the harbour between Bleury and St. Denis, sandwiched between the English west end and the French east end, an ethnic buffer zone was being formed.

The glaring disparities between anglophone and francophone Montreal in the fields of education, social services and employment increased as the wealth generated from the control of a pan-Canadian market was reflected in the rapid expansion of the English institutions in response to the new immigration. These proved powerful factors in assuring that the new Canadians would become English Canadians.

This concentration of economic power reinforced the duality of life in Quebec at a variety of levels. At the turn of the century, English Montreal boasted four daily newspapers and two city-wide weeklies. While none of these papers consistently defended the interests of either the majority of anglophones or the legitimate national aspirations of Québécois people, their mere number assured at least a variety of opinions. By 1914, Sir Hugh Graham controlled all the English press in the city, save for *The Gazette*.

Adequate studies of the sociological impact of the national oppression of Québécois on the various social strata of the anglophone community in Quebec have yet to be done. However, the fact that the only major industrial region in the country where the Communist Party failed to make any headway in the 1930s was Montreal is an indication of the extent to which a deliberately fostered ethnic identification can mitigate class consciousness.

The rapid expansion of the two major financial groups that operated out of Montreal[39] (Bank of Montreal and Royal Bank), came to an abrupt end with the Great Depression. Capital which had been exported during the previous decades by the recently consolidated monopolies in banking, transport, insurance and public utilities was repatriated.[40] Significant problems were encountered by the province's principal manufacturing industry — pulp and paper[41] — while the province's largest manufacturing industry, in terms of employment (textiles) cut wages and shut down factories despite their high protective tarifs.[42]

With respect to the long-term economic development of the province, perhaps the most significant aspect of the 1930s was not something that happened, but rather something which failed to happen. Relatively little Montreal-controlled capital was invested in mining. With the exception of the Timmins area, the capital used to develop the mining industry was either Toronto based or American. As the western economies pulled themselves out of the Depression by gearing up for war, the profits accumulated increasingly in Toronto rather than Montreal. Within a very short time, the financial capital of the country had shifted to Bay Street.

The military conquest of Quebec in 1759, and its subsequent integration into the economy of the British Empire, laid the basis for the national oppression of Quebec. Although the early attempts by the colonial authorities to maintain this oppression (through the fostering of narrow ethnic and confessional identification) were in large measure a success, the rapid social and economic transformations of the Canadian Industrial Revolution accentuated class contradictions within both the anglophone and francophone communities. While anglophones only infrequently supported the struggle against national oppression during the nineteenth century, struggles over economic issues repeatedly transcended national divisions.

The fights against the destruction of traditional artisanal trades, for a shorter working day, for better wages, and for unionization frequently involved both anglophone and francophone workers and leadership. The consolidation, at the beginning of the century, of the upper stratum of the bourgeoisie, which was overwhelmingly English Canadian, accentuated the national divisions within Quebec. The inequalities in the social, educational and health fields increased and, over time, this exacerbated inequities in job opportunities and class mobility.

* * *

Numerous lessons, relevant to the present, can be drawn from the complexities of the past, but in the context of this collection of essays, perhaps two points merit special reference. They are the source of wealth of the anglophone community, particularly in Montreal, and the economic impact of the recent attempts to redress certain of the more flagrant aspects of national oppression in Quebec.

While mitigated by both class and ethnic considerations, the anglophone community has benefited from the unequal development of the Canadian economy. Much of the capital accumulated in Montreal during this century has been achieved through the control of pan-Canadian and not infrequently transnational corporations. The profits from the CPR's operations on the prairies, the Webster family's coal mines in Cape Breton, the Bank of Montreal's financing of the Reid Newfoundland Company, the Greenshield's ownership of the public utility monopoly in Jamaica, Nesbitt.Thomson's hydro-electric monopoly in Northern Ontario, Sun Life's dominant position in the insurance field in Canada, to name but a few, combined with the monopolies and oligopolies built on the low wages paid to the Quebec workers, created a pool of wealth in Montreal that permitted the financing of philanthropic endeavours. McGill, Bishop's, the Royal Vic, the Montreal General, the Saidye Bronfman, the Douglas, the Royal Edward, the Montreal Association for the Blind . . . ; the list is a long one. The eclipse of St. James Street by Bay Street and the rise to prominence of Calgary and Vancouver as financial centres have altered the networks of profit and power in Canada. But in the debate over the recent spate of head office transfers, much more has been written about the potential loss of a position of relative privilege than the injustice of an economic system that creates and feeds on regional disparities.

Since the Sauvé government of 1959, successive provincial administrations have been forced, by the campaigns led by trade unions and other mass organizations, to redress certain of the grave inequalities in the social, educational and health fields that were discussed in this chapter. The failure of the Quiet Revolution to eradicate these injustices is clear. By whatever yard stick one choses to use — number of hospital beds, average per capita income, number of university openings, rate of unemployment, home ownership — the gap between the anglophone and francophone communities in Quebec remains, and with the cutbacks in government services under both the Bourassa and Levesque administrations, these gaps have widened.

This failure is dialectically related to the first point raised above. The cut-backs and the severity of both unemployment and inflation in Quebec during the 1970s and early 1980s are directly linked to the weakness of the capital accumulation by the Québécois bourgeoisie. With almost no monopolies in the private sector, and few oligopolies, the expansion of the state's infrastructure is limited by the absence of a corresponding growth in the economic base. The recent publication of the economic programme of the provincial government, *Bâtir le Québec,* clearly shows that it has learned this lesson. The building-up of the Québécois bourgeoisie, through the use of the Caisse de dépôt et placement, Hydro-Québec, favourable tax incentives, cut-backs in public services, and selective aid to both the traditional cooperative movement (Caisse Populaire, Québec-Lait, etc.) and small- and medium-size entreprises (PME) with export potential, will be the priority of government during the coming decade.

NOTES

(1) In this text, «Québécois» and «English Canadian» are used as analytical tools. They refer to those people who were/are members of either the Québbécois or English-Canadian nations. A nation being an historically evolved stable community of people formed on the basis of a common language, territory, economic life and psychological make-up manifested in a common culture. While precise dates for the fulfillment of these requirements can not be given, generally, one can speak of the Québécois nation by the first quarter of the nineteenth century, and of the English-Canadian nation by the third quarter of the nineteenth century.

(2) E.J. Hobsbawn, *Industry and Empire* (Harmonsworth, Penguin Books, 1971):49. This is the best single volume history of the British Empire for the period 1750-1914.

(3) Certain small settlements, principally for strategic reasons, were created at Murray Bay, Matapedia and Rivière du Loup as well.

(4) The Northwest Company was formed in 1775, but did not constitute a monopoly of Montreal fur-traders until the absorption of the XY Company in 1804.

(5) Alan Dever, *Economic Development and the Lower Canadian Assembly, 1828-1840.*

(6) Taken from a letter written by the Governor Sir James Craig to Lord Liverpool, May 10, 1810. As reproduced in *Archives canadiennes: Documents constitutionnels 4*, George V, A. 1914, p. 402. Translation by the author.

(7) *British Sessional Papers*, 1826, vol. IV, p. 48.

(8) *Ibid.*, 1831-32, vol. XXXII, p. 229.

(9) J. Greenlaw & P. Orr, «Social Origins of Scottish Immigration to Lower Canada».

(10) The words are those of Andrew Stuart, writing in 1816, as cited in F.W. Terrill, *Chronology of Montreal and of Canada from A.D. 1752 to A.D. 1893*, Montreal, John Lovell, 1893.

(11) This, as well as the rest of the figures, comes from Françoise Noël Smith's unpublished M.A. thesis, *The Establishment of Religious Communities in the Eastern Townships 1797-1851.*

(12) While 74,6 per cent of Lower Canada were Roman Catholics in 1831, only 11,4 per cent of the inhabitants of the Townships were Catholics. Presumably, these include some Irish or Highland Catholics.

(13) In fact, the real percentages are probably higher, because at the time of the census there were over a thousand people living in the work camps of the St. Lawrence and Atlantic Railway, principally in the St. Francis region. The railway employed very few francophones.

(14) H.C. Pentland, «The Development of a Capitalistic Labour Market in Canada».

(15) J.-P. Kesteman, «Les travailleurs à la construction du chemin de fer dans la région de Sherbrooke (1851-53)».

(16) *British Sessional Papers*, 1834, vol. XLIV, p. 296. I am grateful to Jane Greenlaw for bringing this quotation to my attention.

(17) In 1851 the largest town in the Eastern Townships, Sherbrooke, had only 2 998 inhabitants. Trois Rivières, with 4 936, and Sorel 3 424 were the closest in size to Quebec City with its 42 052 inhabitants (41 per cent being anglophones), and Montreal with 57 715 (just over 50 per cent anglophone).

(18) St. Mary Ward was east of the old city at the foot of St. Mary's Current and Griffintown; part of St. Anne's ward was west of the city walls, north of the Lachine Canal.

(19) Both took place in the 1840s. The port expanded after the dredging of Lac St. Pierre and the canal development followed the harnessing of the water power of the new locks.

(20) This is a complicated process that has only begun to be fully studied in the Canadian context, the fully studied in the Canadian context, the best work to date being the M.A. thesis of Joanne Burgess of the U.Q.A.M. on the largest industry of the nineteenth century Montreal, that of shoemaking. A précis, under the same title as her 1977 thesis, was published as «L'industrie de la chaussure à Montréal: 1840-1870 — le passage de l'artisanat à la fabrique», *Revue d'histoire de l'Amérique française*, 31,2(sept. 1977). Little work has been done on the flour industry, and one must still rely on the work of A.R.M. Lower for the lumber industry, *The North American Assault on the Canadian Forest*, Toronto, 1937; also *Britain's Woodyard*, Toronto, 1976.

(21) An excellent case study by Margaret Heap concerning the carters and theirs strikes against the exclusive contracts of the Grand Trunk Railway is available in «La grève des charretiers à Montréal, 1864», *Revue d'histoire de l'Amérique française*, 31, 2(déc. 1977).

(22) In both Burgess op. cit. and Heap op. cit., one can see examples of the role of anglophones in these actions. See also Jean Hamelin et al., *Répertoire des grèves dans la province de Québec au XIXᵉ siècle*, Montréal, les presses de l'école des H.E.C., 1970; Charles Lipton, *The Trade Union Movement of Canada 1827-1959*, Toronto, NC Press, 1973; and R. Leahey and T. Cullen's Testimony in *Canada Investigates Industrialism*, ed. G. Kealey.

(23) See the testimonies of R. Leahey and T. Cullen, G. Kealey, ed., already cited in the preceding note.

(24) These terms date from the late Middle Ages and their usage has been studied in the European context by E.P. Thompson and George Rudé. They were an intrinsic part of the popular ideology built around artisanal production. E.P. Thompson, *The Making of the English Working Class*, New York, Vintage Books, 1963 and George Rudé, *The Crowd in History, 1730-1848*, New York, John Wiley & Sons, 1964.

(25) D. Suzanne Cross, «The Neglected Majority: The Changing Role of Women in nineteenth Century Montreal», *Histoire Sociale — Social History*, 6, 12(nov. 1973):216.

(26) *Ibid.*, p. 209. The institutions were: St. George Society, Y.W.C.A., Protestant House of Industry and Refuge, Women's Protective Immigration Society, and the Montreal Day Nursery.

(27) John S. Moir, «The Problem of Double Minority: Some Reflections on the Development of the English-Speaking Catholic Church in Canada in the Nineteenth Century».

(28) Notably the McGill Normal School, the Montreal School of Nursing and the High School of Montreal. The latter did not close its doors until June 1979.

(29) In 1851, there were 42 000 in Quebec and 57 000 in Montreal; by 1901, there were 68,800 in Quebec and 267,700 in Montreal. Source: *Rapport des Archives du Québec*, 1922, p. 27.

(30) Based on figures compiled by the Groupe de Recherche sur la Société Montréalaise au dix-neuvième siècle at the UQAM from census data. The compilation is mine. Totals are out due to rounding. West wards: Ste. Anne and St. Antoine. Centre Wards: St. Laurent and St. Louis. East wards: St. Jacques and Ste. Marie.

(31) Gilles Piédalue, *La bourgeoisie canadienne et le problème de la réalisation du profit au Canada, 1900-1930*.

(32) Only two francophone families made it into either of the groups, the Forgets and the Rollands.

(33) Although I consider that the interpretative parts of Allan Greer's «The Pattern of Literacy in Quebec, 1745-1899», *Histoire Sociale — Social History*, 11, 22(nov. 1978) are open to serious question, his statistical material on the Buller Commission (1830s) and later census data clearly show that the anglophones were consistently more literate.

(34) A. Metcalfe, «The Evolution of Organized Physical Recreation in Montreal, 1840-1895», *Histoire Sociale — Social History*, 11, 21. Of the thirty private or commercial athletic facilities in Montreal between 1860-1895 (within the city limits), the breakdown by ward is as follows: Ste. Anne 6; St. Antoine 15; St. Lawrence 1; St. Louis 4; St. Jacques 3; Old City 1; and Ste. Marie 0. (p. 160).

(35) In 1917, when non-Catholics were less than 30 per cent of the population of the city, there were 7 314 students enrolled in PSBGM schools above the level of grade 4 and only 6 154 students enrolled at this level in CECM schools. Municipal tax support per pupil for CECM schools was $45 per annum in 1921. It was $87 per pupil in PSBGM schools. Source: Terry Copp, *The Anatomy of Poverty, the condition of the working class in Montreal, 1897-1929*, pp. 61 and 68.

(36) The fight against T B is a case in point. The largest and best equipped hospital in the city was the Royal Edward Chest Hospital — funded by the Burland family as a gift in 1909. It was an English hospital that operated in English. When Hugh Graham gave $100 000 to fund two clinics in 1924, it was equally divided between a clinic in Hochelaga and one in the west. According to the Montreal Health Survey of 1927, francophones had a T.B. rate of 167 per 100 000, while English Canadians had a rate of 95 per 100 000. See Copp, op. cit., pp. 100-103 and Kathy McCuaig, *Campaign against Tuberculosis in Canada, 1900-1950*, M.A. Thesis, McGill University, 1979.

(37) There was a disproportionate number of anglophones in skilled trades at Vickers, Dominion Bridge, Northern Electric, Dominion Engineering, Angus Shops and the G.T.R. In 1931, anglophones were 7,5 per cent under-represented in unskilled jobs and 7,1 per cent over-represented in white collar jobs for the province as a whole. Source: John Porter, *The Vertical Mosaic: an analysis of social class and power in Canada*, p. 94.

(38) Groupe de recherche sur la société montréalaise, UQAM.

(39) In 1930, the principal companies in the Royal Bank group were: Dominion Bridge, Montreal Trust, Canada Steamship Lines, Montreal Light Heat & Power, Canada Power & Paper, Dominion Steel & Coal, and Montreal Tramways Co. The leading companies associated with the Bank of Montreal group were: Royal Trust, Dominion Rubber, Dominion Textile, C.P.R., Bell Telephone, and Ogilvie Flour Mills. Sun Life Assurance Co. enjoyed relations with both groups, but was closest to the latter.

(40) Among the numerous examples that could be cited, perhaps the most graphic was the Bank of Montreal's activities in Mexico. It opened its first branch in 1906, was the largest financial institution in that country by 1926, but closed its operations in 1934.

(41) Gilles Piédalue, «Les groupes financiers et la guerre du papier au Canada 1929-1930», *Revue d'histoire de l'Amérique française*, 30, 2(sept. 1976):223-258.

(42) Justice Turgeon, *Royal Commission of Inquiry into the Textile Industry*, Ottawa, King's Printer, 1938-39. See also the first chapter of the CNTU's history *En Greve*, Montreal, Éditions du Jour, 1964.

Education for English-Speaking People until 1964

Alan W. Jones

ALAN W. JONES is Chairman of the Graduate School of Education in Bishop's University; he has served on the Protestant Committee of the Superior Council of Education and is at present the Chairman of AQEM (Anglo Quebec En Mutation).

Quebec's educational system is different from all others. It is confessional, that is, its schools are either Protestant or Catholic. This article attempts to provide the background to the development of schools for English-speaking children prior to the creation of the Ministry of Education in 1964. Therefore, it must deal with both Protestant and Catholic schools for English-speaking children. The reader is asked to do two things. First, he should discard the notion that English equals Protestant and French equals Catholic, for a moment's reflection will show that it is possible to be both English and Catholic or to be both French and Protestant. Second, he needs to admit the possibility that there are other ways of looking at the foundations of education than the one taking its origin from the U.S.A. in the nineteenth century, and so widely held today, namely that the provision of education is unquestionably a function of the state, and that the state should provide common schools in which the children of all members of the community served by a given school are brought together for a common purpose laid down by a secular authority. Without these mental adjustments, the development of education in Quebec will be incomprehensible.

The first recorded English-speaking settlement within the confines of the present boundaries of the Province was at Rupert House in the seventeenth century, but it was natural that the numbers of English-speaking people here were not large until after the Cession of New France in 1763. Then, immigrants came both from the British Isles and from the English-speaking lands to the south of us. Within the period from the Cession until the Rebellion of 1837, there were the administrators, soldiers and traders (such as James McGill) who settled mainly in the urban centres of the St. Lawrence Valley. Then there were the pioneer fishermen of Quebec's eastern seaboard. The Robin family, for example, had a plant on the Baie des Chaleurs in 1764 to serve the cod fisheries there. Farmers from England and Scotland settled unoccupied lands away from the seigneuries of the St. Lawrence Lowlands so that the Eastern Townships, the Chateauguay Valley and the Ottawa Valley acquired English- speaking communities. The migration was made more complex by the loyalty to the Crown felt and acted upon by many of those uprooted by the Revolutionary War. Thus, Loyalist settlements were founded on the Gaspé Peninsula, notably at Paspebiac, in 1784,[1] and there was a Loyalist component in the settlement of the Eastern Townships in the 1790s. A further complication was the migration, beginning in the early years of the nineteenth century, of Irish men and women, who, although they came from a rural environment, tended to congregate, as Irish migrants often do, in the cities. In short, the English-speaking people coming and settling in the years from 1763 to 1837 were diverse in origin, occupation and belief. This lack of homogeneity was emphasized by the scattered distribution of settlement.

All immigrants bring with them a notion of what education ought to be. Usually it is a carbon copy of that to which they are accustomed. In this diversity of immigrants it is useful to see three distinct concepts of education: that from England, that from the northern states of the U.S.A. and that from Ireland.

Officially, England's education was under the control of her Church, so that, for example, Anglican bishops licensed schoolmasters. More than this, to be properly English meant being Anglican, for to be loyal to the King meant also to be loyal to the Church of the land he ruled. In theory, education had to have an Anglican basis. In practice, the working classes in England got only as much education as the squirearchy chose to give them out of charity. The middle classes often sent their sons to the endowed grammar schools where they were supposed to get a classical education, but these schools had often sunk into lethargy. A more practical education could be had at schools and academies set up outside the «system» by Non-Conformists. Such private ventures usually died with the proprietor.

Migrants from the United States, whether Loyalists or not, brought with them a different view of education. They were accustomed to citizens taking the initiative in providing education as a civic duty. They were more willing to produce a workable compromise on matters of religion in school by excising what was controversial or distinctive. Also, they did not see the use of taxes on schooling as inappropriate.

By contrast, Irish immigrants would see education as Catholics have always seen it. That is, education must be part of the work of the Catholic Church in caring for and raising her flock. It is an aspect of pastoral care and has nothing to do with the secular state.

These ways of looking at education are irreconcilable, but each may be discerned in the medley of approaches to education seen in Quebec in the period 1763-1837. In examining the history of this period, it is illuminating to abandon the customary chronological approach and examine the way in which each theory contributed to the development of education.

The accepted English theory, which bound together Church and State, explains the official declaration in 1763 that the Anglican Church, including its schools, would be supported by grants of land. It shows, too, why the Bishop of London was supposed to license any schoolmaster coming to Quebec from England. Nevertheless, the lethargy in England was paralleled by inertia in Quebec, and no real attempt to build a system on this theory was made until Quebec had her own Anglican Bishop. Consecrated in 1793, Jacob Mountain wanted to station Protestant English schoolmasters in every parish to teach English free of charge, together with writing and arithmetic at a small fee, claiming that such a policy would break down the barrier between the English and French within a few years.[2] This concept of providing free schools was embodied in the Act of 1801 «for the Establishment of Free Schools and the Advancement of Learning in this Province». It was left to the people of each parish to decide whether they wanted to build a school, but the number of parishes opting to build one, and then to hand it over in accordance with the Act to a quasi- government agency (the Royal Institution for the Advancement of Learning) in return for support was, understandably, small.

The unofficial English practice of allowing schools to be set up as private ventures, because the official «system» did not work properly, was also transferred to Quebec. Newspapers of the period carried discreet notices announcing to the public the schoolowners' academic wares. By 1790, there were at least six such schools in Quebec City educating some two hundred pupils. We know little about these schools for their records disappeared with their proprietors, and newspaper announcements concerning them are likely to be as trustworthy as most advertisements.

The influence of American thought can be seen in the Report of the Dorchester Committee issued in 1789. Despite its name, the Committee, which was to investigate the shortcomings of educational provision and to suggest remedies, was chaired by Judge William Smith, a Loyalist from New York. It recommended the establishment of a complete state system of education, with a free elementary school in each village or parish, a secondary school in each county town and a «University of the Province of Quebec» in Quebec City. The University was to teach the Liberal Arts and Sciences but not Theology, and was to be open to all, regardless of denomination. Nothing came of the scheme.

English-speaking Catholics would not see the need for government committees to deal with education. By 1819 the English-speaking Catholic population of Montreal included about thirty families in the congregation of Bonsecours Church. The opening of the «Salle des petites Irlandaises» by the Sulpician fathers in 1823 indicated the way in which the Church viewed its duties. By 1837, the Congregation of Notre Dame was also involved in the education of Irish immigrant children, and the Bishop of Montreal, Mgr Lartigue, had established a school for them in the basement of the sacristy of the cathedral.[3]

In this period from 1763 until 1837, no one theory of education had met with complete success. The Dorchester Committee achieved nothing, and the Royal Institution for the Advancement of Learning little, in relation to the scale of the problem. Even the pragmatic attempt to put power and money into the hands of local communities by the Syndics Act of 1829 had foundered after an encouraging beginning.

In the turmoil amongst the Province's rulers following the 1837 Rebellion, education came high on the list of solutions to the unrest. The possibility of bringing everyone together and systematically assimilating French-speaking Canadians into the English-speaking population by the instrument of education was advocated as the final solution to the problem by Lord Durham and his associates. The disinclination of French Canadians to be assimilated according to an American model is understandable, but beyond the terms of reference of this article. What is important for an understanding of the development of education for English-speaking people is that attention was focused on education as a function of government.

The Act of Union of 1840 formally united Upper and Lower Canada, and legislation of the first session of the Parliament of the United Canadas set up a state system of education. From the start the two Canadas found themselves to be incompatible in matters educational, and within a few years had agreed to separate, so that Canada East (i.e., Quebec) had its own system of education quite distinct from that of Canada West (i.e., Ontario). Rather than follow in detail all the changes and revisions of the early 1840s, it is convenient to describe the consolidating Act of 1846, under which Quebec's public education operated and grew for more than a century.

While today it is often thought that only fanatical bigots insist that education should have a religious basis, it seems not unreasonable for parents, or a group of parents, to want to pass on their culture to their children and to argue that, as the culture is based upon religion, education too must be founded upon that religion. In 1846, therefore, Quebec had not only a system of common schools under locally-elected school commissioners and supported by local taxes, but also the provision that religion would be taught in the schools, a provision that accords with the importance of religion in the attempts we have seen at providing education up to that date. Nevertheless, Quebec's population did not all belong to one religious group and so the Act of 1846 allowed dissent. This meant that the school commissioners would see to the provision of religious education in the school under their jurisdiction, but any tax-payers might dissent and set up their own school, which would be supported by the taxes of these dissentient tax-payers. Naturally, as Protestants were in the minority in the Province as a whole, such dissentient boards were frequently Protestant, but since it was a question of dissent *at the local level*, this need not be so, and, if Catholics were in a minority and dissented, then the dissentient board for that locality would be Catholic. A few of each breed have withstood the vicissitudes of time, though in small numbers: for example, in 1977, there was a Protestant dissentient board at Baie Comeau and a Catholic dissentient board at Portage du Fort.[4] In Quebec City and in Montreal, the principle of dissent did not apply in the Act of 1846: in each of those cities there was to be a Catholic Board of School Commissioners and a Protestant Board of School Commisssioners. Nowhere was anything said about the language of instruction.

This administrative edifice may impress us as important as we look at it from our own bureaucratic era. More important in getting things done was local ability and initiative. Arthur Buller's sweeping and insulting remarks in Lord Durham's Report about the state of education were based upon a most superficial enquiry. The Report states categorically:

> It only remains that I should add, that though the adults
> who have come from the Old Country are generally

more or less educated, the English are hardly better off than the French for the means of education for their children, and indeed possess scarcely any, except in the cities. [5]

This is hardly borne out by the existence of a number of academies owing something to the New England model, such as the Charleston Academy at Hatley whose Preceptor, Zadock Thompson, a Master of Arts, had, in 835, published *A Geography and History of Lower Canada*. Twenty years later, local initiative had increased the number of academies to fourteen in the Eastern Thowships alone, with an enrollment of about a thousand pupils.

Amongst English-speaking Catholics, local initiative had to deal with a new wave of immigration. The rapid increase of immigration from Ireland during the eighteen-forties was such that large numbers of English-speaking Catholics, often destitute, sick, half-starved and barely surviving the Atlantic crossing were landed in Quebec. That they needed assistance in providing themselves with the basic necessities of life simply to survive was obvious. Education could not head the list of priorities. Progress was sometimes slow, but the work of the Christian Brothers, who had come to Quebec in 1837 and whose vocation was directed to the provision of education for the poor, provided a nucleus around which education for English-speaking Catholics could grow.

By the time of Confederation, Quebec's educational system based upon the Act of 1846, but leaving much to local initiative and enterprise, was one that allowed for difference of opinion regarding answers to ultimate questions, and accorded equality even in matters of finance to those who dissented from the majority position. This concept was written into the document that served Canada in lieu of a constitution for more than one hundred years. Section 93 of the British North America Act begins:

> In and for each Province the Legislature may exclusive-ly make Laws in relation to Education, subject and according to the following Provisions: . . . Nothing in any such Law shall prejudicially affect any Right or Privilege with respect to Denominational Schools which any Class of Persons have by Law in the Province at the Union. . .

There being Protestant and Catholic schools in the Province at the Union, as long as the British North America Act remained in force, no act of the legislature of the Province of Quebec could prejudicially affect the rights which Protestants and Catholics had to such schools. It must be understood that the guarantees in the matter of schooling were religious and not linguistic.

As regards the development of a central authority for education, Quebec's experience differs from that in all the other provinces. Back in the 1840s Canada East and Canada West each had their own Superintendent of Education, but the climate of opinion was such that J.-B. Meilleur, the Superintendent for Canada East, was never able to build up his office so that it might be compared with that strong central authority created by Egerton Ryerson, the Superintendent for Canada West, in the fast developing lands to the west of the Ottawa River. Similarly, although Quebec established a Ministry of Public Instruction immediately after Confederation, it is significant that it lasted only eight years, and that after 1875 the central authority for public education was the Council for Public Instruction, a nominated body, which, it was alleged, would take education out of the realm of politics. It is also significant that the 1875 Act, drawn up in the years immediately following the firs Vatican Council, gave all the Catholic bishops a place ex-officio on the Council of Public Instruction. Furthermore, it gave control of all matters pertaining to Catholic education to the Catholic Committee of the Council, and control over all matters pertaining to Protestant education to the Protestant Committee. Quebec's education had divided itself into two systems. How separate they were can be seen in the failure of the Council of Public Instruction to meet as a whole after 1908.

Usually in Quebec, one hears and reads about «the French system» and «the English system», but it can be seen that such terms refer to entities that do not exist. Nor is it a question of «the English system» being almost congruent with the Protestant system. In the nine decades between the abolition of the Ministry of Public Instruction in 1875 and the creation of the Ministry of Education in 1964, Quebec's different education systems grew undisturbed by any major change in structure. In 1966-67, the pupils were distributed as follows with respect to language and religion:[6]

	In Public Schools	In Private Schools
French-speaking Roman Catholic:	1 227 217	97 796
French-speaking Protestant:	5 039	939
English-speaking Roman Catholic:	101 107	9 130
English-speaking Protestant:	123 611	10 476

It is striking that the number of English-speaking Catholics almost equaled the number of English-speaking Protestants. Nor is it a question of English-speaking Catholics being concentrated so exclusively in Montreal as to render French-speaking and Catholic synonymous in the rest of the Province. The farming lands of the Ottawa Valley, for example, have a numerous English-speaking Catholic population. Then again, as the province industrialized, most industrial towns attracted English-speakers, both Protestant and Catholic, each community being sufficiently vigorous to support its own school. Shawinigan and Trois-Rivières are examples of pulp-and-paper towns, and Val d'Or an example of a mining town that drew a considerable number of anglophones.

As the English-speaking people had grouped themselves into two distinct communities for their schooling, and as the schooling in each case was based upon a distinct theory of education, there is no common theme to the history of the two between 1875 and 1964. For English-speaking Protestants, there were two major issues to be dealt with during this period: first, the question of consolidation and second, how to accommodate those who were neither Protestant nor Catholic. For English-speaking Catholics the perennial question was: how to survive in a system in which they were outnumbered twelve-to-one by French-speaking Catholics.

In 1902, Sir John Adams, Professor of Education in the University of London, examined the Protestant education system of the province. To the system in Montreal he was complimentary. There, the community was wealthy enough to put up good buildings and to pay teachers well. Outside Montreal there were three types of school: the academy, the model school, and the district school. The academy was often excellent, with a good staff working in a satisfactory building. The model school, which by the Regulation of the Protestant Committee, had to give instruction in algebra, geometry, French and Latin as well as the elementary subjects, often did not justify its name. Usually, it was to be found in a community insufficiently energetic or not wealthy enough to run an academy properly. Regarding the district school (which was the ordinary village school providing the four grades of the elementary course), Adams wrote:

> Speaking generally, these are very bad. They consist of three parts: the schoolhouse proper, the woodshed, the outhouses. The schoolhouse is almost always built of wood, generally clap-boarded, and often painted a dark purplish red. Even the literal log-cabin is not lacking. The number of windows varies from three to eight [. . .] The rule is that when one enters from the road one finds oneself directly in the schoolroom, facing the teacher who is seated at her desk on a slightly raised platform. Between the door and the teacher is the stove. On both sides of the room the desks are arranged so that the children face each other [. . .] The floor is usually made up of broad planks full of nails and knots. In most cases the building is weather-tight, but I saw several schools that let in the rain through the roof, and permitted the wind to make itself felt within the room [. . .] The woodshed is usually quite suitable, for here the needs of the case appeal to the practical Commissioners (sic). The outhouses as a rule are not very satisfactory, either from the point of view of sanitation or of refinement.

As 60 per cent of the district schools enrolled fifteen pupils or fewer, were usually taught by an unqualified teacher and might be open for only a few months a year, Adams recommended consolidation.[7] A start was made at Kingsey in 1905. As the years passed and the means of transporting children improved, the process gained pace, so that the size of rural schools and the area they served increased. The process of «regionalization» which was generated by the Quiet Revolution, and so lies outside the scope of this article, should be seen as a continuation of this trend into an era of more advanced technology. Just as there was considerable debate in the Kingsey case in 1905 about the merits of a community losing its local school in exchange for participation in a larger one at a distance, so the question has been argued throughout rural Canada. For English-speeaking Quebecers, though, there is an additional difficulty. Since they are a minority, their small numbers in a particular locality may mean that their children have to travel immense distances daily.

The problem of what to do about those who were neither Catholic nor Protestant arose after Confederation and usually had to be tackled by the Protestant community. It was immigration that gave Quebec her first major non-Catholic, non-Protestant group: the Jews. Inevitably, an immigrant group coming to Canada in the late nineteenth century, and knowing neither English nor French, would choose to learn English because it was the language of commerce. Jews would also prefer the Protestant to the Catholic school because religious observances were less time-consuming and less obvious in the former. While numbers were few, some workable *ad hoc* arrangement was easy enough to arrange, but when a host community sees the numbers rising, it feels threatened. Would the admission of Jews to a Protestant school diminish the «protestantness» of the school?

This question is at the heart of the debate that went on in Montreal for the first three decades of this century and ended in 1930 with a Jewish School Commission being set up in that city, but making an agreement with the Protestant School Commissioners for the education of Jewish children. Subsequently, other non-Protestant, non-Catholic groups immigrating to Quebec tended to look to the Protestant system for the schooling of their children, and this helped to generate the belief that the Protestant system was no longer Protestant but secular.

English-speaking Catholics, like everyone else in Quebec, have their rights in education based upon religion and not language. Unlike the English-speaking Protestants, they have been unable to dominate the school boards that provide the education for their children. Without any constitutional guarantees, they have had to rely for survival upon the generosity of French-speaking Catholics in allowing them a measure of autonomy. Even in Montreal where, as with the English-speaking population in general, they are congregated, and where legislation in 1928 «established a semi-autonomous administrative committee» for English-language schools within the Montreal Catholic School Commission, they cannot enjoy the same independence that English-speaking Protestants enjoy. Besides this vital difference in administrative structure, there are two other major points to note about English-speaking Catholics in Quebec in the twentieth century. First, they gradually ceased to be dominated by the Irish. Catholic immigrants from Italy or Poland, for example, would opt for English-speaking Catholic schools. By the 1950s it was possible to find a Catholic school in Montreal where the language of instruction was English and in which sixteen nationalities were represented, but where hardly a child had an Irish name. Second, there was the question of whether the course of studies provided in English Catholic schools should be simply a translation of what was approved for French Catholic schools, or whether there should be a distinct programme.[8]

Just as English-speaking people developed their schools about a number of different educational theories, so in higher education there was no uniformity, but a variety of institutions growing out of the initiative of particular groups. Loyola College was obviously Catholic and the University of Bishop's College equally obviously Anglican. Sir George Williams College grew out of the Y.M.C.A. movement. Quebec's best-known English-language institution of higher learning, McGill University, named after James McGill, the trader who willed part of his estate to the founding of a college, grew up under the aegis of the Royal Institution for the Advancement of Learning and quickly became non-denominational.

Looked at from outside at the beginning of the Quiet Revolution, Quebec's education may seem to institutionalize the centrifugal forces within the Province. Protestant separates from Catholic. English-speaking separates from French-speaking. At the same time, since Quebec was less influenced than many other parts of Canada by American theories of educational organization, her educational system stands apart, and is based upon a different premise from that held in much of the rest of the continent.

NOTES

(1) Wilbur H. Siebert, «The Loyalist Settlements on the Gaspé Peninsula», *Transactions of the Royal Society of Canada*, 8(March 1915):399-405.

(2) Thomas R. Millman, *Jacob Mountain First Lord Bishop of Quebec:...*, p. 171.

(3) Paul Gallagher, *A History of Public Education for English-speaking Catholics in the Province of Quebec* pp. 30-33.

(4) Quebec, ministère de l'Éducation, *Répertoire des organismes et des écoles*, pp. 177, 187.

(5) Gerald M. Craig (ed.), *Lord Durham's Report: An Abridgement...*, p. 71.

(6) Roger Magnuson, *Education in the Province of Quebec*, p. 20.

(7) John Adams, *The Protestant School System...*, pp. 7-9.

(8) G. Emmett Carter, *The Catholic Public Schools of Quebec,* pp. 70-79.

Part II

CONSCIOUSNESS OF SELF, OTHER, AND OF QUEBEC

There is considerable evidence to suggest that, as individuals, anglophones are far ahead of their institutions in coming to terms with the new Quebec. In other words, many individuals willingly seek radical solutions to their progressive marginalization vis-à-vis the larger society. If they don't leave the province, they accommodate. It is indicative that the most comprehensive review and analysis of the relevant academic literature on the changes recently undergone by English-speaking Quebec — that of Michael Stein which he has revised for this volume — was written from a «psychological» as opposed to a «structuralist» perspective.

Accommodation takes place principally with respect to language. Use of French by anglophones in their interactions with francophones is patently on the increase. However, acquisition of the appropriate language skills is still not assured by the classic English-language educational system. Consequently, two options exist: one, of immersion programmes within the English schools and, the other, quite simply, of placing children in French schools. Because of its artificial environment, the former has the disadvantage of maintaining a certain social isolation from francophones, while the latter incorporates the risk of a child's English language and cultural heritage suffering. Some parents seek a compromise in assuring a primary education for their children in the French system and a secondary education in the English one.

The dilemma that is created by the educational system is symptomatic of the general issue of the insertion of anglophones in Quebec society. While the acquisition of French language skills ensures an ability to function more adequately in Quebec, it does not necessarily lead to creative participation and implication in the larger society. If the second language does not serve as a vehicle for the transmission of certain values, then integration (with a sharing of the aspirations of the majority) is not assured. Thus, many anglophones who have passed through immersion programmes, while fluently bilingual still see themselves as situated outside the mainstream of Quebec society, unable to define their own place and role in it and even reticent about calling themselves «Quebecers» or «Québécois». Their strategy appears as strictly utilitarian in nature, lacking in empathy and devoid of any real committment to the dominant culture. Eliminating the «us» and «them» from day-to-day conversation is something not everyone manages to do for it requires more drastic measures.

It is no doubt these circumstances that have led some anglophones to choose to «cross the boundary» — in terms of education, marriage, residence and work environment — as described by McLeod Arnopoulos. For such individuals, integration is usually total. It is, no doubt, from their ranks that the fifty to sixty thousand anglophones who voted for the Parti Québécois in the last two provincial elections are drawn. However, these individuals are, in many respects, marginal people. First, and foremost, many come from outside Quebec — Ontario, the United States and Britain — or are of immigrant background. Native Anglo-Quebecers appear to be much more reticent about making such moves, conditioned no doubt by the weight of the past and a certain order in which they were unequivocally *majoritaire*. Secondly, in crossing the boundary, these individuals become invisible in the sense that, functioning within the francophone majority, they are without an anglophone constituency to speak to or inspire.

In the final analysis, whether the absence of such a constituency is to be explained in terms of the kinds of individuals they are — recent migrants, marginals and loners — or because of structural arrangements is unclear. Certainly, an early generation of marginals, the Anglo-Catholics, did assume an important brokerage role. Whatever the reasons for this difference, the implications of it are clear. Individual accommodation, while widespread, has not led to a spontaneous and generalized re-definition of the status or allegiance of anglophones, and it is not clear that it will in the future. At the most, one can, perhaps, envisage the gradual erosion of an old Quebec *anglophonie* as such «transfuges» multiply and, with it, the undermining of anglophone institutions, the latter having been long abandoned by the more resourceful, innovative and even influential members of English-Quebec society. On the other hand, it is conceivable — although admittedly not very likely — that, as a result of some kind of creative distillation of history and minority status, there will emerge an anglo-Quebec cultural consciousness which would serve well both its bearers and the larger society.

Changing Anglo-Quebecer Self Counciousness

Michael Stein

MICHAEL STEIN. Presently professor of political science at McMaster University in Hamilton, Ontario, Michael Stein has taught at both Carleton University in Ottawa and McGill University. While at McGill, his interest in Canadian and Quebec politics led him to the question of transformations of political consciousness among English-speaking Quebecers. Subsequently, he worked as a senior research consultant with the Pépin-Robarts Commission.

When invited in 1982 to up-date his 1979 text, Professor Stein decided to leave it as is. He reported to us, however, that, in his view, the phase of «awareness and action», which he refers to in his article, is continuing to this day with, it would seem, an increased concern amongst anglophones regarding their future place and role in Quebec; and an amplified polarization between the «federalist camp» and those who believe in integration into the new Quebec through accommodation.

Introduction

Since the historic election of November 15, 1976, the anglophone community in Quebec has been experiencing a profound psychological transformation. This change has almost completely escaped the attention of social and political observers, whose gaze has been riveted on the internal division between «federalists» and «independentists» within the francophone community. Yet, the responsiveness of the anglophone community may have an equally crucial and durable significance for the ultimate outcome of the internal Quebec debate. The English Quebecers are consistently used as a reference point for francophones of all persuasions in their efforts to evaluate the progress they have made in their struggle for greater social and economic equality within the Quebec and Canadian milieux. They are frequently a primary target of both francophones in Quebec and anglophones in other parts of Canada for their alleged smugness and sense of superiority, for their tendency to live apart from their francophone neighbours both physically and spiritually, and for their economic success, often at the expense of the francophones. In discussions about the future of Canada, they are often discounted as a negligible and even expendable quantity.

In this essay*, I shall address myself to two principal questions:

1) What was the self-image, within the provincial political context, of anglophone or non-francophone Quebecers (including anglophones proper and non-francophone immigrants)[1] in the past, and how has it been changing? What impact did the election of a Parti Québécois government on November 15, 1976 and its re-election in 1981 have on this self-image?[2]

2) What effective provincial political role might they play during the coming years?

In its self-analysis of its own role in Quebec, the anglophone community may be described as having gone through at least two distinct phases since the end of World War II: 1) a phase of self-confident «majority group» consciousness; and 2) a phase of majority-minority group image dissonance and defensiveness. Since the assumption of power by the Parti Québécois in November 1976, and particularly since the passage of that government's controversial language legislation, Law 101, in August 1977, the anglophone community has entered a third phase, which I have previously labelled 3) a phase of minority group positive self-awareness and action.[3]

* This paper is an updated and expanded version of Michael B. Stein, «Le rôle des Québécois non-francophones dans le débat actuel entre le Québec et le Canada», *Études Internationales*, 8, 3(juin 1977):292-306. I would like to express my gratitude to Stanley Ehrlich for his research assistance for the revised and updated version, and to Balbinder Dodd for his aid in the original draft. I would also like to thank William Coleman of McMaster University for his valuable comments on an earlier draft.

The Phase of Self-Confident «Majority Group» Consciousness

The first phase of self-confident «majority group» consciousness had existed for a long period of time prior to the Quiet Revolution of the 1960s. Indeed, it can be traced back as far as the period after 1763 immediately following the Conquest, when British merchants and officials established their economic and political control over the «habitants» remaining in Quebec. The height of this «majority group» feeling must undoubtedly have been reached during the period between 1830 and 1865, when those of British origin actually were in the majority in the City of Montreal,[4] the Papineau Rebellion had been crushed, and the English merchants had formed an alliance with the French clergy to ensure that the Union with Canada West would work without its objectionable assimilationist overtones.

At the time of Confederation, the first period of extensive urbanization occurred, and by the first census of 1871, there was again a majority of about 60 per cent French in Montreal itself — in the province as a whole the high French-Canadian birth rate had ensured that the overall numerical advantage of French Canadians would remain at about 80 per cent. This balance between French- and English-speaking Canadians of about 80 per cent to 20 per cent in the province as a whole, and 60 per cent to 40 per cent in Montreal itself, remained virtually unchanged for almost a century, until well after the beginning of the Quiet Revolution of the sixties.[5]

The self-confident «majority-group» consciousness of Quebec anglophones was marked by a sense of their superior educational and cultural backgrounds, their higher overall average incomes, and their commanding positions in the economy of Quebec. There has also been an identification with the English-speaking *political majority* at the national level and the Federal government which reflects it.[6] Quebec anglophones tended to regard the *Federal government* rather than the Provincial government as their instrument and their protector, and they looked to the rest of English-speaking Canada for support and sympathy when they felt their «rights» were being circumscribed. Finally, there was an identification with the *majority culture* of English-speaking Canada and North America since Quebec anglophones read many of the same newspapers, periodicals and books, were exposed to the same radio and television programs, viewed the same films, and identified with the same sporting and recreational events as other English-speaking people on this continent.[7]

These basic attitudes translated themselves into several important institutional and behavioural manifestations. They include completely separate anglophone community institutions in isolation from their francophone neighbours, and a print and electronic media which, in its local coverage, concentrated almost exclusively on events within the anglophone community.[8] The media neglected almost completely the francophone milieu, and deprived Quebec anglophones of an opportunity to attune themselves to changes occurring in the

110

francophone community.[9] In addition, there were relatively few anglophones who were functionally bilingual and an even smaller number who were able to converse and write fluently in French, deficiencies which reinforced a trend to anglophone isolationism.[10] In the political-administrative sphere, Quebec anglophones relied primarily on covert elite pressure on Quebec governmental and administrative leaders to attain political favours. This pressure was exerted primarily through face-to-face and telephone contacts between anglophone business and community leaders on the one hand and francophone cabinet ministers and senior officials on the other, often through the intermediary of key anglophone MNAs.[11] They had very little direct representation in the higher echelons of the Quebec public service. After the death of Duplessis, almost all anglophone partisan support went to the Provincial Liberals.

During the Quiet Revolution, which followed the Duplessis era there was general anglophone adaptation to, and even enthusiastic acceptance of, most of the major reforms in the fields of the economy, education and language, including bilingualism at the Federal level; although the latter was probably a belated concession by Quebec anglophones in the face of a recognized threat to their status.[12]

The non-francophone immigrant community began to arrive in Quebec in large numbers prior to World War I. The early immigrants, including Jews, Germans, Poles, Ukrainians and Russians, attended Anglo-Protestant or Anglo-Catholic schools for the most part — in some cases, because no alternative was permitted — and integrated most fully with the Quebec anglophone community. Those non-francophone immigrants who arrived in large numbers somewhat later, such as the Italians, tended to retain their European mother tongues for longer periods, and also established a greater degree of autonomy vis-à-vis the anglophone community. The Italians, like the Irish to a degree before them, had closer social and cultural ties and a higher rate of inter-marriage with the majority French community. At the same time they desired to achieve upward economic mobility, and tended, therefore, after World War II, to send their children primarily to English-language Catholic schools.[13] Their attitudes and behaviour, therefore, did not differ markedly from those of the economically dominant anglophones, whose leadership on political and economic matters they tended to follow.[14]

The Phase of Majority-Minority Group Image Dissonance and Defensiveness

The self-confident «majority group» psychology of the Quebec anglophones had first begun to be shaken by some of the important changes which were taking place in Quebec during the Quiet Revolution, including: 1) encroachment on the hitherto autonomous operations of Anglo-Quebec local institutions and social services by government efforts at reorganizing and standardizing educational structures (Laws 62, 28, 71), government regulation of professional and charitable institutions (Law 65), regrouping of municipalities, and the creation of regional and metropolitan governments. Thus, the anglophones were no longer a self-governing community, but were subject to the will of the governing francophone majority, which had now adopted an interventionist posture; 2) the rise and growing strength of the independence movement in Quebec, including the unification of all splinter groups under the banner of the Parti Québécois and the leadership of René Lévesque in 1968, and its attainment of 23 per cent of the popular vote in the provincial election of 1970; the temporary threat to the constitutional-legal order in the FLQ Crisis of October 1970; and the establishment of the Parti Québécois as the Official Opposition with 30 per cent of the vote in the provincial elections of 1973. These events forced many Quebec anglophones to face the possibility that they might no longer be able to depend on the Federal government or other English-speaking Canadians for the protection of their rights, should an independent Quebec become a reality.

However, the first real watershed in transforming attitudes came with the passage of Bill 22 by the Liberal government in July of 1974.[15] Law 22, or the Official Language Act, made French the sole official language of the province; and, in the eyes of most anglophones reduced English to the status of a minority or second-class language. This itself was a severe psychological blow to them since they had always regarded official use of their language as an «acquired right». It had been at least partially entrenched in the Canadian Constitution through Article 133 of the BNA Act (which specifically accorded protection to English in the legislature and courts of Quebec). A second major objection was raised against the limitation on parental right of choice of language of instruction for their children, directed particularly at the non-francophone immigrant population. Freedom of choice in language of instruction had been guaranteed to all Quebecers by Law 63, passed in 1969 by the Union Nationale government over much francophone nationalist protest. A third major objection was raised by some anglophones against the requirement that firms of a certain minimum size doing business in Quebec include enough French in their daily operations to earn a government-awarded «francization» certificate; failure to comply involved facing such punitive measures as loss of government contracts, fines, etc. Finally, there were many opponents of the Law who objected to it on constitutional grounds or in terms of human rights, arguing that it violated the fundamental guarantees for English language and minority educational rights provided in sections 133 and 93 of the BNA Act, contravened the principle of bilingualism enshrined in the Federal Official Languages Act of 1969, and accorded too much discretionary authority to officials in Quebec City to interpret or apply the generalized provisions of the Act.

The validity or non-validity of these objections is not at issue in this paper — although in my view, apart from the provisions related to language tests for non-francophone immigrants, the Act was, on the whole, moderate in tenor and a useful means of buttressing the French language and culture in Quebec in the face of real threats to its long-run survival. What is important to understand is that, globally, these measures were perceived by a substantial majority of both the anglophone and non-francophone immigrant communities as the first direct attack by the Quebec authorities on their status and even as a threat to their survival. Many anglophones reacted with extreme emotion and bitterness, and some manifested fear and a degree of paranoia. There were angry meetings held to protest the Bill, during which the Premier, the Minister of Education, and the anglophone ministers in the Bourassa cabinet who were present were severely criticized.[16] Almost all briefs presented by the anglophones to the Education Committee of the National Assembly were highly critical and extremely emotional (and, one might add, generally ill-prepared, poorly documented, badly defended, and devoid of constructive suggestions for amendments). All efforts to oppose the Bill, including the «backbenchers' revolt» by Liberals Springate and Ciaccia, the constitutional challenge in the courts, and a radio campaign conducted by John Robertson and George Springate on CFCF Radio to support a petition to repeal the legislation, came to no avail. Subsequent efforts to block implementation of language testing provisions at the school board level, which had been designed to integrate immigrant children into the French sector, achieved a measure of success, but they failed to convince the Bourassa Liberals to eliminate the tests altogether.[17]

An even greater blow to the anglophone «majority group» psychology came with the election of the Parti Québécois on November 15, 1976. The decision by Premier Bourassa to call the election after only three years of his mandate had elapsed caught most anglophones (as well as francophones) by surprise. In the early days of the campaign, the anglophones seemed prepared to vote massively against the Liberals and in favour of the rejuvenated Union Nationale Party, buoyed by the fresh political image of their new leader, Rodrigue Biron. There was also a smattering of support for two «new» third parties, the municipally-oriented Democratic Alliance and Jérôme Choquette's Parti National Populaire. This disaffection had arisen in part from the opposition to Law 22 and, in part, from the highhandedness, alleged corruption, and economic mismanagement of the Bourassa government (including its inept handling of Mayor Drapeau's costly and wasteful Olympic Games extravaganza). A poll was conducted by Maurice Pinard and Richard Hamilton, two McGill professors, about midway through the campaign which found that about 80 per cent of Quebec anglophones and 65 per cent of Quebec immigrants felt some dissatisfaction towards the Bourassa Liberals — this compared to a dissatisfaction rate of 65 per cent for Quebec francophones. Although a very high proportion of all voters (about 40 per cent) were still undecided as to which party they preferred at that point, 49 per cent of anglophones then willing to indicate their choice planned to vote for the Union Nationale, and only 31 per cent opted for the Liberals. Eleven per cent indicated a preference for the Parti Québécois and 9 per cent divided their support among the smaller «third» parties. More strikingly, the first significant division between anglophones and non-francophone immigrants in political attitudes and behaviour manifested itself. Among non-francophone immigrants willing to declare themselves, 28 per cent favoured the Union Nationale, 28 per cent leaned to the Liberals, and the largest proportion, 31 per cent, actually favoured the Parti Québécois at this juncture.

In the interim period (November 5th to 15th), much pressure was applied by the Liberal machine to regain the support of these groups on the grounds that a vote for any party other than the Liberals was a vote for «separatism». This appeal had worked admirably in 1970 and 1973 helping the Liberals to amass over 90 per cent of the non-francophone vote in the province. On November 15th, it appeared to work among these groups once again. Anglophones on the West Island voted overwhelmingly for the Bourassa team, sending ten of eleven Liberal candidates to the National Assembly (Pointe Claire, the eleventh riding, elected a Union Nationale candidate). The three central ridings of the city containing large proportions of non-francophone immigrants also sent Liberal candidates to the National Assembly. Almost everywhere else in the province, the tide had turned strongly in favour of the Parti Québécois which won 41 per cent of the popular vote and 71 seats. The anglophone community appeared completely isolated, out of step, and politically impotent for the first time in Quebec history.

The stunning PQ victory left many Anglo-Quebecers in a state of near paralysis marked by dismay, incredulity and fear. Business in Montreal ground to a halt as local members of the Anglophone-dominated industrial and commercial sectors paused to take stock. It was widely reported that vast amounts of savings were flowing out of the province, and the contents of many safety deposit boxes were being emptied and placed in banks located in areas bordering Quebec. There was much speculation about the new Parti Québécois government under René Lévesque, the future of the province and the country, and above all, personal assessments of one's future place within or outside Quebec.[18]

These anxieties were intensified when the Parti Québécois introduced its own Charter of the French Language in Quebec as a replacement for the Official Language Act of the Liberals in April 1977. Bill 101, as it ultimately came to be known, was actually introduced in three phases: 1) a White Paper, tabled on April 1st and fiercely debated throughout mst of the month of April, 2) Bill 1, the Charter of the French Language, tabled on April 28th and subjected to intensive private and public examination and criticism during its brief existence. It was withdrawn for tactical political reasons on July 9th, and 3) Bill 101, a slightly revised version of Bill 1, which was tabled on July 13th and only briefly debated before its passage into law on August 20th.

Law 101, like its predecessor Law 22, declared French to be the official language of Quebec. But it went much further in implementing this principle. Among its major provisions (including some which merely replicated Law 22), it recognized the fundamental right of every person to have the civil administration, semi-public agencies and business firms communicate with him/her in French; it declared French to be the official language of the Quebec legislature and courts (although unofficial English texts of legislative bills, enactments, and court judgements would also be made available, and English would be permitted in court proceedings under certain conditions); it made French the language of the civil administration, including government departments and agencies, and provided that written communications from the civil service with other governments and with «artificial persons» in Quebec be in French; it required public utility firms and professional corporations to provide services in French, and to use that language in their public texts and documents; it required employers to draw up all contracts and all written communications for their employees in French, and prohibited them from dismissing an employee solely on the basis of his insufficient knowledge of a language other than French; it forbade the use of a language other than French on signs, posters and firm names, in the labelling of most products, in contracts, catalogues, order forms, etc. (with certain exceptions); and most controversial of all, it required that formal instruction be conducted in French for all children in kindergarten, elementary or high school, except for the following: those who were already receiving their instruction in English in Quebec at the time that the Act was passed, those whose elder siblings were receiving such instruction at that time, those who were already living in Quebec at the time that the Act was passed and whose parents had received English instruction outside Quebec, or those who had moved to Quebec after the Act was passed but one of whose parents had received English instruction in Quebec. These provisions were to be enforced by an enlarged Office de la langue française, by francization committees formed in all business firms employing more than one hundred persons, and by a general watchdog commission (Commission de surveillance) for the French language.

The reaction from the anglophone community was predictably very negative and, at first, also very vocal. The original White Paper was strongly condemned in many quarters as a repressive, highly discriminaroty, even culturally genocidal document. One group, calling itself the «Preparatory Committee for an 11th Province», ran a full page advertisement in the now defunct *Montreal Star* entitled «Enough Mr. Lévesque» and threatening to establish an eleventh province of West Quebec.[19] Even moderate anglophones expressed their concern. For example, one hundred and fifteen prominent educators, businessmen and professionals signed a statement addressed to Mr. Lévesque which was also published as a full-page advertisement in *The Montreal Star* under the title «Quebec is our Home». It called on Quebecers to support their opposition to certain aspects of the new language policy.[20]

However, the initial strong and overt character of the protest did not persist, as it had in the case of Law 22. Between the time that the Bill was tabled and public hearings began, there was little direct confrontation between the Government and the anglophone minority. When the hearings opened on June 7th, a large number of formal briefs were tabled and several were subsequently presented by anglophone groups which severely criticized different aspects of the proposed legislation. However, before a genuine opposition party filibuster could be organized, the Government withdrew the legislation and reintroduced it in a slightly revised form as Bill 101. It thereby succeeded in undercutting its opponents both within the legislature and in the public at large.[21]

There were several other reasons for the failure of the anglophone community to mount a successful protest against Bill 101 in addition to the skilful legislative manoeuvring of the PQ government. First, the anglophone community had virtually no leverage with the *Péquistes*. There was no elected PQ member representing its interests within the National Assembly, and no prominent anglophones in the governing extra-parliamentary party. The PQ had an overwhelming majority which did not rest on any anglophone support. There was, therefore, no real hope of getting the Government to modify or withdraw its legislation. Secondly, there was almost complete polarization of the Quebec population along ethnic and linguistic lines in their attitude towards the legislation. Most francophones, apart from those belonging to the business community, were in broad sympathy with the objective of strengthening the French language and culture; there was very little substantive support for anglophone positions even among those francophones who had opposed the election of the Parti Québécois.[22] Thirdly, the media and public relations campaign, in support of the legislation, was brillantly orchestrated by the Government (and particularly by the chief sponsor of the legislation, Cultural Affairs Minister Dr. Camille Laurin). It generally avoided direct confrontation in public meetings between government and majority party leaders and the most vocal opposition groups within the minority anglophone community; it cultivated those elements within the francophone population whose positions on the language question had not yet firmly crystallized, such as urban blue-collar workers, rural farmers or small-town tradesmen and shopkeepers; and it attempted to soothe and placate more moderate opponents by assuring them of the Government's good faith on the question of their continued economic liberty and prosperity and their ultimate linguistic and cultural survival.[23]

The result was that by the time the language legislation was passed, anglophone opposition had virtually petered out. There were some threats by the Anglo-Protestant and Anglo-Catholic school boards to refuse to implement the educational provisions for the impending school year; a group of lawyers promised to initiate court action against the legislation; and there was a flurry of individual organizational initiatives designed to develop greater solidarity among the normally divided minority ethnic groups. Nevertheless, the prevailing feeling among anglophones was rather one of hopelessness and despondency. Whatever combativeness remained was reoriented towards fighting legislation preparatory to the Referendum, which was just then (August 20, 1977) being tabled in the National Assembly.[24]

The attitudinal and behavioural patterns that we have described above reflected a gradual and intensifying state of dissonance between the strong residual «majority group» self-perception which anglophone Quebecers had retained from their past, and their growing awareness of the reality of their current «minority group» status and political impotence.[25] This dissonance manifested itself in a number of ways. In the early stages, it was expressed in excessive emotionalism, particularly evident in the anti-Bill 22 protests, but also reflected in occasional paranoid outbursts against the Parti Québécois.[26] In later stages, it was replaced by feelings of impotence and despair. It was apparent that the anglophone community needed to alleviate this psychological dissonance by redefining its self-image and forging a new role for itself in Quebec, unless it decided to opt out of the province entirely (a choice not available to most members of the minority community for purely economic reasons).

The Phase of Minority Group Positive Self-Awareness and Action

The third phase of Anglo-Quebecers self-consciousness began shortly after the election of the Parti Québécois government, and intensified after the passage of Bill 101. It may be labelled «minority group positive self-awareness and action». It involved an acceptance of the fact that the anglophone community was numerically much weaker than the francophone community, and therefore subject to the constraints of all political minorities operating within the rules of the democratic political game.[27] This did not mean that it would meekly surrender to an overwhelming majority, withdraw from the political, socio-economic and cultural life of the province, and ignore the assertion of individual or collective rights of democratic citizens. It implied, rather, altering certain attitudes and modes of behaviour to make them more adaptive to the altered power configuration of a province governed by a new more nationalistic and independentist-minded elite.

The first step in this new phase demanded a cold look by the anglophones at the reality of their altered political power position. Claims had been made prior to the November 1976 election that they were sufficiently numerous and strategically located to prevent a Parti Québécois victory if they acted as a bloc. An examination of the results of the 1976 election belied these assertions. It revealed that the anglophones actually had the potential to block a PQ victory in twenty-five ridings at most, or about 23 per cent of the provincial total. Moreover, surveys conducted about midway through the election campaign indicated that the previous near-unanimous opposition of anglophones to *péquisme* and to independence in the elections of 1970 and 1973 had broken down to a degree. In certain ridings containing large numbers of non-francophone immigrants, particularly the «mixed» Italian-French ridings in north-east Montreal, there was considerable support accorded by these groups to the Parti Québécois, if not for the independence option itself.[28] Even if all anglophones had managed to unite behind a single federalist party, such as the Liberals or Union Nationale, they would not have had enough numerical leverage to counteract the significant swing in the popular vote in francophone and «mixed» ridings which occurred on November 15th. They were likewise powerless to prevent the huge shift in seats produced largely by the exigencies of the plurality electoral system.

A second step in the process of reassessment involved an attempt to define and activate a new and more positive political role for Quebec anglophones. There was a need initially to build bridges between the various ethnic groups comprising the minority language community and to construct a more unified set of community structures. It would then be necessary to operate these new structures in political tandem with corresponding structures in the majority francophone community.

The effort at self-renovation actually began first in the political arena, and took the form of constructing common political fronts, movements and pressure groups. The first important group of this sort to emerge was the Quebec-Canada Movement, a grass roots organization based on a $ 2 regular membership card, and encompassing federalists from both language communities. It began to organize in the Ottawa-Hull region on the initiative of Liberal MNA Michel Gratton soon after the November 15th election, and spread rapidly to other parts of Quebec including most anglophone areas. Its objective was to promote the advantages of a Quebec remaining in Canada and to help unite federalist parties and groups in preparation for the Referendum struggle. By the time the debate over Referendum legislation had begun in September 1977, it could already claim over 100 000 members.[29] In the initial stages of the post-1976 political reorganization, it assumed a leading role among unity groups, and anglophones were prominent among its leadership. At a later stage, it became embroiled in a dispute with these other groups and the political parties over its acceptance of a grant from the Federal government, which, however, was rapidly resolved.[30] By the fall of 1978, it had firmly aligned itself with other federalist groups and parties under the umbrella of the Pro-Canada Committee. It performed a major function, therefore, as a bridge between Quebec anglophones and their federalist francophone counterparts in the immediate post-November 15th period.

More central to anglophone Quebec concerns was the Positive Action Committee (PAC) formed in January 1977 by a Montreal lawyer, Alex Paterson, and a McGill University philosophy professor, Storrs McCall. Its explicit objective was to help unify Quebec anglophones and involve them more actively in the Quebec political process. It took an active role in formulating a moderate and constructive anglophone response to Bill 101; later, it provided the major input to the federalist critique of the Referendum legislation. This, in turn, led to the formation of a Pre-Referendum Committee to prepare the way for a unified federalist effort in the referendum campaign. The Positive Action Committee was initially conceived as an organization of anglophone educational, business and professional elites in Montreal, but it gradually built a mass base and even claimed a membership of about 25 000 by early 1978.[31]

There were a number of other organizations designed to activate anglophone and other federalist Quebec groups, including the Council for Canadian Unity, Participation Quebec, Rallye Canada, and Decision Canada. They were almost all absorbed in the umbrella organization initially called the Pre-Referendum Committee, and later renamed the Pro-Canada Committee which was created in response to Bill 92, the PQ's 1977 Referendum Act.

The actual union of the unity groups and federalist political parties occurred in December 1977 at a meeting in Quebec City convened by the Council for Canadian Unity. No less than seven unity groups and seven Federal and Provincial federalist parties were fused into a single organization; in a follow-up meeting an executive committee of twenty-eight members was created, headed by Claude Castonguay, the former actuary and Bourassa cabinet minister who was viewed as a relatively non-partisan figure in Quebec. Among the members on the governing body, in addition to the political party leaders, were representatives of the Quebec-Canada Committee and the Positive Action Committee, including several anglophones. Five sub-committees were established to coordinate activities among the groups and to direct the financial and organizational concerns of the Referendum campaign down to the poll level. [32]

This apparent unity of organization and purpose among anglophones and federalist francophones did not, however, last very long. In April 1978, a rift had developed between the executive committee of the Pre-Referendum Committee and one of its major constituents, the Quebec-Canada Movement which was largely responsible for organizing the campaign itself. The Movement had applied for and been awarded a $ 265 000 Federal government grant to help fund its organizational and informational activities. When spokesmen for the Quebec Liberal and Union Nationale parties called upon the Movement to refuse the grant, its members rejected the intrusion, voted unanimously to keep the money, and threatened to secede from the umbrella committee. The issue was soon resolved in a compromise, but the Quebec-Canada Movement was forced to relinquish its former role of principal organizer and coordinator of the Referendum campaign. [33] The anglophone element within the Movement, though not predominant, was disproportionately larger than its numerical strength within the umbrella organization as a whole. The dispute, therefore, had the effect of reducing the overall influence of the minority community in the federalist political camp.

A more important development affecting anglophone political involvement occurred simultaneously in April 1978 with the election of Claude Ryan, the former editor of *Le Devoir*, to the leadership of the Quebec Liberal Party. Ryan's election had the immediate effect of rejuvenating the dispirited Liberals; he also made it clear that he intended to assume the major leadership role within the provincial federalist camp. When Claude Castonguay stepped down as president of the Pre-Referendum Committee in August 1978, pleading pressure of business, Ryan succeeded in installing one of his closest advisors, Michel Robert, a Montreal lawyer, as the new president of the renamed Pro-Canada Committee. The role of the Committee was to be reduced to that of a clearing-house of information among the different unity groups and parties. The political parties were to reassume the major organizational responsibility for the Referendum at the riding level, and to lead the Referendum battle itself. [34]

This initiative by Ryan and the Quebec Liberals met immediate resistance from the other federalist parties in Quebec, such as the Union Nationale and

Créditistes, whose membership ranks were gradually being depleted by the Liberal revival. After several months of internal squabbling, Robert moved to disband the Pro-Canada Committee in February 1979. Although a successful last ditch effort was made to retain the structure of the Pro-Canada Committee, its overall effectiveness was reduced virtually to nil.[35] This also effectively eliminated any meaningful independent role for Quebec anglophones in the Referendum struggle, since anglophone representation within the higher decision-making echelons of the Quebec Liberal Party continued to be very weak.

There was one other forum for potential political involvement and cultural integration of the anglophone community established in the post-1976 period: the Council of Quebec Minorities. This was a federative body composed of about one hundred leading non-francophones drawn from over eighty minority community organizations and associations in the province. It was organized largely on the initiative of leaders of the Positive Action Committee and Participation Quebec.[36] It first met in May 1978 and set its objective: the promotion of understanding between the majority and minority communities, the fostering of bilingualism, and the furthering of the common interests of the minorities.[37] Among the major groups represented on the Council were the Consiglio Italiano Educativo, the Confederation of Indians of Quebec, the Provincial Association of Catholic Teachers and the Federation of Anglo-Protestant Parents of Quebec. Shortly after its creation there were indications that incipient divisions had manifested themselves over the appropriate strategy to follow in relation to the governing party and its supporters, namely opposition or cooperation.[38]

These efforts at anglophone political involvement and cultural integration have not, therefore, proved very fruitful thus far.* In the meantime, the strength of the anglophone community is gradually being eroded by a growing exodus of its younger and more dynamic elements.[39] There continues to be an urgent need, therefore, to redefine and reorient anglophone strategies and behaviour patterns in the cultural and particularly political spheres. In this respect, experience since 1976 may be instructive.

In the first place, the process of reconstructing and reorienting the anglophone community so as to maximize its political potential has proceeded in a structurally incorrect manner by attempting to build community cohesion and political alliances from the top down, rather than the bottom up. The Quebec-Canada Committee, the Positive Action Committee and the Pro-Canada Committee were all efforts at creating political structures originating either outside the anglophone community or in small elite groups within the community and extending these structures down to the mass level. The problem with this approach is that it rests too heavily on the initiative and perseverance of a few «single-issue» minority group activists, whose involvement with the community may be ephemer-

* The editors wish to remind the reader that this specific article was written in 1979.

al and subject to vicissitudes in leadership, events and personalities. It would be wiser to build on already existing structures within the various community groups, such as ethnic associations, cultural groups, religious associations, or educational institutions. The movement represented by the Council of Quebec Minorities appears to be a positive step in this respect, if it can overcome its initial fragmentation and develop more cohesive structures and unified community stances.

Secondly, in political matters, the anglophone community has leaned too heavily recently on the direction provided by francophone elites within the major political parties, movements or interest groups, rather than on its own capacity to develop and exercise leadership based on grass roots support. Prior to the 1970s there was a tendency to rely on the brokerage skills of leading anglophone elite actors who exercised considerable leverage behind closed doors over the francophone political elites. This was the dominant political pattern during the phase of «self-confident majority group» consciousness. In recent years, with the declining influence of these «elite brokers» over increasingly assertive and independent francophone political leaders, a serious leadership vacuum has developed within the anglophone community. The continued fragmentation of the different ethnic groups within the minority language community has further contributed to this void.[40] It is not surprising, therefore, that the community has placed its trust in those francophone leaders and their advisors whom they regarded as most sympathetic to minority group demands. Thus, Robert Bourassa and his immediate entourage of anglophone advisors were regarded as the protectors of anglophone interests; when these interests appear to have been betrayed, as was the case with Law 22, disillusionment quickly set in. The subsequent political fragmentation weakened the anglophone community's impact within the Quebec social and political order. There is a danger that a similar pattern might unfold if anglophone support and confidence is given exclusively to Claude Ryan, and he is likewise later found wanting.*

A more sensible approach would be to develop a stronger indigenous political leadership which would be capable of maximizing the minority community's input into the political process. It is very difficult, however, to evolve such a leadership cadre during a period of demographic decline and community instability. If the hemorrhage within the anglophone community of particularly the young community college and university graduates could be slowed or stopped, then it might be possible to build such a core group. This could be done by creating an inter-community network of ethnic, religious and educational elites, whose support would rest on their sector's rank and file membership. They would be assisted by a group of secondary level leaders whose major energies might be devoted to political organization. It should be possible to organize within all the major political parties on a constituency-by- constituency and poll-by-poll basis. There is a need for a kind of «wardheeler» mentality in this connection, such as exists in many large cities in the United States and in other parts of Canada.

* Editors' note: This is precisely what appears to have happened.

Anglophones can play an important role in the post-Referendum period. For example, they can test the sincerity of the Quebec government's invitation to non-francophones to play a more active role in the «new» Quebec by integrating themselves more fully into an overall provincial social, economic and political network. A positive first step is to pursue the original efforts within the Council of Minorities of cooperative-minded groups. They include attempts to break down the institutional separation between anglophones and francophones; exposing the minority community more fully to the French-language media, artistic and cultural activities; accepting and furthering the process of bilingualization and francization already initiated to a degree within the community; and attempting to act as a bridge between Quebec and the rest of English Canada by interpreting francophone developments and demands sympathetically to other Canadians.

(1) Throughout this essay, the terms «anglophone» and «non-francophone Quebecer» will be used interchangeably, except where a clear distinction is intended between those who are essentially English-speaking (including Anglo-Celts, Jews, Germans and other early immigrant arrivals), and those who still widely use their language of origin (such as the more recent Italian, Greek and Portuguese immigrants). In such instances, «anglophones» refer to the former group and «non-francophone immigrants» (sometimes called «allophones») refer to the latter. These terms are recent additions to English vocabulary in Quebec, being derived from the French. They are not very precisely defined, and are not always used in the same way in the two major language communities. This very broad definition of the term «anglophone», which encompasses a diversity of ethnic groups, seems justifiable within a social-psychological (as opposed to structural) perspective, that is, one which focuses on attitudes and perceptions rather than institutions.

(2) Because of the dearth of available research material of any kind of the anglophone community in Quebec, this paper relies, to a significant extent, on personal *impressions* as opposed to hard data.

(3) These concepts were first applied by the author to the anglophone community in Quebec in Michael B. Stein, «Le Bill 22 et la population non-francophone au Québec. . .» and more fully developed in the article cited in the asterisked note, on the first page of this text.

(4) See Richard J. Joy, *Languages in Conflict*, p. 104.

(5) *Ibid.*, p. 86 (Table 41), p. 105 (Table 54). See also Norbert Lacoste, *Les caractéristiques de la population du grand Montréal*, and «Les traits nouveaux de la population du 'grand Montréal'«. Of course, despite this overall aggregate balance, important changes occurred in the internal composition of the two language groups during this period, including the overall decline of the Anglo-Celtic component of the anglophone population and the proportionate increase of non-francophone immigrant groups. The persistence in attitudes, therefore cannot be attributed (only or primarily) to stability in the demographic characteristics of the population.

(6) See for instance, R.E. Simeon and D. Elkins, «Regional Political Cultures in Canada», Tables # 1, p. 406, # 2, p. 407, # 3-6, p. 410-411, and p. 414.

(7) Support for this observation may be found in Andrew Sancton, *The Impact of French-English Differences on the Governmental Structures of Metropolitan Montreal*. A similar point is made in Gary Caldwell, *English-Speaking Quebec in the Light of its Reaction to Bill 22*, pp. 17-18. I would like to express my gratitude to both authors for making these unpublished materials available to me.

(8) A similar pattern of separate institutions was fostered by Quebec francophones.

(9) This observation is based on personal impressions, and requires empirical documentation. Among studies which treat related aspects of anglophone/francophone media coverage of bicultural relations for Canada as a whole, see Jean Bruce, *A Content Analysis of Thirty Canadian Newspapers (Jan. 1 to Mar. 31, 1965)*, Arthur Siegel, *Canadian Newspaper Coverage of the FLQ Crisis. . .*, and the latter's article in this collection.

(10) Joy shows that in 1961 in the westernmost suburbs and west-centre sections of Montreal, 59 per cent and 52 per cent of the population spoke English only. The respective populations of these areas were 85 000 and 307 000. See Joy, *op. cit.*, p. 104 (Table 53). See also Richard Arès, «Les langues parlées chez les groupes ethniques de Montréal», *Le Devoir*, 16-18 July 1974.

(11) This observation is based on reports and information generally familiar to Quebec anglophones. For a similar perspective, see Caldwell, *English-speaking Quebec in the Light of its Reaction to Bill 22*, p. 12.

(12) The qualification was suggested to me by Kenneth McRoberts in a personal communication.

(13) See Jeremy Boissevain, *Les Italiens de Montréal, l'adaptation dans une société pluraliste*, Ottawa, Information Canada, 1971, chapitre IV.

(14) For example, in the Saint-Leonard school crisis of 1967-69, the Italian community looked to the parents' association headed by an Anglo-Catholic, Robert Beale, and to the anglophone media in Quebec for leadership. See John Parisella, *Pressure Group Politics: A Case Study of the Saint-Leonard School Crisis*, M.A. Thesis, McGill University, 1972.

(15) For a detailed discussion of anglophone attitudes and behaviour in relation to Bill 22, see the author's case study in *Choix*, and in John R. Mallea (ed.), *Quebec's Language Policies...*, p. 243-261. See also Gary Caldwell, *English-Speaking Quebec in the Light of its Reaction to Bill 22*.

(16) See Tetley's article in this collection.

(17) The anglophone-dominated business community, though initially quite antagonistic to Bill 22, was mollified considerably by the modifications in the legislation introduced at the reading stage. The later regulations, which were framed to accommodate many of the business community's suggestions, also won their broad support.

(18) *Ibid*. See also Stanley M. Cohen, «Jewish Concerns in Quebec», *The Canadian Zionist* (Jan. Feb., 1977), pp. 10-12, 15.

(19) *The Montreal Star*, April 30, 1977, p. A-13.

(20) *The Montreal Star*, April 30, 1977, p. A-9.

(21) *The Gazette*, July 9, 1977, p. 1.

(22) This initial impression of a favorable francophone attitude toward Bill 101 has been buttressed by most subsequent polls, which indicate that over 50 per cent of the Quebec francophone community supported the language Bill.

(23) See, for example, *The Montreal Star*, May 3, 1977, «Laurin tries again to allay English fears».

(24) See, for example, *The Gazette*, August 13, 1977, p. 7 («As Battle of Bill 101 subsides, PQ turns its guns on referendum law»).

(25) On the theory of cognitive dissonance, see Leon Festinger, *A Theory of Cognitive Dissonance* (Stanford: Stanford U. Press, 1962), chapter 1.

(26) An example of such behaviour was the threat by Charles Bronfman, president of Distiller's Seagram and owner of the Montreal Expos, to move Seagram's and the Expos out of Montreal if the Parti Québécois won the election. He recanted and apologized for his remarks the following day. See *The Montreal Star, November 15, 1976, p. A-3. See also Peter C. Newman, Bronfman Dynasty* (Toronto, McClelland & Stewart, 1978): 275-276.

(27) Festinger speaks of reducing dissonance by «adding new cognitive elements». See Festinger, *op. cit.*, pp. 21-24. Acceptance of the fact of one's minority group status would be an example of such a cognitive element.

(28) According to a post-1976 election analysis by Maurice Pinard and Richard Hamilton personally communicated to the author by Professor Pinard.

(29) *The Gazette*, September 14, 1977.

(30) *The Gazette*, April 10, 28, 1978. See also below, note(36).

(31) Interview with Storrs McCall, co-chairman of the Positive Action Committee, February 26, 1979.

(32) *The Gazette*, January 16, 1978.

(33) *The Gazette*, April, 10, 28, May 8, 1978.

(34) *The Gazette*, September 4, 1978, p. 3.

(35) *The Globe and Mail*, February 27, 1979, article by William Johnson.

(36) *Le Devoir*, 13 mars 1978, p. 7.

(37) *The Gazette*, May 20, 1978, article by Gretta Chambers, «Can anglos accept minority status?»

(38) Interview with Michael Yarosky, director-general of the Jewish Community Research Institute, February 26, 1979.

(39) *Le Devoir*, 25 mars 1978, 6 mars 1979. See also Andrew Phillips, «English college crowd will quit Quebec: Study», *The Gazette*, March 22, 1978.

(40) On this point, see G. Caldwell, *English-Speaking Quebec in the Light of its Reaction to Bill 22*, p. 18.

What's in a Name?
Problems of Group Identity in Quebec

Edouard Cloutier

EDOUARD CLOUTIER is a permanent member of the department of political science at the Université de Montréal. He has also been affiliated with the Centre d'études canadiennes françaises at McGill University. He is primarily interested in the socio-political analysis of Quebec with particular regard to ethno-linguistic relations and has, in this capacity, served as an adviser to the Minister of Inter-governmental Affairs, Mr. Claude Morin.

Every year, students attending my introductory lecture to a course called «Le Québec et le Canada» given by the French Canada Studies Programme of McGill University, kept asking me to provide them with definitions of such terms as «English Canadian, French Canadian, Québécois, francophone, anglophone», etc... I must confess that, despite numerous efforts to single out and clarify the various properties of these collective appellations, neither students nor professor felt very satisfied with the result, primarily because it seemed that the people falling under each designation varied considerably depending on who was using the designation and to what end.

It is, of course, easy to refer to official documents such as citizenship laws and census tract dictionaries to define such concepts as «Canadian», «Canadien», or French and English «mother tongue» and «ethnic origin». Even though significant quarrels persist among scholars and researchers as to the exact meaning and usages of these terms, one can at least find some generally agreed upon and relatively precise characteristics on which to base definitions (i.e., a citizen of English mother tongue is one who answered «English» to the question: «What is the first language you learned and still understand?»).

These academic definitions, however, are used almost exclusively in scholarly papers and are, consequently, of little help in describing and analyzing the sociological significance of their utilisations in every day life by most people, including scholars. One only has to glance at any form of writing (except, again, some academic statements on precise topics dealing mostly with demography) or lend an attentive ear to any form of oral communication (including, again, classroom exchanges) to notice the great variety of (sometimes incompatible) meanings given to such words as «Canadian», «English Canadian» and «anglophone».

Such variety led to a certain amount of confusion in the classroom which simply could not be dispelled by explaining that the meaning of collective names depended very much, in a fluid social situation, on the person who was uttering the name and on the circumstances (to whom, or in front of whom, he was speaking) under which the utterance was made. My perplexed students kept asking: «But what do you mean when you speak of French Canadians, anglophones, etc., in this classroom?» And I kept answering: «It depends on the context» until, one day in 1977, I decided to turn the tables around and make *them* spell out what they meant by such words. So started the exploratory experiment which I will now proceed to report on.

First, I told the students that some basic common references must be established so that all participants in the experience would know what we were talking about. Consequently, it was agreed that the Canadian census definitions of «mother tongue» and «ethnic origin», which I wrote on the board, would be adhered to by all.

Second, I wrote on the board three lists of French and English collective names, provided by the students themselves, which they thought were used by people of French, English and other origins and/or mother tongues, to designate themselves and other groups. It turned out that people of

a) French origin and/or mother tongue (whom we will call *Francos*) could be called: *Canadien français, French Canadian, Français, French, Québécois, Quebecer, French Québécois, French Quebecer, Canadien, Francophone, Frog, Franco-québécois, Pea Soup* and various other combinations and spellings;

b) English origin and/or mother tongue (*Anglos*) could be called: *Canadien anglais, English Canadian, English, Anglais, Québécois, Quebecer, English Quebecer, English Québécois, Québécois anglophone, Anglophone Quebecer, Canadien, Anglophone, Bloke, Anglo-québécois, Anglo, Tête carrée* and, again, various other combinations and spellings;

c) Origin and/or mother tongues other than French or English (*Neos*) could be called all of the above names plus a number of appellations like: *Néo-québécois, New Quebecer, Néo-Canadien, New Canadian, Canadien, Italien, Polish-Canadian*, and so on.

These lists, the students were told, were meant as mere suggestions upon which they could draw to answer an upcoming questionnaire. It was made very clear that they were not exhaustive and that any other name they thought proper could be used in their answers.

Third, the questionnaire was written on the blackboard and expressed orally in French and English (to make sure everyone understood). It asked the students to put down in writing:

a) Their self-identity:

The group to which he/she thought he/she belonged, according to the census tract definitions just established (Group A — «Francos»: French origin and/or mother tongue; Group B — «Anglos»: English origin and/or mother tongue; Groupe C — «Neos»: other origins and/or mother tongues).

b) Their self-designation:

The name which she/he generally considered the most appropriate as her/his own collective designation.

c) The designation of groups:

The name which she/he thought was most generally used by members of one group (i.e., designators) to talk about themselves or about members of another group (i.e., designees).

Interpretive propositions

Created as a pedagogical tool to impress upon students the complexities of assigning collective names to people, my exercise turned out to be much more useful than expected. As will be demonstrated, it provided very good analytical material for reflection on the relationships between Anglos and Francos in Quebec.

My analysis rests on the general assumption that valuable knowledge of the relationships between groups of people can be gained by studying the vocabulary that is used by members of these groups to collectively designate the groups. The present study concentrates on two basic questions. First, do people use a unified vocabulary to name the group to which they belong (self-designation) and the groups to which they do not belong (designation of others)? Second, are there correspondences between, on the one hand, the vocabulary used by members of one group to designate themselves or members of another group and, on the other hand, the vocabulary used by members of a different group to designate those under consideration by the members of the first group?

The generalized recognition of unified designation for a given group has to be considered as a major component of that group's potential capacity for action and reaction with regard to other groups, as is, of course, the generalized recognition of a unified designation for the other groups. If, for example, one analyzes a society in terms of class relationships, it is clearly insufficient to establish, on the basis of certain criteria (i.e., ownership of the means of production), the «objective» existence of certain classes. One must also establish the degree of consciousness which people have of their belonging to a class and of others belonging to another class. (Many Marxists, in fact, argue that class consciousness is an integral part of class affiliation). A very good indicator of such consciousness is the cohesiveness of the vocabulary used by people to collectively designate themselves and others.

There is no doubt that any study of present-day Quebec society and politics would have important short-comings if it failed to treat the ethnic and linguistic factors in the formation and the dynamics of social relationships. It is my argument that the consciousness of these factors, and therefore their contribution to group actions and reactions based on them, can be measured by the degree of cohesion in the utilization of collective appellations to designate Francos and Anglos. I will thus examine the self-identity of students (considered as subjects thereafter), their self-designation and their designation of Anglos and Francos with the intention of measuring the cohesiveness of collective appellations within each group and the degree of «sharedness» of these appellations between the groups.

It is also my argument that the components of the designations say a great deal about the perception of self and of others, and, consequently, about the relationship between self and others. In the case of Anglos and Francos in Quebec, the designation of groups can include one or two of the following components:

Canada (as in «Canadian» and «Canadien»), Quebec (as in «Quebecer» and «Québécois»), Franco (as in «Canadien français, Français, francophone», or «Franco-québécois»), Anglo (as in «English Canadian, anglophone, English-speaking Canadian» or «English Quebecer») and Neo (as in «Neo-Canadian» or «Neo-québécois»). The first two components relate to territorial and political entity allegiances, the third and fourth to ethnic and/or language allegiances, and the last to the relative recency of the allegiance. Therefore, in addition to the cohesiveness of collective appellations, I will also take into consideration the nature of the allegiances to which they refer.

Finally, it should be clearly kept in mind that the results presented hereafter are strictly heuristic in nature, pertaining, as they do, to a very specific, and rather small, group of subjects.

Self-Identification of Subjects

The seventy-two students attending the course on the day the experiment was held classified themselves in the following manner: 40 in group A (Francos), 14 in group B (Anglos), and 14 in group C (Neos), while 4 chose not to put themselves in any group and were, therefore, eliminated from the study. The fact that the course was taught partly in French and partly in English explains the high proportion of students in group A and the low proportion of students in groups B and C, relative to general enrollment at McGill University. These numbers also point out that we are dealing here with very distinctive subjects: young people of French origin/mother tongue enrolled in an anglophone institution, and young people of English and other origin/mother tongue attending a bilingual course in an anglophone institution. I shall keep these characteristics in mind when concluding the analysis.

The collective names by which subjects chose to designate themselves appear in Figure 1. This figure reveals that there is a consensus (29 out of 40) among subjects of group A as to their self-designation. This is not the case for subjects of groups B and C. Thus, members of group A referred to the Quebec component of their designation 30 times, to the franco component 10 times, and to the Canada component 7 times, whereas the frequencies for group B are 4 Quebec, 8 Anglo and 8 Canada and, for group C, 1 Quebec, 4 Neo, 1 Franco, 1 Anglo, and 9 Canada. In addition, two subjects in each of groups B and C chose French designations («Canadien» and «Québécois») while none of group A chose English designations. Finally, four subjects (one in B and three in C) did not designate themselves.

I interpret these figures as meaning that Franco subjects demonstrate a greater vocabulary cohesion than Anglo or Neo subjects, and that they are, therefore, more likely to share a common self-perception.

The data also indicate that Franco subjects preferred the Quebec component over the Canada component by a ratio of 30 to 7, whereas Anglo and Neo subjects reversed this preference by respective ratios of 4 to 8 and 1 to 9 in favour of Canada, so that the groups differ not only in regard to the degree of cohesiveness, but also with respect to its direction. In this last case, it is worth noting that Anglo subjects show more of a tendency than Neo subjects to adhere to a Quebec component in their self-designations. It is also worth noting that Anglo subjects are more apt to use linguistic/ethnic components (8 out of 20 components) than do Franco and Neo subjects (10 out of 47 and 2 out of 16, respectively).

Self-Designation of Francos According to Subjects

Here, we shall analyze the answers to the following question: «How do people belonging to group A and living in Quebec call themselves?» Figure 2 provides the data by subjects' group, a quick reading of which reveals very clearly that about 8 out of 10 subjects, without regard to their self-identity, agree on the term «Québécois». This means not only that Franco subjects are very cohesive in their self-designation, but also that such cohesiveness is widely recognized by Anglo and Neo subjects.

The self-designations which the subjects of group A think Francos of Quebec use correspond very closely to the designation which the subjects of the same group assign to themselves (Figure 1). The accent is put first on the Quebec component (33 times), second on the Franco component (6 times), and third on the Canada component (5 times). This would tend to indicate that subjects of group A generally find harmony between the way they call themselves and the way people in their own group call themselves. Note also that the self-designation of Francos is recognized by all subjects as referring mostly (more than 80 per cent of components) to territorial/political entity components.

SELF-DESIGNATION OF SUBJECTS BY THEIR SELF-IDENTITY

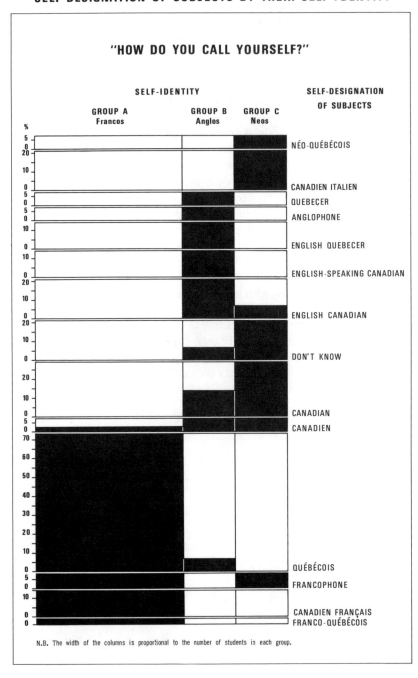

"HOW DO YOU CALL YOURSELF?"

N.B. The width of the columns is proportional to the number of students in each group.

SELF-DESIGNATION OF FRANCOS
ACCORDING TO SUBJECTS' SELF-IDENTITY

"HOW DO PEOPLE BELONGING TO GROUP A AND LIVING IN QUÉBEC CALL THEMSELVES ?"

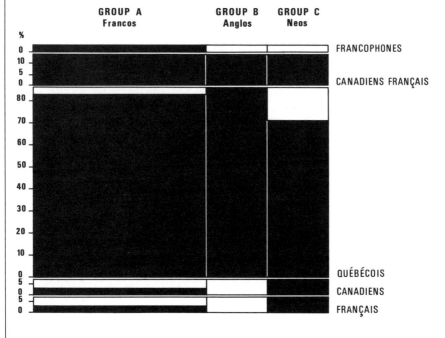

N.B. The width of the columns is proportional to the number of students in each group.

Self-Designation of Anglos, According to Subjects

The question asked: «How do people belonging to group B and living in Quebec call themselves?» The answers, tabulated in Figure 3, indicate that subjects of group B do not agree among themselves on the self-designation of Anglos in Quebec (13 subjects produced 8 names). In other words, there is collective lack of vocabulary cohesion to designate members of the group.

There are, in fact, significant differences between the frequencies of names used by subjects to designate themselves (Figure 1) and the frequencies of names which these subjects think Quebec members of group B use to call themselves (Figure 3). Whereas, in the first instance, the Anglo and Canada components each come up 8 times and the Quebec component 4 times, in the second instance, the Canada component is down to 4 times, the Quebec component up to 6 times and Anglo component keeps to the same relative level with 9 mentions. It thus seems to subjects of group B that the Anglos of Quebec have less of a tendency to call themselves «Canadians» and more of a tendency to call themselves «Québécois» than the Anglo subjects themselves.

More subjects of group C than of group B are inclined to believe that the Quebec people of group B refer to themselves as Anglos. On the other hand, one finds fewer subjects of group C than of group B who think that these people include a Quebec component in their self-designation. Subjects of group A are relatively dispersed with regard to the self-designation of Quebec Anglos (40 subjects referred to 8 names). A majority of them, however, point to the Canada and to the Anglo components as the self-designation of these people.

Neo subjects are more inclined to think that the Anglos of Quebec use the ethnic/linguistic component to designate themselves (12 out of 17 components) than are Anglo and Franco subjects (9 out of 19 components and 24 out of 59 components respectively).

Generally speaking, the analysis of these results shows that there is no perceived consensus, either within or between groups of subjects, as to how the Quebec Anglos call themselves (apart, that is, from the Anglo component of the self designation), the greatest disparity having to do with Franco subjects being much more inclined to retain the Canada component of the appellation than Anglo and Neo subjects.

Designation of Anglos by Francos, According to Subjects

Let us now look at the subjects' answers to a more complicated question: «How do people belonging to group A and living in Quebec call people belonging to group B and living in Quebec?» The answers, found in Figure 4, permit the following statements.

Firstly, a general consensus exists between subjects of all three groups that the Francos of Quebec call the Anglos of Quebec «les anglais», although the consensus is of uneven strength between the groups (13 out of 14 in group C, 28 out of 40 in group A and 8 of 14 in group B).

Secondly, subjects of all three groups are virtually unanimous in retaining the Anglo component of the designation.

Thirdly, subjects of group B are proportionally more numerous than those of groups A and C in thinking that Franco *people* refer to Anglo *people* by the Canada component. With regard to this, it is interesting to note that, in Figure 3, a great proportion of the Franco *subjects* did think, erroneously it seems, that the Anglo people referred to themselves by the Canada component.

Designation of Francos by Anglos, According to Subjects

Subjects were also asked: «How do people belonging to group B and living in Quebec call people belonging to group A and living in Quebec?» Their answers, reported in Figure 5, demonstrate three patterns.

One, there is some consensus within and between the three groups on choosing «French Canadians» as the appellation given to Francos of Quebec by Anglos of Quebec. Note, however, that the proportion of subjects choosing «French Canadians» drops as we go from group A (34/40) to group C (9/14) to group B (6/14).

Two, Anglo subjects are more susceptible than Franco and Neo subjects to think that Quebec Anglos use the Quebec component in designating Quebec Francos.

Three, likewise, Franco subjects are more susceptible than Anglo and Neo subjects to thinking that Quebec Anglos use the Canada component in designating Quebec Francos.

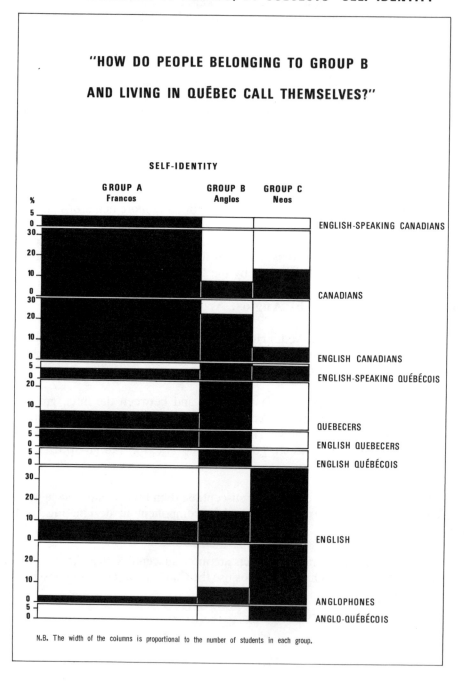

"HOW DO PEOPLE BELONGING TO GROUP B
AND LIVING IN QUÉBEC CALL THEMSELVES?"

SELF-IDENTITY

N.B. The width of the columns is proportional to the number of students in each group.

138

DESIGNATION OF ANGLOS BY FRANCOS
BY SUBJECTS' SELF-IDENTITY

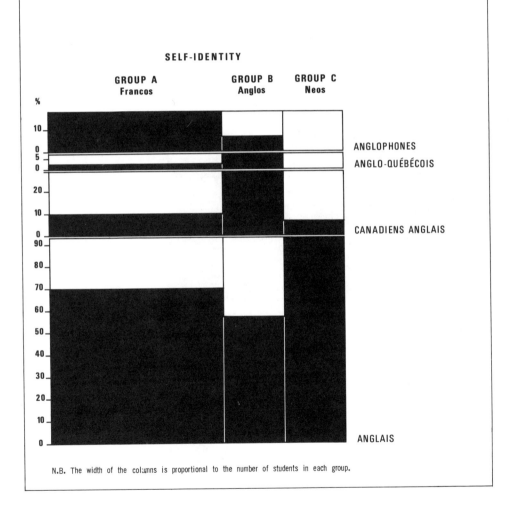

"HOW DO PEOPLE BELONGING TO GROUP A AND LIVING IN QUÉBEC CALL PEOPLE BELONGING TO GROUP B AND LIVING IN QUÉBEC?"

N.B. The width of the columns is proportional to the number of students in each group.

DESIGNATION OF FRANCOS BY ANGLOS
BY SUBJECTS' SELF-IDENTITY

"HOW DO PEOPLE BELONGING TO GROUP B AND LIVING IN QUÉBEC

CALL PEOPLE BELONGING TO GROUP A AND LIVING IN QUÉBEC?"

SELF-IDENTITY

GROUP A	GROUP B	GROUP C
Francos	Anglos	Neos

FRENCH CANADIANS

QUEBECERS

FRENCH

QUÉBÉCOIS

FRENCH QUÉBÉCOIS

FRANCOPHONES

N.B. The width of the columns is proportional to the number of students in each group.

140

Tentative Conclusions

Several tentative conclusions may be drawn. Firstly, the Francos of Quebec are perceived as being in general agreement on their collective name, which name others are also seen to recognize. Furthermore, this name refers more often to a territorial/political allegiance (Quebec rather than Canada) than to an ethnic/linguistic allegiance.

Secondly, the Anglos of Quebec are not perceived as being in agreement among themselves on their collective name, and this would tend to indicate a relative difficulty in collective conscience formation. Furthermore, apart from its Anglo component, there are important disagreements between the groups of subjects as to the Anglos' self-designation, the Franco subjects being more inclined to think it refers to Canada, the Anglo subjects to Quebec, and the Neo subjects to neither of these. This indicates an important misunderstanding between members of the three groups with regard to the Anglos who are thought to appear mainly as Anglo-Canadians to the Francos, Anglo-Quebecers to the Anglos, and simply Anglos to the Neos. Finally, the ethnic/linguistic reference appears to be given a greater recognition in the Anglos' self-designation than in the Francos' self-designation.

Thirdly, there is general agreement as to the way Francos of Quebec designate Anglos of Quebec, by putting the accent on the ethnic/linguistic component of the designation. Thus, the Francos are generally seen as underlining this Anglos' component more than the Anglos themselves do.

Fourthly, the Anglos of Quebec are thought to designate the Francos of Quebec mainly by the «French Canadian» appellation, thereby accentuating both the Franco and the Canada component, with, however, an important difference in that Francos seem more inclined than Anglos to think that Anglos refer to them as Canadians.

To be more than tentative, these conclusions would have to be replicated with a great many more subjects. In particular, subjects other than students would permit generalization of the results to the adult population. I would imagine that, with older subjects, the configurations of self-identities and self-designations would vary considerably, on account of the different socialization patterns that existed prior to the sixties in Quebec with regard to collective appellations related to ethnicity and language.

On the basis of my knowledge of students at the Université de Montréal and at the Université du Québec à Montréal, I would not, however, expect the results to be much different if students from French language universities were tested in the same way.

Anglophones Who Are Integrating Into Quebec Society

Sheila McLeod Arnopoulos

SHEILA McLEOD ARNOPOULOS is co-author with Dominique Clift of *The English Fact in Quebec*, the French version of which won a Governor-General Award in 1980. A journalist with *The Montreal Star* for ten years, she won several awards for her writing on immigrants and on non-unionized women in the labour force. An authority in the field of English/French relations, she is the only anglophone member of the Quebec government's Conseil de la langue française.

As Montreal becomes increasingly French-speaking in every aspect of life, there is more and more pressure upon the city's 700 000 anglophones to become not only bilingual but also bicultural. Until recently, much of the city's English-speaking community felt it should have complete freedom to operate exclusively in English, particularly in the business and education sectors. This was the opinion of the community's traditional leadership which was of mainly British stock. For the English media, the Protestant School Board, and senior businessmen the Quebec English were part of the English-Canadian majority.

In the past, the Province's anglophones survived well with this attitude. English and French societies were so highly segregated that the English could behave as though they were more part of Ontario than of Quebec. The English organized and funded their own schools, social services, art galleries, hospitals and universities, and lived in their own neighbourhoods. Most important, they controlled Quebec corporate life and influenced the course of Canadian business through Montreal head offices.

With the shift of corporate power to Ontario and the West, and the advent of provincial government funding and control of medical, social, educational, and municipal services, the English can no longer remain a self-contained island in Quebec. They are now obliged to become part of Quebec — French Quebec — and this means accepting minority status and the politics of accommodation and compromise. For much of the English community, the idea of accepting minority status and cultural change does not come easily. As a result, certain anglophones — particularly the older generation — are either trying to avoid francization or moving west.

At the same time, hidden away from the spotlight of the press and the eye of the traditional English leadership, are rising numbers of anglophones who are adapting very well to the changes that are now taking place. These English-speaking people are learning French, sometimes moving to francophone neighbourhoods, sending their children to French schools and gravitating toward all-French work sectors. Most are conserving their English identity, that is, they are integrating, and not assimilating, into French-Québécois life. However, they are accepting minority status and the need to be both bilingual and bicultural in today's Quebec.

The more conservative elements in the English community are unaware of these people mostly because the latter have no organized movement such as Positive Action, and do not tend to make statements on the political situation. Most of these anglophones for example did not get involved in the debates over the language legislation (Laws 22 and 101).

The questions which arise are the following: «During this period of English/ French tension in Quebec, what type of anglophone is capable of cultural adaptation?» and «Who are these English-speaking people who can accept minority status and a bicultural life?»

In the late seventies, after the Parti Québécois came to power, I became interested in these questions. At the time, many anglophones felt that there was no point in trying to become part of the French community because they would be automatically rejected. To try to find out whether this was true, I decided to seek out anglophones who had made serious attempts to integrate into the French milieu in some way. First, I did a series of articles for *The Montreal Star*. Later, I expanded the material for a sociology thesis at Concordia University. This study was used for one of the chapters in the book, *The English Fact in Quebec*[1], which I co-authored with Dominique Clift.

For the study, I did research on anglophones who had opted to work in an all-French milieu. According to a special survey conducted by Dominique Clift on the language of work in Montreal for *The Montreal Star* in 1976,[2] about 20 per cent of Montreal's anglophones work completely in French. Some of these English-speaking people work in all-French blue collar sectors. Others are located in high status francophone work environments. It is this overlooked group in the anglophone community that I focused upon.

The research showed that most of the Montreal anglophones who are integrating into the French community are not part of the traditional local English community. The majority are Jews, children of European immigrants, or newly arrived Americans, British, or Canadians from other provinces. These anglophones are marginal to the culture of the mainstream English community. It is this marginality, or lack of identification with the key elements of Montreal English culture, that allows them to assume new cultural colours.

The marginality of these people comes from a variety of origins. Low socio-economic origin and leftist ideology account for some of it, but the most important factor is mixed ethnic background. To explain the cultural adaptability of these people, I drew heavily upon sociological literature on the «marginal man» in works by theorists such as Everett Stonequist and Georg Simmel.[3] Everett Stonequist saw the mixed ethnic «marginal man» as a maladjusted person and a social misfit. Simmel's «stranger», as he calls him, is far more creative; it is this «marginal man» model which was most relevant for the study. Simmel's «stranger» is a «cultural hybrid» and the product of the inter-penetration of cultures that has accompanied the mass migration of the twentieth century. This «stranger» lives in a cultural no-man's land that allows him the flexibility of participating in different cultures and of acting as an important inter-face between conflicting groups.

The study I conducted looked at the experience of Montreal anglophones in three job sectors: French-language universities, the civil service, and business.

French Universities

Bob and Henrietta Cedergren are two anglophones who have integrated into French university life even though they knew no French when they first arrived. Professor Cedergren is a biochemist from Minnesota who came to teach at the Université de Montréal in 1967.

At the university, there is an unofficial rule that newly-hired anglophones get special consideration for the first six months while they learn the language. Accordingly, the biochemistry department let Professor Cedergren do research and teach one course in English while he frantically learned French. The following year, he confidently took on a full teaching load and has been working and living full time in French ever since.

«It took me six months to understand the language and another six months to express myself properly... and I still make a lot of mistakes», he said. Nevertheless, he feels comfortable in the French milieu. He lives in a French neighbourhood, has French-speaking friends, reads French newspapers, belongs to French organizations, and sends his child to a French school.

The only place where Bob Cedergren speaks English is at home with his wife Henrietta who is also English-speaking. When she arrived in Montreal, she also spoke no French, but learned it while she taught English at a French college. She teaches in the linguistics department at the Université du Québec.

The Cedergrens are not unusual. They are typical of the Americans and other foreign anglophones at the French universities who drifted into Quebec with various levels of French fluency and integrated into the French community. Others who behaved in the same way include development economist Ben Higgins who was at Université de Montréal for several years, linguists John Reighard and Kathleen Connors, psychologist George Baylor, architect Colin Davidson... and the list could go on.

Most of these people see themselves as immigrants to a French nation where it is only natural to blend in with the majority. Some voted for the Parti Québécois, sympathize with the independence movement, and look upon Montreal's born and bred English with some suspicion.

Two Ontarians who have become part of the French milieu are economist Leonard Dudley and political scientist Iain Gow. Professor Dudley learned basic French during summer jobs in France and Quebec, but perfected it when he came to the Université de Montréal in 1970. Professor Gow acquired French while working for the external affairs department in Paris. He later took a PhD at Université Laval, and then joined the Université de Montréal in 1964. Like all the English-speaking professors I interviewed, Professor Gow pointed out that although he writes French relatively well, he still makes errors and usually has a French colleague check articles before submission. «Working in French has made the job a little harder. . . but not by a lot», he said, echoing the sentiments of many others in his position.

Although there are few Montrealers of Anglo-Saxon background at the French universities, there are, by contrast, many members of the anglophone Jewish community. Among those at the Université de Montréal are architect Melvin Charney, industrial relations specialist Leo Roback, and psychologist Ethel Roskies. Many studied at the Université de Montréal and were encouraged to accept jobs there when they graduated.

In explaining why they gravitated to a French milieu, some of the Jewish professors said their ties with the English community were never that strong and McGill had not been very welcoming. «Many Jews felt marginal», said Professor Roskies, who pointed out that it didn't really matter what community they were marginal in. Professor Roskies took a BA at McGill University. Despite her fractured French, she went to the Université de Montréal in 1961 to do graduate work, because of its excellent clinical psychology programme. The McGill department, she said, was not keen to accept her because she was married and had children, whereas the Université de Montréal judged her solely on her academic record. «The University of Montreal has always been more receptive to women» she said.

Looking back to 1961, when she first became a student at the university, she said it took a «queer breed of person to cross over the mountain» during those years of the two solitudes. At that time, she said, the Université de Montréal was a very Catholic place. Yet, despite her Orthodox Jewish background and her poor French, she always felt welcomed. Non-francophones such as herself were permitted to write term papers and exams in English, and people went out of their way to help her.

The Civil Service

The civil service, whether at the provincial or municipal level, has never been able to attract many English-speaking people. Various studies show that less than two per cent of senior civil service positions in the Quebec civil service are held by anglophones. Those who form this meagre percentage tend to be a small group of olderr men who entered prior to the Quiet Revolution in order to represent the interests of the English.

One notable exception to this is Alan Wright, a former teacher, who worked for three years in French as an assistant director of curriculum in the Ministry of Education. Mr. Wright joined the public service because he wanted to become immersed in French-Quebec life. He left in 1974, but not because he didn't feel accepted. Another job offer came along and he wanted to broaden his experience. He is now studying toward a PhD degree at the Université de Montréal.

Two other anglophones who have ventured into the civil service sector are Ken Cavanagh, public relations officer with the Montreal Island School Council, and Alex Kowaluk, an urban development expert with the City of Montreal housing and planning department. Fifteen years ago, both were unilingual English. Today, they work almost exclusively in French. Again, both transferred to the French work milieu because they wanted to become more involved in French-Quebec life. In their view, the English community was too restricting.

For Mr. Cavanagh, learning French was slow but painless. When he graduated from Loyola College in 1967, he «could hardly speak a word of French... like so many English kids who went through Montreal's English school system». He became accustomed to French when he took his first job, as an English public relations officer at Molson's Brewery. «I was surrounded by French colleagues», he explained, «and that's when I started to comprehend French.» Two years later, he went to the Montreal Catholic School Commission where, again, he worked in English but was surrounded by French, and that is when he began to speak fluently. He explained that he crossed the most difficult language hurdle when he took his present job with the Montreal Island School Council involving such tasks as writing French press releases, speeches, reports and newsletters. «There were stresses», he admitted, «especially at the beginning. I'll never forget when the Council chairman asked me for a ten-page speech in French for the next morning. I stayed up all night doing it.» Now, however, he is almost as comfortable in French as in English.

For Alex Kowaluk, the transition from English to French was more difficult. After graduating from McGill University in architecture, he worked for ten years with English-speaking architectural firms. When he joined the city of Montreal planning department in 1966, he said he had «about 100 words of French». He left the English work sector because he didn't feel accepted by the traditional English group. «Socially I felt out of step», he recalled. «As an immigrant from Ukrainian working-class background, I just didn't have the right dress, speech and so on. Ideologically, I seemed in a different camp as well... I was class-conscious and tended to oppose their private enterprise values.»

During the period he worked with English firms, Mr. Kowaluk had become friendly with some French artists, and found he was more at home with them than with his English-speaking colleagues. «I could be myself with them... they liked my spirit...» As a result of his contacts with these French-speaking people, he began to consider moving into the French work milieu. He chose the City of Montreal planning department because he felt he could pursue his more community-oriented goals there.

The French Business Sector

During this period of political tension, few English-speaking businessmen would think of moving from an all-English work milieu to a completely French one. But anglophones in French business establishments are becoming more and more common. The Mouvement Desjardins (credit union movement), engineering consulting firms such as Surveyer, Nenniger and Chenevert (SNC), Hydro-Québec and Sidbec all employ anglophones who are quietly working away in French with very little ado.

One anglophone who learned to work comfortably in French at an advanced stage of his career is Terence Dancy, who is vice-president of technology at Sidbec. Mr. Dancy is British-born, but worked in the U.S. steel industry until he was invited to Quebec by Sidbec when it needed special expertise in new steel production methods. He arrived in 1970, at the height of the «October Crisis», but took the political unrest in stride. Although he and his wife knew no French, they immersed themselves in the language and are now fluent. «We felt it was the only sensible thing to do in a place where the majority speak French», said Mr. Dancy. Since Sidbec took over Dosco, the Nova Scotia-based steel firm, in 1968, the proportion of unilingual English executives has dropped from 35 to less than 10 per cent. Interestingly enough, many of the anglophones in the company who have not learned French are Montrealers of long-standing.

Two others who switched from English to French are Irving Ellenbogen and Harry Rapoport. Both come from Jewish working-class, immigrant backgrounds. Mr. Ellenbogen started working in French in 1967 when he joined Hydro-Québec as a programme analyst. In the beginning, his French was poor, «But I didn't let that bother me», he said. «I was quite happy to work in French. I found it a little hard writing at first, but it quickly improved... there are no problems.» Although he works in his second language, Mr. Ellenbogen feels comfortable at Hydro-Québec, more so, in fact, than he did at English-run corporations.

Harry Rapoport is an engineer with Surveyer, Nenniger and Chenevert (SNC) and has been there for more than fifteen years. Until the late 1960s, SNC was staffed mainly by English-speaking engineers, although two of the three partners who set up the firm were French Quebecers. With the Quiet Revolution and the arrival of French-trained Quebec engineers, the company, which now has over 1 000 employees, slowly became more French. During the past five years, Mr. Rapoport has worked on a number of all-French projects, though he could have continued working in English. He found it difficult at first, because his French was not as good as his English. «I often had a headache at the end of the day because I wasn't used to working in French», he recalled. «It was a strain.» Mr. Rapoport finds that working in French takes more energy, but he supports the promotion of French as Quebec's language of work, and wants to make the effort.

The Nucleus of a New English Leadership

What role can we expect these anglophone «marginal men» to play in Quebec's future? Are they a negligible minority... or are they perhaps the beginnings of a new type of elite which will gradually replace the departing corporate group?

In the precarious world of English/French relations in Quebec, I would suggest that the «marginal men» are emerging as a new creative interface between the two polarized and isolated communities. As such, they may play an important historical role in the evolution of intergroup relations. In addition to their role as mediators, they may also serve as the anglophone prototype of Quebec in the eighties. These «marginals», it should be noted, are not only bilingual, they are also bicultural.

If the English are to prosper in Quebec over the long term, it seems clear that they must leave their ghettos and circulate in the corridors of both English and French communities in the manner of th francophones outside Quebec. So far, many people in the main stream of the English community are stubbornly resisting this. Once the present political tension dissipates, however, this may change. At that point, the majority of the English, in their attempt to find more comfortable relationships with the French, may discover that the way has already been explored for them by those who today are seen as marginal.

Observers of the situation may well ask why these so-called «marginal» individuals are so silent. What effect can they have if they do not play more public roles? One or two, however, have become public figures. Perhaps the most notable is Abe Limonchik, the former president of the Montreal Citizens Movement, the major opposition party at City Hall. Mr. Limonchik, of Jewish immigrant background, works for a large English corporation. However, he is married to a French Québécoise, and he has always moved with ease in the city's French, English, and Jewish communities. The Montreal Citizens Movement is one of the few organizations where English and French are working together with few ethnic tensions. One of the main reasons for this is the presence of people, such as Mr. Limonchik, who have a foot in many cultural camps, but are rigidly bound to none.

Historian Frederick Teggart, in his study of great men, refers to the historical importance of the «marginal man» or «stranger» type who is not dominated by a set way of thinking and, therefore, becomes an indispensible personality in the contacts between cultural groups. In his *Processes of History*, he makes the following statement:

> Now, while historically, advancement has been dependent upon the collision of groups, the resultant response has taken place in the minds of individuals and so we are led to see that all transitional eras are alike in being

periods of individual mental awakening, and of the release of emancipation of individual initiative in thought and action... That the historical process of individualization of thought is also the form through which advancement proceeds today would be best shown by an extended examination of the biographies of notable men...[4]

At this point, it seems probable that the future «notable men» of Quebec's English community will be these «marginal men» who are comfortable in more than one cultural community. With these people as leaders, the English community may eventually be able to extricate itself from its present conservatism and paranoia and move into a new era.

NOTES

(1) Sheila McLeod Arnopoulos and Dominique Clift, *The English Fact in Quebec*.

(2) Dominique Clift, *The Montreal Star*, Language and Work Series, March 27, 29-31, April 1-2, 1976.

(3) Everett V. Stonequist, *The Marginal Man, A Study in Personality and Culture Conflict*, New-York, Russell and Russell, 1961. Also: Georg Simmel, *Soziologie* Leipzig, Duncker und Humlat, 1908.

(4) Frederick Teggart, *Processes of History* (New Haven, 1918):155-156.

Part III

THE MANY FACES OF ENGLISH QUEBEC

The image of a monolithic, wholly Protestant, Anglo-Saxon and affluent English Quebec is gradually foundering in the heat of the present debate and as a result of the profound mutations the language group has experienced since the second World War. Anglophones are now legion who insist that there is no such thing as an English community, be it geographical, sociological or ideological, but rather a mosaic of groups for whom English is the dominant language or simply the preferred *lingua franca*. Further, it is considered that, over and above language, all that gives this mosaic cohesion is a certain attachment to Canada, a propensity to be highly mobile at the level of the continent and, perhaps, a greater commitment to material advancement through the private sector and the more fluid environment to be found there.

That one had generalized so readily and spontaneously about «the English» in the past was no doubt due to the fact that it was largely people of British origin who had created «the commercial empire of the St. Lawrence» and founded the principal institutions of English Quebec — the McGills, the McTavishs, the McGregors, the McConnells, the Websters, the Prices — with their businesses, newspapers, schools, universities, hospitals and charitable institutions. And yet the harsh English-French dichotomy that such a concept invoked concealed another kind of dualism, the memory of which still lingers on in parts of rural Quebec. This one insisted on a distinction based on religion — of Protestant and Catholic — that had been enshrined in the British North America Act, and the implications of which we are still grappling with today. It was the inter-penetration of these two dualities that created a very special intermediate group, the Anglo-Catholics, who, with no significant autonomous institutions to speak of, have long played an important brokerage role in Quebec society.

The picture has been further complicated by massive immigration, beginning in the late nineteenth century, bringing other groups who sought to co-habit with one or the other of the charter populations while establishing some bases of institutional autonomy. Notable among them were the Jews, marked by differences in dress, language and religion, a profound sense of history and their concern to construct a more just and more democratic society here in the New World. All this is described by David Rome, along with the tensions they have experienced by virtue of being caught in the cross fire between the two charter populations.

The Jews have been followed, over time, by a multitude of other immigrant groups — East Europeans, Italians, Greeks, Armenians, Portuguese, Egyptians and West Indians, to name only a few. While most, sooner or later, sought accommodation with the anglophones, to ensure access to educational institutions and professional networks, this did not necessarily mean total assimilation to that language group, as Rome quite clearly shows in the case of the Jews. Irrespective of this fact, English Quebec is being radically transformed. Nowadays, Anglo-Quebecers are less and less likely to be of British ethnic origin or of Protestant faith. At the same time, the many ethnic groups harboured by the English language are generally weak in terms of separate institutions and little inclined to consensus. In consequence, the situation presents itself as one in which the *institutions* are largely British and Protestant in inspiration; as well as being powerful and vocal, the *caretakers* of these institutions are drawn from a variety of English-speaking countries — South Africa, the United States, Australia, other Canadian provinces, etc. — and are, hence, rarely heirs to the tradition, while the *clients* come from just about anywhere! It is the growing divergences between these three elements that is one of the most problematic features of the new, plural English Quebec.

On close observation, other fissures are evident in the group structure, inspired by geography and social class. Thus, a demarcation of increasing significance appears to be that separating the residents of the Greater Montreal area from the rural (or «off-island») English. Stuart Richards speaks of the particularities, as well as the social isolation of certain remote English communities in the Magdalen Islands. While economic considerations are obviously pertinent, the increasingly cosmopolitan nature of the metropolitan population and, hence, its «shallower» historical and geographical consciousness, together with the sense that most anglophone institutions speak for the interests of Montrealers, compound the feeling of separateness in rural areas.

As for class, it is perhaps the appearance of David Fennario's theatre, the rediscovery in the collective memory of «The Point» (Pointe-St-Charles) and Verdun, and the arrival of an avowedly social-democratic government in Quebec that, together, have, in a curious way, firmly re-established that there are in Montreal the remains of what was once a massive Irish labouring class and a large number of English craftsmen. Though relatively inarticulate, institutionally weak and uncertain in their relationships with their francophone counterparts, they have at least become visible again, having survived Gabrielle Roy's persuasive contrasting of a French St-Henri with an English Westmount, as well as repeated invitations by an anglophone elite to mobilise along ethnic rather than class lines in the defense of linguistic interests. The little-known world of the English-speaking working class in Quebec takes on more consistency upon reading Carla Lipsig-Mummé's contribution.

These multiple and changing facets of English Quebec point to a diversity of interests and ideologies where, depending upon which anglophones one speaks to, a strong sense of place and history transcends a propensity to be mobile and to be indifferent to the past, an appreciation of language as culture and identity contrasts with a strictly utilitarian vision of it as a vehicle of communication, and a certain consciousness of class serves to moderate an awareness of ethnic identity. Everything points to the fact that this pluralism and separation of interests within the language group are on the increase.

Jews in Anglophone Quebec

David Rome

DAVID ROME is archivist with the Canadian Jewish Congress. Although he spent his early childhood in British Columbia, he is a long-term Quebec resident whose intellectual career has led him to all of Montreal's universities, as well as to the Ministry of Cultural Affairs. A very active member of the Montreal Jewish Community, he has written widely on Canadian Jewry.

As so often happens, an examination of a human group displays unexpected complexities. This is true of the Jewish element of Quebec «anglophonie», itself a complex society. Until a score of years ago, the Jewish community was anglophone in its entirety, if only by deliberate and close association. But since then, a growing number of Jews of French mother tongue have immigrated to Quebec, slowly transforming by their very presence the profile of the community and, above all, demanding that some of its basic values and loyalties be modified or at least questioned. However, this is not the first time that the identification of Jews with Protestant «anglophonie» has been questioned. In earlier decades, the school issue and the Depression had both precipitated a certain re-evaluation of identity and loyalties.

The first question we must ask ourselves is how it happened that Jews, most of whom were of neither French nor English linguistic or cultural backgrounds, came to identify so wholly and passionately with English Quebec. In order to find the answer, we need to retrace the history and development of Quebec Jewry.

As with all nations, Quebec reveres its origins and like many, it cherishes a saga of its own Golden Past as an era that evokes a Genesis-Eden linked with a Messianic Return. Jews, with their own ancient heritage, will be the first to appreciate the sanctity and formative power of this interweaving of history, heroics, genealogy, religion, ethos and pride that colour the aspirations of an entire people.

It is little less than tragic that in this *québécois* tapestry of priests, *coureurs de bois*, heroic soldiers and sailors, *voyageurs*, explorers, *défricheurs* and *habitants*, *seigneurs* and pious mothers, Jews have no place. But it was conceived within the framework of the civilization of New France and, in consequence, under those unfurled medieval banners which condemned Jews as the eternal enemy of this world. Strict laws, reaffirmed by the highest authority, forbade Jews to set foot — let alone participate — in the building of a Quebec nation in the New World. Certainly, the same laws also formally forbade the presence of Protestants but, unlike the Jews, a number of them did settle in the new colony.

It takes little imagination to evaluate the implications of this old Inquisition heritage for the new Quebec dream, particularly as it has never been formally disavowed at any stage or by any dimension of the nationalist movement, neither by the religious leaders, nor by the promoters of tolerance, nor by the agnostic elements. Quebec Jews listen in vain for a disavowal of the most absolute anti-Jewish premise. They assume that if political figures sensitive to their own constituencies, who have been able to promote sweeping measures elsewhere, find it imprudent to touch this aspect of the national understanding, it must be because it still has force and because it is interwoven into the fine network of the common memory. They are sensitive to any indication as to the direction Quebec society is likely to take. As an unequivocally French Quebec, is it likely to be wedded to the restoration of the ethnically monolithic society that Catholic France established in the St. Lawrence Valley, with no room for citizens of other origins or faiths, or is it about to create an open society of the kind we are familiar with in North America that recognizes diverse cultural, ethnic and religious backgrounds? The issue is not a new one in Quebec and certainly, in recent years, much thought has been given to it. However, because of its sensitivity and deep significance, many Quebecers are extremely cautious in their responses, and this only serves to arouse anxiety among Jews.

If Jews were absent from New France, the first settlers arrived with the Conquest. Again, a familiarity with Jewish history will only serve to highlight the symbolic significance of this fact. In Quebec, the Conquest evokes much more than a military defeat, a change of regime or of constitution. Rather, it meant the total collapse and destruction of a treasured world, a parallel of the two Destructions of the Temples of Jerusalem which have to this day associated the very words of Jeremiad and Lamentations with intimate Jewish historic experience.

The very coincidence in time of the arrival of a certain type of person with that cataclysmic historical moment at least confirmed the existing identifications of Jew-devil and anti-God. The first meeting of francophone Quebec and Jewish *Néo-Québécois* was not auspicious.

Fortunately, what followed was not as tragic as might have been expected, perhaps because of lethargy or indifference, perhaps because the History of Quebec had yet to be written. So, the Jews who arrived with the British quickly established links with those immigrants who had arrived from France a century before. Moreover, in contrast with their kin in blood and faith who were to follow a century later, the actual coming of the Jewish settlers in 1760-1865 was a simple matter of migrating from English London to English Canada, or from one British colony to another.

They came with the rare privileges of English freedom and virtual equality, of which they were keenly appreciative in the pre-Napoleonic age. They came with the English and as Englishmen, as members of the colony's commercial structure, but not, as many other Englishmen came, as members of its close governmental, capitalist, professional or ruling structure.

In their case, again unlike the situation that was to prevail in the 1880, they scattered — or they were permitted to scatter, or they were welcomed — throughout the Province. They made their homes as firmly in Yamachiche, Berthier, Rivière-du-Loup, St-Denis, Quebec, St-Mathieu and Trois-Rivières as in Montreal. They intermarried with French Canadians, or Indians, as with English women, traded with *habitant* farmers and engaged *voyageurs* for the deep Canadian interior where they were not strangers themselves. Their daughters studied with the Ursuline Sisters and the young men were welcomed as officers by Canadian privates and by Catholic chaplains.

The historic record establishes that there was a subtle but effective avoidance of confrontation or conflict between the two major linguistic groups, carefully superintended in London where necessary; and all tended to intercourse between the various inhabitants of the colony. This was particularly so for the Jews who, although consistently loyalist if not indeed jingoist, operated beyond the confines of power and were not impeded in their relations with the French Canadians by any anti-Semitic discourse by the Catholic Church beyond the Atlantic. Any limitation on their economic, political or social condition could hardly be explained by prejudice in their new land.

In the eighteenth century, the political arena was new to them. It was considered rather as an area for the *Goyim*, the heirs to the earth, and nowhere else were Jews politically active in 1775. So, not surprisingly, Aaron Hart, speaking as a Jew to his children, warned that they should keep far away from the no-win hustings game.

Yet his sons did not hesitate and ran — sometimes they won, sometimes they lost — in such francophone constituencies as Trois-Rivières, Sorel and Champlain. Ezekiel Hart's misadventures in the Assembly, with all the unswerving support from his Catholic constituency, had no touch of anti-Semitism but was tightly in line with the established political tradition of the time of weakening the sitting parties by expulsion on whatever ground.

Indeed, the century that opened so inauspiciously scarcely records a single incident or word of conflict between Jew and francophone.

The history books accurately record the impressive loyalism of Quebec Jews to the English Crown under whose aegis they had come to the country. However, such affirmations should not blind us to the complexities of the situation. Take, for instance, the matter of legal status. With all the liberty that the Union Jack brought, the synagogue was not a recognized house of worship, and that was not the only limitation on the rights in the British Empire at that time. When Aaron Hart died, there was no way his passing could be recorded; his death was almost illegal, as were the births of his children and nearly all his grandchildren.

The struggle to correct this injustice — as it happens a struggle against the English of Quebec — was not just a «worthy cause.» It was a leading element in the quiet war waged by the French Catholics for what such conservative historians as Pagnuelo call religious liberty in Canada, for their liberty to function as a Church. Of course, they backed the Jewish attempt to establish a synagogue, a cemetery, a register of births, marriages and demise, a rabbinate, and so forth. Because of these pressures, religious freedom and equality were established in Lower Canada in 1832 and by virtue of it, citizens' rights are, to this day, more clearly set out in Quebec and Ontario law than in any other Canadian provinces. Out of this limited but important political alliance between Jew and *Franco-Québécois* quite naturally emerged the much more general, and more important, bestowal of all civic rights upon Jews. This was an event that occurred so early in the worldwide chronicle of Jewish civil emancipation as to be inexplicable outside the context of a French and Catholic Quebec that was also a Protestant and British colony.

In a Quebec fighting for its survival and to defend its rights, social equality was an objective and an instrument of struggle. It had accepted the Protestant presence and had yet to develop a fear of strangers. Jews were not alone among «ethnic» neighbours. They were accepted, assimilated, and sometimes converted; bishops did not hesitate to stay at the Hart home. The tiny Jewish community was divided politically, some Josephs and Harts supporting the anti-establishment party.

Papineau, who had secured full rights for Jews, readily adopted a Jew as his lone companion in his European exile. A Kaufman converted into Marchand fought with the Patriotes of 1837; it was only luck that got him out of the dread Montreal prison so that he could eventually become an alderman in Montreal. A Judah representing francophone Champlain in the pre-Confederation Union parliament nearly made the Cabinet and became, in due course, the solicitor for Catholic congregations. Shortly before the end of this period, another Jew was chosen alderman for Montreal, and later, another was editor-in-chief and one of the makers of *La Presse*.

It is this Catholic-Jewish alliance which explains the political dichotomy within the tiny Jewish community of the first half of the 1800s.

* * *

The 1870s were epochal in their consequences for the whole world and for the Jewish people. The invention of racist, biological anti-Semitism, its partnership with the new xenophobic nationalisms and jingoist patriotisms, their partnerships with the Church and its espousal of extreme conservatism, the sudden application of this to the Russian scene with the resultant pogroms, setting off the unprecedented, uncontrollable mass motion of Jews westward, the energy generated by the creation of Germany, the fall of France, the shock of the Paris commune, the Vatican Council — each of these had tremendous impact upon France and upon Quebec.

The Catholic Church became aggressively ultramontanist: intercourse with an infidel became prohibited; Freemasonry became the arch-enemy and somehow became identified with the Jews, even in Canada. The trauma of the domestic French condition was imported into Canada; Quebec awareness became a hatred and fear of «les autres»; the old and the new institutions of the church, not least the pulpit and the press, were frequently put at the service of extremism.

A dominant fact in this development is that the new Jewish immigrants of the period who came from Russia, sometimes impelled by these international forces, were of a totally different social and even religious character than their Canadian kin, some of whom were by now entering their seventh generation here. Their economic background was markedly different from that of the Davids, the Judahs and the Josephs, so were their religious aspirations and their language, while there was very little that could be considered British about their rich social and political traditions. Even their appearance was new to the country. Nor did these distinctions promise to be temporary, pending assimilation.

There was much in the new scenes on the docksides to surprise a relatively homogeneous Quebec society that was fearful of the unbelieving stranger. In spite of this ambivalence, the historic events shaking Europe converted Montreal and Canada into the new address of a large number of Jewish immigrants in flight from the clear and from the forefelt consequences of European reaction, from Stalin and Hitler who were already looming on the horizon. Their movement was not always very coherent to them or to observers. Their destination was the American Dream, with its freedom, equality, peace, stability, acceptance as well as Jewish continuity. By and large, this vision cannot be called chimeric. Possibly for no other group in flight did this expectation of the New World prove itself in hard historic reality. In substance, those who fled, whether to Jerusalem or to Montreal or to New York, survived. Those who remained perished. But for this migration the epic that began with Abraham might have ended with Dreyfus and Hitler.

This New World was constituted, in reality, of a chain of cosmopolitan cities — Buenos Aires, Johannesburg, Jerusalem, London, Adelaïde, Montreal.... In the case of the last, this idea of a New World was set against certain local realities, the nature of which have not always been understood. There were no overwhelming objections to the admission of Jews into Canada from any segment of the population, and the outcries that could be heard in Quebec came more from newly-organized labour than from the nationalists. Consequently, tens of thousands of Jews were admitted in a mounting flow from 1880 to 1914 thereby creating a community that spanned the nation. To all intents and purposes they were guests of the anglophone Liberal government in Ottawa whose conviction was that Canada could benefit from growth-inducing immigration. Failing British (and French?) immigrants, Jews would serve the purpose. Peace and decency would bring about functional assimilation and foster loyalty to Canada, and these strangers would eventually change their sheepskin coats for double-breasted jackets.

Quebec stood aside from the process. What Ottawa was doing was its own business; there is no indication that the Province wished to intervene. It did not necessarily like what it saw, or whom it saw. Certainly, it did not welcome the newcomers. It even warned Protestants against taking the Jewish «scorpion» to their breast. Insofar as these immigrants were tolerated — and they settled in the eastern port in their greatest numbers, as they did in New York — French Quebec was rather pleased to see them enter the English fold rather than its own. However, it never shut its institutions to the Jewish or other immigrants. The Catholic hospitals were open to Jews. Any Hebrew who wished to attend the Catholic colleges and universities was welcomed and exempted from religious exercises. Discrimination of this type is scarcely heard of, even during that period. When, around the 1890s, some Montreal Jews asked for schools of their own, (for which no provision had been made in Confederatiion) the Catholic School Commission devised a procedure — with no condition, intervention or gain — whereby it collected the Jews' school taxes and turned them all over to the latter for their own schooling purposes. The agreement was terminated only at the Jews' request.

When the Protestant Committee of the Council of Public Instruction and the Protestant school boards assumed the burden of educating «the non-Protestants, non-Catholics», they deliberately assumed heavy financial obligations and ran great constitutional risks. The acceptance by law of the Jewish children as Protestants for the purposes of education was an equal risk. French Canada raised no objections as these immigrant groups, whose tongue was neither French nor English and whose faith was not Catholic, progressively entered the Protestant anglophone camp. It offered no gesture of welcome, made no attempt at conversion but rather, slowly but surely, fueled by a mixture of faith and a strong sense of group identity, unleashed an anti-Semitic campaign that in retrospect, with our experience of Hitler, still frightens.

The campaign was organized under the quasi-official sponsorship of the Catholic Church, with *L'Action catholique* and *La Semaine religieuse de Québec* leading the hounds. The creative nationalist Tardivel put his *Vérité* at its service, and only his son's virulence was to surpass his own. The Association canadienne de la jeunesse catholique was among the leaders, and priests vied in inventing, or in digging up from we know not what past, lies and fabrications ranging from ritual murder and accusations of Talmud falsifications, to world conspiracies, to Protocols of the Elders of Zion, etc... At the turn of the century, the Dreyfus case became a Canadian issue as the French martyr to discrimination was tried and condemned repeatedly in Quebec opinion long after he was exonerated in France. When, in 1913, even the Russian courts freed Beilis of charges of murdering a Christian child, the best Quebec press held that this pointed to the dubious quality of Russian courts and the questionable merit of Russian prosecuting agencies!

Again in 1913, the paroxysm of hate against the Jews reached a climax in the Ortenberg-Plamondon trial which is one of the most socially significant in the annals of the Quebec nation; anti-Jewish incitements had come to a head with a public address made by a Quebec City notary and sponsored by a leading Catholic youth group, in that it gave rise to attacks on citizens. Court proceedings were instituted on what were probably very weak legal grounds. Indeed, the court of first resort dismissed the case.

But even more important than the eventual maintenance of the injured party's case was that during the proceedings, an array of churchmen — academicians of astounding ignorance — supported the wildest accusations regarding the Jewish community. It was a frightening confrontation which took place simultaneously with the Kieff case where Beilis was accused of ritual murder, a horrid fantasy also promulgated by the august daily which called itself *L'Action catholique*. The Quebec priests who uttered these accusations against Jews were not silenced by the verdict in the Ortenberg-Plamondon case, but continued to reiterate them for a decade — with no Catholic disavowal or protest, except haltingly by the Liberal government in Ottawa, headed by the Quebecer Laurier, which continued to welcome Jews among European immigrants.

Because Quebec was not alone in agitating against the Jews, and because, for the Ultramontanists, there was indeed someone hiding beyond the mountain, Quebec was informed at a very early stage of Jewish aspirations to the Holy Land. Followed with concern and hostility in Quebec Church circles, this Zionist project was perceived as a plan of action by the entire Jewish people directed against Christendom. So, the expulsion of the Moslems from Jerusalem by the Christian forces in 1917 was judged a sad day for Quebec. Local followers of the Saviour much preferred Mohammedan to British rule over the holy sites, the latter being considered not sufficiently anti-Jewish.

Another international source of hostility was Russia. The powerful Quebec churchmen and journalists were sorry to see the czar deposed even when his government was replaced by Kerensky's Canadian-style democracy. Jews, of course, were elated over the fall of this Haman. When, in 1917, the Communists took over in Russia, *L'Action catholique* felt confirmed in its suspicion of the Jews, little noting that the Bolsheviks set about to destroy Judaism in their lands and in Palestine. From this date, Jews were no longer devil-freemasons; instead they were now devil-communists.

* * *

Confronted by this rejection, the Jewish community had little hesitancy in following the course of most other immigrant groups in Quebec and, indeed, francophone minorities elsewhere on the continent, in choosing to adhere to the politically powerful, economically enticing and culturally overwhelming anglophone universe. In consequence, the story of the Quebec Jewish community in this century can be read as a graph of Anglo-Jewish relations. It must, nevertheless, be stressed that if Jews have thereby become closely identified with the English, it does not necessarily follow that they identify with them. Were it so, Quebec would not have become the heir to the rich Canadian Jewish culture. Had there been integration the culture would not manifest its present vitality.

In the realm of Canadian politics, from the beginning of the twentieth century, partisan figures saw in the Jews and in other immigrants a natural fund of votes for the Liberal Party. Conservatives, by contrast, expressed little interest in them, and political parties in Quebec none whatsoever. The Liberals found support, to some extent at least, among thinking citizens who saw in these new immigrants a pool of progressive ideas centering on inter-confessionality, improved education, and increased tolerance.

There were subtle as well as obvious circumstances that favoured the development of this partisan relationship. For refugees from Russian Czarism, the very word «liberal» was a powerful attraction (as in the U.S. was the term «democratic»), while in contrast, the term «conservative», in its Russian context, repelled. From this alliance emerged a relatively limited Jewish political power in some urban areas, and Jewish «representation» in municipal, provincial and federal government, in Toronto and Winnipeg as well as in Montreal. It also led to the establishment of a tradition — fortunately not of infinite duration — whereby a Jew can aspire to election only from a «Jewish constituency».

However, the crucial arena where a fateful relationship between Quebec Jewry and the core of «anglophonie» was carefully and contractually established, after much debate in excellent good will, was in regard to education within the constitutionally assured confessional system. Here, the issue was clearly not one of language. It was rather the organic, legal identification of Jew and Protestant. (Where were the Jewish theologians at this time?)

French Canada was formally not involved in the decision, except insofar as it was the government of Quebec which assented by legislation to the remarkable agreement between Protestants and Jews. Later, Henri Bourassa and L.A. Taschereau were to point out the dangers for French Catholicism inherent in this arrangement. But this was later, and in the atmosphere of hostility, their prophecy went unheeded. On the Jewish side, the leaders of the community had overwhelming support in their intention to assimilate culturally (but not religiously) with Protestant «anglophonie».

In choosing to migrate to the New World, the Jews were attracted by a political vision, one of the central elements of which was a religiously neutral public school system frequented by all children as equal citizens. Such was perceived as existing in the United States, and it constituted a school system of which the Jews have been the most consistent proponents and, perhaps, the greatest beneficiaries. However, neither of Quebec's two confessional networks conformed to this school ideal. The Protestant school was considered its nearest approximation because more nominal and less proselytizing than its Catholic counterpart. Of course, the Jews never admitted they would be unhappy in a single Quebec national school system with its francophone majority and Catholic personality, but that is another matter!

In their hearts many Protestants agreed with this commitment to a single public school ideal and foresaw that the presence of Jewish children, and even Jewish board members, would advance the advent of this neutral system. Remarkably, no Catholic observer at the time cared about what the Protestants and Jews were doing: not quite «a plague on both your houses» but nearly, and benevolently so. What they did not recognize is that although a Catholic system can thrive beside a Protestant system, it cannot survive beside a neutral system.

For 150 years Quebec Jews had educated their children as they had wished in their synagogue schools, in their Baron de Hirsch schools, in prestigious private schools, and no one had raised the question whether a Jew is a Protestant. But at the beginning of the century, identifying the two became a social ideal. Jewish ideologists, and notably the Labour Zionists, who were opposing too close a political link with either the Liberals or the Conservatives, were, however, also opposed to the organic link with the Protestant school system calling on the same reasoning: Jews should have the distinct educational and political structure which is available under Canada's multicultural constitution. Of course, they went unheeded, and the ultimate cost was high. For the sake of this identification with the Protestants, the Jews sacrificed the possibility of an independent and free school identity as an uncommitted entity in the complex of Quebec society; they forewent the potentialities inherent in an educational system of their own. Further, in the course of time, they became the pillar of financial support of the anglophone school system of Montreal.

Although the children were well treated in the Protestant schools, the Jews failed in both their central objectives. For sociological and other reasons, Jewish pupils remained largely segregated from their Protestant classmates and, of course, totally isolated from francophones. Further, the parents did not realize their ambiguous ambition of sitting on the Protestant School Boards, at least not until half a century later, in 1965, at the end of the Protestant phase of confessional education.

Within the Protestant community the plan to accord Jews a Christian status aroused an interesting debate that was, on the whole, far-minded and far-sighted. Most of the members of the school boards and of the Protestant Committee of the Council of Public Instruction saw it as their duty to accommodate all ethnic groups reaching Montreal, and to ensure the best education for their children in the interests of Quebec society and of its anglophone component. The long-term benefits of such a position would far outweigh the immediate costs and inconveniences they foresaw. The proof of anglophone foresight lies in their success in assimilating all immigration, even Catholic, to their camp; a considerable achievement that bore within itself the seeds of explosion as it came to be recognized as a threat to French Quebec.

Some Protestant leaders, however, foresaw pedagogical difficulties, not so much in teaching Jewish children (admittedly not notoriously slow learners!) or immigrants who lacked an elementary knowledge of English, but rather in transmitting to their own children Protestant lore in the presence of non-Protestant classmates. In other words, they foresaw the early loss of the Protestant character of their school system, which system was the only constitutional entity of Protestantism and of the English language. More specifically, they foresaw that Jewish parents would, in due course, seek to follow their sons and daughters into the school system, as members of the school boards, at which point one might as well bid farewell to Montreal Protestantism.

The civil nature of the Montreal debate with the Protestants contrasts, however, with the anti-Jewish attitudes displayed by many of the same denominations from Ontario and elsewhere in the controversy over the Lord's Day Act in 1906. Then, the aggressive clergy of the Alliance for the Defense of the Sabbath revealed a hitherto concealed hostility towards the Jews that surprised many. Their zeal did, nevertheless, spill over into Quebec with the local associates of the Lord's Day Alliance injecting their antagonism for years into the Montreal school question debate. Nevertheless, the school arrangements were honorably concluded and enshrined in Quebec Law.

For the first twenty years of the century, the Protestant-Jewish school accord functioned well, as predicted. The pedagogues were loyal to their Jewish pupils. The rising costs to the Protestants were tolerated. The Catholics were satisfied to have the alien non-Catholics, non-Protestants out of their kin. The problems created by the presence of the Jewish children within the Christian system solved themselves through an automatic segregation created by the voluntary delineations of areas of immigrant settlement. Within the schools, the teachers were often able to have parallel classes for Jewish children, while in an extreme case, the Baron Byng High School was constructed so that the University Street Montreal High School could function as a Christian school.

Insofar as Quebec Jewry is concerned, the first quarter of the twentieth century was one of the best periods in its history. It witnessed the establishment of a firm and profound cultural, and hence political, alliance between the Jews and the anglophones to the exclusion of the francophones. If, at the outset, the latter community harboured some vicious anti-Semitism, it was followed by a period of extreme quiescence. The stability in the classroom reflected a triumph for the Jewish ideology which had been transplanted from continental Europe and which considered that the historic problem of the accommodation of Jews within the larger society could best be resolved through sharing the lifestyle, educational system and social ideals of an open, democratic nation. In the New World, this was usually identified with Anglo-Saxon American democracy of which Quebec «anglophonie» was perceived as being its natural extension.

However, as the numbers of Jews in Protestant schools increased, tensions became apparent everywhere. Ironically, the crisis broke in 1924 at the very high point of Jewish enrollment; patience for another year just might have reassured the fearful Protestants. But to deal with developments as they occurred... Jewish parents began to claim parental rights to representation in the government of the schools; teachers complained of difficulties in teaching Jews and Christians together; the financial issue was raised... and the whole educational problem of Quebec ignited to the extent that even today the flames have not been put out.

The ensuing conflict was at once grave and civilized. Profound divergences emerged within the Jewish community itself resulting in the creation of several distinct groups, each with clearly articulated positions. Jews and Protestants battled in the legislature, in the newspapers, before a special government Commission of Inquiry, in the courts, and all the way to the Privy Council. Over the years there developed — or was revealed — a profound and unsuspected religious and cultural hostility. Friendships transgressing religious divisions were shattered. Protestants would not have Jews sit with them on school commissions that educated children of both groups. Harsh words were uttered that were neither withdrawn nor disavowed.

Suddenly, from the side, another enemy emerged, one that was not really implicated in the issues at stake but that was nevertheless sufficiently menacing to add further strain to the alliance between Jew and anglophone. In 1930, just as the school problem was finding a solution — with common approval of Jews, Protestants, the legislature and the courts — the highest levels of the Quebec Catholic Church spoke up: under no condition would they tolerate Jews being recognized on any level as the equals of Catholics. With a heavy handedness probably not matched in Quebec history, they forced the abrogation of a new contract and a new law.

Further, the churchmen did more than shatter this fragile arrangement painfully brought together on the level of school organization. Their attitude launched an anti-Semitic movement by Adrien Arcand which, upon retrospect with the passage of years, is most clearly unprecedented on the continent, and with few if any, parallels west of Poland. Quebec Jews were isolated and under attack.

Their situation was unlike that in Ontario. Quebec «anglophonie» scarcely records any act of hostility towards the Jews, in contrast with events on the beaches of Toronto. There was no fascist group speaking English in the Province. But, by the same token, there was hardly any Protestant defence of Jews — indeed, even of democracy — not even such defence as Henri Bourassa and Taschereau sought to initiate. Here, as elsewhere in the world, Jews suddenly found themselves isolated in the hour of domestic and universal threat, and, to this day, the harrowing experience remains engraved in the memory of a people.

No support was forthcoming from either Quebec or Canadian *anglophonie* for legislation against racial or religious hatred. Mackenzie King's stand towards Nazi Germany and Hitler was ambiguous but cordial, and in the years and months prior to the outbreak of World War II, the possibility of Fascism loomed over Canada resulting in the shattered confidence of Jews in the English with whom they had all too recently sought to identify if not, indeed, to merge. Confirmation of this crisis of confidence was provided by the desperate efforts of Jews to rescue as many as possible of their kin who had fled from Germany and Poland. The English at the port of Halifax and in the offices of the Federal government in Ottawa kept the doors shut against them more ruthlessly than ever before. Inevitably, this agony over their kin abandoned to the Holocaust shattered the bond that had been forged between Jews and Protestants over the period 1903-1923.

Through the twenties and thirties Quebec nationalism assumed a form and name that had certain resemblances with Hitlerism, Polish patriotism and the various quislings and brown shirts who shared, beneath nationalist banners, a murderous attitude towards Jews as well as a Holy Writ and a communion in the Protocols of the Elders of Zion. Indeed, Hilter's concordat prompted a Catholic Quebec to defend his ideology and actions for years, until the Nazis betrayed German Catholics in a cynical violation of the Vatican-Berlin Accord.

When the Second World War finally came, and Canada entered the conflict, it was in no sense a consequence of long-held convictions, but rather a sudden veering from a position that could well have led the country to adopt a stance similar to that of Ireland or of South Africa.

A combination of all these circumstances and tragic domestic misunderstandings meant that Quebec Jews were more scarred than other members of Canadian society. If the mortar that had kept Jewry and «anglophonie» together had dissolved, a traditional Catholic and isolationist Quebec had become indistinguishable from sympathy for Hitlerism, only deepening the abyss between «francophonie» and the Jewish community. The cries of «Down with the Jews», heard at anti-conscription rallies, did not go unheard, and if many radical transformations have occurred in Quebec since the 1930s, these lesions have not entirely healed or ceased to fester. The severance of understanding between French Canadians and Jews was complete and seemingly irrevocable.

* * *

The day that Hitler died, fortune gave the human race a new chance. On that day, in Quebec in particular, calculations based on his victory or even survival, or upon the survival of any of the principles for which he stood, were discarded. Within a few years, every vestige of racism was suppressed. The Church, deprived of much of its strength, re-examined, not so much its teachings, as the social implications of its position. Beginning with Archbishop Charbonneau, it diametrically reversed its racist discourse and its xenophobic attitudes. With the passing of Duplessis, national aspirations were transformed into the search for a less repressive, more ethical, Quebec patriotism. The Province no longer vetoed the opening of Canada's gates to survivors and victims of overseas violence. All over Canada the racial barriers banning Jews came down. No longer blinkered, Quebec quickly realized that the immigrants were most necessary and acceptable, and that Jewish ministers and judges did not pervert the law. Further, if at the outset most visible immigrants were Jews, once the floodgates were opened, they were quickly submerged beneath a kaleidoscope of Italians, Germans, Hungarians, Vietnamese, Chileans, Haitians and so forth, all of whom were welcomed.

The welcome mat had been put out too late for the German and Polish Jews. Treblinka got to them first. On the Jewish agenda of post-war Quebec priorities switched from immigration to other problems, notably Israel, and in these changing orientations, identification with «anglophonie» was further weakened in spite of the maintenance of linguistic ties forged in the childhood of native Jewish Quebecers, and of the existence of a common economic culture.

Mid-century constituted a new beginning for Jews, for Quebec and for the world. A fatal threat had been removed, and mankind could once again dream and talk of freedom. It was a dizzy period in which the Jews sought a new equilibrium following the trauma of the Holocaust. Israel, restored after two thousand years, constituted an immeasurable mental and material challenge. Quebec Jewry was radically transformed with the arrival of tens of thousands of survivors from the events overseas. Refugees from a surrealist universe of abysmal horror, they came to the peaceful world of a Quebec that was, by definition, incapable of conceiving this aspect of the multi-faceted four-thousand-year-old Jewish experience. They were the quintessence of a people's tragic history, but also a symbol and consequence of the isolation of an Israel that incorporates the eternal Jewish Messianic hope. Their *vécu* entered into the very dreams and nightmares as well as the speech patterns of every Jew.

The immigrants were also a challenge to the imaginative potential of the new Quebec mentality. The implications posed by their presence were, in fact, well heeded, and exerted no minor influence on the government of the Province. Yet, at the same time, these events led to the crystallization of two powerful heritages, *québécois* and Jewish, something that was not always clearly appreciated and which precipitated a certain discretion in which the intimate and profound changes of heart were often concealed.

The immigrant's own experience of the nationalisms and of the independentisms of this age did not help. Nor did it help that, in mid-century, as fifty years before, no immigration official or social worker explained to any immigrant the pluralist nature of the Canada to which he was coming, and even less of the French Quebec where he would settle. Under the circumstances, it is scarcely surprising that the Quebec Jews have not always recognized the new configuration of Quebec nationalism. In the fervour of the sixties, they overlooked the fact that one of the most significant demands was to accord greater rights and liberties to ethnic groups and to minorities. Canada took an early, and visible, step in this direction with the Royal Commission on Bilingualism and Biculturalism that was set up by the Pearson government. «Why only two cultures?» asked Michael Garber of the Canadian Jewish Congress, while the demands of Ukrainians and others in the West were even more vocal. The Government buckled. The fourth volume of the Commission's report was only a token representation of a deep change that had occurred in the human topography of the country. For English Canada, the message was clear: no longer could immigrant groups be expected to merge into *anglophonie*.

The consequences of this realization for the internal life of the ethnic communities, and in particular for the Jews, were rapid and intense. If the communities were henceforth recipients of massive funding, by the Department of the Secretary of State and other Federal government agencies, their autonomy and liberty of action were thereby endangered. They risked becoming instruments of central government.

For French Canadians the implications were even more menacing. They were no longer one of only two official cultures. The inter-ethnic game was becoming increasingly complex. Bearing in mind a tradition of xenophobia, there was reason to fear a resurgence of racial strife in Quebec, except that the Federal government's promotion of multi-culturalism coincided with Quebec's more generous approach to immigrants, involving a mixture of recognition of their separate identity and assimilation.

On November 16, 1976 reality caught up with «anglophonie». There was panic and fright in the Jewish community, plus ill-considered statements and actions in the months that followed. The groundswell of emigration touched Jews along with other alumnii of English schools, thereby reinforcing the economic influences of the St. Lawrence Seaway and of Alberta oil in the westward shift of power in Canada. Even so, to predict the future of Montreal and Quebec Jewry in the light of these events and circumstances is a hazardous task. Suffice it to say that far-reaching forces are clearly at work.

During the past two decades, a significant number of Jewish immigrants with French as their first language, and not Yiddish, Polish, German or Russian, have arrived. Regardless of their linguistic advantage, they have had to undergo painful adjustments, like the poor and new before them. But time has moved on, and events have endowed them with a complex but genuine role in transforming Quebec Jewry from within, and in its contacts with the larger society. These newcomers have not known the Holocaust, European Fascism and Canada's leanings in that direction, or Yiddish culture. Theirs is an influence born of a Latin, Mediterranean tradition, formulated in a language that speaks to the heart of a French Quebec. All the while, generation follows up on generation on the shores of the New World. Quebec Jewry moves on accumulating the experience of each wave of immigrants, and the ties between Jewry and the host society are reinforced.

The sum of these movements is not easy to discern. However, we might point to the decline of Yiddish as the language of the community and of its literature, to the disappearance of ideologies inspired by its institutions, the virtual unanimity of the major lines of its policies, to the quasi-governmental or at least corporate traditions of its institutions, to the overwhelming role of the Quebec-born among the activitists, to the disappearance of the European synagogual and traditional forms of religion, etc..

In 1982, the youngest Jewish Quebecer is as distant from the era of Groulx and of Arcand as is the youngest *Québécois pure laine*. Rue St-Denis, the Université de Montréal, Lévesque, Ryan, *Le Devoir* are tangible realities for this graduate of French immersion. The absolute peacefulness of the past decade of Quebec nationalism lead him to view with reserve the rigid attitudes of the Jewish establishment and of earlier generations of his people. Visitors to classrooms in Jewish secondary schools are often surprised at the total openness they find there. And through all their healthy questioning about the future, there emerges, almost unexpectedly, a deep love for Montreal, for *their* Montreal, if not, indeed, *their* Quebec.

The English Working Class of Quebec: Fragmentation and Silence

Carla Lipsig-Mummé

CARLA LIPSIG-MUMMÉ is an industrial sociologist presently teaching at Concordia University. Originally a union organiser and researcher, she has worked with farmworkers and garment workers. She has also been involved in the labour education programmes for the Fédération nationale des enseignants du Québec and for the Canadian Labour Congress Labour College. Her home-base is Montreal, where she is currently working on the renaissance of work at home for wages, and on a study of immigrant workers for the Conseil central of the CNTU.

In the debate over the political future of Quebec which has been absorbing us since 1976, and the broader question of cultural decolonization which has been at issue for much longer, the interests of the English working class have been much invoked by various interest groups but left largely undefined by English workers themselves. In the polemics triggered by the presentation of Bill 101 for example, those language pressure groups representing the English corporate and professional elite repeatedly trotted out the case of the English worker to make the point that since all anglophones were not capitalists, none should be «punished» as such. On the other end of the spectrum within the English community, those groups to some degree supportive of Bill 101, and in the main enthusiastic about the Parti Québécois' then untried social project, voiced concern that the least-skilled English workers would suffer at work for their unilingualism, and called upon the Government to ensure adequate language retraining and job security.

The eagerness with which diverse interest groups hastened, by virtue of opportunism or idealism, to define for the English working class its necessary choices, underscores both the silence of English workers themselves and the lack of clarity with which their place in the Quebec structure is understood. I hope, in this article, to raise some questions concerning the historical location of English workers within the Quebec working class and to suggest some reasons for their lack of organized presence in the current political debates.

Let me begin with some definitions. By English Quebecer, I mean someone of British stock residing in Quebec whose first language learned and still understood is English. Although I am less than fully satisfied with this definition, I have retained it because of its prevalence in census and other demographic materials.[1]

The definition of working class is, necessarily, more complex. By working class, I mean all those who work for wages, but do not exercise control over capital or the work of others, as well as all those who work within the institutions of value-formation and for the state, but do not make or execute policy in these systems.[2] In other words, blue and white-collar workers in mining, manufacturing, construction, trade, real estate offices and finance companies, in transportation and communication as well as the support staff in schools, universities, hospitals, welfare agencies, CLSCs, the media and blue-collar employees of the Provincial and Federal and municipal governments.

Marginal to the working class and in «contradictory» location to it are those who «execute but do not create state policy or disseminate but do not control» the formulation of ideas, ideals and values: the mainly professional employees of the media, the schools, the universities and health and welfare agencies.[3]

I would argue that in the final analysis, one's class origin determines occupation, which in turn determines class identity, the most important single factor in the formulation of political options. This does not mean that other factors do not influence political perceptions — certainly language, culture, sex and community may act to modify in the short run the factor of occupation, and in individual cases may overturn it. Nor would I argue that individuals always, or even usually, intervene in politics in function of their «true» class interests. Rather, I think that, where a political project proposes or causes significant changes in the economic *rapport de force* — as certainly the Parti Québécois has already begun to do — the outline of the interests of the social classes begins, over time, to crystallize in relationship to the emergent social order, and a central core of these interests may be more easily identified than is usual. What are the interests of the English within the working class of Quebec, and how did these come to develop?

While quite a lot of research has been done recently on Quebec's class structure, most of it has focused on the emergence of a state-employed francophone petty bourgeoisie and on the relationship of the Parti Québécois to the fractions of a national bourgeoisie. We know, however, little of the internal composition of the working class, still less of the role of English workers within it.

What we do know is that Quebec's working class is criss-crossed by fissures which are the historic result of external economic dependence as well as of the role of immigration in the economy. The first of these fissures splits the economy into several sectors, each dominated by a different type of capital, and splits the working class into at least three groups, each identifying its interests and strategies in function of the type of capital predominant in its industry. The second of these fissures crosscuts the first, fragmenting the working class into ethnically exclusive streams. Let me examine each of these in turn.

Over time, economies such as ours, in which foreign capital comes to play a directive role, tend to fragment, for foreign capital within particular industrial sectors usually absorbs national capital, leaving particular industrial sectors dominated by international capital while others remain — residually — in the hands of national capitalists. Over time it becomes possible to identify an internationalized sector of an economy (in which the production process is internationally integrated and the market is international), a national sector (in which production is only nationally or regionally integrated and markets are usually domestic), a sector in which state capital is pre-eminent, and finally a mixed sector in which state capital combines with one of the other fractions. While the particular industries in which one or another form of capital dominates vary from country to country, in general extractive industries, those concerned with fuel and with heavy machinery production as well as those demanding the most sophisticated technological software, usually come under the control of international capital. What is left in the hands of national capital are two sorts of residual industries: the classical industries of the early Industrial Revolution, poorly competitive, technologically backward, labour-intensive and unstable; and the purely artisanal concerns, which structure of production has not basically changed since the nineteenth century. It is understandable that workers in each of these three economic sectors, to say nothing of employees of the state, should define their interests differently — their objectives and the limits to what they can extract from their employers differ so dramatically.

The crystallization of separate paths for the working class can be traced back to the end of the nineteenth century. It is not without significance that the period 1870-1920, in which American capital began to develop and transform those of Quebec's raw materials which would be the future motor of the economy, was also the period in which the new forms of industrialization transformed the shape of the labour force, saw the first massive wave of modern immigration, began the fragmentation of economic sectors by source of capital, and crystallized ethnic participation in the economy into exclusive, competitive streams.

In the period between 1870 and 1920, industrial production began seriously to take root in Quebec.[4] That process of transformation worked upon an economy which had, during the nineteenth century, been characterized by, on the one hand, pre-industrial artisanal production and, on the other, by mass employment in the construction of transportation facilities. Artisanal production was characterized by a relatively rudimentary division of labour, by a work force at least 50 per cent English, Scottish, Welsh and German, and by few workers each highly skilled and responsible for the performance of many of the tasks associated with the complete product and exercising considerable individual discretion over the performance of his or her craft.

On the other hand, the pre-conditions for industrial production were laid down by the thousands of unskilled Irish workers who built the canals and railroads.[5]

Into this essentially artisanal economy, foreign capital introduced two processes of change. On the one hand, beginning with steel in the last decades of the nineteenth century, large-scale, truly industrial extractive and transformative concerns were introduced. These new industrial concerns were characterized by a highly complex division of labour, by the mass employment of semi-skilled workers (drawn from the skilled, unskilled and agricultural francophone population), by a fragmentation of the task allotted to each worker, and by the absence of any history of artisanal production within the industry.[6] In other words, by 1900 a method of production had been introduced into Quebec in the form of new industries which themselves had no artisanal past to evolve from.

On the other hand, a second change occured because the method of industrial production operated as an attracting pole influencing many of the formely artisanal industries, partially but imperfectly industrializing them. By the 1870s, partial and imperfect industrialization had begun in the textile, garment, boot and shoe, and other light secondary industries.[7] Thus, by the beginning of the twentieth century, there were three forms of production in Quebec, each lodged in different industries.

The ethnic mix and distribution of Quebec's modern working class had begun to crystallize around 1920. We can identify four waves of immigration straddling that watershed date. The first had begun in the 1820s and continued to the 1880s, bringing skilled German, Scottish, English and Welsh craftsmen to partially fill Quebec's earliest industrial positions. The second began after 1848 and continued for three-quarters of a century, bringing Irish labourers to work in the most unskilled of outdoors jobs, digging canals and building railroads. The third wave of immigration, began in the first decade of the twentieth century. It brought southern, central and eastern European as well as Scandinavian unskilled, semi-skilled and skilled workers to compete with francophones for production jobs in the quasi-industrial urban industries as well as for the skilled positions in the mines; to compete with anglophones for the skilled jobs in textiles and garments; and to compete with the Irish for the labouring jobs. The fourth wave of immigration, stretching from 1945 to the present, focused on encouraging professionals as well as potential entrepreneurs. It will be discussed later.

Each of these waves of immigration transformed the ethnic geography of the working class. If the first wave established Protestant British craftsmen among the vanguard of the nineteenth century working class both in numbers and in vigour when unionization was concerned, the third wave pitted immigrants against francophones for unskilled and semi-skilled jobs, and immigrants against anglophones for highly-skilled craft occupations in those industries which were either still artisanal or in the process of imperfectly industrializing. It did not set anglophone against francophone for jobs in any sector, but it did serve to encapsulate English Quebec workers at the polar ends of the skills spectrum. At one end, the most casual of unskilled employment continued to attract a large number of Irish. At the other end of the skills spectrum, English craftsmen were found in three circumstances: either they were employed as the skilled minority of craftsmen — machinists, welders, carpenters, fitters, pattern designers — working on the railroads and within heavy industry and the mines; or they remained as craftsmen in the still artisanal industries, often becoming by the end of the 1930s, small businessmen in cabinetmaking, clothing repair, upholstering and electrical repairs; or, finally, the English were clustered in the most skilled crafts within quasi-industrializing sectors. They were, for example, typesetters in the newspaper industry and master tailors in the mens' clothing industry. All told, outside the labouring jobs in which Roman Catholic English workers continued to be heavily represented, by the 1920s Protestant English Quebecers still retained leading positions in those craft and artisanal occupations which had been the motor of the nineteenth century economy and had dominated the industrial labour force before its transformation. As well, they were moving into skilled jobs in the new industries.

In sum, English artisans of the nineteenth century became a leading component of the labour aristocracy of the early twentieth, practising their crafts in those industries coming under the sway of international capital as well as in those which were artisanal or industrializing and under the dominion of national capital.

Within the fifty years that followed, however, English workers had, with some significant exceptions, vanished from the skilled jobs in heavy industry in the sector dominated by international capital, and from the quasi-industrialized national sector industries: from autos, steel, rubber, chemicals, but also from garments, textiles, hats, boots and shoes. They remained present in skilled positions in heavy machinery if these were organized on a craft basis. They «reappeared», if one may use the image, proletarianized in the heavy industries, but not in the light secondary industries, as assembly line workers in the main. They retained their importance in the really small artisanal concerns in furniture-making, upholstery and repair, in electrical repair and services, in contracting services for homeowners, and in clothing repair and alteration, although the line between artisan and entrepreneur was often blurred, and one individual might move from employment as a craftsman to owner of his own business and back again over a lifetime. Outside of this last category, blue-collar English workers continued to practise their crafts only when it was possible to be organized and recognized as separate from semi-skilled workers: as electricians, welders, fitters, carpenters and plumbers in the railroads and construction- related industries, and as machinists in heavy industrial plants if these were organized on a craft basis.

So much for the dwindling of the importance of skilled work in industrial settings for the English craftsman over the recent decades. In what other jobs are English workers found today?

They are employed in the mainly semi-skilled jobs in dwindling proportion.[9] In 1951, 34,88 per cent of the English male labour force and 25,91 per cent of the female worked in manufacturing. But in 1971, those percentages had dropped to 29,59 per cent and 16,62 per cent respectively.

Within manufacturing, the English have largely left the light secondary industries where women and migrants now predominate. For example, in 1971, fewer than 3,9 per cent of the clothing trades' labour force was English. In food and beverage production, the percentage of English in the total labour force was 8,5. In wood, primary metal production and mineral products as well — better paid, more technologically advanced but with little recognition of skills specialization — English male workers represented less than 11 per cent of the male labour force. Only in electrical products, pulp and paper, in printing and publishing, in transportation equipment and in metal fabricating did the English male worker represent more than 11 per cent of each industry's labour force. In two of these — printing and publishing and electrical products — English males represented 20,25 per cent and 28,4 per cent respectively of the male labour. The former is a craft-organized field, long an area of skilled English employment, and the latter is organized by craft and by industry.

So much for manufacturing and male workers. In the other traditionally male working class industries — construction, logging and related forestry occupations, fishing and trapping, and mining — English workers contributed little. In 1971, English construction workers represented only 6,16 per cent of that industry's male labour force, 4,05 per cent of forestry and 12,5 per cent of mining, but 21,6 per cent of fishing and trapping, a tiny and shrinking sector of employment.

Only one large industry, transportation (and in particular railroads), had a significant percentage of English employees: 17,8 per cent in 1971.

In all sectors, the English participation rates, in comparison to the total English male labour force as well as to each industry's labour force, had been steadily dropping since 1951.

In the traditionally female working class occupations, English women were steadily vacating the jobs they had historically held. In contrast to women of other ethnic groups, in Quebec, English women had never worked in large numbers as machine operators and floor girls in the garment industry. In 1971, only 2,3 per cent of that industry's workers were English women, as compared to the 42,6 per cent of French women. Manufacturing as a whole grew by 16,7 per cent between 1951 and 1971 in Quebec, but provided employment for 9 per cent fewer English women in 1971 than it had in 1951. Interestingly, English women were far more likely to be employed in clerical jobs in heavy «male» industries such as wood, primary metal and mineral products, than were French women or women of recent immigrant groups. In fact, English women in clerical jobs in heavy industry could be said to be the only significant group of non- francophones employed in that sector.

Another traditional source of female employment, retail trade, had doubled its number of women employees since 1951. But English female participation shrank in two ways: as a percentage of the total number of women employees in that industry, it decreased from 13,6 per cent in 1951 to 11,55 per cent in 1971, and as a per cent of the English female labour force, it dropped from 10,1 per cent in 1951 to 9,5 per cent in 1971. Again, hotels and restaurants more than doubled their employment of women between 1951 and 1971, but provided work for only 3,89 per cent of English women in 1971 as compared to 6,52 per cent in 1951. Finally, personal services, whose labour force increased by less than one thousand in the two decades, saw the percentage of English women participating drop from 8,3 per cent to 5,9 per cent. Its female labour force actually declined by just under three thousand. Within the industry's female labour force, virtually one-third of the decline was attributed to English women.

In other words, since the end of World War II, both the male and female English working populations were moving out of traditional blue and white-collar jobs, usually faster than, and sometimes in the opposite direction to that of the Quebec labour force as a whole. Essentially, the English working population moved in two directions towards the margins of the traditional working class. First, it swelled the ranks of the casual labourers — drivers' helpers, night watchmen and temporary shipping clerks. While only 2,28 and 1,27 per cent of English men and women were so classified in 1951, the percentages were 8,03 and 11,25 respectively in 1971. Second, it moved into those jobs located at the borders of the working class and the bourgeoisie, in those occupations which I have called «contradictory» because their occupants exercise some control over the work of others and/or formulate and execute government policy.

These «contradictory» occupations are located largely in the health and social welfare industries, in education, Provincial and Federal civil services, and in municipal governments and various other services available to the business world. They have more than tripled in numbers employed since the mid-fifties. They can be separated into two major categories: those which entail direct or indirect employment by the state, and those which are employed by or in the private sector.

«Service to business», therefore, stands apart from the other industries and occupations. The English, and particularly English males, are far more heavily represented in these concerns than is any other ethnic group, and employment of this sort has almost doubled in its importance for the English labour force as a whole since 1951.

Direct and indirect state employment represent large and growing sources of work for the English, just as they do for the French in Quebec. Immigrants are largely absent from these fields. Thus, for example, English numbers in the education field approximately tripled during the twenty years in which total employment in that field tripled. In health and social welfare the growth of English employment also kept pace with the growth of employment in the field as a whole. That French employment grew more rapidly is less important than two other contrasts. Firstly, the English are relatively rarely employed in any direct government service at all (they represent only 4,5 per cent of all direct provincial employees); secondly, the contrast between ethnic participation in state-related sectors is less striking than the comparison between male and female rates, regardless of ethnicity. For women of both major ethnic groups, these sectors represent the largest source of employment, the field which has attracted the largest number of new entrants, and the one towards which those shifting out of traditional working class occupations have gone. 26,98 per cent of English women and 29,85 per cent of French women worked directly or indirectly for the state in 1971. Males are, in contrast, far less often employed by the state: only 6,4 per cent of English men and 7,49 per cent of French men in 1971, in spite of the fact that these figures represent an increase of over 100 per cent for each group since 1951.

In sum, the vacating of traditional working class jobs by English Quebecers seems to be occurring at a faster rate than that affecting Quebec as a whole. English women workers seem to be shifting towards some form of public employment and English males towards private sector white-collar employment, particularly in those industries which service the business community. For both male and female English workers, the shift towards service employment has been complemented by the dramatic growth in the reserve army of the casual unskilled. Craft work, that bastion of English employment in the early twentieth century, is of less importance to the English labour force, and English craftsmen play a correspondingly smaller role within this stratum of work. The portrait is of a working English population located at the poles of the skills and status spectrum, with very little presence at the centre in that cluster of industries and occupations which are the traditional source of working class employment.

So much for shifts in the distribution of English workers since the end of the nineteenth century. Given that we know how the English working class has evolved in terms of industrial distribution, some explanations concerning its general silence on the political issues of the day may be given.

The ability of English workers — or of any minority — to intervene *as workers* in political debates is determined by two factors. First, they must have some collective awareness of their identity as English workers as distinct from other workers. This need not be on any larger scale than the plant or office, but it must crystallize collectively. Second, there must be some union or other work-based association which they must influence or work through as a vehicle for formulating and publicizing their position.

These two pre-conditions are not available to all English workers. First of all, English workers are often clustered in non-union sectors or sectors where unionism is weak.[10] While they may have staff associations or some such, these never become vehicles for politicization unless they are in the process of transformation into unions. Second, English workers scattered in assembly-line jobs in industrially-organized plants are unlikely to identify their interests as being distinct from the francophones doing the same work beside them, and if they did, their numbers would be too small to make much difference. Industrial unions are fairly egalitarian structures, and the similarity of work performed, coupled with their recent history of militancy, combine to make ethnic integration more likely than polarization, and coordinated action in pursuit of economic goals is a more pressing priority. This is another way of saying that English production workers do not feel estranged enough from their French co-workers to agitate as a separate English minority.

English skilled workers organized into craft unions face other, equally formidable, impediments. While they are overrepresented in several craft unions in relationship to their participation in the labour force, in none are they close to a majority. The craft structure which scatters members over hundreds of work sites, mixed in with members of other unions, to be regrouped only by virtue of similar craft and only when meetings are called, both provides a potent obstacle to the crystallization of any minority group identity within the union and makes it easy for any determined internal group to capture and manipulate the policy-making structures. In other words, although English craftsmen might be thought to be more prone to crystallize as a pressure group within their unions, craft structures make it exceedingly difficult to succeed.

It is only in the language-related occupations that the conditions for the crystallization of an English working class pressure group are met.[11] In that most significant cluster of occupations — the state-related service sectors — in which English workers regroup in increasing numbers, the ability to see English workers as a group apart and to use the union to further their ethnically specific goals, becomes possible. In health, in welfare, in education, service is segregated by virtue of the language of its provision. Here, English workers get and keep their jobs by being able to work in English and have developed a commensurate sense of their separate collective identity. Further, where they are unionized (in the hospitals and schools), their unions are overwhelmingly English and immigrant in membership and usually (with the exception of the CEGEPs), isolated from the main (francophone) body of the union movement.[12] It is workers in these fields who define their interests in opposition to the transformation of Quebec into a culturally homogeneous society: quite literally, their livelihood depends upon the maintenance of externally buttressed, artificial biculturalism. It is, therefore, entirely logical that, as far as English workers are concerned, only the public and parapublic employees — in the Protestant and English Catholic school systems, and the English welfare agencies and hospitals of all religious persuasions — voice systematic and even desperate opposition to the Parti Québécois cultural project. English workers employed elsewhere in the economy have neither the motivation nor the mechanisms to develop a defensive sense of minority status and act to neutralize the project.

There is, however, an added significance to the locus of organized English opposition to the cultural decolonization of Quebec. The state sector and employees of the English and French service networks are in competition for budgetary allocations. Such competition must, in the middle term, serve to undermine (if not destroy) the solidarity of the Common Fronts. Whether or not the state-employer encourages it, it can only benefit in the future rounds of public sector negotiation.

In recapitulation, then, I think it correct to say that by the 1980s no such coherent entity as an English working class exists. Rather English workers are now scattered through-out the working class in such ways that only where the provision of services in English is the condition of employment are they regrouped in sufficient numbers to intervene as a language pressure group... That this crystallization of identity should be based on competition with francophones located at the same place in economic order will lead, I am afraid, to a real weakening of the abilities of Quebec workers in general to confront the employers of the state and the private sector in the immediate future.

NOTES

(1) I think the category «English Quebecer» is more realistically defined if it moves beyond the narrow and sometimes simplistic definition by virtue of blood. Rather, I see English Quebecer as a socio-cultural category with strong economic bases describing not only a language and an ethnic group, but a culture as well which, together, act as a pole of attraction to other, later immigrant populations. The definition of English Quebecer as one whose origin is the British Isles (in Quebec at least) excludes immigrant groups such as the German and the Finnish as well as pre-World War I Jewish and Italian immigrants, even when these have long since fully assimilated to that pole. Further, in the use of this ethnic-origin definition, the Irish are considered of British stock which glosses over, to put it mildly, the considerable cultural and political differences which, before 1920, existed between the British and the Scottish on the one hand and the Irish on the other, as well as their continuingly divergent occupational paths. It also seems to ignore the sizeable number of Irish Catholics who integrated with the francophone majority in the nineteenth century.

(2) Frik Olin Wright, *Class, Crisis and the State* (London, New Left Books, 1978):96-97.

(3) *Ibid.*, p. 97.

(4) André Gosselin, «L'évolution économique du Québec: 1867-1896», *L'économie québécoise* (Presses de l'université du Québec, 1969):106-107.

(5) Noël Vallerand, «Histoire des faits économiques de la vallée du Saint-Laurent: 1760-1866», *L'économie québécoise* (Presses de l'université du Québec, 1969): 56-59.

(6) On the integration of rural francophones into these industries, see Everett C. Hughes, *French Canada in Transition*.

(7) Canada, *Royal Commission on the Relations of Labor and Capital in Canada, 1899*, pp. 314-320; 364-365.

(8) By leading positions, I do not necessarily mean numerical superiority, but proportional overrepresentation coupled with strategic placement in the industry.

(9) The occupational and industrial data which follow are calculated, unless otherwise indicated, from the 1971 Census, Bulletin 3.4-3 and the 1971 Census, *Economic Characteristics: Industrial Trends 1951-1971* (Cat. 94-793) Table 6, pp. 21-4.

(10) Particularly finance (banks) and retail trade.

(11) Printing and publishing is one industry in the private sector where the language in which work is carried out could lead to a crystallization of an English working class pressure group.

(12) That isolation is indicated by the fact that primary and secondary school teachers employed by the PSBGM, and English Catholic teachers employed by the CECM, plus hospital workers, professional and non professional, in all the major English hospitals are organized in unions unaffiliated to any of the three Federations. English-language social workers in the parapublic agencies tend not to be unionized at all and, while university teachers at Concordia and McGill participate in FAPUQ, Concordia is newly unionized, and McGill is the only non-unionized faculty.

Development Plans, Salt Mines and the English Community of Grosse Isle, Magdalen Islands

Stuart Richards

STUART RICHARDS is now an officer of the Regional School Board of Gaspesia after having been principal of the Grosse Isle Intermediate School. He is himself a native Magdalen Islander. Educated at Bishop's University, he is presently completing a Master's degree and writing a thesis on the history of Protestant Education on the Islands.

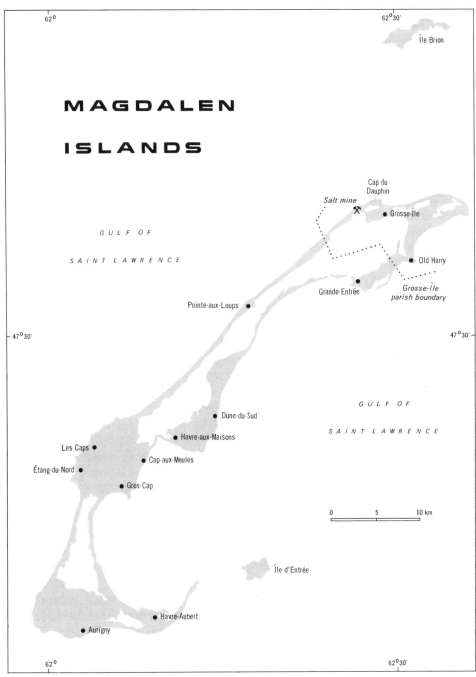

MAGDALEN ISLANDS

Île Brion

Cap du Dauphin

Salt mine

Grosse-Île

Old Harry

Grosse-Île parish boundary

Grande-Entrée

Pointe-aux-Loups

G U L F   O F

S A I N T   L A W R E N C E

Dune-du-Sud

Havre-aux-Maisons

Les Caps

Cap-aux-Meules

Étang-du-Nord

Gros-Cap

G U L F   O F

S A I N T   L A W R E N C E

0   5   10 km

Île d'Entrée

Havre-Aubert

Aurigny

Source : Department of Mines and Technical Surveys, Ottawa

191

Stretching across sixty miles in the Gulf of St. Lawrence are the Magdalen Islands, known as les Iles de la Madeleine to most of their inhabitants. They comprise twelve islands, six of which are linked by sand dunes and marshes. Offshore lie the isolated islands, ranging in size from a few hundred square feet to a few square miles. Only one of these isolated islands is inhabited: Entry Island (Ile d'Entrée). This island is populated by approximately two hundred people of Scottish descent.

The population of the Islands in 1978, as calculated by Provincial government officials, was between 16 500 and 17 000. Of these, approximately 6 per cent were English speaking. Most of the latter group arrived in the early nineteenth century from England, Scotland and Ireland.

Traditionally, the anglophone and francophone populations have remained separate by settling on different islands. The physical structure of the islands has helped in this segregation by virtue of the numerous natural boundaries. Pursued since initial settlement over 150 years ago, it results, today, in a situation where the anglophone population is found in two municipalities — Grosse Isle and Entry Island. The francophone population presently occupies the islands of Havre-Aubert, Cap-aux-Meules, Havre-aux-Maisons, Pointe-aux-Loups, and Grande-Entrée.

The organization of the population along linguistic lines has caused many problems in the evolution of the islands' economy. These problems will become apparent and play a very important role in the following discussion.

It is not the purpose of this paper to provide an exhaustive study of the history of the Magdalen Islands or even of the Anglo-Madelinot population. Rather, it is concerned with looking at one community — Grosse Isle — comprising approximately five hundred anglophones, this with a view to identifying certain internal and external influences that have been critical in its evolution, and in order to identify the problems presently confronting it in its struggle for survival.

In order to properly understand Grosse Isle, it is necessary to consider, firstly, the historical traditions and roots of the people and, secondly, the traditional economy.

The first English settlers came to the islands in the 1820s. They came at a time when the hunting of the walrus and seals was nearing an end, because of over-exploitation. Consequently, these early settlers turned to both sea and land for their livelihood. Fishing became the principal commercial activity and farming became a supplementary activity.

This life-style dictated that every individual had to get involved in the business of sustaining the family to which he belonged. The men and older boys usually concerned themselves with fishing while the women and younger members of the family took care of the activities of gardening, animal husbandry, and lighter tasks around the homestead. Each family became a small enterprise unto itself.

It would be a mistake, however, to overemphasize this occupational pluralism. Certainly, fishing, farming, sharing of tasks among members of the family and, in some cases, migrating to the Maritime provinces to increase opportunities for wage labour, all occurred as complementary activities. However, it was the fisheries that sustained the community, materially, spiritually and physically. All of life and thought revolved around fishing and the successful exploitation of marine resources.

The fishing industry took up the greater part of the year. In the winter months (January-February-March) the boats were made ready, old traps were repaired, new traps were constructed, and engines were overhauled and repaired when necessary. In April, herring fishing would begin. During May, June and July, the men would be hard at work in the lobster fishery. From July to September, they turned their attention to mackerel and cod.

This dependence on the sea became a way of life rather than just an occupation. The sea, the fish, the gear, and the weather were as much a part of what the fishermen said as did. At work or relaxing, at home or at the neighbours, talk would eventually, one way or the other, always get back to fishing.

This form of life-style and occupation persisted pretty much intact until the 1950s. While it is impossible to determine how well Grosse Isle fared compared to other island communities, it is safe to say that the community was comparatively well off. This judgement is based on the impressions of many people and their thoughts about «them days».

It is interesting to note that Grosse Isle, during the years immediately preceding and following the 1950s, in most people's opinion, was a prosperous and thriving community. This was not the case with all English-speaking communities on the islands. The anglophones of Grindstone (Cap-aux- Meules), who were very much associated with entrepreneurial and business occupations, were experiencing a decline in their influence and were, for all practical purposes, being assimilated into the francophone majority.

However successful Grosse Isle was as a community, things were beginning to change, and the effects were starting to be felt in the early 1960s. These changes can be listed as follows: 1) the increase in the offshore fishing fleet, and 2) the decrease in the landings of fish by inshore fishermen.

This change in emphasis of the fisheries was most discernable in the case of cod and herring. The modernization of the offshore fishing fleet in the early fifties and the introduction of long-liners, seiners, and draggers in the Gulf of St Lawrence and around the islands led to a depressing situation vis-à-vis the herring and cod fisheries.

In a mere eleven years, from 1952-1963, the total number of offshore boats registered in the Magdalen Islands increased from 5 to 163. In the same period, the total catch of fish for the Islands went from 1,8 million pounds to over 50 million pounds.

This dramatic increase in fish landings was to have an important and devastating effect on the inshore fishermen. In 1958, the total Magdalen Islands landing of cod and herring was 30,5 million pounds. By 1965, the cod landing was decreasing by approximately 1 million pounds each year. In the early 1970s, this decrease was becoming very alarming to inshore fishermen. In 1975, the total Magdalen Islands landing of cod and herring was 7,5 million pounds.

The offshore fleet expansion was aimed at expanding Quebec's share of the Gulf fishery, increasing the productivity of its workers and stabilizing the employment of the offshore fishermen and the processing plant workers. What this expansion did do, in fact, was to deplete the Gulf fishery, not only for the offshore fleet but, more importantly and tragically, also for the inshore fishermen. The tragedy of the whole expansion programme rests in one fact: it destabilized the livelihood of thousands of inshore fishermen around the Gulf, in Gaspé, the Magdalen Islands, Nova Scotia, New Brunswick, Prince Edward Island, and Newfoundland.

Government Intervention

By the early 1960s, both the Federal and Provincial governments were beginning to realize that many small communities were in trouble. The first direct intervention of the Federal government to help remedy the deteriorating economic situation of these many inshore fishing communities was to extend the unemployment insurance coverage to the now «seasonally unemployed» fishermen. The fishing industry immediately took on another function. As well as providing a cash crop, it also allowed people to obtain the required number of «stamps» which would make them eligible to draw the unemployment insurance benefits.

The decrease in fish stock coupled with the increase in transfer payments in the form of unemployment insurance benefits led to a decrease in the effort expended on fishing. The traditional and diversified economy and life-style was gradually replaced by what has been called a commercial employment/unemployment combination.

This commercial employment/unemployment combination in a relatively short time becomes a very secure form of life. The transfer payment aspect of this provides families and individuals with the same kind of security as sustaining activities under the occupational pluralism model. It also allows people to continue a way of life — fishing — that they are familiar and happy with, and, finally, it allows the people to continue living in the community of their choice.

194

Although this transfer payment approach of government has certain positive effects, it also leads to many undesirable attitudinal changes in a community. It obviously has a very strong influence on young people. Generally speaking, it does not reward effort and initiative. Rather, it ensures a guaranteed income provided there is a certain limited amount of effort. It often leads to apathy on the part of people — an apathy about initiative and job satisfaction. If and when this apathy occurs, it is particularly distressing to a community's vitality and dynamism.

This dependence on government transfer payments usually leads to a lack of interest in, and consideration of, the regional economy and its vitality. It no longer becomes necessary to link into and become part of a regional life style. Isolating oneself is usually the result of this outlook. During the 1960s, this seemed to have happened to Grosse Isle. The community was secure in an economic sense. Consequently, the amount of contact with the regional, or francophone, population was at a minimum.

The BAEQ Plan

The Provincial government was also becoming aware of the distressing situation in many small communities, and it, in turn, began its «war on rural poverty». With the assistance of the Federal government, it created the Bureau d'Aménagement de l'Est du Québec (BAEQ) (or: the Management Office for Eastern Quebec), whose mandate was to study the problems of Quebec's most «economically depressed» region and to develop concrete proposals for their solution.

The Magdalen Islands became a prime focus of the new commitment to action. In 1966 and 1967, the BAEQ published its «development plan for the pilot region», including two volumes devoted exclusively to the Magdalen Islands. Part of the plan was intended for Grosse Isle. For this reason, a brief consideration of it will be undertaken.

The main thrust of the BAEQ plan for the islands, in terms of economic growth and development, rested on three points: 1) the modernization and rationalization of the fishing operation and the mechanization of the fish processing industry, 2) the development of tourism and local agriculture, and 3) the reorganization of the infrastructure and services, which meant the centralization of services and people.

The vision of the future, then, was of one large centre, Cap-aux-Meules, around which most of the population would be organized. The fishing industry would be based on big boats, offshore fishing, and mechanized processing plants.

The most controversial recommendation of the plan was that concerning the reorganization and centralization of services and people. The eastern end of the islands (which included Grosse Isle) would be closed and the population relocated in the western part, that is, near Cap-aux-Meules.

This recommendation met an island-wide outcry of disbelief and anger. As a result of this, the issue of relocation of people was not pressed by BAEQ officials. However, it was not forgotten by the planners in Quebec, who had taken the plan seriously, and it was to appear again in 1972.

The BAEQ plan, and the discussion concerning it, should have taught a lesson to the population of Grosse Isle, that lesson being: 1) that government officials were concerned about the amount of transfer payments being used to support the community, 2) that avenues of communication between the anglophone and francophone populations of the islands were extremely poor, if in fact they existed at all, and 3) it would be necessary for Grosse Isle to become more involved in the regional insertion process if its inhabitants were to have any meaningful input into further discussions on the future of the Magdalen Islands. The sad commentary is that these lessons were not learned, at least not by the majority of the people. Generally speaking, people went back to their previous apathetic state, firmly convinced that they had put the plan and its recommendations «on the shelf» forever.

How mistaken they were. In November 1972, the basic philosophy of the BAEQ plan was again presented in another development plan — *Plan d'aménagement d'ensemble des Iles de la Madeleine* (Master Management Plan of the Magdalen Islands). This plan was written by a consulting firm of urban planners, Gaston St. Pierre, and it eventually came to be known as the St. Pierre Plan. Without going into a detailed study of the proposal, it is necessary to look at the general aims and some of its specific recommendations, especially, as they affected Grosse Isle.

The St. Pierre Plan had a three-fold purpose: 1) to identify the physical and human resources available to the islands, and the various limits and possibilities for their development, 2) to draw up an actual development plan, and 3) to supply each municipality with an «appropriate» zoning plan.

The general direction of the plan, as perceived by the anglophone community, was similar to that proposed by the BAEQ, six years earlier. The population was to be organized around three regional economic zones — Cap-aux-Meules, Havre-Aubert and Grande-Entrée. Thirteen of the eighteen small fishing ports would be closed and the remaining five ports would be expanded. There would be an increased effort at exploiting the offshore fisheries from these five remaining ports. Finally, there would be promotion of industrial efforts and investment in the three «built up» areas of Cap-aux-Meules, Havre-Aubert and Grande-Entrée.

The section of the plan that dealt with Grosse Isle was almost exactly the same as the BAEQ proposals, the difference being, this time, that the population would be relocated around the municipality of Grande-Entrée. An ecological reserve was to be created on Grosse Isle and environs. It was also suggested that the abandoned homes of the relocated people of Grosse Isle and Pointe-aux-Loups be used for tourist lodgings.

As can be expected, the reaction of Grosse Isle was not favourable to the St. Pierre proposals. Moreover, this time, it was more organized and sophisticated than had been the case six years earlier. Immediately after the proposals were made public, the Municipal Council, with support from all the population, appointed a citizen committee to act as a pressure group and demand more information and an explanation. Both organizations wrote to the Ministry of Municipal Affairs, the Islands' deputy in the National Assembly, and other Government departments, requesting help and explanations. At the same time, the Municipal Council adopted a resolution in which it asked the Minister of Municipal Affairs not to approve the section of the development plan for the Magdalen Islands that concerned the communities of Grosse Isle, Old Harry and Pointe-aux-Loups. It also asked for another study of the area and an explanation of the reasons for relocating the people elsewhere.

One of the interesting side effects of this concerted action by the community against the plan was the realization that twice in six years they had been faced with a development plan proposing the elimination of their community. Consequently, they decided that they would write their own plan for Grosse Isle, a plan that would start with the premise of the continued existence of the community. The elected officials took this proposal to the County Council level of government and received support from the other municipalities.

All this effort seemed to pay off as far as Grosse Isle was concerned. The officials of the Department of Municipal Affairs began insisting that the St Pierre Plan had no official status; it was merely a working document. This revelation had an unfortunate effect upon the community. No longer was it necessary to fight for Grosse Isle and, consequently, the Planning and Development committees of the community were disbanded, and the alternative development plan was not written. As had happened six years earlier, the people of Grosse Isle became very secure in the conviction that they had won another battle in their fight against outside intervention. However, their peace was short lived. By the fall of 1973, salt, mines and SOQUEM were becoming household words in Grosse Isle.

SOQUEM (the Quebec Society for Mineral Exploration) became formally involved in the Magdalen Islands in 1972. At this time, it purchased the rights of a private prospector to continue the exploration work on the western part of the islands. By the end of the year, SOQUEM had identified the existence of a large commercial salt deposit on Havre-Aubert.

During the next year, the drillers began to move their equipment to the eastern part of the islands that is, Grosse Isle. By the summer of 1974, ten exploration holes had been drilled in this area. This drilling established the existence of two deposits — one beneath the North Dune about one-quarter of a mile from the community of Grosse Isle, and the other beneath the entire island of Grosse Isle. These deposits ranged from 100 to 3 200 feet below the surface.

Exploration continued into the spring of 1975, when the company attempted a seismic survey requiring the detonation of underground charges in Grosse Isle. By the summer, Grosse Isle had been chosen as the best place for a mine. However, before a decision could be made, certain other factors had to be investigated. These included: 1) determining the actual amount of salt of different qualities, 2) establishing the best methods of mining, 3) carrying out a cost analysis of return on investment, 4) making arrangements for financing, and 5) determining the site of a deep-water port at Grosse Isle.

Finally, in June of 1976, SOQUEM announced that it was prepared to go ahead with the project at Grosse Isle. It would begin by sinking an exploratory shaft in order to answer some of the outstanding questions, questions that needed answering before a final decision could be made about the mine. At about the same time, officials of some Provincial government departments indicated their commitment to the project by pledging support in the construction of the harbour, and by offering to become the principal buyer of the salt — presumably for the highways of Quebec. Soon after these announcements, LOUVEM, a wholly owned subsidiary of SOQUEM, was given the responsibility of overseeing the excavation of the exploratory shaft. Preparations were being made by the end of the year for construction to begin.

The initial reaction of Grosse Isle towards this new intervention was varied. There were some people who became involved in the mining project — by working as labourers, by renting accommodation, and by providing certain basic services. Generally speaking, these people were favourably inclined towards the project. On the other hand, some people were fearful of the impact of the mine and port facilities on the local fishing industry. In the middle, the majority of people were taking a «wait-and-see-attitude». There was, however, no strong reaction, or certainly not the united reaction that had occurred after the BAEQ and the St. Pierre plans were announced.

Local Involvement

It was about at this time (1976) that the Adult Education Department of the Regional School Board of Gaspesia, under whose jurisdiction the Protestant schools of the islands fall, began thinking about community development and how it could facilitate the process. There had been similar attempts in previous years, associated with the Planning and Development committees of the community that had been created out of the uproar over the St. Pierre Plan, but they had met with very little success. However, the time seemed ripe now and a part-time coordinator and animator was hired to work with the community.

This coordinator found himself working with the Municipal Council, which was struggling with the mine project. It will be remembered that the community had no definite opinion about the project and this only made the councillors' jobs more difficult.

After much discussion and soul-searching on the part of the local elected officials, it was generally agreed that there remained many unanswered questions about this project. In fact, people were completely in the dark about it. This, then, became the focus of the Council's direction. It began by asking for information. After a short period of time, it became increasingly obvious that government and company officials were not expending much effort in this direction.

During this time, the Council, with the help of the coordinator, began formulating areas of concern about the project. Such concerns included: 1) the number of jobs that Grosse Islers could expect in the mine and the related activities, 2) whether or not the salt would be stock-piled and the effects of this, 3) the possible effect of mining on the fresh-water table, 4) the effects of the construction of the port facilities on the local fishing bottom, 5) the life expectancy of the mine, 6) the question of waste disposal, and 7) the problems associated with the large influx of highly skilled workers in terms of housing, etc. This is by no means an exhaustive list of the preoccupations, but it does serve to point out the grave necessity of having information. It became obvious that many of the questions could not be answered unless proper impact studies were to be done. This, then, became part of the Council's demands. The Council also insisted that the community be involved in these impact studies.

During the spring and summer of 1977, the Municipal Council began to consider ways which would induce the officials of both the Government and the Company to provide information. The Council began making known its concerns to the other communities of the islands, and as a result, received support from the Comité de l'Environnement des Iles de la Madeleine. It also began contacting the press, and eventually, the *Montreal Star* carried an article on the project.

After a great deal of effort, and with support from various individuals and organizations, the Municipal Council convinced the Conseil Consultatif de l'Environnement to hold public hearings on the mine-harbour project which was slated for Grosse Isle. These hearings eventually took place (after a couple of false starts) on January 24, 25, and 26 of 1978.

Due to the impact of these hearings on the community, the effects will be considered here in some detail. The first obvious result of the hearings was the report* that was submitted to the Minister responsible for the Environment. Some of the highlights of this report were:

1) There were serious deficiencies in the procedure intended to produce decisions concerning the installation of the various elements of the mine-harbour complex.

2) The final decision should take into account the interests of the people of the Magdalen Islands, of Quebec as a whole and, also, the protection of the environment.

3) There was a lack of coordination among all concerned parties. Thus, a coordinating committee should be set up to ensure representation by the developers, the government departments and the local government, as the representative of the people of the islands.

4) Adequate information was not available for the public, and Magdalen Islanders had a «right» to such information.

5) Magdalen Islanders have been unable to participate in, and have not been consulted effectively about, a project that may very well alter many facets of their society and economy.

6) Socio-economic and cultural studies should be carried out in collaboration with government agencies and the local population.

The less obvious, but equally important, consequences of the hearings were those concerning the population itself. These hearings affected it in such a way as to reshape its image, both of itself and of its place in the region.

One of the immediate results was the degree to which the local population supported the efforts of the Municipal Council. Although certain groups of people supported the project, the vast majority of people visibly supported the Council's stand. This was to give courage and needed support to the elected officials.

The educational value of the hearings cannot be overestimated. Men, women and children of the community were presented with models of procedures

* Quebec, Conseil consultatif de l'Environnement, *Environmental Implications of the Proposed Mine- Harbour Complex of the Magdalen Islands*. June 1978.

for conducting meetings, of public speaking, and of decorum. Many people, often for the first time, found themselves face to face with those «mysterious» officials of government departments. They also realized that when local people spoke of their community, many «outsiders» were listening.

Another of the visible effects of the hearings involved a growing self-confidence. Often people perceived the information that was being presented by government officials as being erroneous and sometimes insulting of their intelligence. All of this served to give them confidence in the knowledge that they were the experts concerning their community. They knew what they wanted and they had to tell the so-called «experts» from the «outside».

The public hearings performed two very important functions, which developed more or less incidentally. First, there was the emergence and strengthening of a local leadership at the community level. This leadership centered primarily around the elected officials of the Municipal Council with the addition of several individuals from the community at large. Second, there was the emergence of a workable relationship between the anglophone and francophone officials of the islands. During the hearings themselves, many francophones supported the positions taken by the Council, and it was increasingly realized that all islanders, anglophones and francophones alike, had similar concerns. These two developments were to play a very important part in the workings of the Plan d'aménagement des Iles.

In August 1977, in keeping with the decentralization theme of the Provincial government, the County Council (a regional government made up of all the mayors from the municipalities) was presented with the challenge of getting involved in the «management» and development of the islands' resources. This was a pilot project with a different philosophy from either of its predecessors — the BAEQ and St. Pierre plans. This time, theoretically at least, the direction should come from the municipalities of the islands.

By November, the County Council had accepted this challenge and had hired four coordinators to begin work on the Plan. The coordinators had been presented with the mandate of initiating discussion around the aspects of the islands' economy. This was no easy task.

The public hearings of January, in fact, solved many of the coordinators' dilemmas. Firstly, they emphasized the fact that the mine-harbour project should become part of the development strategy. Secondly, the hearings convinced the coordinators that any meaningful discussion of «an islands' development strategy» must include representation from the anglophone community. Finally, the example of public discussion during the hearings could be used in the structuring of the Plan d'aménagement des Iles.

Therefore, during the early months of 1978, islanders found themselves faced with another plan. This time, however, it was being initiated from the local level. Its purpose was to look at the islands' resources and to suggest constructive approaches for their development with a view to promoting increasing self-sufficiency.

The structure which eventually evolved was to form discussion groups — called modules — around each of the resource areas. Each module was constituted of a diversity of people who were directly concerned. For example, the agricultural module would include farmers, independent producers, and representatives from each municipality.

The involvement of Grosse Isle with the Plan d'aménagement des Iles, during the early months, was intense and meaningful. The representatives of the community who sat on the mine-harbour module were actually exercising leadership. They began setting the terms of reference for this module. At the same time, there was a realization, on the part of the module members, that the task which they had set for themselves was so large and complex that it was necessary to create sub-committees. Again, at the insistence of the Grosse Isle representatives, sub-committees were created around different aspects of the project. For example, four sub-committees were mandated to look at respectively, the mine, the port, the lagoon, and the socio-economic study which had been recommended by the Conseil Consultatif de l'Environnement.

The socio-economic study became one of the very important areas of concern for the Grosse Isle representatives. They certainly did not want a study which would be similar to those which had been presented in previous years by the BAEQ and the St. Pierre plans. Consequently, they began pushing for the right of islanders to dictate the terms of reference for the study. Finally, after much discussion, the government departments who were to finance the study, agreed. Hence, a coordinating committee was set up to oversee the hiring of professionals and also to coordinate the activities of the latter.

Even though Grosse Isle representatives played a very important role in the setting up and steering of the mine-harbour module, there were still serious deficiencies in the degree of participation in the other modules. In some cases, there was no representation at all. Two reasons can be offered for this lack of participation. Firstly, the mine-harbour module was obviously the most important during the initial stage of the plan. This project, because of its direct influence on the community, was to receive priority, and all available energy was aimed in this direction. Secondly, the community did not have the required number of bilingual people to sit on the other modules. In fact, the community was hard-pressed to find a couple of people to act as translators and resource people. The bilingual people who were available, and they could be counted on one's fingers, were being worked to the limit. Unfortunately, this problem still exists and is severely hampering the participation of Grosse Isle in the entire plan.

After the Salt Mine

By the summer of 1982, the salt mine was in place, some 125 people were working there, and production was imminent. Independently of the consequences of the presence of the mine, it is this writer's conviction that the public hearings (January 1978) around the issue of the forthcoming mine and the initiation of the Plan d'aménagement des Iles were the two most important events — at least of a local origin — in the recent history of the community of Grosse Isle. The events leading up to the public hearings had shocked people into the realization that Grosse Isle had to start taking care of itself. These hearings permitted a forum for public debate, not only on the salt mine, but on the community as well. They created an atmosphere in which people started to look at themselves and began articulating where they wanted their community to go. It also allowed people the opportunity to gain enough confidence in themselves to do something about their community and its future.

The Plan d'aménagement des Iles provided a structure which allowed the anglophone population to get involved in matters regarding the Magdalen Islands as a whole. Although this structure has not delivered what it promised, participation in it has forced the anglophone community to articulate, probably for the very first time, its aspirations and expectations.

It would, however, be foolhardy to suggest that this process of stock-taking is completed. Grosse Isle tends to become apathetic in its outlook after periods of crises, as the experience with the BAEQ and the St. Pierre plans have shown. This time, the community leadership is convinced that there should not be a relapse, although it must be said that recent political developments — such as the proposed school reform — have led to a level of anxiety and pessimism as to the direction being taken by Quebec society as a whole — which makes it difficult to sustain confidence.

If the community is to maintain the vitality and growth that it experienced in the mid-seventies, the process of articulating its aspirations and needs must continue. There is a firm conviction that the maintenance of the fishing industry and the associated life-style is paramount in any effort towards greater economic viability and self-sufficiency. There is also the realization that the fishing industry, which is not being heavily regulated, is not sufficient to satisfy the ever-growing population needs.

Ways and means must be found to complement fishing, and the salt mine has not been a sufficient solution. Scarcely a fifth of the approximately 125 jobs at the mines are in the hands of the residents of Grosse Isle, and related service sector employment does not benefit them at all. Other possible complementary activities which are based upon local resources and skills are boat building and agriculture. Yet boat building for a stable fleet and greenhouses for a strictly limited clientele present almost no opportunities for growth. Other developments in the secondary industry sector, such as the diversification and improvement of fish processing, seem to have largely benefited other island communities.

Nevertheless, the local leadership became and remains convinced that meeting the needs of Grosse Isle depends upon the community getting involved in planning at the regional level. But to achieve a permanent presence in the regional milieu as well as long-term local self-sufficiency, certain conditions must be met. One of these is a bilingual leadership confident of itself in its dealings with the francophone milieu. Attendance at the francophone «polyvalente» by a significant proportion of young anglophones may be the prelude to an expanded basin of bilingual persons. As for the question of confidence, the assurance in dealing with francophones gained in recent years, remains and is reflected in the very productive relationships established at the local level. At another level, however, confidence is faltering. Increasingly the anglophones of Grosse Isle are questionning the capacity of francophones to assure the future of Quebec without recourse to stultifying centralization and a suppression of local particularities and cultural differences.

The question of confidence is capital. For Grosse Isle to survive, it must be sure of itself. It must have direction without being rigid, it must have self-assurance without being presumptuous, and it must have a meaningful role to play in the Magdalen Islands as a whole. This requires that individuals and institutions must be involved at the community level. There must be meaningful community discussion in order that its leaders feel they are not simply defending individual points of view, but rather the sentiments and ways of life of an entire community.

Part IV

INSTITUTIONAL EXPERIENCES AND CRISES

According to sociologists, the survival of any collectivity, and particularly any minority group, depends to a great extent on the viability and diversity of its institutions — whether it is characterized by a high degree of «institutional completeness» or not. To the most casual of observers, English Quebec possesses just such institutional completeness — schools, universities, radio, television, newspapers, financial and commercial institutions, medical, legal and other professional services, political structures, etc. — in sum, a multitude of institutional contexts in which control is vested in anglophone hands and where the particular interests of the anglophone population are served. Hence, the long-term survival of the language group is seemingly assured.

Closer examination reveals, however, that many of these same institutions have experienced numerous crises in recent years which have been damaging both for their proper functioning and for the population they serve. These crises are reinforced by a very marked tendency amongst anglophones to withdraw from institutions shared with the majority, and consequently by the intrusion of what is perceived as a harsher and harsher duality: the duality of «French» government versus «English» business, of the Montreal Board of Trade versus the Chambre de commerce du District de Montréal, of francophone public service versus anglophone private enterprise, of English versus French schools, of Catholic versus Protestant school commissions. . . the list is never-ending. Because of this manifest duality, the crises are commonly perceived in dialectical terms, of «us» and «them», with the problems of one (the minority) being a consequence of the actions of the other (the majority). Once the polarization has occurred, re-establishing a working relationship and some level of integration is no easy task as the attempts to attract more anglophones into the Quebec Public Service clearly illustrate (see Allnut).

The rupture and the crises are consecrated by the silence of the anglophone intelligentsia and media. The assertions of the institutional leadership are rarely questioned or discussed and the analysis rarely debated. No impartial observers seem to be present to diagnose the crises, indicate the parallels between them, provide an historical dimension, a certain sense of perspective. Few doubt that Sun Life of Canada was «driven» out of Quebec or that there is «no place for anglophones» in the Quebec Civil Service. The reasons for this silence are difficult to discern, although some would attribute them to the estrangement of a significant proportion of journalists and academics who, being new and transient to Quebec, lack the necessary sense of history, involvement and intuitive understanding of events. Because of the situation, the crises are, at best, lived out in isolation and, at worst, treated as some kind of diabolical conspiracy on the part of the francophone majority.

The scenario is a dismal one, as are the implications. Yet these institutional crises are not the fruit of hazard. They are yet another manifestation of the tensions that Quebec «anglophonie» is presently experiencing — of coming to terms with an assertive majority, Quebec nationalism, and the growing power of the State. If anglophone institutions fail to cope with the crises, keep insisting on resolving them solely through constant confrontation and, ultimately, departure, and if the intelligentsia fails to conduct more penetrating analyses of events, then Quebec «anglophonie» may ultimately be deprived of the professional leadership necessary for its long term survival, and most importantly, *it will not have been consulted in the process*. Sun Life had already lost 30 per cent of its business in Quebec by June 1979 shortly after its combative decision to transfer its head office to Toronto; a decision which led to families being uprooted and, furthermore, to a situation where the viability of one of the last major private-sector enterprises in Montreal where one could work exclusively in English — The Sun Life — is being placed in the balance. Needless to say, the Sun Life is, perhaps, not alone in this visceral reaction to events. Even so hallowed an institution as McGill University has considered, on more than one occasion, a cynical abandoning of the province and people that has provided its very life blood for generations in favour of «greener pastures» in Ontario.

Fortunately, all is not yet lost and there are now evident signs of more measured and wide-ranging reflection. The Sun Life «affair» constitutes something of a bench-mark in the debate — witness the economic and constitutional ramifications as drawn out in the texts of three members of the Economic Department at McGill University (Brecher, Kierans and Naylor) which are reproduced here — as well as the public initiative taken by the lawyer Richard Holden to prevent the company from transfering its head office to Toronto. Among the churches, the United Church has distinguished itself in recent years by its honest soul-searching and questioning with respect to not only francophone aspirations, but also to its own place and role in a new Quebec (see Mair). Finally, from the very beginning of the recent controversy on a planned educational reform, anglophone boards, spokesmen and educationalists have been in the thick of the fray.

To provide the thread that weaves together particular experiences and crises with the aim of creating a sustaining set of values — an English Quebec cultural and intellectual tradition and a flow of indigenous experience — is to act courageously in these times. William Tetley, whose experiences are described elsewhere in this collection, was one of the very few who ventured in this direction. He sought, during six and a half years in the Liberal Cabinet «. . . to convince English Quebec to accept the French fact, thus becoming a real part of Quebec, and to defend English rights in Cabinet. The task. . . was exhilarating but often misunderstood and very often unpleasant. People are much more understanding and appreciative now . . .».

In a time of majority status, the sustaining power of an intellectual tradition was, perhaps, not necessary. However, when a population and the institutions it has created find themselves in a minority status, the existence of such a tradition is essential to survival. There is, at long last, indication that some individuals are aware of this fact and are prepared to provide some intellectual and spiritual leadership and debate, and that the media are prepared to communicate their concerns. It remains to be seen whether the managers of the institutions will listen to them. Holden lost his battle to keep Sun Life in Quebec; Tetley's position on language legislation was far more consistent than that of the English educational establishment and he is much better appreciated out of, rather than in, power...

The Protestant Churches

Nathan H. Mair

NATHAN H. MAIR is currently personnel officer for the Montreal and Ottawa Conference of the United Church of Canada. He is the author of two books on the history of moral and religious dimensions of education in Quebec Protestant schools which have been published under the auspices of the Protestant Committee of the Superior Council of Education. He was also, for ten years, director of studies at the United Theological College, McGill University.

A few days after the election of the Parti Québécois in November 1976, the Executive of the General Council of the United Church of Canada issued a statement which included this declaration:

> We recognize there is something new and, to some, even exhilarating in the Canadian situation today. We see this as a time of opportunity, not of frustration, of hope, not of despair. There is an opportunity for open dialogue between partners on the Canadian scene.[1]

The statement reaffirmed the policy of the Church with regard to French Canada, formulated in 1972. This policy held:

> That the crucial factor in the shaping of future political structures must be the deliverance of French Canadians from any sense of subjection and that such deliverance requires an openness to a reconsideration of the present structure of Confederation.[2]

In 1977, a special task force commissioned by the United Church to undertake a detailed study of the subject, delivered a report which spoke of events in Quebec as an opportunity:

> We have a rare opportunity to make our laws (perhaps our constitution), our social, economic, political and religious institutions reflect the reality of our life together, as well as our aspirations.

> . . . we also call attention [. . .] to collective rights, to the rights of communities and peoples. In this we include the right to take what measures are necessary for collective survival and fulfilment. We call for safeguards of both individual and collective rights in a situation full of conflicting interests. At the same time, we are convinced that the defence of self-interest is not necessarily the way of the Gospel, which testifies to the dying of self and to being born for others.

> . . . there is the opportunity, by way of referendum, for *the people* of Quebec to make a choice [. . .] to have some measure of control of its destiny. . .

> . . . there is opportunity for the majority to take further control of the levers of decision in Quebec. Along with that goes the chance to do so by building a society in

which all the elements of the population have their appropriate and legitimate part to play.

> To the English in Quebec, whatever its future in or out of Canada, there is an additional opportunity to discover and demonstrate the role of a responsible minority. We are convinced that the English-speaking people who belong to Quebec and are at home there have a very important contribution to make, and that they will discover how best to make it. [3]

Some church orators in those days spoke about the «exodus experience» in which the French Canadian people of Quebec were involved; these had left the land of bondage, were no longer engaged in mere survival, but had grasped the way to their fulfilment as a people.

The Canadian people in general probably did not hear much about these sentiments of church leaders. It is questionable whether many of those who were aware of them agreed. Did they nevertheless reflect the views of the majority of United Church people or other English Protestants in Quebec? Probably not. Much of the language in the statements could be dismissed as emanating from brothers and sisters in other parts of Canada, who were removed, somewhat, from the battle zone. There were a few radicals and idealists, of course. The true feelings of most Quebec anglophone Protestants were better expressed in short, sad sighs about «the time of trial to the church as a whole» and in statements such as:

> The election of the Lévesque government is the most telling element in the life of the church in the Montreal and Ottawa Conference. Bill 101 is now law and is seriously hampering the recruitment of ministers for the Quebec part of the Conference. Many of our churches have felt the loss of families, as people have left for Ontario and the West. The church in our Conference is living in a time of great uncertainty as we wait for the referendum. This uncertainty has led to tension that has affected all aspects of the church's life. [4]

If Québécois were now on an «exodus pilgrimage» to the «Promised Land», English Quebecers (and most Protestants were in this group) have had time and energy to think only of survival. The referendum of 1980 may have given to the majority of English-speaking Quebecers a moment of encouragement, but the re-election of the Parti Québécois in 1981, the enforcement of the provisions of Law 101, and rumours of changes to come in the educational system have afforded added proof that their alarm is justified. Quebec Protestants continue to feel abused and are using «fightin' words» about their rights under the B.N.A. Act. Few are «exhilarated», and many seem not very open to dialogue with French-speaking

Canadians upon the subject of the latter's nationalistic hopes. The reason for this Quebec English Protestant «defensiveness» may perhaps be clarified by reference to the demography of the Province, to the history of English values and institutions, and to recent Quebec events.

* * *

According to the 1971 national census, about 500 000 persons in Quebec said they were Protestants. They formed about 8 per cent of the total population. Roman Catholics composed about 87 per cent (about 7 per cent of these were anglophone, 6 per cent Italian and other non-anglophone ethnic groups), Jews 2 per cent, Orthodox 1 per cent, and others, including «no religion», the balance. The denominational breakdown among Protestants was:

> Anglican — 181 875
> United Church of Canada — 176 825
> Presbyterian — 51 785
> Baptist — 37 820
> Lutheran — 23 845
> Jehovah's Witnesses — 17 130
> Pentecostal — 8 535
> Unitarian — 2 715
> Salvation Army — 4 030
> Others — 23 030

Some 100 000 of Quebec Protestants stated, in the census, that their mother tongue was French. (Many of these are simply «non-Catholic» and are not committed to a particular Protestant denomination.) It appears then, that only 400 000 Protestants in Quebec may be counted as «English». Who are they?

Certainly not all Protestants are of the old-fashioned white anglo-saxon variety; there is at least one vigorous black congregation; there are also Chinese, Japanese, Korean, Armenian, Hungarian, Yugoslav, Portuguese and other «ethnic» congregations. Many blacks, and a few Chinese and others are within the current membership of congregations which used to be almost wholly white anglo-saxon.

The number of persons in Quebec who are descendants of the «White anglo-saxon Protestants» of yester-year may be more than 300 000. These figures are cited because they may help to dissipate some misleading images which are often used to characterize Protestants in Quebec. Quebec Protestants are a multi-denominational, multi-ethnic, and multi-lingual people. They are distributed through all the economic levels, though the white anglo-saxon-celtic portion (but by no means all of these) tend to be found in the middle and upper-middle classes. In proportionate terms, their significance is rapidly declining. The social power of Protestants has also diminished. In the past, Protestants, though a numerical minority, were able and accustomed, to practically impose themselves on the Quebec economic or educational scene.

Indeed, much of the history of Quebec's institutions must be viewed in the light of the peculiar situation in the Province in which the two groups, French and English — each of whom deemed themselves minorities — made provisions to ensure their survival. The French Canadian people resisted every attempt, conscious and unconscious, of the ruling British to assimilate them. The Church was their bulwark and it received immense authority to preserve the culture and to shape the mind of French Canada.

The Protestant immigrants to the Province brought precisely those ambitions and values (pride in individual initiative and resourcefulness, stress on the importance, were — until the late 1950s — largely ignored, anglicized or segre-experimental attitude to the discovery of new truth) which were often discouraged by Quebec-Catholic morality, but which were needed to exploit the opportunities of the new country and to raise a modern industrial nation. The English, therefore, took economic control of Quebec, leaving the French to dominate in provincial politics where their numbers made this logical. Many Protestant churches, particularly in the cities and small industrial towns, thrived as the temples of the owners and managers of industry and of financial institutions.

The schools of the Protestant community symbolized the cultural unity of the British-Protestant population of Quebec, and were counted upon to maintain and extend that culture, as well as to equip the rising generation for useful and profitable worldly callings. Francophone Protestants, being few in number and importance, were — until the late 1950s — largely ignored, anglicized or segregated. Though the relation between the Protestant churches and Protestant schools was not organic nor official (such as existed in the Catholic sector) the assumption of the need of collaboration between Church and school remained a significant reality in Quebec far longer than in other sections of Protestant Canada. The Protestant school system was by law *Protestant*: Protestant clergymen were official visitors and were very often chosen to sit on the *Protestant Committee* and on school boards, frequently as chairmen; Protestant worship and Bible study were encouraged as a normal part of the school curriculum. The provisions of section 93 of the B.N.A. Act and of the provincial educational laws of 1869 and 1875 assigned to the Catholic and Protestant communities in Quebec effective responsibility and authority over the public schools which either *de jure* or *de facto* pertained to the two confessions. (Jews have been counted legally as «Protestant for school purpose» since 1903, but only within the last decade have been able, everywhere in the Province, to sit as members of school boards).

* * *

216

The Quiet Revolution of the 1960s signalled the end of the historic arrangements defining the relation of English and French, Catholic and Protestant in Quebec. A new nationalism had emerged which emphasized the necessity of Québécois becoming «maîtres chez nous», not only politically but economically as well. If Quebec were to change to meet the demands of the modern age, then it should do so with the destiny of French Quebec in mind.

There was initially strong support in the Protestant churches (and among English-speaking Quebecers generally) for certain aspirations of the French Canadian people. Most agreed with Gérin-Lajoie that the educational system had to be reformed if equality of opportunity for all were to be provided. It was felt that as long as Protestant institutions were safeguarded, it would be a distinct step forward for the Province to build a coherent and unified educational administration under a minister of Education, such as existed in the other provinces. Also, it was widely held among English Protestants that greater economy in the use of resources and increased government responsibility for the financing of education was desirable, and (though this was not said aloud) that a modernization of Catholic education to meet the presumed excellence of the Protestant schools was overdue. Protestants assisted in the creation of the new educational structures.

Then, amidst rumblings about the need for an independent Quebec, a new francophone priority was crystallized. The birth-rate had declined with the adoption of new social values. French-Canadian culture was thought to be seriously endangered, existing as it did within a heavily anglophone North America (a fact television now constantly reminded the Québécois). It was well-known that immigrants to Quebec usually chose English-language schools. The Gendron Commission was given the task of studying this problem. It recommended that for the sake of the survival of the French language and of the Québécois identity — as a people in charge of its own social and economic destiny — it was essential that laws be made to promote and ensure the use of French: French should become the normal working language of the Province.

At the same time, English Protestants had, since 1964, been discovering the width of the communication gap between themselves and those who spoke the other language. French-speaking Canadians not only spoke a different tongue; they thought differently, prized different goals, possessed a different set of values. Anglophone educationalists, for instance, were astonished at how little the anglophone and Protestant interest figured in the total educational picture. Teachers who, despite many internal wars, had experienced the old Protestant system as something of an extended family, now knew themselves to be part of a large and impersonal organization for which they felt little kinship. The English began to fear for their future in the new Quebec in which the culture, interests, and goals of the French section of the population would dominate.

* * *

The closing-in of the Protestant churches upon themselves to center on survival strategies (though it must be admitted that many a congregation has not for years been in any other than a survival stance) must be viewed then, as a not unnatural response to the reduction of English and Protestant power; particularly with respect to those two special areas, business and education, which had given them a special place in the social system of Quebec, and which ensured their existence as a distinct and important people.

Many Protestant congregations and church groups are characterized today by an attitude of anxious self-protection and by the withdrawal of concern and interest from outreach ministries. Programmes and services which generations of Protestants have supported with finances and with volunteer leadership on boards (hospitals, libraries, colleges, social service institutions) are now finding it difficult to maintain their activities owing to the shortage of leadership and money. Many congregations are likewise drained and will not survive if the trend continues. The shrinkage of resources in the Protestant community and the reduction of the scope of their work has thus made it very difficult for the churches to be objective about the Quebec situation or anticipate their possible future role.

Not all Protestants have viewed the future so bleakly. In the early summer of 1977, one church court heard the report of a committee which called for «a Christian perspective» on the situation in Quebec. This «manifesto» affirmed:

> ...the new sense of hope that has come to inspire our francophone fellow-citizens...

> ...that Christians are called to involve themselves in affairs of human communities, and without pride or quest for power to assume responsibility for society.

> ...the need for «a new breed of anglophone» [...] committed to the good destiny of this province and its unique contribution to Canada...

> ...that we are prepared to live in Quebec as part of a minority [...] a creative element [...] to support the vision of a better society...

> ...that it is essential [...] to preserve the French language, culture and heritage and that [...] government may need to resort to what may seem strong or artificial measures...

> ...that the Church of Jesus Christ transcends racial, national, linguistic and other particularities yet liberation is always worked out in the specifics of daily existence...

218

The report lamented:

> . . .the tendency of some of our anglophone brothers
> and sisters to give way to feelings of personal anxiety,
> resentment, [. . .] apathy, so that they miss the oppor-
> tunities implicit in our present situation. . .

> . . .the continuing spirit of narrow racial, economic and
> other interests, which gives priority to self-preservation
> and to the fostering of ends which deny Christ's call to
> human solidarity. . .

> . . .the tendency of some to construe this as a struggle
> for the maintenance of French Canada and not for our
> country as a distinct entity on this continent and a
> creative force in world affairs. . .

> . . .the failure of some Christians to rise above cultural
> and traditional loyalties to higher loyalty of faith in the
> universal Lord [. . .] and the assumption, on the other
> hand, that faith ought simply to ignore the particular-
> ities of nation, race, speech and culture. . .[5]

Considerable discussion followed the presentation of the «manifesto» and there
was some apparent support. Finally, a resolution was passed to table the motion of
approval. The *ad hoc* committee that had created the manifesto was dissolved a few
months later, and the concern with which they had been entrusted («the future of the
Church in Quebec») was recommended as an agenda item for standing committees.

Some good work has since been accomplished by these committees, but an
opportunity for the corporate Church to say something significant at an important
moment in Quebec's history was missed. This even typified the uncertainty (one
might almost say «paralysis») of the denomination with respect to decisive action
on this subject. The church communities, reflecting the attitudes of the English of
Quebec in general, felt too threatened by the movement of events to be objective or
to take many risks.

More hopeful signs are now appearing, however. Some of these no doubt
reflect strategies for survival rather than courage and commitment to Quebec. In
this list might be included: appointment of special officers to help the churches deal
with English-French relations, signs and letterheads bearing the names of churches
and institutions in French, national church conventions invited to assemble in
Quebec, stepped-up programmes of French-language education promoted or supported by the churches, requirements that clergy achieve some mastery of the
French language.

However, there are deeper currents as well. A report received by the Anglican General Synod admits that:

> The gradual development in a French milieu, of an Anglicanism which has been largely a chaplaincy to a unilingual Anglo-Saxon-Celtic population, has not helped to promote dialogue.[6]

Also:

> Large numbers of Anglicans are committed to the priority of French and are seriously equipping themselves [...] Anglicans are among those who are selling their houses and leaving [...] but others are staying...[7]

Dialogue, a ministry of the United Church of Canada, has taken as its priority task the equipping of anglophones to participate meaningfully in Quebec society. There is also hopeful activity in the theological colleges. The Anglican bishop of Montreal reported at the annual synod of the diocese of Montreal on April 27, 1978 that:

> Our Montreal Diocesan Theological College has taken a stand about staying here [...] With the appointment of [...] the full-time Principal [...] we made a commitment to training men and women for ministry in Quebec [...] in the language of the majority [...] as well as in English.[8]

The United Theological College now has a francophone principal, Dr. Pierre Goldberger, and has begun a complete re-orientation of its policies and programmes to effect full participation in the new Quebec context. The Montreal Institute for Ministry, sponsored by the Anglican, Presbyterian and United Colleges at McGill University, has held several study programmes on the role of the Church in Quebec. Here and there in congregations are to be found individuals, study groups, and working committees moving beyond the discussion of anglophone rights to probe the question of Protestant responsibility. They are asking what conclusions may be drawn for our task in Quebec when we consult those beliefs and values on which the Protestant identity is based.

Deep in Protestantism is rooted the belief that «no man has seen God at any time», that is: no culture, system of ideas, person, or groups of persons on the earthly scene may set themselves up as infallibly representing the divine. If they do so, they become idols or ideologies rather than bearers of truth. The Gospel, indeed, clothes itself in particular cultural forms and is communicated through persons who are bound to a time and a place. But it can never be finally identified with these. The living voice of God, Protestants believe, speaks through contemporary events and persons in the same Spirit (though not with the same «words» or concrete messages) as He spoke of old and as is communicated uniquely in Jesus the Christ. But the content of the message is forever new. It speaks of the future while remembering the past. Thus, Protestants are most true to themselves when they forgo worldly securities and are open to learn new truth, from whatever quarter it may come, and to enter upon the adventures of faith to which God calls them.

Under such rubrics, the over-identification of Protestant with anglophone interests in Quebec can only distort the message of the churches. Their first task is to ask of anglophones (and francophones) an account of the ultimate purpose of their institutions and cultural forms. Survival may be a compelling human need, but it is not an ultimate one. Cultures, like persons, are of time and place; they own a death. Surely their inner force comes from serving a purpose greater than themselves. The Protestant spirit thus calls for serious reflection and self-evaluation of all institutions in terms of their ultimate goals. Protestants, in the legitimate pursuit of justice, may well protest aspects of Law 101, but the collective and individual rights of Quebec's francophone citizens will also be of concern to them. A Protestant message of particular relevance today is that which reminds us that privileges and rights are not ends in themselves, but are meaningful only in terms of the responsibilities and services their possessors are enabled to perform. Indeed, the spirit of Christianity is more accurately displayed by individuals in their seeking justice for others, rather than for themselves.

One of the more helpful statements known to the author concerning the possible future role of the Protestant churches in Quebec has come from Douglas Hall of the Faculty of Religious Studies of McGill University. Dr. Hall, who was one of those responsible for the «manifesto» described earlier, writes:

> The mandate to the Church in Quebec, then, is to expose itself anew — perhaps really for the first time — to the realities of its context. It must let go of the ideological version of Christian faith which has insulated it against the actualities of the culture in which it has lived for centuries, and determine to develop its «Gospel» gradually, slowly, tentatively — only in response to «the new Quebec». This new mandate has in some significant measure, it seems to me, begun to be heard and accepted [. . .] We have only gone a little way into this uncertain place — this *terra incognita* that is «the new Quebec». We recognize that we are strangers in this land. We have a great deal of listening to do before we can earn the privilege of speech. . . [9]

Only the future will reveal whether it was possible for Quebec Protestants in the 1980s to exert a moral leadership among the English-speaking population and to find creative ways of contributing significantly to the future of Quebec.

The matter may, of course, be decided by forces and events of which we now have little inkling. The emergence of third-world nations which now demand a greater share of the world's riches, and the sudden possession of immense economic leverage by the oil-producing nations of the Middle-East and elsewhere may bring about events which will force a different definition of Quebec's task. The emergence of new cultures, new economic orders and new value-systems may make old nationalisms archaic and may rearrange the present patterns and relationships in Quebec and Canadian society. In almost all of the Protestant churches, important decisions will be forth-coming concerning the shapes of ministry needed to engage the modern secular world.

New patterns of Christian witness will have to be created in order to respond to changed learning modes and to ways of communicating which must continue to appear in the wake of technological advance. The Church may not be strong in numbers in the future, especially if sufferiing, risk and adventure in the faith become the order of the day. But will the Protestant churches in Quebec do more than survive? Will they be able to open up to Quebec, Canadian, and world citizens more possibilities for a full life and thus to glorify their Lord? The answer is probably in the making today.

NOTES

(1) «Statement Regarding Canadian Unity in the Light of Recent Political Developments in the Province of Quebec», The Executive of the General Council of the United Church of Canada, p. 18.

(2) *Ibid.*

(3) *Record of Proceedings of the 27th General Council of the United Church of Canada.* Aug. 21-30, 1977 (The United Church of Canada, 1977):292-293.

(4) «On the Way — Sur le Chemin», *Record of Proceedings of the Montreal and Ottawa Conference of the United Church of Canada*, 1(1977-78):32.

(5) Douglas J. Hall, «Being the Church in Quebec Today».

(6) Reginald Turpin, «The Church in Quebec», p. 8.

(7) *Ibid.*, p. 11.

(8) Rt. Rev. Reginald Hollis, «The Bishop's Charge», *Proceedings of the One Hundred and Nineteenth Annual Synod of the Diocese of Montreal*, April 1978, p. 21.

(9) Douglas J. Hall, «A Generalization on the Theological Situation of Protestantism in Quebec».

The Quebec Public Service

David Allnut

DAVID ALLNUT. Director of public relations at Concordia University, David Allnut spent the period from 1973 to 1976 working in Quebec City for the former Liberal government, first as executive assistant to three Education ministers and, later, as administrative assistant to Robert Bourassa. He recently completed a Master's thesis on minorities in the Quebec Civil Service at the École nationale d'administration publique, Université du Québec.

A report on anglophones in the Quebec public service twenty years down the road will seem like an obscure treatise on dinosaurs. The concept will be an anachronism, if it isn't beginning to be already.

In the summer of 1978, Patrick Kenniff, a Quebec City lawyer and assistant dean of law at *Université Laval* was appointed assistant deputy minister in the Department of Municipal Affairs. His appointment was billed in the media not so much as a great step for the municipal affairs department, but as a «plus» for the anglophone community. Anglophones had risen one rung higher in the Quebec public service and Kenniff was perched on the top rung.*

Of course, Kenniff was annoyed by this reading of his appointment. He had earned the job because of his expertise — he was the best available in the minister's judgement, he assumed. He was not the best anglophone, but the best, period. Furthermore, like an increasing number of anglophones in Quebec, he was not sure what the term «anglophone» meant in his case anyway. His work had been conducted for years in French, his family and social life was French, and the only aspect of his life that seemed to justify the anglo tag was his history. He grew up in the west end of Montreal and attended Loyola College. Names no longer mean very much: if former parliamentary reform minister Robert Burns could pass as a francophone, so can Patrick Kenniff.

For more and more of the few anglophones who do work in the Quebec public service, the anglo tag is useful for historical purposes, but that is about all. «You almost have to become French», says Harold Hutchison, a member of the revamped Public Service Commission, «if you want to work for the Quebec government.» This is a fact that anglophones face at both provincial and municipal levels.

For 16 years, Hutchison has worked for the Quebec government in Quebec City. When he began, the *Chronicle Telegraph* was still a daily newspaper serving a shrinking but still sizeable anglophone community. Over the years, the daily paper became thinner, its publishing schedule cut down gradually from daily to weekly. Many anglophones were pulling up stakes, regrouping with other anglophone clusters elsewhere in the Province. But there were other anglophones, who were moving increasingly into the francophone community; moving as individuals as old English groups began to disband, and discovering their conversations animated not by the *Chronicle Telegraph* and *The Gazette* of Montreal, but by the capital city's *Le Soleil* and Montreal's *Le Devoir*.

Hutchison's parents are English, his grandparents Irish. When asked at the time of his latest appointment in 1979 about his experiences as an anglo in the Quebec public service, he suggested the question was a non-starter: «I don't think

---

* In 1980, Kenniff rose even higher when he became the deputy minister of the Department.

you can consider me an anglophone. I always worked in French and have for years. Most of my life is French.» Hutchison, in fact, went to French schools for most of his education.

Attitudes undermine the concept of the «anglo public servant», and so do the statistics on this shrinking band which refuses to see itself as a band at all. In May 1979, there were only 521 anglos among the 73 185 full-time and part-time employees assigned to forty-six major government departments, agencies and boards; most of which recruit under the aegis of the Public Service Act. Others, like Hydro-Québec, recruit their own staff directly. At the so-called senior level of the public administration, up to and including deputy minister, anglos figure in just twenty-eight positions. Similarly, there are 110 anglos at the «professional» level. Among the blue-collar workers in government service, 370 were on record as anglophone.

In most cases, change has been considerable: there are in percentage terms many fewer anglos working in Quebec's public service than was formerly the case. The tremendous growth of the public service in the 1950s, but more significantly in the 1960s and the 1970s, has been accompanied by a shrinkage from approximately 7 per cent to 0,7 per cent today of anglophone participation in the public administration. Absolute numbers of English-speaking public servants have grown marginally as the public sector has grown in leaps and bounds.

The reduced amount of anglophone participation accounts, to some degree, for the increasing insignificance of the very term «anglo public servant». In the years where anglos numbered 7 per cent of the public work force, many identified with a visibly English element, both in the Quebec City community and in government where English was spoken much more than today. Today, that element is invisible, a sparse scattering of anglophones who in fact behave mostly as fancophones.

It is difficult to come by hard figures concerning the ethnic or linguistic background of functionaries before the 1960s. Quite often then, it is the reminiscences of long-time civil servants that testify to anglo presence decades ago. Roch Bolduc, the chairman of the Public Service Commission, is one of this breed. Considered one of the half-dozen great mandarins of the Quiet Revolution, he has been in and out of most key public service jobs in his long career in Quebec City. He recalls the period when the old Department of Mines «had at least four administrative units composed almost exclusively of English-speaking Quebecers. They dealt mostly with technical matters. In Finance, two units dealing with such matters as debt management were exclusively English, since they had to deal with banks in the rest of Canada and the United States.»

Education has always attracted a significant number of anglophones for two reasons. First, previous to the creation of the Department of Youth and then the Department of Education in the early 1960s, education was under the control of the

Department of Public Instruction composed of two distinct Catholic and Protestant committees. Each religious group thus controlled directly all aspects of education concerning its own network of confessional schools. As is still largely the case today, the Protestant population was composed almost exclusively of English-speaking Quebecers who, in turn, manned the civil service posts in Quebec under their jurisdiction. In the 1950s then, the Protestant service accounted for thirty to thirty-five anglophone civil servants; whereas there were as many as four times that number of francophones working in the Catholic education branch.

When the Department of Education was formed out of this dual bureaucratic structure, many of the anglophones stayed on and some of them are still there today, albeit in less important positions.

Secondly, the nature of the Department's clientele assures some anglophone representation. Education is the only area of government where the taxpayers need be treated differentially, linguistically, on such a massive scale. Academic planning must take into account the language in which services are being offered.

Of the two-hundred-odd senior posts in the entire civil service in the mid-1950s, ten to fifteen, Bolduc says, were occupied by anglophones. As for the overall non-francophone Quebecer presence in the contemporary civil service, more accurate figures are available thanks to an inventory of «ethnic» civil servants conducted in March-April 1979: in addition to the 521 English referred to above, there were 798 French (from France), 134 Italians, 16 Greeks, 34 Germans, 24 Portuguese, 32 Spaniards, 154 of other European origins, and 262 of other ethnic origins.

The English presence is numerically notable only in fourteen of the forty-six departments and agencies surveyed. Indeed, «notable» may be hyperbolic: of the fourteen, the Department of Revenue has the highest percentage of anglo-employees — 0,6 per cent!

Hence, although 13 per cent of the Quebec population indicated in the 1976 partial census that English was its mother tongue, anglos represented only 0,7 per cent of the civil service work force. The other non-French cultural communities accounted for 6,2 per cent of the population, but for only 0,9 per cent of provincial civil service workers.

The under-representation of cultural minorities in the civil service has not received much attention, especially where anglophones are concerned, partly because they have not been viewed as downtrodden and worthy of special attention. Anglophones have been traditionally drawn to the private sector where salaries were relatively good and the language of work their own. It is interesting to note, incidently, that anglophones are embarrassingly absent in major municipal civil services in Quebec, notably Montreal; and perhaps more surprisingly, in the Federal government work force within Quebec's borders.

Francophones, on the other hand, especially those who wanted to work in their own language, moved in different directions; one being the public service as it grew to play an increasingly important role in the economy and in society in general.

* * *

Although Quebec's minority employment record in the public sector is unenviable, other provinces too suffer from varying degrees of under-representation of minorities. In Ontario, for example, where francophones comprise 10 per cent of the population, francophones occupy only 5 per cent of the public work force. In New Brunswick, francophones account for 39 per cent of the population and only 21 per cent of the public jobs. The federal Commission on Bilingualism and Biculturalism pointed out another interesting aspect of minority employment when it released its report in 1969: notably, that minority groups in high-salaried positions won these jobs either because of their knowledge of languages or skills otherwise unavailable in the majority community. Minority employees were not as a rule all-purpose administrators capable of moving from department to department as challenges arose.

In the provincial public service system, one finds a similar situation: namely, minority employees working in either highly specialized positions or in manual and clerical staff jobs, and as such, outside the mainstream public service career system.

The Gendron Commission pinpointed some of the problems in 1971 — in particular, under-representation of non-francophone minorities and the fact the non-francophones who did work in the civil service tended to be found in lower salary categories. However no action was taken until 1978 when the péquiste government announced its intentions in its *Cultural Development Policy for Quebec*.

In the much celebrated (or decried, depending on where you sit) White Paper on Quebec culture, the government called on Quebecers to broaden their links with minorities. «The government must begin by setting an example in its administrative services and its very structures» the report said. Referring to the Gendron Commission's remarks on low salaries and under-representation of minorities, the White Paper added: «The present government intends to tackle the causes of this irregular situation. The bodies responsible to the government should in any case make every effort, through their composition and their action, to promote true equality and significant relations among Quebecers of every origin.»

Among the twenty task forces established to develop and implement legislation after publication of the White Paper, was one specifically devoted to making the civil service more representative of the population as a whole.

Although bureaucratic inertia and politicing prevented the committee's work from being properly completed, the government did unveil a «Plan of Action for the Cultural Communities» in March 1981, the major component of which were provisions for substantially augmenting minority representation in the civil service. The measures aimed at correcting the present undesirable situation are indeed novel, some of them at least, albeit modest and cautious. The most daring change would allow candidates for positions to respond to juries' questions in English, on the assumption that ability to understand questions posed in French is indicative of some working knowledge of the official language.

Unfortunately, this plan for equal employment opportunity is only one of three the government has brought forward in the last few years. The others are aimed at women, notably absent at the senior levels, and the handicapped. A fourth plan, for native people, is also in the works. The problem, put simply, is that there will not be enough vacant positions to provide for the aggregate objectives of the women's cultural minorities, handicapped and native people's employment programs. Not to mention, of course, the white francophone male, whose legitimate career aspirations require that some room be left for him to move into or up the ranks of the civil service.

* * *

We have talked in general terms of why «anglo public servant» is an anachronistic term. But why is it that anglophones, even if they remove that linguistic label from their lapels, refuse to enter Quebec's public service in greater numbers?

For obvious reasons, incumbents have to have a real capacity to speak and write French, especially in Quebec City which is surely as French a city as anywhere in the francophone world, Paris included. These days, one can no longer fudge about being bilingual. One's ability to work in French is tested every minute of the day, in addition to which Law 101, the French Language Charter, requires all employees in the public administration to communicate among themselves and with their French-speaking publics in the one official language, French.

This stricture alone prevents many «semi-bilinguals» from entering public service here, although years ago it was to some degree possible for this group, and even those of lesser French-speaking abilities, to work in the service.

Behind the obvious barriers, however, more subtle forces are at work. The «old-boy network» that anglos employed for generations on St. James Street where school ties and McGill University degrees provided employment cachet, is at work today in the public service. The difference is that ties to the school of *Hautes études commerciales (HEC)*, affiliated to the *Université de Montréal*, bring back the silver more often than do McGill and English private school ties. A well-placed HEC graduate is more likely to look favourably on a candidate whose background and training he already knows and respects.

The other aspect to the recruiting system that militates against increasing anglophone presence has to do with the way job competitions are held. Since vacancies are offered to those with relevant experience, and since the most relevant experience is offered in most cases within the public service in the first place, vacancies tend to be filled by insiders..., 98 per cent of the insiders being francophone, of course. Certainly this was the case in 1974, when a government recruiting study found that 48 per cent of the positions offered at the upper levels had already been unofficially filled at the time of the competition. And when it came down to filling the vacancies, for which one out of two applicants were outsiders, 81 per cent of the jobs went to insiders already working for the government!

The system naturally favours francophone appointments in the upper echelons. Unfair as the system may seem, its hiring practices are biased in favour of the people it is most familiar with, namely its own. A tried and true practice the world over....

Perhaps Quebec's past governments can be cited for failing to alert minorities to job opportunities. Figures on advertising vacancies in the print media would seem to justify corrective action. Between April and December 1978, the government announced 600 competitions in *Le Soleil*, 400 in Montreal's *La Presse*, 250 in *Le Devoir*, but only 75 in *The Gazette* and 35 in *The Montreal Star*. One has to discount *The Star* since it was on strike for most of the period covered, but figures for *The Gazette* would suggest the government policy is out of line. It should be noted that all these advertisements appear in the French language only. Consistent with the B & B findings, advertisements directed at anglophone media have been geared largely to recruiting highly-specialized personnel, for energy, mining and manufacturing sectors, or translation staff. Concedes Public Service Board chairman Roch Bolduc: «Maybe we should advertise all the jobs equally in all the major Quebec media, English as well as French. Of course, we have budget restrictions that would affect that.»

Given the fact that the system already reinforces a francophone recruiting bias, because the public service tends to hire its own, and given the effect of the «old-boy network», it would seem grossly unfair to maintain this unbalanced approach to the non-francophone community in the government's advertising policy. The government is not, apparently, the only culprit. It has not yet been proven, officials point out, that anglos and members of other cultural minorities *want in*. Between February 1980 and February 1981, seventy competitions were advertised in *The Montreal Gazette*, and six other English newspapers in Canada: only sixty-two persons applied for the various positions.

In this connection, it is worth noting how francophone and anglophone universities have contributed to the process. Francophone institutions have always developed many of their training programs with a view to meeting the needs of Quebec's public service, either provincial or municipal; and to a lesser degree, francophone schools have kept watch on federal needs too. The *École nationale d'administration publique*, run by the *Université du Québec*, is without doubt the francophone community's biggest commitment to the training of public administrators.

The degree to which the news of Concordia University's School of Public and Community Affairs has been trumpeted suggests how anglophone institutions are latecomers to the notion that they have a job to do in providing adequately trained candidates for civil service roles. The idea comes late in the day because of the anglophone community's traditional orientation towards the private sector; the idea of training future civil servants for Quebec comes very late indeed. Most anglos in Quebec who have followed courses in public administration have thought in terms of careers in the federal civil service. Many have graduated without being able to master «the official language». Concordia's boast that its school of Community and Public Affairs is the first anglophone school of its type to graduate bilingual candidates for careers in Quebec constitutes a remarkable statement given the fact that it comes twenty years after the Quiet Revolution began.

One does not have to go back very far to the days when French was taught as an abstract subject. «Speak *proper* French, not Quebec French.» The concept of one's working life being conducted in French became abstract at one and the same time. Even if a few had a realistic grasp that French was not an abstract subject and working in French was a pos? sibility, only a fraction of this group probably envisioned a full day of work and play, business and social functions, acted out in the language one was being inadequately taught a few hours a week. Surely if anglophones generally had had such a view of their futures, they would have done their homework, figuratively and literally.

* * *

Given the fact that Quebec City, the site of most public service activity, is French, almost entirely so, anglophones entering public service must shift gears

233

completely and *live* in French. It goes without saying that many cannot, indeed many will not because they simply don't wish to the latter tend to demonstrate the same vehemence that characterizes many francophones who do not want to live in an «alien» culture. One observes today the notion that bilingualism, is not the same as biculturalism, and while some welcome living in the other world, others resent it because it is forced. Sad as it may be, bilinguals are often as clannish as unilinguals. Suffice it to say the culture shock experienced by an anglo Montrealer moving to Quebec City can be as traumatic as it can be rewarding. Some cannot, or will not, make the switch.

Pierre Martin, until recently a senior official in the Premier's own department, the Executive Council, encountered this problem. He was the Quebec government's chief talent scout and was dealing with men and women who command 50 000,00 $, 60 000,00 $ and 70 000,00 $ a year in their present jobs. He *was* looking for anglophones, but faced stiff opposition to a Quebec City move on the part of most prospective candidates. One, slotted for a top job in one of the biggest departments, told him he would be glad to accept as long as he did not have to move to the capital.

What is not explained by recruiting or cultural phenomena might be by financial considerations, although this has changed since the mid-seventies. The private sector, still home to most anglophone professionals, paid better; and if the private sector did not siphon off potential Quebec public servants, the federal public service might, because it paid better than its Quebec counterpart. According to a Quebec government study, average salaries in 1975 were 3 400,00 $ less in the public sector than in the private sector.

Ironic as it may seem, the Liberal's Law 22 and now the Parti Québécois' Law 101 have probably contributed to the anglophone community's reorientation away from the federal capital towards Quebec City. A combination of factors seem to bear this out. First, the National Assembly legislation has had much more direct bearing on the citizen's life than anything the Federal parliament has produced in recent times. While defence estimates and food prices are discussed in Ottawa, personal futures are being weighed in Quebec City, and anglophones feel the pressures directly when they look around at their shrinking social circles.

Wether the pressures are real or imagined, anglophones train their eyes on Quebec City more and more — in Quebec, however, for the first time in decades, they had no representatives in the National Assembly, at least not in the first term of the present government. Secondly, in conjunction with Quebec's perceived stronger influence, the Federal government's reluctance or incapacity to act to restore the pre-Bill 22 status has taught many anglophones that they have to marshall their arguments in Quebec City if they want to be heard at all. The third point that might be made here is that a sizeable contingent of anglophones has decided to leave Quebec, leaving behind a reduced community of anglophones, a greater proportion of whom are prepared for change, or at least prepared to join the debate in Quebec City.

All this makes the anglophone much more aware of not only the political process in Quebec, but of the machinery of government as well and the employment opportunities that might be pursued therein.

Quite apart from political forces, various groups, some of them francophone, have expressed concern about the dwindling numbers of anglophones in the Quebec public service. One such group, the *Centre des dirigeants des entreprises (CDE)*, a business group, in a 1973 brief to the former Bourassa government, called on legislators to arrest the trend of decreasing anglophone representation in the public service and to reverse it by appointing more anglophones to senior level positions to allow «the English population to participate more and more in the evolution of Quebec.» More recently, *Participation Québec*, and later the Council of Quebec Minorities, took up the cause.

Even the best of intentions can founder, and so far, no government has successfully pursued the goals set forth in the recommendations made by these various organizations.

Premier Levesque, when he was unseated leader of the opposition back in 1974, suggested in an interview with a *La Presse* reporter that he could not see any reason why bilingual anglophones could not work in the public service, adding «except for reasons of climate». Mr. Levesque took pains to explain that for several years francophones increasingly subscribed to a «national» feeling about Quebec in addition to holding a cultural allegiance, and that «Canadian-first» anglophones might be troubled working in an atmosphere shaped by these loyalties.

Distinctions such as those outlined by Mr. Levesque are, for reasons I stated a little earlier, becoming clouded, especially for those anglophones determined to stay in Quebec. In the same interview, Mr. Levesque added that there was not much to cry about however, given the fact that the Federal civil service and key private enterprise sectors were as open as ever to anglophone job seekers. Wasn't it normal, if perhaps deplorable — he asked in that very Levesque style — that the indigenous (francophones) hang on to the one big employment outlet they have, at least until the «colonial» situation has been corrected?

Without advancing counter rhetoric, anglophones should expect to see more welcome signs out in government as Bill 101 progressively wrenches the anglo hand of «colonialism» from the controls of private enterprise and successive provisions of the law come into force. If parallel activity — opening up the public service to anglophones and, for that matter socalled «allophones» — does not come about, the situation will be both abnormal and deplorable. Miracles will not occur overnight. The Government's equal employment opportunity programme needs explicit political backing throughout the Cabinet, and it is not yet evident that the cause of the cultural minorities enjoys the same support there as does the plight of women. Even with the best of intentions, it will take as long as ten to twenty years before representation of cultural minorities in the public service approximates their proportion of the general population.

* * *

It would seem to be in the interest of the Government to ensure that a greater number of anglophones and other minority groups participate in the public service. If nothing else, it is one way to win over a segment of the community to the cause of Quebec, even if one's definition of the cause does not necessarily coincide with the Government's definition. The point surely, in the last analysis, is to have various parts of Quebec society work out a common sense of purpose, of community.

The more the public service acts as a catalyst in the process that mingles our communities, and in so doing, attempts to make non-francophone groups more represented in its ranks, the more this society will feel as one.

I am not suggesting that representation of minority groups should be necessarily proportional because such a policy would lead to the indignities associated with quotas. One sees departments blossoming into legalized token collections, instead of resource pools of real talent. No, what I refer to is the need to lift the subtle obstacles. I shall refer to a personal example.

In the autumn of 1975, when Raymond Garneau, then Finance Minister, was given the additional portfolio of Education just vacated by Jerome Choquette's resignation over the language issue, I was appointed his executive assistant. The appointment was only temporary — ministers were shifting around fast and furious in Education in those days. Notwithstanding this, you could hear in the corridors that snake through the huge Government «Complexe G», remarks on how funny, how strange, to have named an anglophone as executive assistant in such a culturally-oriented department as Education. One can understand the attitude, even explain it I suppose, but one can also wonder if it is right.

It occurred to me that the wisecracks were misplaced, but they do prompt me to wonder about my assumptions concerning my own «angloness». True, I was raised in an English home and did not master French until my twenties. Yet as I write this report, I find «concours» comes more easily to mind than competition. My wife is francophone, our children are francophone, and our homelife is almost entirely so.

The best way to close, I suppose, is to borrow Harold Hutchison's earlier remark and apply it to myself: «Actually I'm not sure you can call me an anglophone». . . I leave it to other contributors of this collection to consider the implications.

236

The «Sun Life» Issue

Eric Kierans

Irving Brecher

Thomas Naylor

ERIC KIERANS. Economist and a former minister in Liberal governments at both the provincial and federal levels, Eric Kierans was closely associated with the transformations initiated by the Quiet Revolution. He recently retired from the economics department of McGill University.

IRVING BRECHER. Member of the McGill University economics department for many years, Professor Brecher is, since June 1981, Chairman of that department. He has also served as vice-chairman of the Economic Council of Canada. His academic interests are oriented towards Canadian economic policy and problems of the Third World.

THOMAS NAYLOR is associate professor of economics at McGill University.

The following three texts provoked by the Sun Life's decision to move to Toronto were reprinted in the *McGill Journal of Political Economy*, no 3 (1978) after originally appearing in the *The Gazette*. They are presented here exactly as they appeared in the *Journal*, the Kieran's text being followed immediately by the Brecher rejoinder, both of which are, in turn, commented on by T. Naylor.

A Case for Provincial Autonomy

Eric Kierans

Something of benefit will be gained from the Sun Life affair if, in studying the background to management's decision to move to Toronto, people in the rest of Canada come to understand more clearly the forces that are shaping political directions in Quebec. A provincial politician, attempting to protect and to further the interest and welfare of his community, will find two general restrictions on his capacity to plan. The first constraint, of course, is defined by the powers exercised by the federal government while the second resides in the present helplessness of provincial governments to achieve economic objectives against the resistance to change of corporate concentrations of power. Provinces vary in the depth of their hostility to either or both of these limitations on their ability to achieve particular community objectives.

At the end of the Second World War, the federal government was determined to find a «peace-time equivalent» to the win-the-war objective that had served to unite Canada industrially and economically, if not militarily. Anxious to continue the wartime measures of control over the tax and spending powers, Ottawa believed that it had found the formula «equivalent» with a White Paper on Employment and Income, presented to Parliament in April 1945, by the Rt. Hon. C.D. Howe, which defined federal objectives and «stated *unequivocally* its adoption of a high and stable level of employment and income. . . as a major aim of government policy.»

No one has ever questioned the objectives but many, particularly in Quebec, rebelled against the attempt to continue the arbitrary powers of the war years while pursuing these aims.

When the White Paper explicitly laid down that the goals *must be wholeheartedly accepted by all economic groups and organizations as a great national objective, transcending in importance all sectional and group interests* the stage was set for the federal-provincial confrontations over jurisdiction, sovereignty and priorities that have continued to this day.

What did Duplessis want and what has every Quebec premier wanted ever since? They want back some measure of provincial control over economic affairs, realizing full well that an economically dependent province would have no chance of managing and directing its social, political and cultural priorities. Beginning in 1945, Canada was organized, organized from the top and from sea-to-sea, into a unitary state with a national outlook and policy that evolved not as a whole which was the sum of its parts but a new entity that was distinct and separate from sectional interests and values.

The pluralism of preceding generations disappeared without debate in Parliament and new policies were presented to federal-provincial conferences as so many faits accomplis. To the extent that varying provincial priorities existed, and this was not admitted, they were subsumed in the overall national pattern.

Exhilarated by its role as a charter member of every international agency that ever existed, Canada jumped into the world of international trade, capital flows, take-offs and interdependence without taking the elementary precaution of first building the foundation, a balanced economy at home. Participation in world trade and global integration of capital, labor and resources comes after a nation has secured its home front and, by its domestic policies, attained a reasonable level of employment, productivity and control over its own affairs.

Canada made the cardinal mistake of going international first and gearing growth to global output as a specialized supplier of raw materials to the labor, capital and entrepreneurship of others. At home, we invited economic penetration and domination by importing machinery, component parts, technology and selling our land, resources and domestic markets for the ready money needed to balance our accounts.

One should pay for what one buys but we have so arranged our affairs that we must pay for all eternity in dividends, management services and dependence on international prosperity. The profits and surpluses that would enable us to invest in our own future now accrue to others. When 70% of the profits in the resource sector, or 50% in the manufacturing sector, accrue to a few hundred large foreign-owned firms with their own fish to fry, what do Canadians have left with which to speculate and to invest in new frontiers? National policy has used the global corporations as the instrument by which Canada has gained a satellite status in an interdependent global economy. As a consequence, we are now more vulnerable to international cycles and dependent on the favour of the very giants that we have created. The cosmocorps can go anywhere and do anything while the federal politicians and bureaucrats who helped to make them great can only sit at home and fume. *Ottawa's challenge is to find a way of stepping out of its own history and starting all over again.*

Is it any wonder then that provinces are now taking the initiative and seeking to create balanced economies at home and to secure the profit base for more stable and diversified growth in the future? Thus Alberta with its Heritage Fund, Saskatchewan with the ownership of its potash resources and halting attempts in Quebec to be the home, in fact rather than fantasy, of the asbestos industry.

The greatest adjustment to Ottawa's vision of a nation, where economic activity was specialized, rationalized and impersonal, obviously has to come from Quebec. Since values, culture, traditions and language are notably different, there was much more to submerge and mould into the common interdependence that Ottawa demanded.

Quebec tried to adapt and that is what the Quiet Revolution was all about. The educational system in the province was completely revamped, at enormous cost to traditional cultural and spiritual values, to provide the flow of technical, managerial and administrative skills that the 20th century demanded in its public and private bureaucracies. Accused of being out of the mainstream with a classical system of education unsuited to the times, (and this is debatable), the province made a massive effort of accommodation.

One would have expected that, in all fairness, this effort would have been recognized by the business community and that the inequalities of opportunity which were so blatant would diminish and positions of authority and responsibility would be open to all. Education widens horizons, multiplies options and broadens the range of choice open to young men and women. If they find no opportunities to use their knowledge, exercise their skills or take part in decisions and activities that add up to a meaningful existence, they will look for the change in institutions and government that will overturn the inequality and unfairness. This is what has happened.

It would be a serious error to interpret the retreat of Sun Life to the unilingual ramparts of Toronto as the signal for a wholesale withdrawal of head offices from Montreal. The point about the whole affair is that the Sun Life has to pull out of Quebec. It has no choice for it has become an anachronism, a completely English-speaking operation in a French-speaking community which it has never recognized. *Maître-chez-nous* was supposed to go away.

Turning a blind eye to the changes that have been sweeping the province for the last generation, the Sun Life is in no position to wait for the regulations governing head office operations or to open negotiations. They would have to ask for a complete exemption from Bill 101, a concession that no government could grant.

Nor would there be any basis for a blanket exemption when one notes the samll percentage of French-Canadians among the 1800 head office employees, grouped almost entirely in the support levels of secretaries, messengers and filing clerks with virtually no representation in middle, upper or top management.

Any attempt to make substantial changes in management structures quickly would result in administrative chaos. The magnificent indifference of management to its environment has caught up with Sun Life. Quebec will never again provide the unilingual, anglophone base on which the Sun Life management had gambled.

Other firms have learned to adapt to changing circumstances, to manage their affairs better and, at the least, to keep their options open. One would expect many of them to stay.

Canada could not possibly continue on the basis demanded by the White Paper on Employment and Income, the submergence of regional and provincial interests and the transcendence of an overview, a National Going Concern that would organize all of us. Heartlands create hinterlands and regional pressures are now rebelling against this conception of a core with its outer satellites. Smaller political units can be more sensitive to differing characteristics and perhaps they will be persuaded to concentrate on the utilization of their existing manpower and resources to proovide employment and output at home instead of chasing the will-of-the-wisp benefits of global interdependence prematurely.

Quebec is seeking to recover possession of itself and so, I feel sure, are other provinces. In addition to protecting the special community defined by its own language and culture, it is searching, like the other provinces, to build a more complete and balanced economy at home. If the provinces are looking inward, it may be because the federal government has looked outward far too long with only high employment and inflation rates and an unfair distribution of wealth and incomes to show for it.

We are reaching for a new federalism in Canada that will spring upward from the provinces and regions. The federalism that was imposed on us in April, 1945, is at an end and it would be wisdom to recognize this.

Kierans on Sun Life:
A Prescription for Canadian Dismemberment

Irving Brecher

The Kierans article is a remarkable effort which must not go unnoticed. Wooly economic and political theorizing is always deplorable; when it comes from a well-known public figure, it is also dangerous.

We have here all the makings of an engrossing Western movie, 1930s vintage. The plot is totally uncomplicated, the villains are vividly identified and the hero rides into the sunset with new worlds to conquer. The whole thing would, in fact, be a joke if it were not so deadly serious.

Now let us dig a little more deeply. There are three big black-clothed villains in the piece: the Government of Canada (or «Ottawa», to use a favourite swear-word), the so-called «global corporations», and the Sun Life Assurance Company in particular. The hero, or rather the heroes, are the provincial governments, and, more specifically, the province of Quebec — all dressed in dazzling white.

Actually, Sun Life gets only minor billing in the Kierans scenario. It is written off as an «anachronism, a completely English-speaking operation» that has turned «a blind eye to the changes that have been sweeping the province for the last generation». This particular attack I leave for others, including the Sun Life, to assess, since I have no special knowledge of the Company's operations or of its attitude and policies vis-à-vis the aspirations of francophone Quebec. What I find much more interesting is the fact that Professor Kierans sees no connection between the Sun Life problem and the deep malaise imposed on the Quebec community at large by a Bill 101-obsessed provincial government which views the suppression of basic anglophone, and indeed francophone, individual rights as a key prerequisite to progress for that mysterious thing called the «collectivity». It would be nice to know whether Professor Kierans includes such suppression in the «changing circumstances» to which Quebecers must learn to «adapt».

But let us turn to the main theme of the Kierans story. Bluntly put, it is that ever since World War II the federal government, in typical Machiavellian fashion, has been using the employment and growth goals primarily as a device for aggrandizing federal power at the expense of the provinces; secondly, that the federal government, in some sort of conspiracy with the global corporations, has seriously damaged the Canadian economy by opening it up to international trade capital flows before this country had achieved a «reasonable level of employment, productivity and control over its own affairs»; and thirdly, that the only way out for Canada is a «new federalism» that gives the provinces all the powers necessary «to provide employment and output at home instead of chasing the will-of-the-wisp benefits of global interdependence». What we end up with is a recipe for pouring the old wine of economic nationalism into a new bottle: start with the usual dose of anti — Americanism, but then sprinkle generous amounts of «Canadian satellite status in the world economy», and top it off by substituting provincial goals for virtually all nation-wide objectives. This is not only economic nonsense; it is an invitation to national suicide.

To a very considerable extent, every government — at any level — strives to protect and expand its powers. But to suggest that this was the dominant force behind Ottawa's postwar adoption of employment-oriented and social-welfare policies is to ignore the fundamental fact that millions of Canadians were demanding economic and social benefits on a scale so massive as to be feasible only through federal financing and the exercise of federal know-how in those fields. Over the years, of course, the realization has grown that provincial governments can and should play a more important role in such programs, and that they must have the financial strength to do so. Huge resource transfers to the provinces have, in fact, been made, and they are deeply involved in the implementation of broad social and economic programs. This is an argument for maximizing the effectiveness of public policies; it provides no basis for arguing that the federal government should abdicate its major responsibilities for promoting national unity and national economic welfare.

The Kierans case for a closed Canadian economy is really something to behold. It would be more understandable, though not necessarily more valid, if he were talking, instead, about Pakistan or Nigeria or Jamaica. Canada's problem is not that it «jumped into the world of international trade» too soon, but rather that it has not jumped far enough or fast enough. For much too long, high Canadian import tariffs and severe foreign restrictions on Canadian exports have blunted this country's productive efficiency. They have also fostered much of the heavy foreign investment in Canada that has caused a good deal of Canadian disquiet. It is far more realistic to view the tariff-investment link as a matter of ill-conceived trade policy than as some kind of conspiracy to impose «satellite» status on the Canadian economy. In any event, whatever the economic meaning of such celestial terms in this interdependent world, we have succeeded in becoming a pretty rich satellite. The multinational corporation is here to stay, whether Professor Kierans likes it or not. Surely, the challenge is not to pretend that it will go away, but rather to harness its benefits and minimize its costs. There are no easy solutions, but this much is certain: going it alone in a protected, isolated market — the Kierans way — will seriously erode, if not destroy, our capacity to sustain Canadian living standards in the world of the 1980s and beyond. What we need is bold new initiatives towards a more effective Canadian integration into the world economy, not a parochial program for getting out of it.

We come now to the «pièce de résistance». While the Kierans recipe is wrong-headed and dangerous of the world front, it spells disaster in the context of

Canadian unity. Here we are being dished up a «new federalism. . . that will spring upward from the provinces and regions». In actual fact, it is a recipe for a new isolationism to be implemented by sovereign provinces or regions in some mysterious entity called «Canada». I have already referred to the massive transfers of resources and responsibilities that have been made from the federal government to the provinces over the past three decades. Indeed, many Canadians have begun to wonder whether this process can go much further without destroying the fabric of Confederation. This, apparently, is of no concern to Professor Kierans. On the contrary, he must be envisaging further large one-way transfers, for how else could every province, as he puts it, «build a more complete and balanced economy at home»?

On the question of what important powers should remain, wholly or partly, with the federal government, he is conspicuously silent. The Kierans approach is, rather, to blame Ottawa for all of Canada's economic ills; and to give the provinces whatever freedom they require to pursue their own particular ends, presumably oblivious to the implications of each region's policies for other regions and for the country as a whole. Quite foreign to this system is any concept of a federal presence strong enough to protect minority rights, to promote national development, or to engage in a meaningful process of redefining and reallocating federal and provincial powers. It would seem impossible to provide a formula better designed to impoverish Canadians and balkanize the country.

Kierans Versus Brecher: A Third View

Thomas Naylor

Before the dust kicked up by the recent public clash of my colleagues, Professors Kierans and Brecher, completely settles, it might be worthwhile for readers of the *Gazette* to be made aware that not all McGill economists share either Professor Kierans's nostalgia for the days of «state rights» or Professor Brecher's naive and dangerous faith in centralised political power. Both have advanced arguments in defense of their respective positions which do not bear up under scrutiny. Let us begin by reviewing Kierans's original position and correcting some major historical inaccuracies that apparently led his logic astray.

Kierans begins his argument by specifying two constraints under which provincial politicians must operate — the authority exercised by Ottawa on the one hand, and the concentration of corporate power on the other. The first is imputed to the effects of world war two: the source of the second is never analysed. In point of fact, these constraints, on closer analysis, turn out to be one and the same — with important consequences for some of the political recommendations that follow from Kierans's argument.

The concentration of economic power in a small network of interlocking big business concerns paralleled the centralization of political power in Ottawa, and both grew up in a mutually accommodating fashion from the socio-economic conditions of the second world war. Conduct of the war required that close planning by the federal government partly displace the market mechanism as the instrument for determining the allocation of national resources. Concentration of fiscal resources and spending responsibilities in federal hands followed as a matter of course. It also entailed — here by choice, rather than necessity — the ceding of large amounts of planning power as well as responsibility for delivering the goods, not to duly constituted provincial governments, but rather to a group of large corporations whose political and economic power was accordingly much enhanced.

This alliance of corporate and federal political power during — and after — the war was in several important respects a departure from previous experience. Prior to the war some sort of rough and ready corporate federalism existed. Transportation conglomerates and the great financial institutions typically focused their attention on the federal levels of government where the primary constitutional authority for their «regulation» lay. Manufacturing and resources companies, with a few important exceptions such as the iron and steel cartel, not only wielded relatively less economic and political power, but tended to focus it more on the provincial level of authority where the spheres of constitutional influence that most concerned them — control of natural resources, direct taxation, labour relations —

were vested. Moreover, in the field of providing social overhead capital, a division of powers existed that, while often hazy, was at least functional. The federal government had assumed the power to lay down the infrastructure, particularly railways and the like, necessary for the transcontinental economy under construction before the World War, while in the 1920s the most important spheres of government capital spending were for highways and electrification, uniquely provincial concerns. The Second World War destroyed the balance in both economic and political terms.

Out of the war came an integrated big business elite in which the traditional spheres of economic influence vanished; out of it too came a clique of bureaucratic mountebanks in Ottawa accustomed to a greatly expanded field of federal authority; and out of it came a welding of these two groups into a permanent mutual admiration and accommodation society. Not only were provincial political powers eroded, but the new corporate integration and concentration process meant that the exercise of authority over the business sector by one level of government automatically intruded on the constitutional competence of the other level. Thus, for example, federal taxation of an integrated manufacturing — resource corporation's income simultaneously affected its rate of exploitation and utilization of the natural resource base of the province in which it operated. While certainly some interdependence of federal-provincial decisions regarding the business sector was present before the war, the scale was vastly enhanced by the parallel movements of political and economic power the war engendered.

It was not simply by affecting business income and spending patterns that the bloated post-war federal powers encroached on provincial reserves. The intrusion was even more in evidence in the provision of social services. Two factors were central to the rise of a federal welfare state. On the one hand the federal authorities, business and political, had drawn the obvious lessons from the aftermath of the First World War which had spread paranoia about a possible «Bolshevik» insurrection in Canada. Added to their memories of the «Winnipeg Commune» was the stark reality of the power of the organized left in the unions and among unorganized workers that grew during the depression years. The federal welfare state was conceived of, on one level, as a device for buying off social discontent and undermining the political influence of the left. It had the rather interesting additional advantage, given the memories of the Great Depression and the possibility of a post-war slump, of transferring extra spending power to the federal government, helping to create a larger domestic market for federal debt instruments by the enforced investment of a portion of workers' incomes, and at the same time assuring that the burden of supporting the unemployed in a future depression would pass from the upper middle class and the corporate sector, to the working class itself. Intra-class and inter- generational transfers would replace inter-class and intra- generational transfers when hard times arrived.

Such, it seems to me, is a more accurate view of the forces behind the post-war centralisation of political power in Canada than that propounded by

Kierans. If it is accepted, then it serves as well to throw into question the next major tenet of his argument, namely that the post-war federal state, glutted with illegitimate powers and responding to the prompting of the corporate elite, embarked on a premature opening of Canada to the forces of international integration. Thus «Canada jumped into the world of international trade, capital flows, and interdependence without taking the elementary precaution of first building the foundations, a balanced economy at home. Partnership in a world trade and global integration of capital, labor, and resources come after a nation has secured its home front... «The result apparently was Canada's sudden regression to satellite status and a much enhanced vulnerability to external influences, political and economic. Thus, big business, Kierans seems to argue, is international business: it concentrates power within Canada at the federal level, then robs even that level of authority of the ability to control the socio-economic development of the country. The result has been a recent resurgence of provincially based demands for the restoration of the constitutional *status-quo-ante-bellum*, and thereby for a resuscitation of some measure of popular control over our social and economic destinies.

Coming from a native Montrealer, a veteran senior politician, and a formerly prominent financier Kierans's views are remarkably flavoured with small town populism. One can well understand Brecher's desire to criticise them, even if he did so for all the wrong reasons.

The first, and most important fallacy in the Kierans view is the supposition that a minor country has ever or could ever, under the present rules of the game, «secure the home front» before engaging in international integration. Countries like Canada were *created* by multinational corporations and by the international movement of capital and labour. The multinational corporation is as Canadian as imported apple pie. From the earliest days of white settlement responsibility for colonization and government as well as commercial development was vested in the hands of the directors of great chartered trading companies of France and England. The Canadian economy created by these companies and the succeeding web of imperial-colonial trading regulations was accordingly a marginal part of the world economy from the start, completely dependent on the decisions of an overseas corporate-political elite. The nature and mechanisms of external control have changed — the fact of it has not. To argue the «good old days» scenario is thus to commit a double error: it assumes that external control is new, which it is not; and it assumes that the provinces are more likely to try to combat it, which they will not.

While external control is a constant factor in the history of Canadian economic development, its particular manifestations have changed. Under the aegis of the multinational corporations' efforts to achieve global integration, the centres of economic gravity of North America have been shifting. In Canada industrial and commercial development has traditionally followed two main axes of development. A transcontinental axis dominated by Montreal tapped the natural resource industries, particularly agricultural, of the West and oversaw an east-west flow of commodities and capital that made Montreal the transportation and financial centre of Canada. On the other hand the axis of manufacturing development followed the main contours of American industrial growth, concentrating on the Great Lakes area and predicated on a spill-over of American manufacturing capacity into the Windsor-Montreal belt. Thus Southern Ontario and the Toronto region became the locus of most of Canada's secondary industrial growth.

Since the war the axes of development changed. Continental integration ruptured a transcontinental economy already badly shaken by the Great Depression; and the rise of the integrated manufacturing-resource company, often foreign controlled, to corporate leadership refocused the main flow of economic activity to Toronto and environs. Toronto, already dominating the industrial heartland of Canada, began to displace Montreal as the financial and commercial centre of Canada as well. The result over the post-war years has been a steady flow of corporate headquarters to Toronto. Sun Life's decision to move is only the most recent manifestation of an on-going phenomenon.

At this point it is useful to make reference to Brecher's criticisms of Kierans's arguments, one of which is that Kierans fails to see the link betwen Sun Life's withdrawal from Montreal and some sort of Bill 101 malaise under which Quebec's investment climate reputedly labours. However, as I read it, contrary to Brecher, Kierans seems to claim that Bill 101 is a symptom of a general provincial rights resurgence which in Quebec takes on a special character because of the accompanying question of national self-determination. It was, according to Kierans, Sun Life's refusal to accommodate itself to the particular dimensions the provincial resurgence takes in Quebec that led to its decision. Both protagonist and antagonist in this debate seem to me to be quite wrong. Both have refused to recognize the crucial distinction between a «reason» for a corporation's actions, and a «pretext». Sun Life's decision to move seems to have been inevitable. It was one of the most important financial corporations to grow up in Montreal as part of a transcontinental axis of development that simply no longer exists. There is no reason to think Sun Life's decision to set up shop elsewhere was prompted by any different a set of considerations than motivated dozens before it — save perhaps for one small item. In doing the inevitable, Sun Life chose to make a public spectacle of itself in a crude and transparent effort to further discredit the incumbent government.

Professor Brecher undoubtedly would disagree. To him the Sun Life departure and Bill 101 itself are symptomatic of the state of affairs engendered by a government that «views the suppression of basic anglophone, and indeed francophone rights as a key prerequisite to progress for that mysterious thing called a collectivity.» Most of us, I am sure, would not find the notion of collective social existence, or the need for individuals to make sacrifices for the communal good, quite so mysterious as would economics professors who tend to spend an appalling amount of their time in a textbook world of invisible hands guiding the dog-eat-dog competition of social atoms. But even ignoring this slight problem of ideological perspective, one cannot but be struck by the inconsistent reasoning involved in

Brecher's argument. It is increasingly common — but not for that reason any the more excusable — for attacks on Quebec's national resurgence to take the form of denying to Quebec the right to legislate in such a way as to remind minorities of their minority status, while at the same time granting this right to the federal government. By endorsing the right of the federal government to intervene, and indeed, exhorting it to do so, Brecher assumes federal power will be used to *defend* minorities while Quebec's power must be used to *offend* them. Apart from the obvious rejoinder — try that one out on a Pacific Coast Japanese-Canadian — one can only balk at the nature of the logic that leads to the apparent belief that if the «natives» are given some measure of political control, they will spend their time not attempting to rectify social inequalities and develop and balance the economy, but rather in the perverse pastime of persecuting ethnic minorities.

Clearly then Brecher has a different view of the nature and functioning of the federal government than has Kierans. To Brecher, the impetus to growing federal power came not from the refusal of the federal mandarins to surrender their emergency powers at the end of the war, but rather to the fact that «millions of Canadians were demanding economic and social benefits on a scale so massive as to be feasible only through federal financing and the exercise of federal know- how in these fields.» He thus proceeds from a correct premise — the post-war mass demand for economic security — to a false conclusion — that only a highly centralised system of government could meet that demand. As to the vaunted «federal know-how», it is necessary to recall that until the post-war period, social programs were conceived of and executed by the provincial governments, and that «federal know-how» at the end of the war reflected in good measure federal appropriation of provincial ideas and personnel. True, the provincial programs had been of limited scale, a limit determined in large measure by financial considerations. But to argue from the *fact* of limited provincial fiscal resources to the *need* for federal leadership is an exercise in paralogism, which slips an extra, erroneous, premise into the debate from under the table. Federal power came first, and with it federal fiscal resources. At the end of the war, given that the federal government *had* appropriated the lion's share of available fiscal resources, it could have followed two courses of action — either return to the provinces what was constitutionally theirs, allowing them to administer social programs, or insist on further expanding central government powers by controlling social programs itself. Because it *did* opt for the second, rather than the first, of the two alternative policies is no reason to suppose, as Brecher does, that it *should have or had to follow such a course of action.*

Citing the massive intergovernmental transfers as Brecher does, hardly belies the point about the unwieldiness and overcentralized character of the Canadian federation. If anything, it does the opposite. Federal grants in aid of specific programs launched by the provinces, far from being a healthy manifestation of «cooperative federalism» act simply to further extend federal power. Just as in the case of foreign «aid» payments to many developing nations that Professor Brecher is well aware of, these intergovernmental transfers further constrain and regiment the fiscal freedom of th recipient government by forcing it to channel its spending into areas that complement and supplement the type of programs that the donor government has decided to support. In the case of a federal system it serves as further proof that financial powers are *overcentralized* in relation to spending responsibilities, thus further undermining the constitutional division of power.

Brecher next turns his attention to an effort to counter Kierans's expressed distate for the process of international integration currently superintended by the multinational corporation. My reading of Kierans's argument, again contrary to what Brecher seems to imply, is that at no point did he suggest autarky as an economic objective: the evil is not international integration *per se* but whether the terms under which that integration takes place are determined by a democratic national authority or a tiny foreign oligarchy in control of the so-called multinational corporations, the technocrats' euphemism for American big business operating abroad. Brecher's argument thus becomes that the American corporate elite are better judges of what pattern of production and distribution in a country is most conducive to that nation's welfare than the elected representatives of the population of the country concerned. As to his unsubstantiated assertion that the multinational corporation is «here to stay», one can only reply that this kind of mixture of ideological incantation and economic soothsaying, by itself is no guarantee of objective realisation, especially in a world where a multitude of nations are moving briskly to control and even eliminate the economic and political power of the multinational corporation. However, there is no doubt that the multinational corporation will be a problem for Canada for some time to come; so too will be liberal economists with their blind faith in free trade and free capital flows. That is just all the more reason for the rest of us to heed Kierans's advice and start looking for more serious means of countervailing its power than we have at present.

Parenthetically one might point out another logical curio in Brecher's eulogy over the multinational corporations. In the 1950s and 1960s when Canada's living standard was second highest in the world, its unemployment rate running about four percent, and prices reasonably stable in the face of a satisfactory growth performance, economics professors routinely taught their students to genuflect before the altar of free international enterprise — all this in conformity with their discipline's zeal for fobbing off specious correlations of effects in the guise of analyses of causes. Now with our living standard about eight highest, inflation at nine percent, the unemployment rate — using the federal government's carefully falsified statistics — running at about eight percent, manufacturing capacity utilization at under 80%, and the spectre of resource based economies like northern Ontario regressing to empty slag heaps as direct result of *administratively* ordained changes in corporate investment priorities, we still hear tales of the multinational firm's corporate cornucopia. Strange logic, even for an economist.

In conclusion it is difficult to avoid the opinion that both Brecher's impassionately confused defense of centralized federalism and the power of the multinational corporation on the one hand, and Kierans's rather naive exultation over «states rights» on the other equally miss the mark. The federal government has clearly been a pliable instrument in the hands of the corporate elite since the war. Yet can we seriously expect provincial governments, even if bolstered by the return of their proper powers, to behave in a strikingly different way? Provinces are potentially more amenable than the federal government ot two types of control — from their populations at large, and from certain members of the business elite with a pronounced stake in one particular province. The fact that the federal government always has to perform some kind of juggling act between different sets of corporate demands means that in meeting the requirements of corporate-controlled economic development as a whole, it has some scope for resisting the unconscionable demands of this or that particular member of the privileged set of corporate citizenry. The provinces have much less scope for autonomous action. It is no accident therefore that buccaneer capitalism, of the grab-and-run type, the sort that graced Quebec under its late Liberal government or Newfoundland under the last years of the Smallwood regime, recurs more frequently at the provincial than at the federal level of government. The extra flexibility of provincial political responses as a result of their smaller scale therefore can be an instrument of good or evil, more often the former. Furthermore, merely transferring more power to the provincial government as Kierans calls for, is unlikely to do more than eliminate their flexibility of response to the popular base by enhancing bureaucratization without really challenging the structure of corporate control. When smiling Bill Davis, the businessman's friend, calls on the federal government to shelve the first anti-combines law with any real teeth in Canadian history, in the interests of improving the investment climate for business, are we hearing the voice of provincial populism or that of a set of giant automobile corporations who control the Ontario speciality plants through long-term supply agreements of dubious legality? Surely between Brecher's unabashed lauding of the multinational corporations and the federal mandarins who serve it on the one hand, and Kierans's plea for redistributing political power within the context of a given structure of economic power on the other, we are presented with a Hobson's Choice. Far better we begin the task of conceiving of a third option.

Part V

THE EDUCATIONAL ESTABLISHMENT

Educational institutions have long been central to English Quebec society, and this has become even more apparent in recent years. It is this centrality which has led us to give considerable attention to the English language educational system in this collection — witness Jones' background statement in part I where the emergence of the «system» is outlined.

Educational institutions, of course, assume a central role in any industrialized society, but there are additional historical and sociological reasons which account for their salient position in English Quebec. Constitutionally, they are the only publically financed institutions which impinge on the daily lives of the vast majority of the population; and their existence, at least with respect to their Protestant nature, is firmly entrenched in the British North America Act. In fact, English common schools, as Jones indicates, got off the ground before French common schools, and until very recently, they enjoyed a comparatively better tax base. Historically, English Quebecers were very committed to their schools, devoting the time and resources necessary to create a public system which they considered — not entirely without reason — to be one of the best in the western world; and to which they subsequently became very attached. Under the circumstances, it is not surprising that the parallel system of private educational institutions was poorly developed. The contrasts between the English and French systems are in this respect considerable.

Yet, perhaps of more consequence in the elevation of the school system to such a central role has been the weakness of other mainstream institutions of a public nature in English Quebec. The Church was, necessarily, highly fragmented — Catholic, Anglican, Presbyterian, Baptist, etc. — and no single faith succeeded in establishing its ascendancy over the anglophone population. Furthermore, in recent years, the various religious institutions have lost the self-confidence and even the man-power necessary to make this possible. Elsewhere, the English component of the Quebec civil service atrophied and the business milieu contracted, consequent upon the continentalization of production and the shift in the centre of gravity of the Canadian financial world to Toronto, and more recently, to the west. Hence, there emerged, by default perhaps, a situation in which the only institutional complex with resources and staying power in the post-war period was the educational one. For reasons touched on by Caldwell in his background discussion of demography, the clientele continued to thrive — at least until the passing of more stringent language legislation in the form of Laws 22 and 101 — while the prevailing liberal and universalistic systems of values made it easy to import the human resources necessary to run the system.

The Quiet Revolution, and the modernization it engendered, served to strengthen the English institutions. Until then, they had been largely locally based and locally financed. Educational restructuration and reform made immense new public resources available to an already well-established English-speaking educational system. But more significantly, the centralization inherent in this structuration, particularly for the Protestant system, created what had never existed in

English-speaking Quebec since the withdrawal of the British troops: a province-wide centralized and publically supported network. In addition to the formal school system and the presiding Department of Education, there came into being, or were strengthened, a host of para-educational organizations spawned by the modernization of educational structures in Quebec: teachers unions, associations of administrators, teachers associations based on subject matter, not to speak of associations of school boards and parents associations. On the local level, school facilities were centralized over immense distances in order to improve services and to compensate for the dispersion of the English-speaking clientele. However, this latter innovation had the effect of isolating students from their own, often linguistically mixed, communities and of erecting a distant and powerful technocracy quite removed (literally) from local control.

Inevitably, the educational system became a political base and subsequently, an actor, of great significance: during a certain period, the director-general — and not the elected president — of the PSBGM became the most weighty political personality in English-speaking Quebec. In fact, in the late sixties and early seventies, 6 000 Fielding Street, in the West Island, the seat of the Protestant School Board of Greater Montreal (PSBGM) and the Quebec Association of Protestant School Boards (QAPSB), was the centre of political gravity in (at least) Protestant Quebec. Faced with the prospect of a government «fait accompli» on educational reform, the Protestant «system» is presently in the process of raising the population.

However, school board administrators are not, and cannot be expected to be, the interpreters and guardians of the wider public interests, in this instance, the longer-term future of English-speaking Quebec. They were, as almost any organizational leadership would be, almost exclusively concerned with short-term institutional interests. In the case of educational institutions, this parochial self-interest may well have been reinforced by the fact of their being staffed at higher levels substantially by people not native to Quebec, and therefore with very little social ground to stand on other than that of «their» institutions. Hence, the crying of wolf three times on linguistic legislation (see Tetley), a late and reluctant recognition of the importance of French language training, a defensive and reactive response to the Montreal Island school restructuration question (see Bissonnette), and an aloofness, if not indeed total disembodiment, on the part of the universities (see Roy).

Nonetheless, given its very centrality as the major institutional support of English-speaking Quebec, the educational milieu has a potentially creative role to play in the present moment of truth, above all in those parts of Quebec where the educators are the only English-speaking elite present. Innovation in the development of French-language immersion programme (see Lambert and Tucker), and an increasing willingness on the part of some elected officials within the system to affirm themselves publically are encouraging indicators. In the same vein, repeated efforts to collaborate with francophone counterparts on the current education reform issue are a sign of new and less isolationist posture.

Yet, paradoxically, the greatest challenge the system must now face comes from within. Having realized that the English system does not prepare the young in a way that would permit them, if they so chose, to be successful in Quebec, the English elite — a disproportionate fraction of which lives off this same educational milieu — has now largely abandoned the system. Children of prominent business-men, professionals, director-generals, and University professors are sent to French Catholic schools in Quebec, both private and public, or to private schools in Ontario; while university-aged off-springs frequent, in increasing numbers Queen's, Western, Toronto, Trent, University of New Brunswick and half-a-dozen other institutions in neighbouring provinces... not infrequently with financial support from Quebec sources.

Graduates of Early French Immersion

Wallace Lambert

Richard G. Tucker

WALLACE LAMBERT, in collaboration with Richard G. Tucker, pioneered in the area of bilingual education for anglophones in Quebec and is a prominent international scholar in the field of language learning. He is presently professor of psychology at McGill University.

RICHARD G. TUCKER is Director of the Center for Applied Linguistics in Washington, D.C. He formerly worked with Wallace Lambert at McGill University. His published research includes studies in language learning and teaching in both monolingual and bilingual settings.

Introduction

The present demand for the development of new or varied approaches to second language teaching represents one very visible manifestation of Canada's rapidly evolving language practice. Although The British North America Act of 1867 designated English and French as the two official languages, the French language has, in fact, traditionally been relegated to a minor position — even in the Province of Quebec. Over the years, English had become firmly entrenched as the working language of business and industry.[1] The eruption of terrorist activities in the early 1960's revealed the latent resentment felt by many French Canadians over the inferior ascribed status of their language in this supposedly bilingual country.

The ensuing ten-year period was marked by rapid change in language policy at both the federal and provincial levels of government. Pinault and Ladouceur[2] pointed out that more action had been taken in the previous ten years to guarantee the maintenance and development of French as the *de jure* and *de facto* working language of Quebec than during the preceding 190 years. For example, with the passage of Law 101, all English-speaking children must acquire a demonstrable working knowledge of French within their school curriculum; a working knowledge of French has replaced Canadian citizenship as a requirement for professional licences; and the Government has exerted direct pressure on large companies and industries to collaborate with it to make French the working language of employees at all levels. At the federal level, bilingualism is now a prerequisite for advancement, and direct financial incentives are being offered to individuals who possess bilingual skills.

Simultaneously, in the Atlantic provinces, in Ontario and in parts of Western Canada, small groups of French Canadians have once again become vitally concerned with the preservation of their cultural identity. They are demanding government support to initiate or broaden programmes of French education for their children, many of whom now claim English as their native language.

Meanwhile, the teaching of French to English-speaking children has typically produced disappointing results. Even in Quebec, where French is introduced in the early primary grades as a second language (FSL) and remains compulsory throughout high school, students pass examinations in French language and literature without being able to carry on a simple conversation. After studying French for seven to twelve years, the majority are definitely not equipped to function in a French milieu.

With the growing demand for more effective programmes of second language teaching, many educators have begun to consider the adoption of some form of bilingual instruction. Bilingual programs emphasize the use of the second language or target language as a major medium of instruction. This approach is based upon the belief that children can assimilate, quite easily, information via a second language while simultaneously acquiring a knowledge of the code itself.[3]

One form such efforts have taken is «early immersion». What follows is an abridged version[4] of a report on the graduates of St. Lambert early-immersion programme.[5]

Methodological Considerations

The pupils in the original pilot class of the St. Lambert «Early Immersion» or «Home-to-School Language Switch» project have now graduated from secondary school.* For this report, we asked these young people to look back on their schooling and to appraise its effects on their lives. We also asked their parents to do the same.

There was something very special about the schooling of these students because during kindergarten and grade 1, their entire contact with teachers and subject matters took place in French, which was essentially a foreign language for them since they all came from homes where only English was used, and since very little contact with French-speaking Canadians took place in their neighbourhoods. They were given the chance to learn French, indirectly through the course materials taught, and directly as a subject matter from their French-speaking teachers. During grades 2, 3 and 4, they continued in a mainly French learning environment, except for two daily half-hour periods of English language arts and for courses in physical education and plastic arts which were taught by native-speakers of English. The amount of instruction time given to English increased at grade 5 so that during grades 5 and 6, the last year of elementary school, the proportions were roughly 60 per cent English, and 40 per cent French. Thus, the elementary school program was structured as to proportions of time given to French immersion, but for the first few years, many «experiments» were conducted in the process of finding appropriate teachers, materials and modes of instruction. The pilot-class felt the full weight of this experimentation.

The programme for secondary school was not as well regulated, although attempts were made to provide appropriate follow-up or maintenance courses in French and to offer certain subject matters in French. As we will see in this report, the students and parents were generally not satisfied with the follow-up program.

* * *

Each year, the students in the early-immersion French programme were tested for their progress in French, in English, and in subject matters; their standing on measures of verbal and non-verbal intelligence; and their attitudes towards

* These students graduated at the end of the seventies.

English- and French-speaking people. They were compared with English-language-schooling and French-language-schooling control groups, each composed of children from the same socio-economic background, of the same intellectual level, and, in the case of the English-speaking controls, from homes with comparable attitudes towards French-speaking Canadians as those in the immersion programme.

No attempt was made to select only those with high academic promise so that in the immersion classes as in the comparison groups, I.Q. scores varied widely and a small proportion of children with diagnosed «learning difficulties» were kept in each sample. Also, it is important to note here that although the groups described here were essentially middle class, the programme was not intended exclusively for middle-class children. In fact, the same immersion programme has been followed by children from working-class backgrounds,[6] and the favorable results of immersion hold as well for them as for the more favored social groups.

The results of our year-by-year testing have been presented in a series of reports.[7] On the basis of these detailed comparisons, we found that from kindergarten through grade 6, the children in early immersion classes progressed extremely well in all aspects of French language skills, relative to the French-speaking controls; they were also able to learn content subjects (such as math, science and social studies) using the French language as well as the comparison groups; they showed no signs of falling behind their age equivalents in any aspects of English-language development; they were not impaired intellectually, judging from their performance on measures of intelligence — in fact, by the later grades, they pulled ahead of the comparison groups on measures of «divergent thinking» or «creativity»;[8] and their attitudes towards French people and towards the French-immersion programme were favourable throughout the elementary years. We also found that as the proportion of time spent in French-language instruction decreased from grade 3 to 6, their progress in development in French-language skills slowed down as well.[9]

* * *

This report picks up the same young people, now graduating from secondary school, after a gap of five years, since our regular testing stopped at grade 6, when students moved on to secondary school. During this gap, most students took the follow-up programme in French offered at secondary school. In the final two years, they also took secondary school-leaving exams in French-as-a-subject matter, and in some cases, exams on French-language skills designed for French-speaking secondary school students.

Questionnaires designed to elicit information on competence and use of French, assessment of different programmes to teach French, and plans for the future were given or mailed to all those who had started school in a French-immersion kindergarten twelve years previously, as well as to their parents. Questionnaires were also completed by those pupils and their parents who had been in the original English comparison classes — those whose parents had entered their children in a conventional English-language programme in Montreal's public schools which had a programme of French as a second language (FSL), one period per day from kindergarten on.

In this programme, the children studied French approximately forty-five minutes per day as a subject. The children were first introduced to oral activities with an emphasis on listening to the language and learning various songs, drills, short dialogues, etc. This FSL programme used a relatively traditional audio-lingual approach in which the children first listened, then mimicked, then practised what the teacher said until they gradually were able to produce utterances unaided. For the most part, the French as second language classes were strictly language-arts classes, with no attempt made to teach context via the language. The comparison-group parents living in the Westmount community did not have an early immersion programme available to them as an option. Thus, they were «forced» to enroll their children in the traditional English classes. In the St. Lambert community, parents were essentially assigned by lot to the experimental or control groups. Six of the English-comparison students had taken the «late» French-immersion option at grade 7, which meant that the bulk of their grade 7 schooling was conducted in French with teachers whose native language was French. In this report, we will treat the English-comparison group as a whole, without differentiating those with grade 7 immersion experience. The grade 7 immersion option was not open to those in the early immersion programme.

Results: Students' Questionnaire

Since the questionnaire included straight-forward questions as well as opportunities for extended comments, we will, in this abridged paper, present the findings in both an objective form, that is, with allusion to statistical counts[10] of reported levels of skills in the French language and use of the language in the community, etc.; and a subjective form, relying on the extended comments made by students and/or their parents as to their feelings and personal views about various aspects of the school experiences.

The comparisons to be made permit us to assess how well the programme of «early immersion» in French has served these English-Canadian young people as a preparation for coping with the bilingual demands of today's Quebec or other bilingual areas of Canada. In other words, we will try to determine how well immersion-schooling prepares English-speaking students to function at work, in school, and in social relationships in a bilingual society.

One of the general conclusions we arrive at is that these young people are indeed very well prepared to function in French, much more so than those without the early-immersion French-language experience. At the same time, however, we also conclude that even with a substantial bilingual preparation, many of these graduates have trouble making contact with the French world around them, and that disappointments may be engendered, precisely because they have developed the capacity to function easily in a bilingual community. We even wonder whether some form of this type of disappointment, coupled with mounting employment problems, may prompt many of these young people to think of making their lives outside of Quebec. What this means is that our analysis of the results will focus as much on the students' perceptions of the social atmosphere of contemporary Quebec, as on the surface meaning of their replies to our questions.

We begin by summarizing the students' and parents' responses to our questionnaire, with brief references to the statistical outcomes. At the same time, we will refer repeatedly to the personal commentaries added to the questionnaires.

On reading these «family» impressions,[11] one sees how a novel educational experience like early-immersion schooling actually involves parents as well as pupils, and brings about important reciprocal influences at every step. As we will see, pupils and parents sometimes have different expectations about the outcomes of such an educational experience although, in general, there is substantial agreement within families as to what went on and what came from the experience.

Table I presents the basic background information for the two groups of grade 11 students, the «early immersion» group labeled as EI, and the English-schooling comparison group labeled as EC. From the original classes, we will be dealing with 17 early-immersion students and 21 English-schooling controls, with roughly equal numbers of males and females. Originally, there were 22 students in the EI class at kindergarten and 34 students in two separate kindergarten classes of EC children. We made every attempt to contact all of these students, either directly if they were still in Montreal, or by mail. Nearly all the students were at grade 11 at the time of the survey, and all of them came from English-language homes, with no other language as a home or working language.

As of grade 11, all of the EI students had been in public schools since kindergarten. In fact, the vast majority of the original class moved along year-by-year as a unit, a rarity in these days of streaming and ability grouping. In contrast, a significantly larger proportion of the EC group had entered private schooling. (X^2 (df, 1) = 3,82, p< .05). This difference might simply mean that the EC families, many from Montreal's Westmount area, were less sure of the secondary school education available to them, compared to that available in the St. Lambert area. On the other hand, the difference could mean that the EC families, representing as they do the same social-class standing as the EI families, had found more need than EI families to turn to private schooling; as though in their eyes, public schooling was inadequate in certain respects, specifically in language teaching, as expressed in

TABLE I — Students' Views at Grade II — Background Information of Students

	Student Group	
Sex	Early Immersion (EI)	English Control (EC)
Male	10	11
Female	7	10
$X^2 = 0,01$; df = 1; n.s.		
Present Grade Level		
Grade 10	1	2
Grade 11	15	17
Grade 12	1	2
$X^2 = 0,37$; df = 2; n.s.		
Public versus Private School, at Present		
Public	17	15
Private	0	6
$X^2 = 3,82$; df = 1; $p < .05$		
Native Language		
English	17	21
(100%, both cases)		

the questionnaires. On the other hand, the commentaries suggest that the EI students appreciated the «special attention» they received as the «pilot» class of this new form of education, and the cohesiveness of the group. Apparently, it was this satisfaction, along with the regular progress being made in French that satisfied the EI parents as well; otherwise, they, too, might have chosen private schooling in similar proportions.

* * *

We now turn to the results and, in the first instance, to those concerning French-language competence. However, the statistics for group-comparison on French-language competence are, for reasons of space, not presented here. In reviewing the comparisons, it should be kept in mind that the EC students followed a conventional English-language programme with French as a second language from kindergarten on, that is, they had received an average of 45 minutes per day of instruction in French as a second language. In other words, in comparison with typical programme of second or foreign language training available in the United States, or even in other parts of Canada, the EC students had a very rich programme of French study.

We are relying here on the *perceptions* these young people have of their competence in French, and although these could be admittedly subjective and possibly biased, it is our opinion that in giving their ratings of competence, these students use as a frame of reference what a fully bilingual person in Montreal is like.

As a group, the graduates of the early-immersion programme feel that they can speak, understand, read and write French at relatively high levels compared to the EC students. In terms of degrees of competence, the EI students feel they handle each aspect of the language «quite well», whereas th EC students say they can handle French only «well enough to get by.» In each instance, there are statistically reliable group differences in perceptions of competence in the French language, and each of these favours the EI group.

It is clear that the graduates of the EI programme feel much more competent in their ability to function in French, in the community, than the EC graduates. As a group, they feel more able to attend a French-language university, to take employment where French is required, to perform daily errands in French, to ask and give directions in French, and to attend essentially French-only social gatherings. Interestingly, both groups feel equally able to read French newspapers, whereas the EI students again feel more competent to understand French T.V. and radio programmes.

With respect to the actual usage made of French outside of school, it is not surprising that neither the EC nor the EI students use French with parents, brothers and sisters or schoolmates. This finding is consistent with the views the EI students have previously expressed: for them, there is something «phoney» in using French with English speakers even when they are bilingual. Nor do the groups differ in the frequency of attending French films, listening to French radio, watching French television or reading French newspapers or books. Both groups indicate that they rarely, if ever, turn to any of the French media. As seen in the commentaries, both EC and EI groups appear to be swamped by the impact of the American media, from films and television to periodicals and books. One wonders, in fact, how in this setting the value of some other media source such as Canadian French-language programmes can have impact.

The groups pull apart, however, on an important subset of items dealing with the use of French in the broader community with French people. The EI students «almost always» use French with their French teacher, while the EC group does so only «sometimes ($p < .01$). The EI students use French more often with French-speaking friends ($p < .01$), and more often with French-speaking neighbours ($p < .01$). They also find more day-to-day opportunities outside of school to speak French than do the EC students (p< .01). The picture that emerges here is that once a certain level of language skill has been attained, another linguistic world starts to open up. The main point, though, is that there are important differences between EI and EC groups in their willingness and/or ability to *find* opportunities to use French in the French community.

This difference between the EI and the EC groups in ability to make social contacts with French-speaking people is reflected as well in the responses to the questionnaire. When they meet a French-speaking stranger, members of the EI group are more likely to start up a conversation in French (on the average, they do so «often», while the EC students do so «sometimes», p<.03). What is perhaps more interesting is that French-speaking people are also more likely to strike up a conversation in French with the EI students («very often») than they are with the EC students(«sometimes»,p<.02), and the EI children are more likely to communicate back in French than are the EC children (p<.01). It would be interesting to follow this pattern of differences in greater detail, for one gets the impression that the children with early immersion experience react more like French speakers, possibly sending out better signals of their ability and willingness to communicate in French.

Nevertheless, there appear to be limits as to how far these English-speaking young people can go in their social relationships with French speakers. When asked if they attend parties where French alone is spoken, only a small minority of the EI or the EC students answer that they do. Likewise, when asked if they take part in other activities in the community which call for a knowledge of French, at least half of the students in each group say that they do not.

But it is not that either the EI or EC students actively avoid situations where they have to speak French; however, EI students do find more occasions than do the EC's to come into social contact with French people. For instance, they are much more likely to use French for errands (p<. 02), and for asking and giving directions (p<.02). And, although both EI and EC students mention that they have French-speaking friends, there is an important difference in the form of linguistic interaction that takes place with these French friends. The EI students never use English, but instead, either French or some combination of French and English. Few EC students use French in these situations (p<.01).

The questions then arise: Why don't these contacts with French-speaking friends, based on mainly French language communication, lead the EI students further into the French-Canadian society? Why are so few of the EI students invited to mainly French parties or other community activities conducted in French? Later we will attempt to explain these apparent limits on the possibilities for social interaction.

* * *

The final set of questions asked the students to look ahead and sketch out their plans for the future. After secondary school, the vast majority of both groups plan on college or university training; and they are aiming for either professional or white-collar occupations. When asked where they will likely be living in four years time, the majority of both groups do *not* see themselves living in Quebec.

When asked if they plan to continue to improve their knowledge of French, the majority of both groups say that they will. This general interest in improving their French skills may reflect a generally positive attitude towards the French community. Gardner and Smythe[12] have found that favourable attitudes and an «integrative motive» toward learning the language of another ethnolinguistic group promotes in students the intention to continue the study of that language, as well as the actual implementation of these intentions. Still, a surprising minority of each group does not plan to continue with French, as though certain of these students may be discouraged about the value of going further with the language. Perhaps their attitudes have taken a negative turn, in Gardner's sense of the term.

However, when asked if they are intereted in learning another language other than French, there is an important group difference. The EI students show more interest than the EC's in another language ($p < .06$). This could reflect a difference attributable to the taste of success: the EI students have already seen in their own experiences that one can master a second or foreign language and, perhaps as a consequence, they are more ready and interested to try another. The important message for language educators is that the development of high-level skills with one foreign or second language can increase the desire to learn other languages.

Results: Parents' Questionnaire

The questionnaire was also given to each parent. We observe first, that the parents of both EI and EC students are all native speakers of English; and for the most part, they have misgivings about their lack of skill in French, placing themselves a bit above the reference point «barely enough to get by», but below the «well enough to get by» point with regard to their ability to speak, understand, read, and write French.

These findings are interesting because the same parents, in our interviews some thirteen years ago,[13] told us that they were disappointed with their own lack of competence in French in spite of some seven or more years of public school instruction in the language. In fact, a large part of the interest of the EI parents in exploring other ways of learning French for their children appeared to stem from their own frustrations with the language at school. But it is difficult to understand how these parents, mainly long-term residents of Quebec, would not have progressed further in their command of the French language since some 80 per cent of the population of the Province are French-speaking. One could interpret this lack of competence as a reflection of the greater prestige of English over French in North America. Of course, one could interpret the same findings as a reflection of the general lack of interest in the French language and the desire to have English overpower French as a working language even in Quebec. We might offer another possible interpretation: that neither the French Canadian nor the English Canadian has made really serious efforts to open up their respective societies to enable the other ethnolinguistic group to learn the other language or to learn about the other people. This interpretation comes to mind because we found that the EI and EC students apparently encounter numerous barriers for intergroup relations, and it could well be that their parents had similar encounters a generation earlier.

The vast majority of both groups of parents have encouraged their children to participate in activities, outside of school, where French is the dominant language, such as going to the theatre, taking athletic and sports instruction in French, etc.

The vast majority have also encouraged their children to use French in the community by, for example, asking directions in French, seeking out French-speaking playmates, etc.

Further, the children's comparatively richer experiences in French have had some impact on the parents' attempts to improve their own competence in the language; in fact, about a third of the parents say that they were so influenced.

Finally, when the parents try to reflect on, and assess, the language programmes their children followed from kindergarten through secondary school, a very striking difference emerges: the parents of the EI students almost unanimously consider that the early immersion experience was successful whereas the vast majority of parents of the EC students see the conventional French as a second language programmes as unsuccessful ($p < .001$). Furthermore, the vast majority of the parents of the EI students said they would choose the early-immersion programme again, while the EC parents were uncertain as to what they would choose as an alternative ($p < .02$).

The Extended Comments of Students and Parents

The comments spontaneously added by students and parents are the subject of the present section. They constitute a rich supplement to the questionnaire responses because in them, one can often capture feelings and attitudes that are otherwise not expressed. We have already drawn on this source of information for examples of the feelings of students and parents, but here, in Table II, we have compiled numerical counts of certain reactions that recur as themes in these free

270

commentaries. In doing so, we find that although they agree in general with the questionnaire response, in many cases they go far beyond in the attitudes expressed.

TABLE II — **Themes Emerging from Commentaries: Comparisons of EI and EC groups***

		Early Immersion Students (N = 18)	English Comparison Students (N = 22)	Early Immersion Parents (N = 16)	English Comparison Parents (N = 20)
1) Student's working	Yes	33	9	25	5
experience with	No	55	77	44	80
French language.	No Info	11	4	31	15
2) Student capable of	Yes	72	22	75	20
working in French.	No	6	18	6	20
	No Info	22	60	19	60
3) Student capable of	Yes	28	9	56	5
studying in French	No	22	27	19	20
institution.	No Info	50	64	25	75
4) Student's attitude	Positive	72	41	88	70
toward integrating	Negative	17	14	0	5
with French speakers.	No Info	11	45	12	25
5) Motivated to stay	Stay	39	18	38	30
or leave the	Leave	56	73	38	30
Quebec scene.	No Info	6	0	25	40
6) Student's satisfaction	Satisfied	72	27	81	20
with potential to be	Little hope/				
fully bilingual.	Too late	6	45	12	50
	No Info	22	27	6	30
7) Student has French	Yes	50	27	38	30
speaking friends.	No	33	50	38	10
	No Info	17	22	25	60
8) Private vs. public	Public	100	64		
schooling.	Private	0	36		
	No Info	0	0		

* Entries are percentages.

In Table II, we have presented a number of recurring themes along with comparisons of the reactions of EI and EC students and parents. Because the contents of these comments varied widely and were voluntary, statistical analyses were not appropriate. Coding of the responses would have been difficult and we had no way of evaluating those cases where no information was offered. Certain trends are, nonetheless, clear.

What we find is that some 33 per cent of the EI students have already found occasions to work in French in part-time or summer jobs, compared to only 10 per cent of the EC students. Overall, some 70 per cent of the EI students feel they could work in French, versus 20 per cent of the EC students; and in general, the parents agree with their children in these instances (items 1 and 2 in Table II). Some 28 per cent of the EI students also feel they could carry out their college and university studies in French institutions, compared to only 10 per cent of the EC students who feel that capable in French (item 3).

Incidentally, some 56 per cent of the EI parents feel that their children could enroll in French colleges; this means that there is a much larger number of parents than students who feel the latter could succeed in a French institution. Even though this suggests that the EI parents may exaggerate their children's capacities in French, the main point is that about a third of the EI students do feel capable of entering French language colleges for advanced training.

One recurring theme dealt with students' interest and motivation to become more a part of the French-speaking world around them in Quebec. We found a decidedly more favourable attitude toward integrating with French-speaking Canadians among EI than EC students (72 per cent versus 41 per cent). This more favourable attitude may be an outcome of their greater ability in French.

Incidentally, this is another instance where the views of the EC parents are not in line with those of their children: 70 per cent of the EC parents feel that their children are favourably disposed to integration with French Canadians while only 40 per cent of the students themselves express such an attitude (item 4, Table II). This discrepancy is interesting to us and we wonder why students and parents have different perspectives on this important issue. Apparently, the parents are more prone to give the socially expected reaction.

We also counted the number of students in each group who felt motivated either to stay in Quebec or leave, in face of the uncertain political and economic future of the Province. Here we find that some 40 per cent of the EI students are anxious to stay in Quebec (item 5, Table II), compared to 20 per cent of the EC students who are similarly motivated to stay. (Note here again that the EC parents have an inflated view of the feelings of their children on this critical issue: 30 per cent of the EC parents project that their children will stay versus 18 per cent of the students who say that they are likely to stay.)

We are impressed most by the fact that some 56 per cent of the EI students, with their capabilities in the language and their desire to integrate with French-speaking Canadians, are thinking of making their lives outside Quebec. This is all the more striking when we realize that over 70 per cent of the EI students are of the opinion that they could easily become fully bilingual, given opportunities to practise their French; compared to only 27 per cent of the EC students, who are more inclined to the view that it is too late for them to become fully bilingual (item 6, Table II). Here, the parents agree with the students' assessments of their bilingual potential. Furthermore, some 50 per cent of the EI students say that they have French-speaking friends (with whom, as already noted, they tend to use French), compared to only 27 per cent of the EC students (who tend to use English or English and French as the language of communication: item 7, Table II).

Finally, in item 8, we see reflected again the fact that our sample of EI students has stayed in the public school system, and also stayed together as a group, whereas 25 per cent of the EC families turned to private schooling. This greater use of private schooling might reflect a general concern on the part of the EC parents about their children's future in Quebec, including the need for comprehensive training in French that one gets in private English language schools in Quebec (cf., the commentaries of students and parents), and the desire to offer their children a more personalized education. What is interesting is that the EI families may have been more satisfied with public schooling because, with the immersion programme, they were assured of progress in French, the support and security of a well-knit peer group, and a generally more personalized education.

There are other interesting comparisons to be seen in the commentaries. One that struck us as important has to do with the attitude of EI students and/or parents towards being enrolled directly in French-language schools which afford English-speaking children the chance to be with French-speaking children and communicate with them in French. What we find is that the EI students and their parents seem more open to, and accept as normal, the idea of going one step beyond immersion to «submersion», that is, to actually attending French-language schools. The general attitude that one finds in the commentaries is that even though the immersion programmes has been successful, students could progress even further by having direct experience in French schools with French youngsters. The major point is that this idea emerges spontaneously from families with immersion experience, more so than from the English comparison families; as though the former had few concerns or misgivings about losing ground in English or of personal identity by taking such a step. The statistical evidence for this conclusion comes from the fact that five students and two parents in the EI group mention the submersion option while there is only one such suggestion from an EC student and one from an EC parent. The suggestion from one family is that schools be integrated, half French- and half English-speaking students in each class, alternating languages of instruction. However, in the EC group, there are three other instances where «submersion» experience is suggested as a valuable addition; but in each of these cases, the parents are judging from experiences with *other* children in the family who either had early immersion schooling or, in one case, schooling in a private French high school. Thus, the total for those with early-immersion experience in the family who spontaneously suggest, as an alternative, sending their children to French schools is 10 (7 students and 3 parents) versus 2 (1 student and 1 parent) for those without early-immersion experience in the family. The idea we see emerging is that parents and students with immersion schooling experience are generally satisfied with it and take the idea of going a step further towards integrated schooling in the other language community as natural and appropriate.

Conclusions

These, then, are the conclusions we arrive at from our analysis of both the objective and subjective responses of these two groups of high-school students and their parents:

1) There is a very clear appreciation for the early immersion experience on the part of the EI students and their parents who, in the vast majority, say that they would choose the immersion option if they had to do it all over. This general satisfaction on the part of the EI parents — in spite of their dissatisfaction with the follow-up programmes at the secondary school level — stands in sharp contrast to the general disappointment of the EC parents with their children's language programmes. It is the EC parents who are more prone to direct harsh criticism at the school system for having failed them and their children; they also turn more to private schooling, perhaps as an assurance for their children's future.

2) In general, the students with early-immersion experience express a feeling of well-being, self-assurance and satisfaction with their level of attainment in French which is much more advanced than that reached by the English comparison students. This sense of attainment shows itself in various ways: (a) the EI students have already had more part-time and summer working in French, (b) the EI students feel much more capable of working in French, (c) they feel more capable of studying in French at the college or university level, and (d) they are more eager to study other languages, as though the taste of success with learning French and the realization that one can master a foreign language stimulated a more general interest in learning other languages.

3) The EI students as a group also show a more positive attitude towards French-speaking Canadians and a greater willingness to make contacts with French-speaking friends; we are informed as well that they are much more inclined to use French with their French friends.

4) Also, a larger proportion of the EI than of the EC students express a desire to stay in Quebec, even though a majority of both EI and EC students think in terms of leaving the Province in the next few years.

5) A much larger proportion of EI students feel that they could, with experience in using the language, become fully bilingual. These feelings are shared as well by the respective groups of parents. The EC students, on the other hand,

give the impression that they have little hope of really mastering French or that it is too late to expect that degree of competence.

6) Having experienced immersion schooling, both the EI students and their parents are more inclined to see the merits of going even further in forms of immersion to the point of full contact with French students in French-language schools. Rather than viewing «submersion» in a total French school as a radical step, one which might adversely affect a child's identity and native language competence, it is seen more as a natural and obvious extension of early immersion by a substantial number of EI students and their parents.

7) On balance, the contrasts between the EI and EC groups that have emerged here portray the early immersion experience as a means of developing high degrees of skill in the French language; a feeling of confidence among graduates that they could work, study, and live in a French environment as well as in an English one; a belief that they could, given simple opportunities to use French, become fully bilingual, and a willingness and desire to meet and integrate with French-speaking Canadians.

At the same time, the analysis has brought to light various hurdles that these well prepared and motivated young people face if they try to penetrate the French world around them in Quebec. Some of these hurdles are very likely rooted in the English-speaking society itself which may not provide models and examples of ways to make contact with French-speaking people. On the other hand, some hurdles are very likely rooted in the French-speaking society of Quebec which, also, may not provide models of how one could encourage and follow-up on gestures of personal interest coming from English-speaking Canadians. Furthermore, this group of English-speaking students, graduating from secondary school in the late seventies, enters a society that is divided and polarized along ethnic and linguistic lines to a greater degree than that experienced by their parents or grandparents. One wonders how these youngsters can learn to live cooperatively as Canadians, when the schools they attend are segregated along religious and linguistic lines. In such conditions, children could reasonably ask why it is that the society apparently does *not want* them to learn the other language or to get to know members of the other ethnolinguistic group. In an important large-scale investigation with French-Canadian secondary-school students, Gagnon[14] found that the vast majority thought that it is only natural that both major Canadian groups learn each other's language; and that, in their views, the language would best be learned though schooling plus personal contacts. Gagnon also found that over 70 per cent of his sample would be very appreciative of occasions to visit English-language settings. Today, young people might wonder why society makes it so difficult for them to learn the other language or make social contacts with the other group.

* * *

Because these hurdles could be a source of frustration, it is important that educators and policy makers give thought to helping these students understand their society and letting them have a hand in improving it. We have found here that there are few ways these students can use French outside school; that they would like to be more involved in basically French activities, but usually are not invited; that friendships with French speaking young people are not common or easy to establish; and that the majority of both EI and EC student groups are thinking of moving out of Quebec in the next four years. In spite of current political policies in Quebec that limit the chances of French-speaking Canadian students to become as competent in English as the EI students are in French, still there likely are numbers of French-Canadian young people who have similar desires for social contacts, but who face comparable societal hurdles in their attempts to make contact with the English-Canadian society.[15] From the perspective of both groups, then, we begin to understand how easily ethnic and linguistic segregation can isolate subgroups within a society. Some argue that the problem is found in most complex, ethnically-plural nations.[16]

It could be argued that this societal wariness of social contacts across ethno-linguistic boundaries represents a search for peace and comfort that comes from being in a setting with one's «own kind».[17] If this is true, then overly enthusiastic attempts to penetrate these boundaries may be disturbing for either group. Applied to the Canadian scene, this would mean that young people who have mastered the other group's language must test cautiously how far and how quickly they can make social contacts that will be acceptable to the other group.

Perhaps the most important conclusion to be drawn from this investigation of the early-immersion experience is that we have been forced to place this innovative form of language training in a broader societal context, and this leads us to a realization that we must now seek out solutions for problems of social segregation and cleavage within Canadian society. The beginnings of a solution seem to stem naturally from the early-immersion experience itself, especially from what the EI students are asking of their society: an opportunity to put their competence in the other language to meaningful use. French-Canadian students may be asking the same — that is, similar opportunities for social contact across the common ethnolinguistic boundary. As parents, educators or political leaders, we must listen and try to understand what these young people are asking. The solutions needed are likely to be found in the questions being asked. It is our opinion that Canada, and especially Quebec, provide researchers with a wonderful field station for finding solutions which can draw on the goodwill of these two streams of young people.

NOTES

(1) D. Lieberson, *Language and Ethnic Relations in Canada*.

(2) Pinault and Ladouceur, *National Language Policies* . Undergraduate Research Paper, McGill University (Montreal), 1971.

(3) Richard G. Tucker and A. d'Anglejan, «A New Direction in Second Language Teaching», R.C. Troike and N. Modiana, *Proceedings of the First Inter-American Conference on bilingual Education* (Arlington (Va.), Center for Applied Linguistics, 1975):63-72.

(4) Questionnaire and appendices, as well as some of the references, have therefore been amputated.

(5) The research was supported in part by grants from the Ministry of Education of the Province of Quebec to the South Shore Protestant Regional School Board, and from the Canada Council to W.E. Lambert and G.R. Tucker.

(6) Wallace E. Lambert, Richard G. Tucker and A. D'Anglejan, «Cognitive and Attitudinal Consequences of Bilingual Schooling...»; G.A. Cziko, *The Effects of Different French Immersion Programs...*; G.A. Cziko, *The Effects of Language...*; M. Bruck, J. Jakimik and G.R. Tucker, *Are French Immersion Programs Suitable....*

(7) Wallace E. Lambert and Richard G. Tucker, *Bilingual Education of Children...*, W.E. Lambert, W.E. Tucker and A. d'Anglejan, «Cognitive and Attitudinal Consequences of Bilingual Schooling...»; M. Bruck, W.E. Lambert and G.R. Tucker, «Bilingual Schooling...»; M. Bruck, W.E. Lambert and G.R. Tucker, «Cognitive Consequences of Bilingual Schooling...».

(8) S. Scott, *The Relation of Divergent Thinking to Bilingualism...*; J. Cummins, «The Influence of Bilingualism...».

(9) Wallace E. Lambert and Richard G. Tucker, *Bilingual Education...*; I.V. Spilka, «Assessment of Second-Language Performance...».

(10) Actual statistics and the tables from which these findings are drawn are not presented in this rendering of the report (the editors).

(11) These spontaneous comments from each family are available in full, albeit anonymously.

(12) R.C. Gardner and P.C. Smythe, «The Integrative Motive in Second-Language Acquisition».

(13) Wallace E. Lambert and Richard G. Tucker, *Bilingual Education....*

(14) M. Gagnon, *Attitudes à l'égard de la langue anglaise*.

(15) *Ibid*.

(16) A. Rabushka and K.A. Shepsle, *Politics in Plural Societies....*

(17) Wallace E. Lambert, «Language as a Factor in Intergroup Relations».

School Restructuration on the Island of Montreal:
A Missed Opportunity for the Anglophones

Lise Bissonnette

LISE BISSONNETTE is presently the editor-in-chief of *Le Devoir*.

English version by R. Clive Meredith and Audrey Pratt of the
Direction de la traduction, ministère des Communications du
Québec

Throughout the history of minorities, the subject of schooling has always held an important place. The blackest dates in the saga of the francophones outside Quebec are those of the battles related to education: battles against legislation to ban French-language instruction, and battles to maintain existing French-language institutions or establish new ones. Every community projects itself through its schools; and it views those schools as its principal means of survival and complete development — in short, as a necessity. Its other cultural institutions it can take or leave, but its schools are where the most fragile elements of that group, the children, are introduced to its culture. By that fact alone, they act as buttresses.

Quebec's anglophone minority is no exception to this rule, although its experience is unique, and this uniqueness is only now beginning to appear. School disputes are still something quite new to this minority. Until the middle seventies, Quebec's anglophones were in an exceptionally comfortable position; now, that position is beginning to change, and school disputes are part of a rude awakening. Quebec's anglophone minority has always seen itself as a minority with the status of a majority. It could not see the writing on the wall, nor was it ready to do battle; indeed, it was convinced that it was indestructible, nay impregnable. For this reason, when the right time came, it refused to agree to certain changes which today would have allowed it to maintain its positions, and it became a victim of its own defence strategies.

In this regard, no experience has been more instructive than the attempt at the so-called «school restructuration»[1] on the island of Montreal in the late sixties and the early seventies. Quebec's greatest concentration of anglophones live on the island, and it was there that this group missed an opportunity to associate itself with the changes which were sweeping Quebec, and thereby to ensure, in a rational manner, its own development.

A Refusal to Associate

To begin, let us put to rest a myth. The Quiet Revolution of the early sixties was anything but a settlement of accounts with Quebec's dominant minority. One of the key pieces of reform born of that period was the Report of the Royal Commission of Inquiry on Education, the *Rapport Parent*. That report did not view the school system from a political point of view. Concern for effective teaching methods came before any concern for what the present government calls «affirmation collective». It is at that moment, still relatively «neutral» politically, that the anglophone community, falling back on its own positions, manifested its refusal to join in the common effort. Paradoxically, it may have itself introduced «politics» where «politics» did not exist.

In those days there were forty-one school boards on the island of Montreal. The Parent Commission wanted to put some order into this multiplicity, and to rationalize the structure. Accordingly, it recommended that the school boards be grouped into seven «unified» school boards — comprising schools which, depending on enrolment, could be Catholic, Protestant (or, even, non confessional) and French or English. This slicing up of school boards would have been done strictly on a territorial basis.

Already in 1966-67, in the course of the Superior Council of Education's hearings on the recommendations of the Rapport Parent, almost all the organizations representing the anglophone community[2] came out against the «unified» school boards. The anglophones were in the majority on the Protestant boards and they could see no advantage in disturbing the status quo.

In 1968, the Government of Quebec set up a «Comité de restructuration scolaire» to study the special problem of the island of Montreal. This committee tried to skirt the issue by proposing the creation of language commissions, nine of which were to be French and four English. The idea of deconfessionalization was resisted in both the francophone and the anglophone camps. Nevertheless, in 1969, the Union Nationale government tabled Bill 62 which reintroduced the concept of unified school boards. Opposition to this Bill persisted until the party was defeated in April 1970. The next government took up, with Bill 28, where the previous one had left off, proposing again «unified» boards. Opposition being fierce and politically explosive, the Liberals abandoned their plan in July 1972, opting instead for a step-by-step solution to the problem. With Law 71, they set up a school council for the island of Montreal, and it was left to that council to decide what kind of reorganization was needed. In the meantime, the idea was to reduce the school boards to eight, six Catholic and two Protestant.

Over a span of six years (1966 to 1972), a problem which had started out as an organizational one became a highly political one. It had become, literally, a «power struggle».[3]

The defence strategy adopted by Montreal's anglophone community was in no way surprising. Their community was the strongest, and the status quo played in their favour. There were no new worlds to conquer (an exception to the general rule regarding minorities); and the school situation in Montreal provided just one more illustration of the power which the anglophone community wielded in Quebec's economic heartland.

Some Statistics

Let us now review the principal aspects of this special situation which prevailed before the committee on school board restructuration began its work.

The 1971 federal census showed that 17 per cent of the population of the island of Montreal was of British origin. But 23,7 per cent of that same population claimed English as their mother tongue, and 27,4 per cent claimed English as the language they generally used. The census also showed that 59 per cent of the island's population was of French origin and 61,2 per cent claimed French as their mother tongue and the language they commonly used. Even though the study of language transfers has revealed a number of subtle nuances — which to a certain degree cancel each other out — it remains quite clear that the anglophone group benefited the most from integration of «other» groups. Indeed, it was these groups which permitted the anglophones to increase their demographic weight.

It has been amply shown that the «others» who opt for English do so primarily — and naturally — with an eye to climbing the social and economic ladder. After all, the facts are there, and difficult to misinterpret. In 1971, anglophones were in the majority in the eleven municipalities with the highest average incomes; and in eight of these, English was used by over 80 per cent of the population. While recent studies showed that income discrepancies between francophones and anglophones in the Montreal region have tended to diminish,[4] impressions, particularly those of new arrivals, remain unchanged. Population concentrations contribute, to a great extent, to the persistence of these perceptions.

The demographic and economic weight of the island's anglophone community had repercussions on the school structure. While English was the natural or adopted language of 27,4 per cent of the population of the island — 10 per cent more than the British-origin group alone — this rate of attraction was increased by the linguistic duality of the school system. In 1971, 37,1 per cent of the island's school population attended schools in the English system, and projections showed that this number would keep rising. In 1975, the remarkable table which follows was published by the Comité de restructuration.

TABLE I — **Changes in the School Populations in Francophone and Anglophone Sectors, Montreal Island School Boards**

Sectors	Years						
	1971	1972	1973	1974	1975	1980	1985
Francophone	62,9%	62,1%	60,9%	59,7%	59,0%	57,3%	56,6%
Anglophone	37,1%	37,9%	39,1%	40,3%	41,0%	42,7%	43,4%

Source: *J.-P. Proulx, La restructuration scolaire de l'île de Montréal — Problématique et hypothèses de solution,* Conseil scolaire de l'île de Montréal.

The proportion of francophones for the years of actual, as opposed to estimated, enrolment corresponds rigorously to the number of French mother-tongue pupils; which means that almost all the «others» registered in English schools.

Furthermore, the demographic weight of the «other» group was constantly increasing, and according to projections, numbers in the two systems would fairly soon be equal. The existing system had served the anglophone minority well, which explains its dislike of the changes proposed in the Rapport Parent, and in legislation introduced between 1968 and 1972.

In October 1974, the Comité de restructuration scolaire de l'île de Montréal resumed its work after being delayed by a number of technical problems. At this point, the passive resistance became active. Three months previously, the National Assembly of Quebec had passed the now famous Bill 22. This legislation made French the official language of Quebec and, for the first time, imposed a type of coercion to redress the massive language transfers which had been taking place in the schools. For months, heated debate raged between the predominantly anglophone supporters of «freedom of choice in the language of instruction» and the nationalist elements which, at a minimum wanted to see all neo-Quebecers in French schools. The Bourassa government finally decided that pupils who lacked sufficient knowledge of the language of instruction would be refused access to English schools. To implement this ambiguous piece of legislation, the government opted for a system of language tests. Pupils would be tested by the school boards themselves, which had to organize themselves accordingly.

In the summer of 1974, Law 22 was studied in parliamentary commission. There, Montreal's two anglophone-majority school boards, the Protestant School Board of Greater Montreal (PSBGM) and the Lakeshore School Board, mounted fierce, public, opposition. The PSBGM was the stronger of the two, and during the next school year, it refused to participate in the development of the tests, which tests it subsequently boycotted; it also joined the Lakeshore Board in actively contesting the constitutionality of Law 22 before the courts.

Consequently, at the very moment when the Comité de restructuration scolaire de l'île de Montréal was undertaking the essential part of its research and deliberations, the anglophone community's battle against Law 22 was at its peak. The committee found itself having to deal, on the one hand, with the bitter anglophones and, on the other hand, with the dissatisfied nationalist elements who saw Law 22 as merely a half-measure. The political discontent of those few months can be measured better when we remember that the committee's final report was submitted on November 1, 1976. Fifteen days later, a party dedicated to independence would be elected to power. Political polarization was at its extreme.

Law 22 posed a threat to the vitality of the English language educational system; that is, its attractiveness for neo-Quebecers. The authorities were now determined to fight any additional erosion of the system which had always served them so well.

The most relevant statistics from that period show that on September 30, 1975, there were 334 419 pupils enrolled in the primary and secondary schools on

284

the island of Montreal. Of these, 137 058 — or 41 per cent — went to English schools. Almost half of the latter (67 760) fell under the jurisdiction of the Protestant boards, where they were in a solid majority. English-speaking Catholics were more dispersed in the francophone-majority school boards, yet the Anglo-Catholic sector of the Montreal Catholic School Commission (CECM), 40 344 pupils strong, operated under an administration that was relatively autonomous.

The table which follows gives a breakdown of enrolments for both systems by school board. Here, we get a good picture of how concentrated the anglophones were. Thanks to that concentration, they had ample room for manoeuvre, despite the fact that they were a minority on the island.

TABLE II — **Population of School Boards, Island of Montreal, September 30, 1975**

Catholic Boards	French Sector	English Sector
Jérôme-Le-Royer	22 933	7 625
CECM	133 601	40 344
Sainte-Croix	8 150	3 367
Verdun	8 338	1 872
Sault Saint-Louis	12 860	6 395
Baldwin-Cartier	9 872	9 695
Protestant Boards		
PSBGM	1 607	50 786
Lakeshore	—	16 974

Source: *J.-P. Proulx, La restructuration scolaire de l'île de Montréal — Problématique et hypothèses de solution* (Conseil scolaire de l'île de Montréal, September 1976): 325.

The Lakeshore School Board, then, is homogeneously anglophone, while the PSBGM is almost entirely anglophone. At Baldwin-Cartier, anglophones and francophones are equal in number, while at the CECM the anglophones are assured a special status by virtue of their numbers. Slightly more than 19 000 pupils out of a total of 137 000, or only 14 per cent of the total anglophone school population, are in a genuine minority situation.

It would have been a matter of simple logic for the anglophone community to try to consolidate its relatively autonomous position by insisting that the Comité de restructuration divide school boards according to language; but in view of the political situation of the time, spokesmen of the anglophone community saw the language legislation as a threat to their very existence and, as a result, they generally preferred to fall back on the old reliable status quo.

Their analysis was founded on the schooling guarantees embodied in the Canadian Constitution; these were founded not on *language* but on *confessionality*. It is a fact that any Catholic or Protestant minority may withdraw from the jurisdiction of a so-called «common» school board and administer its own schools.

The Comité de restructuration scolaire attempted to find out whether, regardless of the right of confessional minorities to dissent, it was constitutionally permissible for the government of a province to change school territories and types of school boards. However, legal opinions on the subject were divided. Nevertheless, it remained quite obvious that for anglophones, be they Catholic or Protestant, constitutional protection was much more certain on religious grounds than on language grounds. Religion, which for so long had been the custodian of language among francophones outside Quebec, was now assuming the same function in Montreal.

Restructuring: Public Debate

The Comité de restructuration held public hearings in May and June 1975, and the anglophone groups made no secret of their highly pragmatic view of things. During the hearings, the largest Protestant institution, the PSBGM, insisted that schools be structured both on a linguistic and on a confessional basis, with six Franco-Catholic boards, two Anglo- Catholic boards and two Anglo-Protestant boards. In its brief, the PSBGM made it clear that it had been compelled to take this stand because of its concern about Law 22 and the increasing numbers of «separatists». Confessionality, it argued, had proved its effectiveness in protecting the English language. However, five commissioners from the PSBGM dissented: they wanted the school boards to be unified and neutral (their argument being that this would promote «harmony» between the minorities and the majority).

The (Protestant) Lakeshore Board was just as outspoken as the PSBGM; while openly acknowledging that it would have preferred the school boards to be divided according to language, it wanted confessional boards as long as the threat of Law 22 persisted. The Lakeshore Board wanted the status quo maintained until the constitutional conflict over the Official Language Act was permanently settled in court. A number of school committees within the PSBGM and the Lakeshore Board submitted similar briefs to the committee.

The Catholic anglophones took a much harder line. The Anglo-Catholics were part of school boards where the majority was French-speaking, and they received most of the students from other minorities who were integrating into the anglophone community. They wanted separate boards, both confessional and linguistic. Of the forty briefs submitted at the hearings, seven came from this segment: from parents, administrators and even the clergy. A veritable lobby had been organized, thereby creating an impression of numbers — indeed, four of the briefs submitted were identical, give or take a few sentences.

These briefs were, to a great extent, inspired by Montreal's sizeable Irish community, and showed an attachment to confessionality of schools and school structures which was far more direct than in the Protestant camp. When questioned by the members of the committee, however, most of the spokesmen for this group held that if they could not obtain the Anglo-Catholic school boards they sought, they would prefer to join the Protestants in boards divided according to language (i.e., English boards) and try to keep their own schools Catholic. Clearly they wanted to put an end to their co-existence with francophones within Catholic boards.

Of the forty briefs submitted at the hearings, about thirty favoured confessional boards. However, barely six or seven of these saw religion as a fundamental issue, and they were primarily from francophone groups following the stand taken by the Montreal archdiocese.

A number of prestigious francophone groups, such as the CECM itself and the large trade unions, refused to submit any briefs at the 1975 hearings; they claimed they had already made known their position in 1971 when Bill 28 was reviewed in parliamentary commission. Hence, the 1975 hearings in Montreal were largely dominated by the claims of the anglophone community.

Aborted Restructuration

The hearings, then, did anything but clarify aspirations; it was a futile attempt to do the impossible. The seven members of the Comité de restructuration held seventy-eight meetings (including the hearings), and worked for two years. When they finally submitted their report, in November 1976, it was inconclusive. Four members proposed that the school boards be divided along both linguistic and religious lines (Franco-Catholics, Franco-non-confessional, Anglo-Catholics, Anglo-Protestants).

Three of the committee's francophone members dissented, however, and each had a different reason for doing so. Fifteen days later, the Parti Québécois was elected to power. The report became a dead letter.

Nevertheless, between January and May 1977, the Conseil scolaire de l'île de Montréal did study that report in three sittings. It rejected the majority proposal of the Comité de restructuration. In the end — on division and with only a one-vote majority — it resigned itself to recommending that the Quebec government maintain the status quo, with the difference that they made the suggestion that non-confessional schools could be set up within the Catholic or Protestant boards. The restructuring operation was a total failure, and the only reaction from the ministère de l'Éducation was . . . total silence.

Sequels

Bill 101 was assented to in 1977. As far as the language of instruction was concerned, this legislation was far more radical than Law 22. It was intended to set up machinery to systematically block language transfers in the schools. Henceforth, only children already enrolled in English schools and those whose parents had been educated in English in the Province could attend those schools.

It is still too early to assess all the effects of this legislation on enrolments in English schools, but one fact is clear: the anglophone school system has been weakened. Because of the drop in the birth rate, numbers have declined faster than in the francophone system; while with the general francization resulting from Law 101, a great many anglophone parents are enrolling their children in French schools.

Let us now return to Table I. This table shows that in 1975, when the Comité de restructuration was doing its work, the English school system accounted for 41 per cent of the island's school population; this figure was supposed to progress to 42,7 per cent in 1980 and 43,4 per cent in 1985. The most recent statistics on school enrolment — for 1980-81[5] — show that the English system accounted for 37,6 per cent of the island's school population in those years. It had regressed almost to its 1971-72 level.

The actual number of enrolments is steadily decreasing everywhere on the island, but this phenomenon is more noticeable in the English schools than in the French. Between 1979 and 1980, for instance, the francophone system lost 40 800 pupils — 3 per cent of its total — while the anglophone system lost 90 300 or 9,2 per cent. This reversal is most certainly attributable to Law 101, since it first manifested itself the year after the Law was promulgated. Between 1976 and 1977, the French system lost 120 000 pupils compared to 8 000 in the English system.

Demographers attribute this trend mainly to the establishment of *classes d'accueil*, which all neo-Quebec children must now attend, and to voluntary transfers by anglophones to French classes.

The Protestant school boards started out by boycotting enforcement of Law 101 in 1977, but finally resigned themselves to opening their own French *classes d'accueil* in 1978, and their «French sector» is expanding rapidly. While not one French child was enrolled with the Lakeshore Board in 1975, by the time classes opened in September 1980, it had 820. In 1975, there were 1 600 pupils enrolled in French with the Protestant School Board of Greater Montreal. Five years later, that number had risen to 4 000.

The anglophone sectors of the Catholic school boards, especially the CECM, have continued to defy the law and are still admitting «illegal» pupils to their classes — pupils who do not comply with the standards for access to instruction in English. These children, whose parents persist in sending them to English school, today number some 1 500. They come primarily from neo-Quebec families, whereas the voluntary shift to French schools is being made by anglophone families of British origin — especially, it would seem, in the most favoured sectors of Montreal. This behaviour comes of a sense of economic realism given the fact of a French Quebec, and should result in a trickle-down effect among groups which have adopted English as their language of use, precisely because of the economic benefits they would hope to derive.

It is certainly too early to forecast precisely the rate at which Montreal's English school system will decline. (The demographers at the Conseil scolaire say that student population in that system will dip below 70 000 in 1984. In other words, it will have lost half of its pupils in ten years.) Be that as it may, it seems obvious that, as is already manifest in the distribution of anglophone pupils, especially in the francophone-majority school boards, we shall soon have reached a critical threshold from which it will be difficult, highly expensive and, in some cases, totally impossible to provide adequate training and services for English classes.

TABLE III — Total Enrolment for Both Sectors, Montreal Island School Boards, 1980

Catholic Boards	Francophone	Anglophone
Jérôme-Le-Royer	18 008	6 356
CECM	95 595	25 165
Sainte-Croix	6 941	2 170
Verdun	5 802	1 063
Sault Saint-Louis	10 232	4 700
Baldwin-Cartier	11 250	6 961
Protestant Boards		
PSBGM	3 847	33 113
Lakeshore	820	12 322

Source: Pupil enrolment, September 30, 1980. Report to the Conseil scolaire de l'île de Montréal, December 15, 1980.

This explains why, in the autumn of 1981, some of the leaders of the anglophone community, concerned by rumours to the effect that the Minister of Education might be tempted to have another try at «unifying» the school boards, have finally begun to take a serious look at the idea of school restructuration on linguistic bases.

If this idea catches on, Montreal's anglophone community will have finally come to grips with a reality which is hard to acknowledge but which is viable: its minority situation. It would find itself involved in school structures whose main concern would not be to act as a pole of attraction, but rather to guarantee, for those naturally entitled to it — meaning the real anglophones in the region — cultural cohesion and a more homogeneous institutional base. Therein lies the essence of the strength of a minority. Montreal's anglophone community has grasped this a little late — if not too late. Now, in its search for rational school structures which will provide it with the best protection, the community must await the pleasure of a government which has no interest in making haste.

NOTES

(1) Most of the statistics and historical elements in this article were taken from a remarkable work by M. Proulx, sometime executive secretary to the Comité de restructuration scolaire de l'île de Montréal: Jean- Pierre Proulx, *La restructuration scolaire de l'île de Montréal — Problématique et hypothèses de solution*.

(2) *Ibid.*, p. 5.

(3) *Ibid.*, p. 7.

(4) Paul Bernard et al., *L'évolution de la situation socio-économique des francophones et des non-francophones au Québec (1971-78)*.

(5) *Inscription des élèves au 30 septembre 1980*, Report submitted to the Conseil scolaire de l'île de Montréal on December 15, 1980.

Quebec's English Universities Revisited

Jean-Louis Roy

JEAN-LOUIS ROY, publisher of *Le Devoir*, has published widely on social and political change in post-war Quebec. His familiarity with the English university system in Quebec stems from the position he held at the Centre d'études canadiennes françaises at McGill University and his experience as an executive officer of the Fédération des associations de professeurs d'universités du Québec. He has also been a prominent member of the civil liberties movement in Quebec.

Just as we asked all the other contributors to update their articles, so we invited Mr. Jean-Louis Roy to revise his contribution. Mr. Roy preferred to let his article stand as it was written, on the condition that it be explicitly dated. Respecting this wish, we ask the reader to bear in mind that what follows was written in 1979 — before the Referendum — when the present publisher of *Le Devoir* was a professor at McGill University. The editors leave it to the readers to decide the extent to which Mr. Roy's criticisms of the English-speaking academic community are still pertinent.

Existing and yet to come discussions on the status, functions and future of Quebec's English-language universities* should be put in the perspective of three levels of reflection.

For some ten years, a sweeping tide of criticism has been dashing against those seemingly firm, institutional rocks which are the universities of the western world. Now, it is Quebec's turn to assess the significance of its investments in higher education — and to determine whether those investments are profitable. Pleading financial problems, and the need to rationalize and plan everything (from capital expenditures to course content) which contributes to the maintenance and expansion of those institutions of higher learning, the Quebec government is requiring the universities to give a much stricter account of their use of the public funds they receive. When the Green Paper on a Quebec policy for scientific research and the final report of the study committee on the universities are tabled**, the discussions which are sure to follow will lead to more careful planning as regards those activity sectors. Within that context, all of Quebec's universities, French as well as English, will have to re-examine their position in society and within the university system, specify their objectives, and prove the relevance of their institutional choices.

The future of the English universities is one major element of a much broader question: the status of Quebec's anglophone minority.

Early in this decade, a fundamental discussion began within Quebec society. The objective: to break down the false linguistic duality which, until that time, had dominated political and cultural discussions in Quebec. A number of people maintained that ethnic minority rights could no longer be defined on the strength of linguistic duality (French-English). They felt that all the cultures of the different ethnic groups were equal in law, and that this equality was derived from the nature of the various circumstances surrounding their establishment in Quebec. To put the cultures of all these groups on the same level through the use of a single second language was to disrupt the balance of the relationship between the majority and the minorities, and establish a division and an imbalance which no fair assessment of the rights of each of these groups in relation to the others could justify. Hence, the question was asked: considering the differences between the cultural characteristics of the Eskimos, Indians, Jews, Anglo-Saxons and Italians, their history in Quebec, and their respective numbers, who could ever hope to arrange in any kind of order the contributions they have made by their presence here?

* This article was written by a Quebec francophone academic. It is not an in-depth analysis or learned study of Quebec's English universities, but a personal opinion on how the best use can be made of that remarkable group of resources, the English universities of Quebec.

** Editor's note: the report was indeed tabled in April 1979.

The anglophone minority has had to bear the legislative and regulatory consequences of this new awareness. Nor is that all; its secular position has been profoundly altered. In the past, that minority viewed itself, and was viewed, as part of the Anglo-Canadian majority — but living among a minority: the French Canadians of Quebec. This view of things has now been radically changed. Quebec's francophones see themselves as the majority within Quebec. Above and beyond partisan options, this sentiment and this status have become an essential part of political conscience in Quebec. They have led to legislation and regulations which, in recent years, have affected the domains of school and language.

Finally, the outcome of the Canadian constitutional crisis will substantially affect the future of all Quebec's English institutions — and therefore, that of its English universities.

Even though constitutional talks have been going on for more than twelve years, the problems presented by the status and rights of the minorities — both regarding principles and concrete developments — have not yet been solved; and they do not appear to be on the point of being solved. The situation is indeed a difficult one, and there is no political willingness to seek a solution to this major problem facing Canadians. Witness: the recommendations of the Laurendeau-Dunton Commission, on the creation of bilingual districts; the texts prepared at various constitutional conferences; the refusal by the English premiers to look favourably on the Quebec proposal for reciprocity with regard to schooling arrangements; the recent proposal by the Pépin-Robarts Commission that the provinces be fully empowered to develop school and other services able to meet the needs and aspirations of the minorities. All these alternatives have, over the past fifteen years, pointed out that difficulty and that lack of willingness.

This is the context in which questions are being raised about Quebec's English universities — their status, their functions and their future. Also to be considered are the foreseeable effects of Law 101, under which all new Quebecers must enrol their children in the school systems of the francophone majority, and the precise consequences of the English minority's own demographic dynamics. We leave to our specialist colleagues the task of demonstrating up the importance of these matters, while we limit our consideration to the three aspects already mentioned.

First, however, one saliant factor should be insisted on. For almost twenty years now, French-speaking Quebecers have been becoming more self-critical, asking a growing number of questions about their society and their institutions, and searching for new bases and new models for their collective existence and development. The francophone community has been constantly trying to redefine the conditions of its existence, as well as the grounds upon which it hopes to build its relationship with its neighbours and with the international community. A similar process has been notably absent within Quebec's anglophone community.

The anglophone minority has indeed placed itself in a position where its only action is reaction. It has not yet learned how to vigorously and responsibly affirm its status as a true partner in the discussions which preoccupy the majority. It has not yet learned how to define and affirm its existence as a different entity with its own requirements and responsibilities as Quebec's first minority — historically and demographically. The anglophone intellectual community, which consists largely of the English university community, has also failed in one of its essential responsibilities. It has remained apart from the discussions and decisions which have occupied the majority. By so doing, it has isolated Quebec's anglophone minority from the most essential democratic process, to a point here that minority no longer has any identifiable representative within the government or within the Quebec parliament. On many occasions, reference has been made to tthe total absence of anglophones from Quebec's civil service.

It can be said that in the last two decades, Quebec's anglophone minority has not known how to go about affirming itself as a social and political community. It has taken an increasingly negative attitude towards certain elements of the majority and, rather than live up to its responsibilities and cast aside its prejudices in the interests of collaboration, it has chosen to maintain those prejudices.

The attitudes shown by Quebec's anglophone minority led to a paradox: after the War, that minority wanted to see Quebec society modernized; however, as soon as that modernization took place, the same minority began to fear its essential implications. In extreme cases, this withdrawal took the form of profound misunderstanding, and even of constant psychological apprehension.

* * *

How can one explain this failure on the part of Quebec's anglophone academics? Some blame the very make-up of the university system; for instance, they wonder how many members of the staff of these institutions received their first degree from a Quebec — or even a Canadian — university.

Others point to the language barrier — both at the institutional level and at the individual level. They wonder why even today, despite recent, compulsory changes, the public services, administrative staff, and institutional appearance of the English institutions are little influenced by the language of the majority.

Those two factors may provide at least a partial explanation of the gulfs — institutional, and professional — which separate the English intellectual community from its French counterpart.

At another level, the English community has always been assured of its role as a full and powerful part of the Canadian majority, and this doubtless removed some of the urgency from the need to determine precisely its size and strength. Now that this situation has been reversed, it is incumbent on the anglophone minority to undertake this difficult exercise. Otherwise, it is doomed to a struggle — lost before it has even begun — for privileges, «acquired rights», and other realities that are more Victorian than contemporary. Here, again, we are confronted with the failure of Quebec's anglophone academics.

Where are all the potentially serious and useful studies on Quebec's anglophone minority? At a time when that minority is being shaken to its very foundations, we must still speak of it in generalitie, and in some circles, statements about it abound which border on the ridiculous. Is it not the responsibility of that minority's intellectuals to set the facts in their true light? One cannot but come to the conclusion that Quebec's anglophone intellectuals have developped a poor strategy... or have no strategy at all.

The anglophone minority comprises a number of elements: universities, schools, trade unions, businesses, social institutions and volunteer organizations. Had these various elements joined forces, the conditions necessary for a vigorous democratic dialogue with the majority could have been created. Had such been the case, the minority would have emerged in its own and the majority's eyes as an essential component of society as a whole. Of course, this joining of forces would not have been easy: doubtless it would have created its own tensions. But it would have had the inestimable merit of compelling each component of the minority to clarify its own goals and to identify areas where dialogue with the majority was indispensable, areas of potential conflict, and areas where cooperation was possible. This joining of forces and this dialogue never took place.

In the contemporary debate over the future of Quebec society, the anglophone minority is under represented. This is a deplorable situation, both for the minority and for the majority, and the intellectual class (the academics) is largely responsible. The intellectuals remain prisoners of the *laisser-faire* tradition, and have condemned themselves to reacting; and to naive, ineffective protestation. This is to be deplored, and the more so because the issues at stake merit more than an unseemly withdrawal from the field. Some of the minority's traditions, let it not be forgotten, have been at the very heart of Quebec's educational planning since 1963: regional service, the democratization of access to higher education, and decentralization of cultural services.

The situation is to be especially deplored because, in some cases, the research resources of the anglophone minority's universities have been, and still are, superior to those available to the majority.

It is to be deplored further because, at a time when Quebec could have gained much from active participation by the English universities, the human and institutional resources of those universities were not used to their full extent.

Finally, this situation is to be deplored because this self-imposed isolation, this withdrawal on the part of the anglophone academics, deprives the anglophone minority of the chance to clearly comprehend the questions the majority is asking, and that majority's aspirations. The reasons for that withdrawal need to be carefully examined.

* * *

The foregoing comments outline in negative terms what is expected of Quebec's English universities and anglophone academics.

To begin with, one would hope Montreal's McGill University, the largest of these institutions, would tone down its rhetoric. The Sherbrooke Street institution is no longer the only one with an international outlook. All Quebec's universities are involved in international activities. Today, no one institution can invoke international activities to set itself apart from the others, or to ensure itself a special status. In other days, such a status might have corresponded to an objective situation; it no longer does. The same applies to the concept of excellence. Today, excellence is the objective of all Quebec universities, and they all pursue it with equal zeal and tenacity. Besides, what is expected from the universities is self-criticism, not an apologia.

Quebec's English universities like their French counterparts, are 85 per cent financed by public funds. Would that they decide to give priority treatment to that community which, with scrupulous fairness, provides them with considerable resources. In the present situation, such an attitude could mean the pooling of the physical, financial and human resources of two or more institutions of higher learning. It could mean programmes combined or even dropped, and restricted numbers of foreign students admitted. It could mean existing programmes being changed so that their content, at least in part, would prepare students psychologically and socially for a smooth entry into Quebec's private and public institutions. More specifically, we have in mind the training of anglophone students for the Quebec civil service.

We expect Quebec's English universities and academics to criticize firmly the development of Quebec's public institutions and that of Quebec's economic, social and cultural movements. This duty to criticize is one which they share with their French counterparts, and the criticism should be made at the intellectual level, far from any ethnic or partisan considerations. This return to the facts implies a detailed knowledge of Quebec society, an implication which would surely have profound effects on policies concerning the hiring of academic personnel, particularly in the vast field of social sciences. This criticism must be visible, accessible and spoken aloud.

We expect Quebec's English universities and academics to support firmly and consistently the objectively-founded demands of the francophone institutions and of Quebec in general, in those many areas of activity where, for various reasons, Quebec has been badly served — if served at all — by federal policies or the orientations of Canadian federalism. To give but two examples, we are thinking in particular of the Federal government's choice of investments in scientific research and the unanimous wish of francophone Quebecers (reflected by all of Quebec's political parties) to regain control of certain areas of activity — control which over the past quarter of a century has been exercised by the Federal government. This, of course, does not mean that Quebec's anglophone intellectuals need be swept along by the latest constitutional nonsense to come out of Quebec City. Instead, they must become vigorously involved in one of the two great Canadian intellectual discussions: the discussion centred on the conditions for a balanced, operational, democratic relationship between the nations of Canada and Quebec, and the discussion centred on control by Canadians of their financial, commercial and cultural institutions.

It all boils down to this: does Quebec's anglophone community consider itself a fragment of English Canada, or an essential component of Quebec society?

This choice leaves the way open to a vast number of political options. None of the basic alternatives which the coming Referendum will offer is excluded.

If Quebec's anglophone academics were to carry out this necessary reappraisal, they would bring the debate into their own ethnic group, perhaps ensuring the anglophone minority the conditions for a cohesion which it does not now have. They would provide food for public discussion and democratic confrontation within and with the majority (whose complacency and one-sidedness are often at the root of problems). Quebec's anglophone academics would then be exercising their duties as corporate and private citizens, transcending that «wait-and-see» — nay, negative — attitude which they seem to have adopted over the past years.

In undertaking such a reappraisal, Quebec's anglophone academics would finally be acting at a democratic level. In social groups, volunteer movements, political parties, professional and scientific associations, they would no longer count as strangers — misunderstood and inactive — but as full citizens able to bring their own ideas and their own values to collective discussions and decisions. At the same time their institutions would acquire a new credibility and social visibility. These academics would gain power and exercise it — power which would give Quebec's anglophone university institutions a new shape, as institutions forming an integral part of society. They would discover that to be powerful on the outside an organization must be powerful within. Of course, there is a risk that the status who would be disrupted and that relationships within the institutions would be changed. Anglophone and francophone academics might even discover that their interests often coincide.

This is a project that has been hastily put together. Will anyone come forward and breathe life into it? It is a project which presupposes a thorough awareness of those very real transformations which have altered the status of francophones and of anglophones both within Canada and within Quebec. It is a project which presupposes a switch from self-defence to self-criticism.

It seems to me we have a long way to travel — and not much time to get where we're going.

Part VI

THE MEDIA

In a time of rapid change and crisis, it is scarcely surprising that there should be debate and controversy over the role played by the media in the provision of information and the interpretation of events. The English-Quebec media, both printed and electronic, have proved no exception. In recent times, they have been subject to a barrage of criticism coming from all sides, for their sins of omission in failing to report on important events, their complicity in the creation of a common front against the Government of Quebec, their outright partisanry, their quest of sensationalism, their parochialism, their failure to be sufficiently zealous in defence of anglophone interests and of federalism, and so forth. The list of charges is endless, and the immediate victims are the journalists who tread, painfully, the firing-line between the warring parties.

Concern within the profession itself over coverage of the Quebec scene dates back a number of years now. In 1972 the Association of English Media Journalists of Quebec produced a document with the significant title *The English Media in Quebec: A Distorting Mirror of Reality?* (Montreal: Reporter Publications). Back in the late sixties, *The Montreal Star*, in a move to report more effectively and sensitively on Quebec, initiated a policy of employing francophone journalists. When the only English radio station closed down in Quebec City in 1975, CBC moved quickly to take it over and replace what had degenerated into a more or less continuous popular music programming by a radio service integrated into the national network and providing some local news content.

In quantitative terms, the anglophones are well provided for . . . a plethora of radio stations, two television channels and until recently, two daily newspapers in the Montreal area, a well-developed regional press that extends from Abitibi and the Ottawa Valley to the Gaspé coast, and a radio service for outlying communities — the Quebec Community Network — not to mention the proximity, for many, of media originating in the United States or neighbouring provinces. Yet, in spite of this, there are certain major structural problems that find expression in the news and editorial content of the media. David Waters puts his finger on many of these problems, and Arthur Siegel in his communications analysis demonstrates their consequence in terms of content, in newspapers at least. All our media organs appear to be sensitive to the demographic evolution of the anglophone population. Hence, in 1972, the *Quebec Chronicle Telegraph*, serving the Quebec City area and much of Eastern Quebec, shifted from daily to weekly publication. More recently, the *Montreal Star* and *The Gazette*, confronted by a declining readership in the Montreal area, became engaged in a «death struggle» in which, it was claimed — and indeed it came to pass — that only one could survive.

Demographic considerations are, however, of secondary importance compared with the fact that the principal organs of information have been and are still controlled by national interests whose centres of decision are located in Toronto — the Canadian Broadcasting Corporation, Southam (*The Gazette*) and Free Press Publications (the erstwhile *Montreal Star*). Such a reality of power inevitably leads to a perspective on events that is strongly coloured by preoccupations with national unity and the promotion of continental interests. It also creates a situation where management, and even journalists, are drawn from outside Quebec. The reporting of events by such people — frequently linguistically incompetent, and with loyalties and interests that are viewed as being dialectically opposed to those of Quebec — suffers accordingly. Parochial concerns and matters that are seen as affecting the interests and future of Anglo-Quebecers as an integral part and extension of English Canada get highlighted, and other matters get overlooked, notably in the social realm. Thus, the English Quebecers largely ignored the social and medical reforms when they were initiated through Law 65 under a Liberal government, as they almost completely overlooked the activities of the Conseil du statut de la femme (and, in particular, the publication of *Les Québécoises: égalité et indépendance*) or, until very recently, the actions undertaken by the authorized organ of that other official minority, the Fédération des francophones hors Québec. The attention recently accorded to the Jean Commission report on adult education by *The Gazette* is perhaps indicative of a new interest in the total situation in Quebec.

For the Anglo-Quebec journalists, close witnesses to events in Quebec and themselves part of Quebec, the conjuncture is a painful one, as David Thomas testifies. For them, the media and certain extraneous events serve to mobilize people along linguistic lines and to give them «what they want» with respect to information. Presided over by an ownership and management that is patently alien, they see themselves as sandwiched between the two forces. Treated with suspicion and with little chance of promotion to positions of importance in the local media, they find themselves unable to furnish an accurate coverage of important events in Quebec and thus give anglophones what they believe is needed to permit them to judge these events more objectively. At the same time, because of the interpretation of events furnished by the media, these same journalists are often treated by the government as being its unofficial opposition.

For Anglo-Quebec journalists, the solution in the short run is to leave the Quebec-based media and report for English-Canadian media elsewhere on events in Quebec. Because these other media already treat Quebec as something of a foreign country, they feel they have more liberty in reporting and in analysis. Hence, it is non-Quebecers who become the principal beneficiaries of their insights, while the Anglo-Quebecer himself, until recently, often had to turn to the *Toronto Globe and Mail* for competent reporting and in-depth analysis of the Quebec scene!

The English Media and the New Quebec

David Waters

DAVID WATERS. Born in Montreal, David Waters is very familiar with the English-language mass media in Quebec, having worked for the Canadian Broadcasting Corporation, *The Montreal Star* and *The Gazette*. In addition to being elected member of the Quebec Press Council, he was one of the founders of the «Media Conferences». Presently an executive producer with CBC English network in Quebec, he is engaged in originating and establishing programmes designed to assess and analyse Quebec issues.

In 1970, not too long after the October Crisis, the Senate published its findings on the Canadian media, and on page 85 of volume one, it quoted the editor-in-chief of the *Montreal Star*, Frank Walker, as follows:

> We try as a conscious editorial policy to take the surprise out of living[...] the shock value out of things that happen[...] we discuss a trend or predict an event or a change in attitude and by putting that into the paper early enough, stop this constant bump you get by being surprised almost every day.

Few people — certainly I do not — dispute Frank Walker's intentions as a journalist; but many journalists — and I am one of them — maintain that on most vital Quebec questions, both the now defunct *Montreal Star* and the other mainstream media outlets in Quebec failed throughout most of the sixties and seventies to prepare their audiences adequately for the changes that were taking place. Rather than take the «bump» out of living, the mainstream English media frequently made it more difficult for its audience to recognize those bumps and adjust to them.

In making that claim, I am, of course, in part criticizing myself, because I have been an integral part of that mainstream media for more than a decade; but as I hope to show in this essay, the problems facing the media in Quebec go far beyond the individuals involved and are far more serious. Moreover, the present inability to cope with them further complicates the role of the English in Quebec and makes further «bumps» in our collective right all that more likely.

Many of those bumps, of course, have to do with the respective roles and behaviours of the two major linguistic communities in Montreal. During the sixties and seventies, they began to rub up against each other in disturbing ways, and much of the friction was accentuated by ignorance — an ignorance that too often had the media as untutored midwife and arrogant nursemaid.

To explore how and why that was so, one must first put into perspective the fundamental nature of the problem facing the two linguistic communities as the third quarter of this century got under way. At its outset, the two communities appeared to be comfortably settled into their respective isolations. The War and the conscription crisis had begun to recede into the past, and the deal between Duplessis and the English corporate establishment seemed to be working. The isolation of the French community in the last decade of Duplessis was still ensured by that insular fortress of culture and religiosity — the Catholic Church of Quebec — that continued to disdain the modern alliance between utilitarian Protestantism and money-making. The isolation of the English community was fortified by a society that believed science, Latin and a knowledge of British poets were mandatory accomplishments, but that involvement in Quebec politics and an ability to speak French were not.

In such an atmosphere, the English community and its leaders could pursue their business and other colonial interests, and could take under their wing the European additions to their society without challenge or interference. All the two communities needed in times of stress were a few of its members to be sufficiently knowledgeable in the language and ways of the other collectivity to act as bridges of communication and resolution. Certainly, in terms of the English community, those members were rarely its most powerful or influential. Ambassadors of understanding rarely are.

Then, in the sixties, changes in the fundamental isolation of the French collectivity began to manifest themselves to all but the most blind observer. Seeing them is one thing: understanding their significance is another.

Very rapidly, the protective membrane of a cultural and religious nationalism which looked backward to a pastoral golden age broke down. The lure of North-American production and consumption, of the new and glittering post-war empire of the west was too strong. French Canada broke out of its isolation with a pent-up energy that was both applauded and feared, and that was often both assertive and fearful at the same time.

It was assertive in that it was expanding outwards to involve itself in areas that were previously the preserve of others. It arose fear because that expansion outwards into areas of English and American hegemony undermined the old protective barriers and increased the dangers of both the anglicization of the language and a concomitant Americanization of morals and culture. That prospect threatened the *French* character of the Province, a character which had been so carefully nurtured by every generation since the time of New France.

Change too was happening to the English-speaking Quebec community — but with a significant difference. It was not questioning its role in Quebec's evolution, but rather, the nature of its allegiance to other English-speaking centres of culture.

Prior to, and during the war years, its empathy with and loyalty to England and the British Empire were clear: but increasingly, the additions to the anglophone community were from non-British, European stock, peoples, whose children in particular had a natural inclination as North-Americans to look southward to the United States as the pace-setter for their values and aspirations. Concomitantly, as the post-war expansion of higher education gathered steam, English Quebec's institutions increasingly reached southward for their brains trust rather than across the ocean as they had in the past.

Even more important, the coming of television — that glorious gift to the mundane but a bane to the rational intellect — made it clear that English-speaking Quebecers were about to spend more time gaping enviously at the American imagination than at any indigenous exploration of their role in Quebec society.

Even amongst the English business élite — those cautious, conservative erstwhile managers of imperial capital — there was the inevitable awareness of the withdrawal of «Threadneedle St.» from the action and its replacement by the new money-men of «Wall St.».

In this turmoil of change of allegiance, both emotional and financial, the cacophony of change emanating from the French community appeared only as an additional and unwanted harassment. In that sense, the Quiet Revolution may have had its tempestuous moments, but for the most part, it was seen as being of primary significance only to the French community, and perhaps to those few in the English community upon whom some of its aspects directly impinged.

Few in the English population saw a new potential role energing for their community as a protective and essential bilingual buffer zone: on the one hand, sensitive to the francophone community's fears of anglicization as Quebec became increasingly North American in style and activity; and on the other, capable of persuading the expanding financial and industrial inroads of English North America to make the necessary language adaptations to Quebec before harsh and unpleasant steps became necessary. Had the English community taken up that role, Laws 22 and 101 might never have been seen as necessary; but the English community remained indifferent to francophone linguistic concerns, and facilitated instead the continuous anglicization of the growing industrialization of Quebec. To many in the French community, the English in Quebec began to be seen as the insensitive front line of the anglicization they feared. The two linguistic communities were on a potential collision course.

Throughout this period, the English community continued to graduate students from its expanding school system unable, for the most part, to function in the language of the majority of Quebecers.

* * *

In that context, how was the English community to understand what was happening in French Quebec? Unable by and large to read the French press or listen to French broadcasting, it was unusually dependent on what the English media chose to bring to its attention.

How did the mainstream English media report and reflect upon those changes? In brief, the latter misunderstood the French community's uneasiness. They highlghted instead its aggressive assertiveness, implicity tried to slow down the nature of the change, and, overall, defended unceasingly the attitudes and interests of its non-francophone but often francophobic audience. There were, of course, notable examples and periods of exception to that rule, but in looking back, it is clear now that they were just that — exceptions to the general thrust of the role played by the Englsh media.

That role was not one that was primarily imposed by the owners, or by the «establishment», upon media that wished to behave otherwise: on the contrary, it flowed to a much greater extent from the internal media realities that are a result of the mainstream media's relationship to its public.

In examining that relationship and its related media constraints, it may be useful to identify a number of the underlying maxims which have applied in the past, and which continue to apply today, in a way that exacerbates, rather than resolves, the problems facing the English-speaking community and its media.

To begin with, any mainstream English media outlet in Quebec feels implicitly threatened if its public is not comfortable or happy with the product it markets.

The reasons are simple enough. An English newspaper revenues in Quebec are dependent upon a circulation and advertising base that is potentially limited to less than half that of other metropolitan North American cities of equivalent size. The *Toronto Star*, for example, because it is operating in a one language town, has a larger circulation than had the *Montreal Star* and *Gazette* combined. Yet, journalism in Quebec is probably more expensive than in places of comparable population and significance because one is reporting about two linguistic societies without the advantage of their combined circulation potential. Moreover, since there is no demonstrable relationship between the size of circulation and the *quality* of reporting about the «other» community, the result is a media management that is highly sensitive, not so much to the quality of such journalism, but to whether the audience reacts favourably to the overall impact of the product it is marketing. How does the public determine the degree of its satisfaction with a media product? In my experience, the following usually applies.

Readers, listeners or viewers tend to be happy with the media when, first, events *appear* to be reported objectively (that is without upsetting «alien» bias), and second, their interests and attitudes are adequately defended and reflected by it.

The above is particularly true when the area of news bears down on the conflicting interests or concerns of the differing linguistic communities. During the last two decades, English media managers learned only too well that to report on what was happening in the French community with understanding or empathy was not popular with readers, listeners or viewers because it suggested trends which most of them did not want to see happen.

For a brief period in the late sixties, the *Montreal Star* actively pursued the goal of improving its coverage of what was happening in the French community.

312

Among other things, it hired a handful of journalists whose background was not only French, but who had extensive experience in the French media. Their work soon added pith, perception and tone to the *Star*'s reflection of Quebec, but such shifts in tone and perspective were far from universally applauded.

It may have been well received at first by the few editors who urged it, and by the growing corps of young reporters who reflected the more open and aggressive journalistic attitudes of the campus revolts of the sixties, but there were other members of the staff at all levels who felt uncomfortable with the changes for a number of reasons. For some, one of the reasons may well have been a lack of familiarity with French — a reality which was fairly widespread at those levels of the newsroom not required to go out and cover events at first hand. A similar feeling of uneasiness with the change in tone in covering Quebec news began to filter back from the paper's traditional constituency. As Quebec headed into the October Crisis, a sense of backlash began not only to be felt but to be heeded. With the arrival of the Crisis itself, any enthusiasm for an explorative, questioning, «let's look at the other side» kind of journalism faded. By the time November 15th arrived, the *Star*, like the backlash it heeded, had its editorial head sufficiently buried in the sand that it too experienced «bumps» in the night for which it, like its readers, was ill-prepared.

An equally illustrative example can be given from the recent history of mainstream English television in Quebec. The local CBC station (CBMT), in the late sixties, began to hire journalists who felt that better coverage of what was happening in the French community was mandatory, and that moreover, Quebec coverage meant coverage from the perspective of the overall Quebec society and not just from that of the more limited interests and concerns of the English community. On the other hand, CFCF (the local commercial affiliate of CTV) appeared to pursue a policy of identification with and «service» to its target audience. It was hardly coincidental that around the time of Bill 22, CBMT aired an exhaustive series explaining the social and political realities surrounding the language problem, while CFCF's radio outlet, not too long after, spearheaded a campaign to garner the signatures of all those who were opposed to the Bill. Nor was it probably coincidental that during the period of such divergent approaches to Quebec coverage, the ratings of CBMT programmes plummetted while those of CFCF grew steadily. At one point, CFCF's *Pulse* newshour drew more than a quarter of a million viewers, while *City at Six* drew less than a hundred thousand. Needless to say, no commercial media outlet could have tolerated CCBMT's drop in ratings and the consequent loss in revenues from advertising rates for even the briefest period.

There are, of course, many reasons for such viewing patterns other than the different approaches to covering Quebec affairs, but any analysis of causes always comes back to a simple fundamental conclusion: in ratings or circulation, the name of the game is to identify with your public, find out what they want and meet their expectations. Survival for the mainstream private media requires that they not only heed, but court their public's approbation.

It is a situation which sets the stage for hucksterish managerial decisions, and it fosters a management that is uncomfortable with the journalistic messengers that make their target audience unhappy. Unfortunately, journalism at its most meaningful has nothing to do with popularity: on the contrary, it is often about information which may be unpopular for a variety of reasons.

* * *

A fundamental principle of most North-American journalism must be understood here if one is to grasp the impact of the English media in Quebec during the critical last two decades. That principle has to do with «news as voyeurism», rather than «news as uneasy truth». It is important to realize that most of the information funneled through any mainstream media outlet does not confront or challenge the vast majority of readers or viewers in a direct or personal way. Understandably, most of the information is about «others», «elsewhere».

Whether such information is about Vietnam or Iran, Europe or the United States, Western Canada or the Maritimes, news reports are tailored for such a broad audience that implications for any specific group is necessarily absent. Hence few of us feel implicated in such events, and because few of us know much about such events anyway, we not only have little capacity to judge the possible inadequacy of such reports, but are, in most cases, little more than passive spectators whose interest is held by media techniques little different from those of a sidewalk barker giving us a voyeuristic glimpse of other people's troubles. That is as true of the Cronkite news «show» as it is about most newspaper front pages. Part of the result is that we tend to define «true» news coverages as «interesting» and «not boring», as about «others» and not «me», and as «troubling to others» and «not troubling to me».

Such techniques and definitions are hard to apply to vital Quebec news, since it often poses problems for the group to which the reader or viewer belongs. Moreover, it often exposes conflicts which involve us all directly. To report fully and fairly is often to bore the «customer» (who feels he knows a lot already) in ways that the limited chunks of international news never do. Moreover, the Quebecer tends to believe he knows enough about local matters to conclude that there is unacceptable bias in any report which does not accurately reflect his pre-conceived sense of reality.

In Quebec matters, there is an additional aspect that is even more troubling. About many issues the public is already partisan, and in such cases the media for many people is seen more as a vehicle of persuasion than of information. The anglophone businessman is less interested in seeing in a newspaper what French-language lobbyists are demanding than he is in seeing that the public is persuaded that those demands are unwarranted and should be resisted. Undoubtedly the reverse is equally true.

Fortunately, or unfortunately, as the case may be, the media rarely works as a vehicle of persuasion the way people want them to. More often than not, they only appear as persuasive to the already converted, and only produce paranoia and hostility in those who do not share such a point of view. Any journalist who has worked the local scene knows only too well how easily oil is added to the ever present embers of suspicion and alienation.

When one is dealing with Quebec events in particular, there are few readers or viewers who do not have a vested interest in the reality that is being reported. Such interests might be adequately satisfied if a media outlet were able to mirror all important events and all pertinent points of view. Unfortunately, a media outlet is not a mirror: rather, it is a selector and censor which decides what does not get reported, as well as what goes on the front page and what goes on the back page. As to what does not get reported, it is important to remember that the amount of news in a newscast, or in a newspaper, has little correlation with the amount of news that is out there to report about. A half-hour newscast is a half-hour newscast, day in and day out, regardless of the expansion or contraction of news events in the real world. A Montreal newspaper is bigger on a Wednesday than it is on a Tuesday or a Thursday because there are more ads on a Wednesday. The number of ads and the number of copies printed determines the amount of news carried, and the size of staff a paper feels it can afford. That is the inescapable logic of a society that wants to pay as little as possible for the information it receives. Those limitations can have, and have had, a pernicious effect. . . particularly for the English media and the community they serve in Quebec.

There are few media newsrooms in Quebec, for example, that can afford to have more than one experienced reporter in any specialized field. What happens as a result when, for instance, the French teachers' union is meeting at the same time as the Protestant School Board of Greater Montreal? Any comparison of the French and English media makes it clear that the range of events in either community gets a more limited exposure in the other community's press.

Even where a newsroom is rich enough in staff to avoid having to make such harsh choices about what to ignore of importance that may be taking place in the other linguistic community, the importance accorded to that type of news in relation to other news, and the slant that is often given to it, can be equally troubling.

In general, the mainstream English media in Quebec during the last two decades placed a very low premium on non-political news about the French-

Quebec community except, of course, where such news had disturbing implications for the English community.

* * *

The reasons for this are not limited to the factors already mentioned, that is the internal restraints of limited news space and staff, the external constraints of a limited market, and the need to heed the expectations of that market. There has always been the additional factor that in English language editorial rooms in Quebec there has been a surprising number of people in decision making roles who could not function in French and who were suspicious about the changes taking place in Quebec. Consequently, they tended to downplay the significance or value of what was happening in French Quebec.

Some of the reasons for the lack of facility in French in our newsrooms may be understandable enough. A media outlet here handles more news which comes from outside Quebec in the Province about events elsewhere, than that which is generated in the Province here. One does not need to be bilingual to sift and edit copy about Europe, The United States, Africa or the Middle East. In the fifties or sixties, a «Brit» off the boat who had experience in Fleet St. may have seemed a better bet to handle such copy than someone who was a native Quebecer. In the field of television, anyone with BBC or American media experience was on the same pedestal as was a graduate of an American Ivy League university with regard to our educational institutions.

In the last ten years, the ownership of the major English print media in Quebec passed into the hands of chains controlled outside the Province. In broadcasting, outlets are either owned or controlled in Toronto, or are heavily influenced by the fact that Toronto is the dominant broadcasting centre for both news and entertainment. Both CTV and CBC's main newsrooms are located there. It is hardly surprising, therefore, that many of the media managers of the English-Quebec media come from elsewhere and bring to their roles here the practices, policies and attitudes acquired from their experience outside Quebec.

One result is to increase within the mainstream news organizations here a predisposition to see Quebec news as «provincial», and to suspect that the trends in Quebec since the Quiet Revolution are fundamentally wrong. Such newsmen would prefer to rivet their attention on realities at the heart of English Canada, or on patterns and events occurring south of the border.

Nowhere is this tendency more visible than in the «non- political» fields of culture and sports. In these areas, the television medium is the most blatant example. Local production is less important than network production controlled in

Toronto, and both play second fiddle to programmes and events emanating from the United States. The media Americanization of our lives, of course, may be beyond the power of media managers to resist even if they wanted to. It is not because American media reality is any better per se, or even because the public hungers for it that Americanization is taking place: it is a matter of money as well. Ann Landers is not necessarily more gifted at giving moral and social advice to Montrealers than would be an equivalent Canadian or Quebec columnist, but her column can be purchased at a fraction of the cost of paying someone local to do the same job.

Yet, even in areas of cost where media managers have choices, the lines of least resistance which all lead to the centre of the American empire tend to be followed. The *Gazette*, for example, once had a TV critic who focused most of her columns on Canadian television, both French and English. When the choice had to be made to replace her, it was with an American style gossip columnist who fuelled an English-Quebec impression that the only fascinating people in town are the American film stars who pass through it and the local hucksters who dance attendance upon them.

There is more to Montreal and Quebec, of course, than those who fly here because of our film production tax haven and while here, go dance at Regine's; and there is more to Montreal and Quebec than the American programmes that are increasingly our cultural sustenance, or the syndicated columns and articles that occupy so much space in our newspapers. While it is true that, imposed upon that mix, the politics of Quebec still gets considerable play in our media, it is equally true that much of the underlying thrust of Quebec politics may well be misunderstood if so much of the surrounding ambiance of French life here goes unreported.

English Montrealers may well assume, for example, that an explosion of film-making is occurring here. They may be aware that federally-created tax shelters have stimulated investments in English-language films designed for the American market. They may not be aware of the fact that such policies have made it more difficult to find financial support for French-language films; as a result, productions like «Mon Oncle Antoine» may be a thing of the past, and, in consequence there is a growing discontent in Quebec cinema circles. When, and if, it becomes another political thorn in the sovereignty-federalist struggle, will it come as yet another «bump» to English Quebecers?

* * *

In looking back upon the recent history of French Quebec affairs, one is struck by the number of Quebec figures who, by and large, have only been reported in the English media when they have done or said something which impinges negatively upon the English community's sensibilities. It is as if such people, or the groups they often represent, did not have an existence apart from their relationship to the English community's interests or concerns. There are times, of course, when the English media have made efforts to correct that imbalance, but such efforts were sporadic, and perhaps understandably so, given the many factors mentioned above.

In my view, the amalgam of such factors produces a peculiar English media ambiance to coverage of Quebec affairs: a way of looking at and covering events that is sharply divergent in tone and approach to that of Quebec's French media. In many ways, of course, the French media's tone and approach is often excessively Quebec oriented and empathetic, precisely because it is not logistically and spiritually connected into the journalistic umbilical cord of Toronto and the United States.

But it is the English media's ambiance that I am concerned with here because of the impact it has had on English Quebec attitudes over the last two decades.

The problem of ambiance, of slant, of emphasis, of focus, of selection because of limited space, of what one believes to be true, all are the heart of adequate or inadequate public journalism. Moreover, it is not just some of the «facts» or even all of the «facts», but the *way* in which facts are reported that is crucial to effective journalism. It is decisions in these areas, if anywhere, which affect a community's sensibilites and potential harmony to the reality around them.

Here are a few pertinent examples of decisions about coverage of the Quebec reality during the last decade which may well have affected political and linguistic attitudes.

I personally remember well a meeting at the beginning of the decade with Dr. Denis Gendron who headed the Gendron Commission investigation into the status of the French language in Quebec. He had just made public the Commission's report and he stressed to a few of us his fears that the English media, for which we worked, would emphasize what it liked in the report and not what he felt was its essential message and warning. He acknowledged that he was not calling for protective language legislation immediately, but he argued that his findings showed that if rapid and substantial change did not occur in the language of the marketplace, then harsh and restrictive legislation would be inevitable within a matter of years. Change, he pleaded, could occur without legislation only if the English community understood the urgency of the situation.

In scanning the English media coverage at the time, I could only conclude that Dr. Gendron must have been disappointed in it. What was emphasized was the fact that his report concluded that legislation was not necessary at that stage, and although the other aspects of the report were included in the news coverage, the approach did not convey the desperation nor the urgency that the commissioners had come to feel.

Of course the English Quebec media must make its own decisions about what is newsworthy, and about what is more important or less important in any given news event, but the incident I have just presented illustrates a fundamental variance between the perceptions of the two major linguistic communities. The English media, like the community it serves, had, for the most part, refused to accept the thesis that the French language and culture in Quebec were endangered in this part of North America. The Gendron Commission did, as did most of the educated leaders of French Quebec. How one viewed that situation was often a determinant factor in «the way» in which news events in that area were journalistically handled. By consistently viewing and reporting such news from an essentially English perspective and interpretation, the media indirectly encouraged the English community to march to a different drummer than that of the French community in their interpretations of Quebec reality.

The issue here is not whose perceptions were right and whose were wrong. The situation is obviously far too complex for such simplistic conclusions to be more than departure points in a discussion about what changes may or may not be needed to work out a societal problem. Unfortunately, throughout most of the last decade, such different interpretations were not seen as grounds for serious discussions and negotiations; but instead, they grew into entrenched positions allowing only a little room for bargaining and a wide open field for bitter confrontation.

Another significant example was the *Montreal Star's* handling of the 1973 press conference of the Parti Québécois at which the party presented its hypothetical «budget for year one of an independent Quebec» should the party win the election which was then underway. During an election campaign, a pronouncement by a major political party is usually reported in a straightforward fashion, and the rebuttals of the other parties are either reported subsequently or are run alongside it. In this case, the *Montreal Star* led its report with a critique by the head of Bell Canada. That company no doubt had a vested interest in the electoral result and in what the public might think of the proposals of the Parti Québécois, but Bell Canada obviously was not a registered party in the electoral campaign, and why its reaction to the budget proposal should be the lead news, rather than the proposed budget itself, is difficult to explain by journalistic standards. This point was raised by René Lévesque in a letter that he wrote at the time to the *Star*, arguing that fair play had not applied.

That kind of journalistic treatment is usually reserved for groups or ideas whose views editors consider so reprehensible that every effort is made to ensure that any reporting about them does not automatically bestow upon them some form of public legitimacy or respectability. Very few in the English media would have viewed the Parti Québécois in quite those terms.

However, there were clearly some non-journalistic attitudes and perceptions about this relatively new political formation that the English media tended to foster, not only through its editorials and commentaries, but also through the slant of its news coverage. One was that beneath the party's democratic surface, there lurked non-democratic forces waiting to seize power at an appropriate moment. Another was that the main thrust of the new party was not, as it claimed, a positive concern with the future of the Quebec people; but on the contrary, a negative desire to punish and restrict the English for imagined grievances and dangers, and to bring about the downfall of the country.

Unconsciously, at the very least, there was throughout most of this past decade a desire on the part of most of the editors of the English media to question the legitimacy and respectability of what the Parti Québécois represented. For some of them, even if the movement could not be viewed as «downright traitorous», there existed the feeling that beneath it all something very akin to that was involved.

* * *

Such views were no doubt held by a substantial number of people in the English community as well. For them, as for their counterparts in the English media, the electoral results of November 15th, 1976 came as a traumatic shock. How could a wide-based «informed» electorate possibly support something which had such questionable motives and substance? For someone who was poorly informed about the French community, the shock of November 15th may have been understandable: for a journalist with more than superficial political experience or competence, it should not have been — as it probably was not for those who covered the campaign in the field rather than directed it from the confines of editorial offices where comfortable and comforting presumptions can more easily prevail.

The shock of November 15th should have caused a re-evaluation of the quality and adequacy of the information presented in the English media about what was happening in Quebec. In my opinion, that has not happened. On the contrary, if one examines the English media's coverage of events which have taken place since — from Premier Lévesque's speech to the Economic Club in New York, through the Law 101 hearings and the «flights of capital» to the visit of Premier Raymond Barre of France — one can only conclude that, for the most part, the patterns of coverage which marked the first half of this decade only became more pronounced as the decade drew to a close.

The coverage of Premier Barre's visit was particularly telling in that regard. There was little, if any, coverage of the agreements that were signed between France and Quebec during the visit (as if that could not possibly be of interest to

English Quebecers); nor was there much of a serious attempt to report upon the carefully enunciated posture of the French government towards the goals of the present Quebec government. Instead, coverage was concentrated almost exclusively upon the «peculiar» and «disgraceful» behaviour of Premier Lévesque during the «balcony scene» at the official banquet in Quebec City and at the departing press conference. In contrast, the French media led with the accords that were signed between the two governments and gave subsidiary coverage to the Quebec Premier's diplomatic gaffes.

Of course, one could argue at length about whether the French or the English media provided the most appropriate coverage. That such arguments have indeed occurred within the media only highlights the fact that *emphasis* and the *way* in which events are reported are indeed critical elements of any attempts at «fair and balanced» journalism.

The problem is serious precisely because so many members of the two linguistic communities are now so clearly at odds on almost every major aspect of their inter-relationship. It is not only that there are sharp differences in their goals and aspirations, but also in their understanding of the problems. Moreover, the differences have a depth of feeling and volatility that will be severely tested in the years ahead. In the English community, certainly, there is now probably more anger, uneasiness, and even fear than at any time in the last two decades. More is involved here than the desirable differences of opinion which should exist in any vibrant democratic society.

The present level of tension is compounded by the fact that a large portion of the English community (probably about 400 000 people) still cannot function in French. Consequently, they remain restrictively dependent upon the mainstream English media for their information about, understanding of, and relationship to the majority linguistic community.

In that context, what role will the media play in the critical period ahead? Will it seek to rally antithetical feelings, at the expense of understanding and empathy in reporting certain aspects of the «other» community? I suspect that most mainstream media outlets in English Quebec will tend in that direction.

* * *

Yet, in the English community itself, there are also some signs of a steadily improving grasp of the community's troubled relationship with the larger Quebec society. Paradoxically, I suspect that this is due to the escalated tensions of the last few years. One result is that the English community is paying more attention and is thinking harder about Quebec events and their implications than ever before.

Such an atmosphere brings out a wider range of communal voices and leadership, with the result that more facets of a community's concerns tend to make their way through the media funnel. Moreover, the pressure that a wider divergence of informed leadership puts on the media can only be beneficial in improving the quality and care with which mainstream journalism is practised. At the very least, in a situation of heightened communal thoughtfulness, any weaknesses in the accuracy or fairness of contemporary journalism will have less of an adverse impact than would occur if the readers or listeners were passive and indifferent.

Weaknesses in accuracy and fairness there are bound to be. Few people realize that most media outlets do not (and usually cannot) have more than very limited internal mechanisms to safeguard the quality, accuracy or fairness of what they present to the public. News moves too fast, and budgets are usually too limited for it to be otherwise. Even where internal editorial discontent exists with regard to any particular news report, the next day always seems to bring its own more pressing concerns allowing little time for much to be done about yesterday's inadequacies. In the end, the news instincts (wise or inadequate) and the innate fairness, or lack of it, of media people prevail.

In the past, many media people have chosen to believe that if the quality of journalism is inadequate, or if the slant is seriously wrong, then the public, or key sectors of it, will react in a way that will effectively call the flawed journalistic performance into question. I suspect that such an assumption has always been a convenient, self-serving illusion. In truth, factual and contextual errors are committed daily by the news media, and there has rarely been much public reaction. Even where some reaction has existed, it has rarely been substantial enough to result in any serious self-criticism or re-evaluation. The absence of a critical English-Montreal intelligentsia has been particularly pertinent in this regard. It has been my experience that political scientists and academics in English Quebec may have known who the editors of prestigious foreign journals were, but, for the most part, they have been indifferently ignorant and almost snobbishly disdainful of the media in their midst. That has surely been a factor in determining that in the past, the only major watchdog of the media's performance has been the general public's impression of whether the media, like Steinberg's, has been satisfactorily «on their side».

Being on anybody's side, of course, should be restricted to the editorial pages. When it creeps into the newscasts or on to the front pages in response to a public desire that media reflect particular views of reality, or act essentially as vehicles of persuasion, then «bumps» in the community's experience of changing circumstances are bound to occur.

There have been too many such «bumps» in the last two decades. The media can only assist in diminishing their frequency and intensity if the English community increasingly wants its media to play a different role than it has asked them to play in the past. Because of the many constraints mentioned earlier which govern mainstream media's relationship to their public, it would be illusory to expect the media to perform in ways that their public does not desire. There may be journalists and editors who might wish it were otherwise, but experience makes it only too clear that their wishes are unlikely to prevail against the grain of public expectation and insistence.

One hopes that the English community will increasingly understand that the media must do more than reflect *its* sense of events and *its* concerns for the future: it must also reflect with equal understanding the sense of things that the «other» (and larger) community brings to mutual areas of concern. Too much stress on the former role can only exacerbate the present level of uneasiness and alienation; a level that clearly cries out for more of the latter kind of journalistic performance in the very difficult period of adjustment that lies ahead for Quebec's two major linguistic communities.

The Quebec Media and Canadian Unity

Arthur Siegel

ARTHUR SIEGEL, a professor in the division of social sciences at York University, is interested in French-English communications in Canada in particular, and the national mass media in general. He has also worked in the field of broadcasting, wire services and the printed media.

Introduction

A critical aspect of the Canadian unity debate is the role of the mass media in Quebec. The penchant of the Parti Québécois government for holding plebiscites related to the future of Quebec in the Canadian federal union make the French and English press in the Province especially important political actors in the pre-voting periods. The politics of plebiscite is addressed essentially to the people. The vote itself reflects the views of the majority at one particular moment on the highly emotional issue of sovereignty. The mass media are the great battleground for public opinion and, much more so than in a general election, the media are the centre of public debate in a plebiscite. In fact, the media are the plebiscite campaign.[1]

This study seeks to examine the role of the French and English media in Quebec as political actors in relationship to federalism specifically, and to Canadian unity generally. The unique characteristics of the media serving minority linguistic groups — as in the case of the English newspapers in Quebec — will be explored.

Language and Canadian Communications Problems

While many of the problems faced by the mass media in the modern world are shared by a large number of countries, Canada distinguishes herself by having a particular clustering of problems which must be dealt with simultaneously. Thus, firstly, the physical characteristics of Canada are a source of one set of communications problems; the large size of the country and the difficult terrain provide obstacles to the easy flow of communications. Secondly, there is the population dispersion with most Canadians living in a relatively narrow ribbon of land — about thirty to forty miles in width — parallel to the U.S. border and spanning the continent. This situation tends to undermine an east- west or all Canadian route for communications and gives rise to a north-south, or Canada-U.S. pull in the communication exchange. Thirdly, because of the overwhelming size of the U.S. communications industry compared with Canada's, the mass media communications flow tends to be essentially from the United States to Canada with relatively little moving in the other direction; observers speak of this as a cultural invasion that undermines Canadian identity. The fourth of the major Canadian problems in communications stems from bilingualism which has resulted in the development of two distinct media systems: one French, the other English. The independence of the two media systems may be a healthy reflection of bilingualism and biculturalism, but at the same time, the separateness of the French and English communications' networks is costly. It means a duplication of technical facilities, facilities that are already burdened because they have the potential to serve a population far in excess of Canada's twenty-three million people. Even more important than economics are the problems of a bilingual communications network as they relate to Canadian politics and integration.

In examining communications in relation to Canadian identity, Canadians — especially the English-speaking sector — have been preoccupied with the external problems: specifically the penetration of U.S. communications messages into Canada. The question of French-English differences in communications content has been largely overlooked. It is this neglected problem that is of critical importance in the Canadian unity debate.

Efficient internal communication among a whole people seems to be one of the requirements of nationhood. «People are marked off from each other by marked gaps in the efficiency of communications.»[2] In Canada's federal society, the maps of the world — and specifically of Canadian affairs — that are drawn for us by the mass media are an important clue for evaluating the pressures for integration and disintegration. If these maps vary in important ways, and the variations are identifiable with population clusters that have a geographic or political base — then the communications flow has an unsettling effect on integration.

Dual Federalism

Language and cultural considerations in the Canadian communications flow are intimately linked to Canadian attitudes on federalism. This is because the Canadian federal system incorporates two distinct dimensions that are compelled to co-exist within the same constitutional structure.[3] The basic component is organized around the classical notion of a division of powers so that the national and regional governments are each, within a sphere, co-ordinate and independent. The second and distinctive component of Canadian federalism is that we are also a union of two «founding peoples», each fostering its autonomous cultural and linguistic traditions.

Professor James Mallory in *Five Faces of Federalism* uses the term «double-image federalism» to describe the federalism of Canada in recent times.[4] The «founding peoples» aspect of our federal structure is not prescribed constitutionally in the British North America Act. It stems from cultural and political factors that predated Confederation and found a fertile soil in the economic, political and social systems as Canada moved from a largely rural-based society to a highly industrialized nation. In 1979, the Task Force on Canadian Unity noted that cultural duality of English and French was one of the underlying principles of Canada. Prime Minister Pierre Trudeau in his *A Canadian Charter of Human Rights* gave recognition to the principles of dual federalism. The Royal Commission on Bilingualism and Biculturalism came forward with recommendations which held up the viability of the two linguistic and cultural groupings, i.e., the founding peoples, as an essential goal and basic principle of Canadian existence. This French-English founding peoples notion has been developed into a whole series of concepts and formulas for Quebec's position in confederation including «special status» and the «bi-nation state». The aspirations of the Parti Québécois government for the separation of Quebec from Canada is an extreme perception of how the principle that Quebec «is not a province like the others» should be translated into reality.

Communications Analysis

A communications analysis indicates that the unity problems of Canadian federalism to which the political sector is now addressing itself have been evident in the message pattern of the Canadian mass media for many years. If political scientists and students of the media had shown a greater interest in the role of mass communications in the federal equation, Canadians would not have been caught unprepared when, in 1965, the Royal Commission on Bilingualism and Bicultural-ism declared «Canada without being fully conscious of the fact, is passing through the greatest crisis in its history.»[5] The Canadian emergency of October 1970 that is generally referred to as the F.L.Q. (Front de Libération du Québec) Crisis can be seen as a battle for the temporary control of the mass media in Quebec.[6] In 1976, the victory of the Parti Québécois in the provincial general election should not have come as a surprise to students of political communications. The sociologist, Frederick Elkin, in his essay on the role of Canadian communications in the development of a Canadian identity, expressed the view that the content of the English and French media, «although basically following similar lines, often reflect[s] different cultures.»[7] The Canadian Senate Study on the Mass Media (1970) concluded that in journalism, «the traditions, the audience preferences, the mythologies, the economics of publishing and broadcasting — all are shaped by the French Fact, to the extent that the province [Quebec] cannot be viewed simply as part of the Canadian whole.»[8]

In order to find out more about these differences and evaluate their implica-tions in the interaction of mass media and federalism, it is useful to look at four studies that deal with the communications flow in Canadian newspapers and broadcasting. The most exhaustive of these studies focuses on French and English newspaper coverage of the Front de Libération du Québec Crisis in October 1970. The second study examines French and English language newspaper coverage of the Federal-Provincial Constitutional Conference in February 1969. The third study deals with Quebec newspapers only — French and English — and focuses on the coverage of the Quebec provincial election in June 1966. The fourth study deals with the broadcast media, and surveys the similarities and differences in French and English newscasts (television and radio) in May 1977.

Study I. The Canadian Emergency in October 1970 — The F.L.Q. Crisis

The Crisis involved a series of events which began on October 5th with the kidnapping of the British Trade Commissioner in Montreal, James Richard Cross, by the Front de Libération du Québec (FLQ). In the next two weeks, or so, there were to be such other notable and traumatic events as the kidnapping and murder of the Quebec Minister of Labour, Mr. Pierre Laporte, the proclamation of the War Measures Act by the Federal government in Ottawa, and the deployment of armed troops for the maintenance of internal security.

The FLQ Crisis was intimately linked to the French-English confrontation in Canada. In a sense, one can view the Crisis as an attempt to resolve the constitutional question by violence, for it aimed at breaking up the Canadian union as it exists today. Involved in this Crisis were the issues of Quebec's place in the Canadian federation and whether there was to be a federation at all. The way the Government perceived the developments in October 1970, was that the very life of the political system was under attack.

The invocation of the War Measures Act, in effect declaring a state of emergency, marked the first time that the government took this step in time of peace. Matters very much related to the Crisis were civil rights in time of emergency, the role of Parliament during a grave crisis, and the power and role of the Federal government in the emergency. Another very important consideration, apart from the fact that the jurisdiction of the federal government is sensibly enlarged by an emergency situation,[9] is the role of the provincial government which has exclusive constitutional jurisdiction for the administration of justice, which comprises most of the field of «law and order.»

The FLQ Crisis is particularly useful for an analysis of French and English media interpretations of the same political events. A crisis situation tends to reveal basic characteristics of the political and social systems, including such matters as stability, flexibility and responsiveness of the institutions.[10] It is in a situation of this nature that the political system is confronted with the unusual, and its response is likely to bring to the surface characteristics that remain latent in what are regarded as more normal times. In other words, a crisis situation precipitates a moment of truth for the political system. It is also a moment of truth for the mass media. Communications studies have shown that in time of crisis, coverage tends to become more alike and terse, and many differences are submerged in what is regarded as the common interest.[11] The differences that do show up are seen as being of a fundamental nature.

* * *

A multi-dimensional content analysis of a representative sample of twenty-two Canadian newspapers showed that French and English dailies attached similar overall importance to the FLQ Crisis as revealed by similarities in the intensity of coverage.[12] In every other main sphere of analysis — themes of front page coverage, the evaluation of general themes, personality emphasis, geographic sources of stories and editorial positions — there were important differences.

Two news themes — *negotiations* and *manhunt* — were especially important in setting the patterns for the news coverage. The French-language newspapers stressed *negotiations*; which could be interpreted as a compromise approach to resolving the crisis. For the English-language papers, the main theme of emphasis was *manhunt*; these stories dealt mostly with police activities to apprehend the kidnappers and free the hostages. The two different approaches to resolving the Crisis explained the variations of coverage — news and editorial — between the French- and English-language papers. Far more public opposition to the authorities was reported in the French newspapers than in the English papers. The French dailies emphasized personalities; English dailies institutions. The French papers carried more editorial comment, background stories and intellectual comment than did the English dailies.

The differences in the French and English newspaper accounts reflected two distinct patterns of coverage which meant that the FLQ Crisis looked different to French and English readers. We can speak of different patterns of coverage, because the variations in theme-emphasis were not randomly distributed, but rather reflected an organization of information which projected different overall perceptions of what was taking place and what aspects were important in the resolution of the Crisis. The patterns of coverage reflected different values and norms in the French and English newspapers. These values and norms are, in effect, the looking glasses through which the same political events are observed. The major findings are outlined in Table I.

TABLE I — **Characteristics of French and English Language Newspapers observed in a content Analysis of Coverage of the FLQ Crisis.**

(i)   There were basic French-English differences in viewing the political system. English language papers saw Canadian unity as a major objective and tend to take a pan-Canadian perspective in their editorials. Different priorities existed in the French papers: their main concern was Quebec and French Canadian society. Editorials in the French papers generally evaluated developments from a Quebec perspective without giving much concern to the national implications.

(ii) There was a personality emphasis in French-language newspapers in contrast to an emphasis on political institutions in the English press. Seen from a political culture perspective, it is argued that French Canadians may have difficulties in relating directly to the political institutions that are associated with the parliamentary system.

(iii) French-language dailies showed a strong interest in a distinctive Quebec personality on the international scene.

(iv) French-language dailies stressed the historic and contemporary economic and social injustices experienced by French Canadians. The emotional cost of being a minority sub-cultural group in a disadvantaged economic position was reflected in the French press. English-language papers emphasized current economic factors: the effect of the crisis on stock market prices, the value of the Canadian dollar.

(v) In 1970, French dailies had a neutral disposition on separation and appeared to be leaving their options open. English newspapers were highly critical of separatism.

(vi) French papers and journalists projected images of their importance in the political process. English newspapers maintained a comparatively low political profile with the coverage generally depersonalized.

(vii) French-language newspapers were a homogeneous and cohesive group providing a relatively uniform picture of developments. In the English language press, there was no such evidence of homogeneity of coverage; on the contrary, the picture was fragmented.

The homogeneity of coverage observed in the French-language newspapers (Point vii in Table I) was traced to the leadership of the Montreal dailies. It was found that Montreal plays a dominant role in the French press system to such an extent as to create communications bonds which overshadow differences of ownership and regional dispersion of a limited nature. In this way, the Montreal French-language papers exert centripetal pull and the French-language service of Canadian Press provides an organizational support structure for the Montreal dominance.

One Montreal daily, *Le Devoir*, stood out for its uniquely strongly-defined editorial position and equally strongly-defined emphasis on news themes reflecting the editorial stand. As a result of this finding, it was decided to carry out an analysis over time — a day-by-day evaluation of the coverage. The findings here, combined with a number of other findings — such as *Le Devoir*'s emphasis on intellectual journalism, its prestige background, the nature of its news coverage — led to the conclusion that it played a leadership role in the French- language group of papers. No English paper emerged in such a role.

For the English-language press system, there was no single primal city that provided national newspaper leadership during the FLQ Crisis. Variations in coverage were associated with numerous factors, including: metropolitan status, size of city, distance from crisis area, and local characteristics of the city. The findings were seen as a reflection of the fragmented nature of the English press system. The local influences, while noticeable in the French dailies where they applied, were much stronger in the English dailies.

* * *

The findings of that first study indicated that the French press and the English press have different perceptions of their importance in the political process. The French papers projected an image of self-importance in many ways, including: frequent reference to media and journalists, personalized coverage which, at times, included the raising of rhetorical questions which they then proceeded to answer, and editorials written in the first person. The enormous editorial comment in the French papers — all of it signed by persons who are recognized as media intellectuals — and the massive editorial page backgrounding — much of it contributed by academic figures — are reflective of the involvement of intellectuals in the French press system, especially on the editorial pages which are, of course, identified with the ideological perspective of the medium. This would suggest that values articulated in the French dailies are inserted by an intellectually oriented group. The observed characteristic of French dailies whereby they maintained a fixed editorial position once they had indicated an attitude would suggest that the editorial outlook was derived from a larger perspective based on goals that went beyond the Crisis. English newspapers, for their part, maintained a comparatively low profile as far as projecting their own image was concerned, with the coverage generally depersonalized.

Some of the most interesting findings in the analysis related to the differences between the French and English press in The Province of Quebec. In Montreal, for example, the French-language dailies, *Le Devoir* and *La Presse*, devoted three times as much editorial comment (editorials, backgrounders, cartoons) to the October developments as dit the English-language *Gazette* and *Montreal Star*. Not only were the French-language editorials longer and more detailed, but they were also more outspoken on the critical aspects as to how the Crisis should be resolved. Furthermore, French dailies in Montreal carried twice as many editorials as the English papers. Differences of similar proportions were also observed in Quebec City and in Sherbrooke, Que. which had English daily newspapers in 1970.

In each of these cities — Montreal, Quebec City and Sherbrooke — the English newspapers speak to and for a minority language group. (In Ottawa and in Moncton, N.B., the situation is reversed with the French dailies serving the minority linguistic group, a factor which seemed to have a moderating influence on the space devoted to the editorials and the nature of the content.) A conclusion of the study was that newspapers serving the minority language group had a tendency to editorial silence. It is noteworthy that in Sherbrooke and in Quebec City, where the English-language populations were greatly outnumbered by the French-speaking populations, the minority-language newspapers often concerned themselves with peripheral matters and did not really come to grips with what were perceived to be the important issues. The *Sherbrooke Record*, for example, had an editorial on the type of press coverage the FLQ Crisis was receiving in Western Canada. The Quebec *Chronicle Telegraph* used a number of Canadian Press background pieces in the lead editorial column. These were essentially explanatory in nature and not indicative of editorial attitudes of the paper.

A further reflection of «insecurity» in the minority-language newspapers was the kind of treatment they provided for strictly local aspects of the Crisis; the minority-language dailies tended to put these matters on their front pages while the majority-language newspapers relegated them to their inside pages. The local situation and especially any developments that could potentially create local up-heavals were regarded as extremely important by minority-language dailies.

Finally, the first study showed that there was a clear link between the editorial positions of newspapers and the kind of coverage given in the news columns. This association was especially noticeable in the newspapers in Canada's metropolitan cities. The dailies in these large cities had more headline stories, a greater number of stories, more front page coverage, and devoted a greater amount of space to the FLQ Crisis than did newspapers in medium-sized and small cities. Also, the editorial comment was different. The editorials in the metropolitan papers appraised what was going on, they urged action and they argued. Editorials of this kind are regarded as politically more involved than those that merely explain and are essentially background pieces.

Montreal and Toronto papers fitted into the respective French- and English-language patterns (as noted in Table I), but their editorial positions tended to be closest to each other when compared with the largest cities in the rest of the country. In effect, the most influential dailies in Quebec and Ontario formed a «similarity group» when compared with dailies in other regions where newspapers tended to become more hard-lined as the distance from the crisis centre increased.

There was also evidence of a national dialogue in the editorial pages of the metropolitan dailies: excerpts, and sometimes complete texts, of what were regarded as important or interesting editorials were reprinted in other cities. This dialogue in the newspapers of the largest cities was not confined to English dailies, for the French newspapers also took part. The interaction of editorial opinion was especially strong for Montreal and Toronto. This editorial dialogue, and the relative closeness of Montreal and Toronto in terms of editorial positions, can be seen as mediating factors in the overall polarizing characteristics of the French and English press in Canada.

Study II. The Federal-Provincial Constitutional Conference, February 1969

The Federal-Provincial Constitutional Conference held in Ottawa, February 10-12, 1969, was the first such meeting since Pierre Trudeau had become Prime Minister in 1968. The three-day conference produced some changes in provincial attitudes towards Mr. Trudeau's official language bill and towards entrenchment of human rights in the constitution. Despite differences between Ottawa and the provinces on cost-shared programmes and the division of fiscal powers, the February 1969 Conference produced a text of consensus that indicated considerable momentum in the efforts to revise Canada's constitutional arrangement. The Conference provided a unique opportunity for content analysis of the press coverage partly because of the importance of the Canadian heads-of-governments meeting, and partly because of the extensive media coverage of the Conference.[13] The study revealed strong differences in the descriptions provided by French- and English-language newspapers.[14] The major findings are outlined in Table II.

TABLE II — **Characteristics of French and English Language Newspapers Observed in a Content Analysis of Coverage of the Federal-Provincial Constitutional Conference, February 1969.**

(i)   A two nation parity concept was very much in the minds of French-language journalists. Essentially the French papers saw the Constitutional Conference as a meeting between Prime Minister Pierre Trudeau and the then Quebec Premier Jean-Jacques Bertrand: Mr. Trudeau speaking for English Canada and Mr. Bertrand for French Canada. The content analysis revealed a French newspaper perception of polarization between Quebec and the rest.

(ii) English-language newspapers tended to give more extensive coverage to Quebec than other provinces, partly because of the well-defined Quebec demands at the constitutional conference, However, there was overwhelming evidence that the English papers perceived a federalism of provinces and not "nations".

(iii) Quebec newspapers, especially the French-language dailies, attached great importance to an international role and personality for Quebec. The international role issue was almost entirely neglected in the English-language press outside Quebec.

(iv) English papers in Quebec reflected concern about the future of minority rights in that they showed particular interest in safeguards for human rights and language rights. French papers in Quebec and English papers outside Quebec showed little interest in the human rights issues.

(v) The French press attached a greater sense of importance to itself than the English language newspapers. The French-language journalists frequently referred to themselves, their own newspapers and the press as a whole. None of the English papers or reporters reflected such symptoms of "ego".

(vi) French papers displayed more emotion compared with the English press. The attitudinal profile showed French papers speaking of "attacks", "assaults", "disagreements" and "demands". English papers referred to "discussions" and frequently used the term "unity".

(vii) Both the French and English language papers showed strong interest in the financial aspects of federalism.

(viii) French and English-language papers stressed different subject matters in their coverage reflecting different value systems. Quebec papers (French and English) showed a greater interest in legalistic aspects of the constitution than did Ontario papers. French papers discussed international relations, family allowance, medicare, education and telecommunications, matters largely neglected by the English dailies.

Study III. Quebec Newspaper Coverage of the Quebec Provincial Election, June 1966

There was considerable controversy in Quebec about newspaper coverage of the June 1966 provincial elections which saw the Liberals go down to defeat and the Union Nationale of Premier Daniel Johnson return to power. As is often the case, the loser — and in this case it was Premier Jean Lesage — cried foul and among others blamed the press. There were strong attacks on the news media during and after the campaign. L'Union canadienne des journalistes de langue française, launched a survey on the nature of the press campaign coverage. About 1 400 articles from six newspapers — representing about 80 per cent of the total circulation of Quebec — were analysed. The papers were *La Presse*, the *Montreal Star*, and *Le devoir* of Montreal, *Le Soleil* of Quebec City, *Le Nouvelliste* of Trois-Rivières, and *La Tribune* of Sherbrooke. A report was prepared by University of Montreal Political Science Professor, Guy Bourassa.[15] Some of the major findings are listed in Table III.

TABLE III — Characteristics of Quebec Newspapers Observed in a Content Analysis of Coverage of the June 1966 Quebec General Elections.

(1)   Although most space in the Quebec press was given to the Liberals in the election campaign, the party's image came across rather badly.

(ii)   The press tended to present a less favourable image of the Liberals than of the Union Nationale party. Of particular interest is the attitude of the Quebec press toward the separatist groups. It turned out that the separatist Rassemblement pour l'Indépendance Nationale came out best in the election press. The RIN, said Professor Bourassa, "was never shown up in a bad light". While the RIN was shown in the best light, the other separatist party — the right-wing Ralliement National — was far away at the other end of the spectrum.

(iii)   The RIN again led when orientation of headlines was considered. Second favourite was the Union Nationale, with the Liberals third — though, very occasionally, in fourth place after the RIN.

(iv)   In headlines about politicians, the RIN leader had favourable lines relatively more often than the NU leader who was in second place, ahead of the Liberal party chief, Premier Lesage.

(v)   In picture coverage Mr. Lesage only came in fourth place, while one quarter of stories on RIN leader Pierre Bourgault carried his photograph — putting him in first place.

(vi)   The RIN leader was also first in terms of backgrounders or analysis stories. (Union Nationale chief Johnson had twice the number of such stories as Mr. Lesage.)

The study raises some interesting questions about the involvement of the Quebec press in the separatist cause, or some related form of it. The Quebec coverage in the June 1966 election campaign shows that there was a strong support structure for separatism in the press at a time when the politicization of separatism was still in its infancy.

Study IV. French and English Broadcasting: Similarities and Differences, May 1977

The fourth study, carried out in 1977 for the Canadian Radio-Television and Telecommunications Commission, focused on broadcasting in the public sector: The Canadian Broadcasting Corporation-Radio Canada.[16] It found that there were major differences in the descriptions of Canadian society disseminated

337

by French and English newscasts. A multidimensional content analysis that included an examination of themes of news stories, personalities in the news, geographic sources of stories and political classification showed that differences far outweighed similarities. Of 1 785 stories examined, 259 appeared in both French and English newscasts and more than half of these had an international content. A realistic estimate of common ground in French and English newscasts (radio and television) would be about 15 per cent. The theme analysis showed that different subject matters were emphasized in French and English newscasts.

The study found that the French-language Radio Canada network was concerned primarily with Quebec (see Chart I). National news stories out of Ottawa frequently had Quebec content. The rest of the country received little attention unless there was news that specifically related to Quebec. It would appear that in terms of Canada there is a limited perspective in French-language newscasts. The emphasis on Quebec in the French-language newscasts was observed in every phase of the study. The English-language newscasts, for their part, emphasized national news out of Ottawa. Canada's four Atlantic provinces and the west coast province of British Columbia received comparatively little attention.

Even in dealing with international news, there were significant differences between French- and English-language newscasts: English television news devoted more than twice the time that French television news did to the United States, and French news gave greater emphasis to western Europe.[17]

Many of the differences observed between French- and English-language broadcast news (e.g., the French-language concern with Quebec, the emphasis on personalities, international interest) were in line with the differences observed in the printed press.

TABLE IV — Selected Theme Emphasis, by Language

	In English Newscasts	In French Newscasts	In both French and English Newscasts
	Native Affairs	PQ in Union	Summit Conference
	Human Rights	Separatism	War and Peace
A- Political	Armed Services	Quebec Provincial politics	Federal by-elections
	Municipal News	Quebec Provincial economy	
		Language political	
		International relations	
B- Economic/ Environment	Energy Pollution Consumer Affairs	Labour strikes Labour demands Labour settlements	Inflation Unemployment Prices & Wages
	Disasters		
	Obituaries		
C- Others	Sports Entertainment		

Source: C.R.T.C., 1977.

CHART I. *Political Classification of Canadian Stories — 10 Days in May '77* **(based on time).**

TELEVISION

English-TV (C.B.C.)

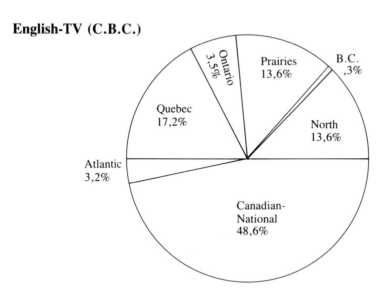

French-TV (Radio-Canada)

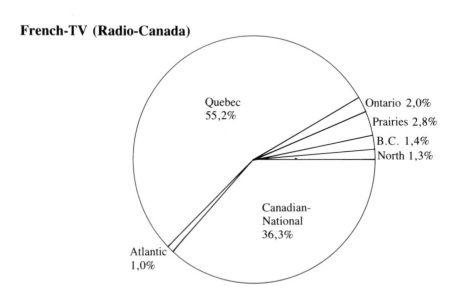

Source: C.R.T.C., 1977.

Conclusions

In looking at the studies together, it can be concluded that the «we-they» perception of Canadian federalism — with parity for French and English Canada — has long been built into the French-language communications system. There are basic French-English press differences in viewing the political system, political institutions, Quebec's international personality, economic and social history and the press as a political actor. Separatism has long been recognized as a viable proposition in the French press, and there is evidence of a media support structure for a separatist political party as far back as 1966. The significance attached to an international personality for Quebec appears to be linked to a Quebec independence posture and is reminiscent of Ottawa using international relations as a stepping stone for achieving Canada's full sovereignty.

Of particular interest is the leadership role in French- Canadian society in which French-language journalists see themselves. The articulation of a clearly defined value system is evident in French-language journalism, a practice that goes back a long time. It may, however, be argued that until about fifteen to twenty years ago, the impact of this was muted in political terms, and the intellectual journalists may well have been at a distance from the readership they were trying to lead. The media are among several social institutions that include the family, the educational system, the church, the peer group and the work environment that are believed to be especially important in shaping the value structure in society. However, the Quiet Revolution in Quebec combined with the youth revolution globally have resulted in diminishing the influence of the church and family in shaping attitudes and as transmission agents of political culture. Also, the educational system has undergone major reforms. It is argued here that the mass media and the new generation of teachers have emerged in comparatively more influential positions than before. It is no accident that the Parti Québécois leadership is made up of an extraordinarily large number of journalists and teachers.

We see, then, the Quebec media today as enormously important political actors. The growing influence of the press and press personalities in French society is closely related to the unity crisis.

There is evidence that the French and English media help to reinforce the bicultural characteristics of Canadian federalism. The homogeneity of the French press system can be seen as a necessary supportive factor for a numerically disadvantaged sector of society. Because of the enormous influence of the printed press on the news content of the electronic press, the French media — newspapers and broadcasting — provide distinctive outlooks towards the political system, institutions, and economic matters, among others. There is no such uniformity of outlook on the part of the English press which, as noted above, is fragmented. Fragmentation and parochialism diffuses the polarizing tendencies of the French and English press systems and can be regarded as a mediating factor. A second mediating factor is the comparative similarity of outlook of Montreal and Toronto newspapers vis-à-vis the coverage in other large cities. Yet a third mediating factor is the existence of a dialogue in the press, most intense at the level of metropolitan papers.

Indications are, however, that these mediating factors are not sufficient to balance the disintegrating pressures that flow from the Canadian media. The evidence shows that the press system in Canada, as illustrated by its performance in the FLQ Crisis (Study I), had an unsettling effect on Canadian integration, or at least did not promote it. This conclusion finds support in Studies II (newspapers) and IV (broadcasting) which also compared French and English media content. The empirical findings reveal that the media reinforce sub-cultural differences rather than contribute to the unification of society by broadening the base of common norms, values and collective experiences shared by its members. The media accounts of the same basic political events are socially divisive because they are organized in such a way as to emphasize particular interests co-inciding with territorially-based language divisions.

* * *

The English-language newspapers in Quebec share common values with the English press in the other regions of Canada. There are some important issues, however, where Quebec dailies — irrespective of language — have common outlooks. This occurs when the interests of the French and English communities in Québec come together. In effect, the English papers in the Province are tributary to the English press in Canada, but not entirely so. The conclusion is based on the findings in the studies dealing with the press coverage of the FLQ Crisis and the coverage of the Federal-Provincial Constitutional Conference (1969).

The English-language press is in an isolated position on a number of important issues. This is especially true on the questions of language rights and civil rights. In addition to this isolation, and partly because of it, there is the sense of insecurity reflected in English-language newspaper content. In the FLQ Crisis, the English-language papers in Québec displayed more anxiety compared with all other papers in Canada — both French and English — in that they gave far greater front page emphasis to stories that dealt with strictly local aspects of the Crisis. In effect, the local events appeared to have potentially threatening implications. Furthermore, the editorial page content was muted in the English-language papers in Quebec; there was a hesitancy to speak out compared with the French-language newspapers in the Province and the English newspapers in the rest of Canada. At a time when the English-language newspapers in Montreal, at the crisis centre, would have been expected to provide a sense of direction to the rest of the English media, they were noticeably silent.

The hesitancy of the English-language press in Quebec to speak out openly on issues of great importance to the English population in the Province has major implications for plebiscite campaigns. Plebiscite politics is likely to become crisis politics. It was noted earlier that in time of crisis, the media become especially important; not only are the media interpreters of political events, but they themselves are also drawn into these events, as important political actors. The role of the media is critical in a plebiscite campaign. The findings here suggest that the English-language media in Quebec may not feel comfortable in this enlarged political role, and they are likely to experience difficulties in coping. The French-language media, for their part, have a rich background in terms of political involvement.

NOTES

(1) Colin Seymour-Ure, «The Press and Referenda: The Case of the British Referendum in 1975», *Canadian Journal of Political Science*, 11(Sept. 1978):3.

(2) Karl W. Deutsch, *Nationalism and Social Communications* (Cambridge, M.I.T. Press; New York, John Wiley, 1953):100.

(3) J.R. Mallory, *The Structure of Canadian Government* (Toronto, Macmillan of Canada, 1971):393.

(4) J.R. Mallory, «The Five Faces of Federalism», P.-A. Crepeau & C.B. Macpherson, eds., *The Future of Canadian Federalism*, Toronto, University of Toronto Press, 1965.

(5) *Preliminary Report of the Royal Commission on Bilingualism and Biculturalism* (Ottawa, 1965): 13.

(6) Daniel Latouche, «Mass Communications in a Canadian Political Crisis», Benjamin D. Singer, ed., *Communications in Canadian Society* (Toronto, The Copp Clark Publishing Co., 1972):302. See also: Arthur Siegel, «The Use of the War Measures Act in October 1970: A Communications Analysis», Paper presented to the inaugural meeting of the Canadian Association of Survey Research, Quebec City, May 30-31, 1976.

(7) Frederick Elkin, «Communications Media and Identity Formation in Canada», *Communications in Canadian Society*, p. 222.

(8) *Report of the Special Senate Committee on the Mass Media* (Ottawa: Queen's Printer, 1970), vol. I, p. 95.

(9) The War Measures Act (Rev. Stat. Canada 1952, c. 288) is a grant of power so sweeping that it conveys to the Governor-in-Council most of the war-time emergency powers made available to the Dominion Parliament under the «peace, order, and good government» clause of Section 91 of the British North America Act. As Professor Mallory has pointed out in *The Five Faces of Federalism*, there is nothing either in the Confederation Debates or the B.N.A. Act which addresses itself to the distribution of powers in an emergency. It was the courts that have made this opening in the federal system, regarding the federal distribution of powers as a peacetime luxury which must be foregone in wartime. Emergency federalism, in effect, makes Canada «a unitary state for the duration». See J.R. Mallory, «The Five Faces of Federalism», P.-A. Crepeau and C.B. Macpherson, eds., *The Future of Canadian Federalism* (Toronto, University of Toronto Press, 1965):7-9.

(10) Crisis was defined as a situation involving the following aspects: (1) a threat to the goals of the political system, (2) outside initiation, (3) surprise, (4) escalation of risks, and (5) time pressure in the sense that the situation is acute, not chronic. See James Robinson, «Crisis», *International Encyclopedia of the Social Sciences*. See also Daniel Latouche, «Mass Media and Communication in a Canadian Political Crisis», *Communications in Canadian Society*, pp. 296-297.

(11) J.T. Klapper, *The Effects of Mass Communications* (Glencoe, (Ill.), The Free Press, 1960):53-61.

(12) Arthur Siegel, «The Norms and Values of the French and English Press in Canada: A Political Evaluation», W.E. Mann and Les Wheatcroft, eds., *Canada: A sociological Profile*, 3rd edition, Toronto, Copp Clark Publishing, 1976. The twenty-two papers used in the study are: Halifax *Chronicle-Herald*, Moncton *Transcript*, Moncton *L'Evangeline*, Montreal *La Presse*, Montreal *Le Devoir*, *Montreal Star*, *Montreal Gazette*, Quebec City *L'Action*, Quebec City *Chronicle Telegraph*, Sherbrooke *La Tribune*, Sherbrooke *Record*, *Toronto Star*, *Toronto Globe and Mail*, Ottawa *Journal*, Ottawa *Le Droit*, Kitchener-Waterloo *Record*, Thunder Bay *News Chronicle*, *Edmonton Journal*, *Red Deer Advocate*, *Vancouver Sun*, *Victoria Colonist*, *Prince Rupert Daily News*.

(13) Reporters who covered the Ottawa conference said at the time that seldom had there been that great a turnout of Canadian journalists for a single show.

(14) Arthur Siegel, *A Content Analysis: French and English Language Newspaper Coverage of the Federal Provincial Constitutional Conference, February 10-12, 1969.*

(15) See Guy Bourassa and Francine Despatie, «La Presse Québécoise et les élections du 5 juin», *Cité Libre*, 17(nov.-déc. 1966):5-32.

(16) Arthur Siegel, «A Content Analysis, the Canadian Broadcasting Corporation: Similarities and Differences in French and English News.»

(17) *Ibid.*

The Anglo Press in the Seventies: Conspiracy or Just Plain Incompetence?

David Thomas

DAVID THOMAS, a member of the National Assembly Press Gallery from 1976 to 1980, has worked as a reporter for the *Canadian Press*, *The Gazette*, *MacLean's* and as a contributing editor to *Actualité*. Like many Quebec-born English-speaking Quebecers, he managed to attain adulthood without speaking French. It was a separatist demonstration in Jonquière during the 1972 election campaign — when Trudeau grabbed and mutilated a placard Thomas could not understand — that he decided that a command of French was essential for English-speaking journalists.

Friday evening, three days before November 15th, 1976, the first relays of deskmen quit the seedy old Gazette building on St. Antoine Street to scurry into Mother Martin's for a drink between editions. The trough was already lined with off-duty reporters, and Chong, the Korean barman, had started the tabs that would run through the evening and into the morning beyond. The end of a week and the imminent climax of a long and odd provincial election campaign were reason enough for some serious fun. But a more immediate cause for commotion was about to erupt back in the fourth-floor newsroom. Alerted by workers in the composing room, a *Gazette* editor had discovered an exceptional editorial signed by Publisher Ross Munro and set to run on the next day's front page, the last before voting day.

It was a curious piece of work: sizzling with syntactic slips, it was, in anyone's memory, *The Gazette*'s first front-page editorial and the first signed by a publisher. Written in the breathless style of a war dispatch from Dieppe, it was titled simply, «An Editorial». More appropriately, and more in keeping with *the Gazette* style of the day, it might have been headded: «Doom Looms». This is how it unfolded the following morning on the unsuspecting breakfast tables of the already nervous West Island:

> The central issue in Monday's provincial election is separation. The Parti Quebecois (sic), who are (sic) dedicated to this purpose, has scarcely mentioned it in their (sic) campaign. It is clever politics to soft-pedal this explosive issue. They camouflage it all by saying there will be a referendum on independence in two years time.
>
> This subterfuge seems to be working. Most people in Quebec want to remain part of Canada, yet our public opinion poll shows the PQ running far ahead, with the strong possibility they (sic) will form the next government unless there is a heavy swing in voters' preference over the weekend...

Munro's empassioned plea rang suspiciously like the Liberals' shrill «Stop separatism» campaign. His panic was, in fact, nourished by Liberal Premier Robert Bourassa who, the night before Munro penned his editorial, had met secretly with the publisher to literally beg an endorsement from *The Gazette*. It was the refusal of Editorial Page Editor Tim Creery to buckle under such crude pressure that pushed Munro and his jitters onto page one. This was not the first time Bourassa had tried to bribe and bully *The Gazette*: a year earlier, he had brazenly offered Munro's retiring predecessor, Mark Farrel, a government sinecure in exchange for the recall of the paper's two National Assembly reporters: Patrick Doyle and myself. So confident was Bourassa of his coup that a few days later he snickered to Doyle:

«We're going to miss you». Farrel, of course, treated the Bourassa proposition as the desperate bartering of a frightened politician who knew his end was near. Munro, on the other hand, was more vulnerable to Bourassa's appeal to the publisher's Canadian patriotism.

To newsroom employees, summoned back from Mother Martin's to read the proof of the editorial, the excited prose of the latter was reminiscent of their publisher's distinguished days as a Canadian war correspondent. Certainly, the editorial seemed to be consistent with Munro's own description of his wartime reporting philosophy, quoted in Phillip Knightley's book on military correspondents, *The First Casualty*:

> I don't think young people today could ever feel the commitment that we had. Maybe it was just jingoism, chauvinism, and stupidity, but we felt that the Germans were going to wreck this world of ours and that we would have to stop them. The troops were committed to it and I think the correspondents were — I certainly was. But it won't ever happen again. The war we were involved in was very clear cut. It really was a crusade.[1]

Whether his editorial was part of a new crusade, or merely an expression of its author's personal anguish for his country, his newsroom staffers reached a quick consensus that, somehow, they must cry out their dissent. . . though not all for the same reasons. Some found the editorial's tone embarrassingly maudlin; others saw it as an unfair attack on the Parti Québécois which some had quite openly favoured in arguments along the bar. As the deadline neared, a statement was drafted and passed around the newsroom for signing. A senior editor volunteered to act as emissary and carry to Munro's fifth-floor office the demand by the non-unionized staff that their statement be printed in the paper. To his credit, Munro accepted the mutinous proclamation as a paid advertisement. Instead, he could have fired the lot.

Printed on page three over the names of its signatories, here's how the ad read:

> Thirty-six members of *The Gazette* editorial staff of approximately 100 last night dissociated themselves from the editorial, signed by Ross Munro, publisher, that appears on page one today.
>
> The journalists, after reading a copy of his editorial, signed the following petition:
>
> «The undersigned editorial employees of *The Gazette* wish to inform readers that the views on the Quebec

election stated on the front page do not necessarily reflect those of the employees of this newspaper who attempted to report and edit campaign news as professionally as possible.»

Economic management and government honesty were clearly defined by a recent public opinion survey — partly commissioned by *The Gazette* — as the major issues of concern to Quebecers. Only seven per cent of respondents identified independence as the major issue.

Readers, probably already confused enough by the flaunted rebellion, were targets of yet another exhortation in the name of *The Gazette*, this time on the editorial page where Tim Creery serenely counselled *The Gazette* readers to vote for federalist candidates, but not to be stampeded:

It is futile, however, to wave the bogey of a vote against the Liberals as a vote for separatism in front of people who know it is not so. Voters are not cannon fodder to be fired against the ruling party's opponents. Voters are all of us, and we better be regarded as intelligent if our system is to survive and flourish.

* * *

Once the euphoria had cleared after his election victory and René Lévesque had recovered his usual pugnacity, many English-language journalists were — given the incidents just described — puzzled by the Premier's obsessive insistence that a «common front» of English media was conspiring to undermine his government. How, they wondered, could there exist collusion among owners, editors and reporters when just one newspaper alone could not manage to present a coherent stance on the eve of a critical election.

Unity of thought was, and remains, infinitely more obvious in Quebec's French-language media — a phenomenon implicitly recognized by politicians and journalists who repeatedly point to the harsher treatment accorded the government by the English media. Significantly, such comparisons were rare during the latter of the Bourassa years when, for media of both languages, it was open season on the government. There were no complaints then from the PQ.

Lévesque has convinced many French-speaking citizens and journalists — and some anglophones sympathetic to his cause — that only the French-language

351

media are honest and fair in their treatment of his government. This is not, however, an opinion shared by all French-speaking journalists. The then editor-in-chief of *Le Devoir*, Michel Roy, wrote shortly after the visit to Quebec of French Premier Raymond Barre that the French-language media had erred by not treating Lévesque's diplomatic gaffes and provincial behaviour with the same directness as the English-language media:

> ... in general, French-language journalists treat Mr. Lévesque with a complacency which leads them to hide his errors, to remain silent about his blunders, to over-protect him in the manner of the sons of Noah who, seeing father drunk, shield him behind the mantle of modesty.

This, of course is not the place to put Quebec's French- language media on trial. It is, however, essential to emphasize that the majority press — the standard against which the English-language media are often judged — itself sometimes strays with the carefree abandon of a *coureur de bois* from the narrow path of journalistic rigour.

The only sensible criterion for judging Quebec's English-language media is how well they serve their public. Do English-speaking Quebecers see, through their media, an accurate image of the larger Quebec society? Conversely, do these same media permit French-speaking Quebecers, or even their own English-speaking clientele to take stock of the rapidly changing situation of Quebec's largest minority?

Did *The Gazette* help English-speaking Montrealers cope with the first uncertain years of Parti Québécois government? Having largely ignored the Party and its strength in the years before 1976, did it recover afterwards? Well, almost a year after the change of power, *The Gazette* was still capable of this:

> Displaying the diplomatic cool that led him from the leadership of an obscure, left-wing political party to the premiership of the province of Quebec, Rene Levesque (sic) skilfilly (sic) foiled with defiant parents last night and vowed Bill 101 (sic) 'is going to stay' the law. [2]

Mispelling Lévesque's name by omitting the accents, mispelling «skilful-ly», and describing in the same breath language legislation as both a «bill» and a «law» are inexcusable enough. But to describe the Parti Québécois as having ever been obscure is to confess laughable ignorance of ten whole years; and endowing René Lévesque with «diplomatic cool» is like calling Lise Payette slinky.

Such an example may seem frivolous, but it illustrates the important handicaps suffered by the English-language media in Quebec. Increasingly, they adopt a parochial perspective, converging on the immediate concerns of a minority. Major events are described in terms of their effects on a small segment of the society. *The Gazette* has become a journal for an ethnic minority in cultural exile, much like the *Mexico City News*.

The reality of minority status also has a more direct impact on the day-to-day workings of the English-language media. No longer does there exist a hinterland of English- language newspapers outside Montreal capable of supplying big-city media with young, Quebec-raised reporters and editors. Added to that is the failure of Quebec's English-language schools to equip their graduates with a sufficient command of French to permit them to work in Quebec. The result is that recruits must be sought outside the Province.

For English-language newspapers in other major North- American cities, importing reporting and desk staff is not a problem; their territories are culturally close enough to make journalists interchangeable parts of the machine. Quebec's English-language media, however, suffer two disadvantages: an essential need for bilingual staff and the withdrawal of Montreal from the big city media circuit of English North America. In Canada, ambitious, young, anglophone reporters see Toronto as the big time, and Montreal is no longer an important way station.

At higher levels, managers still are not bilingual*, with only few exceptions. The incredible result is that the publisher and editor of *The Gazette*, and those of virtually every other English-language media in Montreal, are incapable of reading three of the city's four daily newspapers. Few anglophone editors could order lunch in French. To fully seize the folly of the situation, imagine an endeavour by unilingual French-speaking editors to publish a French-language daily in Toronto.

René Lévesque is unlikely to relinquish the satisfying and simple conviction that the oddities and outrages delivered by the English-language media are the product of a conspiracy by an anglo elite and its puppet media. The messy reality, however, is that the English-speaking community is hardly capable of effective collusion and, since the PQ has been in government, has demonstrated a remarkably pacific tendency to flee rather than fight. Instead of encouraging the English-speaking minority to stay and develop a new strategy for survival, its media, owned and increasingly staffed by non-Quebecers often just passing through, tend to maintain a level of anxiety and ignorance that can only accelerate the departures of anglophones.

The anglo exodus was largely provoked and fueled by doomsaying headlines and editorials and, ironically, it has created a widespread, though probably unfounded belief among journalists that there was no longer economic room for

---

* The editors of this collection leave it up to the reader to judge whether the situation of the 1980's differs from the situation described in this paragraph.

two English-language newspapers. The *Montreal Star*'s demise may have been a case of self-inflicted prophecy.

Because of the anglophone minority's decline as a vibrant, self-renewing community with a coherent set of political myths, its news media — the most visible part of any community — exhibit pessimism and confusion. What Lévesque sees so darkly as conspiracy is, in fact, confusion and alienation.

NOTES

(1) Phillip Knightley, *The First Casualty*, New York, Harcourt, Bruce, Jovanovich, 1975.

(2) As printed in the *Gazette*, on October 4th 1977.

Part VII

THE POLITICAL REALM

According to one of those many cynical jokes that circulated in Montreal in the aftermath of the Parti Québécois victory, the English businessmen of St. James' Street opened up their little black pocketbooks on the morning of November 16, 1976, to find that they no longer had a single phone number in government in Quebec City that they could ring in order to get prompt, and privileged attention on matters that concerned them directly. The party in power included among its numbers a *Néo-Québécois* (a Haitian to boot) and a couple of francophones with the fine Celtic names of Burns and O'Neill but not a single representative of the anglophone world.

Whether the anecdote is true or not matters little. That day marked the end of a very long era, one that dated in all likelihood back to Confederation — see the historical overview of English-French relations in John Jackson's contribution on collective and individual rights. This era had been characterized by anglophone control of certain key ministries in the cabinet and government departments (notably Lands and Forests, Natural Resources and Revenue), plus a refined strategy of *lobbying* that ensured the satisfactory meshing of the political interests of the francophone elite with the economic interests of the anglophone elite. At a more general level, the event reflected the emergence of a much more «capricious» anglophone electorate that had failed to vote *en bloc* for a single political party. Hence, in the political realm, one could justifiably speak of a *crisis* for the anglophones, a crisis that could best be characterized as «a severe loss of influence».

The second time around, in 1981, certain visible changes occurred. On the one hand, two anglophone *péquistes*, Robert Dean and David Payne, were elected to the National Assembly and a third, Henry Milner, to the Executive Council of the Parti Québécois, while on the other, the anglophone electorate clearly re-aligned itself with the Liberal Party. Yet, this has in no way served to resolve the crisis. Such *péquistes* remain essentially marginal people, in the McLeod Arnopoulos sense of the term, with no substantial anglophone constituency behind them. Dean, as a militant syndicalist and ex-vice president of the *Fédération des travailleurs du Québec* (FTQ), threw in his lot with the francophone working class long before such gestures became fashionable; Payne is a British Catholic who came to Quebec via Rome and joined the *classe politique* by virtue of having been active in an English CEGEP union; while Milner is an intellectual and socialist whose decision to assume a militant role in the Parti Québécois has a distinctly cerebral quality about it. As for the anglophone electorate, its support of the Liberal Party is aggressive, and it tends to display anger and hostility at any spokesman — be he the party leader or not — who expresses even the milder nationalistic stands of the kind voiced during the years when the Liberals were engineering the Quiet Revolution. The Party has yet to formulate a vocation for the eighties that is acceptable to the two very different linguistic communities that assure its survival.

The crisis may, in fact, serve to be a salutary experience in the long run in the sense that it has most certainly highlighted a number of major idiosyncracies that have crystallized in anglophone political behaviour in recent decades. The initial political response to language legislation, as revealed in William Tetley's account of events leading up to the passage of Law 22, provides a striking illustration of this.

Insofar as the wider causes of political behaviour are concerned, anglophones have consistently seen their «real» government and interests as residing in Ottawa while judging limited and directed intervention in the political process in Quebec to be, nevertheless, necessary. This preference for Ottawa has its roots in the distant past — a lineage that goes back through the Dominion of Canada and British North America to the British Isles; hence, a government that mirrors more accurately the very foundations of English Quebec. At the same time, it is a government that, in the British tradition, has acted as a defender of individual rights and liberties (which have, of course, invariably favoured the majority!) in contrast with the government of Quebec which has always more or less explicitly sought to defend a linguistic community. Whence the dilemma, for anglo- Quebecers, described by Jackson.

Effectiveness of anglophone intervention in the political process in Quebec was ensured by a tradition of accommodation between the two dominant language groups, but its real strength lays in the particular leverage the anglophones have long exercised over one of the major political parties — the Quebec Liberal Party — to the extent of furnishing almost one-third of its votes in recent elections. This strategic presence, compounded with a marked lack of loyalty with respect to the provincial cause, finally foundered in 1976 consequent on the growing strength of the Quebec state, the abandonment of a policy of accommodation (particularly on matters of language and territorial allegiance), and the temporary dispersal of the anglophone vote. Declining support among francophones ensured the continued exclusion of the Liberal Party from power and reinforced the anguish of its leaders as to which interests should be promoted in the future and which strategies favoured.

For anglophones, what has finally emerged at the provincial level is, in a very real sense, the kind of behaviour that has long characterized municipal government in rural Quebec. No longer able to function as co-partners in the political arena, to determine the language of interaction and to, in a major sense, *control* matters that concerned them, they have simply withdrawn from an active role in the political process. As they are absent at the level of regional government on the Iles-de-la-Madeleine (see S. Richards in this collection) or in the municipal affairs of Percé, so they are now without a voice in the Government of Quebec and in the principal political party on the provincial scene. At the level of local government in rural Quebec, a preoccupation with *survival* has engendered a retreat into the small community. At the provincial level, the same preoccupation has since encouraged a return to the fold of the one political party that appears to offer the possibilities of a return to the *status quo ante* and a strengthening of loyalties to the Federal government through the creation first, of diverse unity groups and, subsequently, of a province-wide official-language minority-group federation massively funded by the Department of the Secretary of State.

Through all these mutations, the political radicals (both secular and Christian) of English Quebec have been notably marginal, if not indeed silent. Bound by the same loyalties to Ottawa, and tributary of an English-Canadian intellectual tradition, they have repeatedly failed to find common ground with the francophone intelligentsia and be nourished by their political ideas and ideals. There are, of course, a few exceptions, notably the *patriote* Wilfrid Nelson and such renegades as Stanley Gray and associated McGill students who assumed an active role in events of the late sixties, but they were in no sense products or architects of a radical tradition such as was familiar to, and espoused by, certain Protestants in Ireland. Torn by the «national question» and a certain continental dimension that imbues their thinking, it is only in Montreal and through the Montreal Citizens Movement that anglophone radicals have been able to collaborate effectively with francophones in the seventies, thereby allowing class to displace ethnicity as an important basis for political mobilization. However, the arena is a notably neutral one in the sense that it generates no conflicting loyalties with respect to place. While rewarding, such action is scarcely enough, and anglophones have yet to determine a strategy of creative political action in Quebec that admits to a minority status and to an espousal, at least in part, of the political aspirations and instruments of the majority. It is almost certainly an appreciation of this fact that has led Henry Milner to shift his attention from the municipal to the provincial scene and to change his preoccupations from analysis to action. It also probably explains the rather hazardous path, in terms of their electorate, that such deputies as Reed Scowen and, before him, William Tetley have chosen to take within the Quebec Liberal Party.

The Language Question in Quebec: On Collective and Individual Rights

John D. Jackson

JOHN D. JACKSON was born and educated in Montreal and now teaches sociology at Concordia University, Sir George Williams Campus. His long-term interest in the French- English language question grew from his personal biography as a Montrealer. His recent research and publications have focused on French-English relations in Quebec and Canada, and on the development of English Canadian-culture.

This policy [Law 101] was a priority, since language is the very ground under a people's feet: by it they know themselves and are known; it is rooted in their hearts and allows them to express their identity.[1]

It is historically and currently true that the anglophone community is part of Quebec. And this community cannot continue to make its full contribution to Quebec life if it is not allowed to be itself.[2]

Article 26 [U.N. Declaration of Human Rights, 1948] declares, as Quebec has historically, that «parents have a prior right to choose the kind of education that shall be given to their children.» Prior right means prior to the state. Collective rights do not come before individual rights.[3]

The above statements illustrate the bases of both the «French» and «English» Quebec positions in the continuing debate on language policies. The first two statements point to arguments based upon a concept of collective rights. Each party rationalizes its position with reference to rights of collective or group survival. The last statement illustrates a countertendency in the «English» rationale where opponents to Law 101 shift their argument from collective to individual rights. It is interesting to note here that both the second and the third statements were made in the same document prepared by the Protestant School Board of Greater Montreal.

That one set of rights should contradict another, contradictions which can only be resolved by a consensus on priorities, or that one set of rights should limit the exercise of another is not a new experience. Most will recall the struggle over housing rights in the United States where the claim of Blacks to live where they wanted to, given appropriate purchasing power, clashed with the claim of Whites to sell to whomever they wanted. The right to freely purchase property in the market place clashed with the right to dispose of private property to whomever and whenever one pleased. We need not belabour the fact that the rights of some limit the rights of others. What is of interest here is the argument over collective and individual rights.

Though the distinction between collective and individual rights is at best cloudy because, among other things, it is individuals who act, make claims and are affected by the claims of others, it would be useful to attempt a clarification prior to proceeding with our discussion. A collective right is a claim which an individual may make by virtue of his or her membership in a social category (e.g., age, sex, ethnic origin, occupation, language, etc.), or an association (e.g., a labour union, an association of manufacturers, a professional association, etc.), or on behalf of a social category or association. A union member in a plant where a collective agreement is in effect has a right to so many paid holidays per year; an employee in a particular political jurisdiction has a right to a particular minimum wage; not so long ago, men have had property rights over women; Protestants in Quebec, and Roman Catholics in Ontario, have had rights to separate educational systems in the public domain. All of these are examples of collective rights or claims made by virtue of membership in a particular category.

In contrast, individual rights refer to equalities of conditions regardless of achieved or ascribed memberships in social categories or associations. All citizens, francophone or anglophone, male or female, Protestant or Roman Catholic, worker or owner have a right, or assume to have the right, to free assembly. All citizens have a right to free movement, property rights, and equal rights before the courts. These claims can be made without reference to one's position in a social system. To say, for example, that women have a right to equal pay for equal work relative to men is to say that sex as a category is to be put aside in favour of equality of conditions for individuals. Two additional points should be noted in passing. The question of the priority of one type of rights over another is always an open question. The Rand formula in Canadian labour relations gives collective rights a priority over individual rights; i.e., a union shop clause takes priority over free association. Zoning by-laws limit property rights in the market place. The second point is that collective and individual rights are generally established in custom and/or law through conflict and accommodation. Rights reflect power relations between categories of individuals, ethnic groups, men and women, owners and workers, and so on.

In this article, I want to demonstrate that language rights in Quebec and Canada are collective rights from whatever side one approaches the question, that these rights historically reflect relations of power between the two major language categories, and that these power relations ideologically and politically express relations between social classes; i.e., relations based on the location of people with respect to the means of production. Finally, I want to demonstrate that language policies signal either a continuation of current dominant — subordinate relations based on language or a change in these relations, but may not signal any change whatsoever in class relations.

Images and Realities

Two images flash through my mind whenever I reflect on language rights. One is an image of meetings of the Council of Quebec Minorities* (meetings which I never attended) where, sitting side-by-side were representatives of Quebec's Black, anglo-Protestant, anglo-Catholic, Greek, Italian «communities». This is

* Which became «Alliance Quebec» in 1982.

only a partial list, but they were brought together because of their common plight, that of being minorities in the new Quebec. The image does give rise to a wry pleasure when one notes that the «English», «English Protestant», or «WASPS», whatever label one wishes to apply, have become a minority like the others. As a colleague of mine pointed out, one has «to marvel at how much more xenophile the English in Montreal are than the English in metropolitan Toronto».[4]

The second image brings to mind the closing scene in an early version of David Fennario's recent play, *Balconville*. The play is located in one of Montreal's working-class neighbourhoods, Pointe-Saint-Charles, where francophone and anglophone workers mix about as well as francophones and anglophones interact in any other «mixed» neighbourhood. Three families, two English-speaking and one French-speaking, share rear balconies. In the closing scene, the three families are finally drawn together in an awareness of their common plight, one which transcends language and ethnic identity. The link between government, property, unemployment and welfare slowly rises in their consciousness after a series of common experiences with housing, work, welfare and neighbourhood. Their common status as victim seems, in the end, to have little to do with language.

The substance of each image is rooted in actual events; one is no less real than the other. Each, respectively, has to do with aspects of the national and class questions. Both have to do with people interacting on the basis of social categories — French and English, Black and Italian, Greek and Jewish and, in the last image, working class relative to state bureaucracies, bosses, owners, and landlords. I present these two images because they pose a dilemma. To pursue the first would limit us to a view which tends to deny the connection between social class and national, ethnic and linguistic categories. To pursue the second, though it does present a more promising lead, may lead us to view national, ethnic and linguistic categories as mere epiphenomena.

Keeping in mind that our objective is to explore the issue of collective and individual rights in relation to the language question, how might we extract ourselves from the dilemma? The obvious answer, to combine the substance of both images, may not be the most fruitful though it would certainly encourage us to direct our inquiry towards the relation between the language situation and social class. An alternative is to take both images as representing *observed* behaviour. The Council of Quebec Minorities did exist, and the presence of «WASPS» in the organization certainly pointed to a real or perceived change on their part in the relative positions of ethnic groups in Quebec. French and English-speaking neighbours do interact in Pointe-Saint-Charles; in some situations, the interaction is based on linguistic affiliations and in others, on class membership. This is to say no more than that the images are rooted in fact. However, facts are not self explanatory. Explanations are located in theories which filter and organize observations of day-to-day activity.

Two notes from the work of anthropologists may help us here. The first states that «direct observation does reveal to us that human beings are connected by a complex network of social relations. I use the term «social structure» to denote this framework of actual existing social relations». [5] The second takes a somewhat different view:

> When we describe structure we are already dealing with general principles far removed from the complicated skein of behaviour, feelings, beliefs, etc., that constitute the tissue of actual social life. We are as it were in the realm of grammar and syntax, not the spoken word. [6]

I don't want to enter into an argument over what is or what is not social structure. Suffice it to say that our two images belong to the first statement; i.e., they are built from observations of social relations — people interacting with people on the bases of ethnicity, language and social class. An understanding of the observations is to be found in the direction indicated by the second statement. What are the general principles of social life underlying the language question in Quebec? How do patterns of language use become institutionalized as «rights» such that a change is viewed by one or other party as a threat to its survival and to the identity and status of its members? If these questions can be answered then I have gone a long way toward meeting my objectives. To formulate an answer requires that we unravel the complicated skein of relationships between class and language which underlie our observations of daily happenings.

Contact, Conflict and Accommodation

Patterns of language use organize daily interaction. In a bilingual or multilingual setting, the answer to the question «who speaks what language to whom and under what conditions?» is also, in part at least, an answer to the question «who interacts with whom, under what conditions and with what frequency?» Languages, as well as other historically developed means of designating people (e.g., age, sex, occupation, religious affiliation) limit the scope of human interaction. Once «who speaks what language to whom, when and where?» becomes institutionalized; i.e., regulated in law or custom as «rights» (it is seldom otherwise in multilingual states), then we might expect that these patterns will be combined with other patterns of social behaviour, especially those which signify dominant-subordinate or power relations between categories of people. Accordingly, the language of the dominant category usually takes precedence over the language of the subordinate category, the members of the former remaining unilingual and the members of the latter becoming bilingual. But, wherein lies the source of the dominant-subordinate relations? Surely it does not lie in the languages themselves such that one is intrinsically superior to another. This is a possibility with respect to certain languages and certain domains of discourse, but not when two or more major world languages with common cultural roots are in question as is the case here in Quebec. So, we must look elsewhere. Since any multilingual setting is a result of contact between peoples, our inquiry should be directed toward certain aspects of the history of French- English relations in Quebec and Canada.

To this end, we should keep in mind that prior to 1760, New France had benefited from over two centuries to develop into an established and self-conscious society, albeit a metropolitan outpost. Furthermore, New France was not the harmonious, pastoral society that some historians have made it out to be. Like other European colonial societies of the time, it was rife with conflicts based on the transition from feudalism to capitalism and, within a capitalist framework, from a mercantile to a manufacturing base.[7] One student of New France described the situation in this manner:

> Canadians were divided between two vocations, a com-
> mercial and an agricultural vocation, and neither one
> nor the other received an exclusive concentration in the
> customs and institutions of the colony [. . .] A commer-
> cial empire and an agricultural colony: two realities and
> two ideals which are antithetical; sustained by two
> political rivals, the administration and the Church.[8]

Related to these two orientations, State, Church, seigneur and merchant found themselves in various coalitions and oppositions with and to each other depending upon the issue.[9] The Conquest effectively destroyed the secular side of French authority, leaving the lower classes of both town and country, seigneurs who stayed, and the clergy to work out an accommodation with the new ruling authority. Nor was the new ruling authority a cohesive force: British merchants in London and in New England were in opposition to the new colonial administration, itself composed of members of the lower nobility. In passing, it is interesting to note that the first Governor of British Quebec referred to the English merchant class as «a set of licentious fanatics.» That they would lean towards the seigneurial class and the higher clergy of French Quebec for support in their opposition to the rising power of the English merchants should come as no surprise. Out of this complex class situation emerged the accommodations between French and English in Quebec. It is this web of relationships, a web tied to an economic base, that sealed the survival of French Canada.

It is clear that the accommodations did not follow a simple linear link between two hypothetical integrated and harmonious societies. Rather, various factions of both French and English classes formed coalitions according to the interests of each. It was indeed a typical colonial case involving an articulation of the elites of both parties, the elite of the subordinate party maintaining its dominant position over its own underclasses as the price for handing overall control to the new ruling authority. It was out of this set of relations that the French language and the Roman Church were «to be preserved in order to counter potential social unrest in the colony». Language and religion guaranteed «the seigneurs class dominance over the peasants»,[10] thus providing British authority with the means for effective control. Language as an issue was rooted in this complex of class relations, not in any predetermined liberal attitude regarding language rights. From 1760 on, various class coalitions formed and disintegrated in response to the changing forces of production.

> The struggle between the [British] administration and the English Canadian bourgeoisie from 1760 to 1800; the struggle of the petite bourgeoisie against the seigneurs and clergy from 1800 to 1840; the struggle between the urban and rural faction of the French Canadian petite bourgeoisie from 1940 to 1960,[11]

have been referred to elsewhere. Running parallel to these coalitions and antagonisms were various colonial policies which either attempted assimilation or prompted the institutionalization of the means for the survival of French Canada.

Assimilation versus Survival: 1760-1840

The first policy act, the Royal Proclamation of 1763, was quite definitely assimilationist in intent. It sharply reduced the boundaries of the old French colony, set up English law and courts, and set aside lands for the support of Protestant clergy and schoolmasters; and this, according to Governor General Murray,

> ...to the end that the Church of England may be established in principle and practice, and that the said inhabitants may by degrees be induced to embrace the Protestant religion, and their children brought up in the principles of it.[12]

A host of problems prevented the fullfilment of the intent of the policy, not the least of which was a growing rebellion in the colonies to the south. There was a fear that the «inhabitants of Canada were united 'in common principle and wish' with the inhabitants of the other colonies».[13] A potential union of class interests, crossing lines of language and religion, could be prevented by gaining support of the French elite.

The Quebec Act of 1774 was to meet this objective. It solidified the alliance between British colonial rule and the French higher clergy and seigneurial class. These retained control over the mass of the French population at the price of democracy and dependency upon British interests. In exchange, the French community in Canada was recognized, and earlier hopes of assimilation put aside. The

370

Constitutional Act of 1791 and accompanying orders-in-council strengthened the separate identities of each community, French and English. Two colonies were created: Lower Canada, largely French in character, and Upper Canada, largely English in character. Each possessed an elective assembly, each assembly subject to the authority of an appointed legislative and executive council. French and English Canada were political and social realities under the control of the British colonial office, via an alliance of the two colonial based elites.

The succeeding complex struggle in which class and national interests were compounded culminated in the rebellions of 1835-38. This need not be treated here except for one important point. A wedge based on national aspirations was driven between Upper and Lower Canadian adherents to the rebellion. Had Papineau and MacKenzie been able to join forces, we may well have had a second American Revolution. But in Lower Canada, for various reasons, the rebellion was perceived in French-English terms, as a rebellion on the part of the French against the Crown, not as an incipient bourgeois revolution.

The measures which followed, among which The Union Act of 1840, not only attempted to control future rebellion, but also contained policy directed toward the elimination of the French fact. After almost seven decades of policy directed toward the strengthening of the two communities as separate entities, the 1840 policies established a single province of Canada, incorporated a legislative council appointed for life and an elected assembly composed of forty-two members from Lower and Upper Canada respectively. English was to be the only official language of government. Representation by population was admitted. Significantly, the population of Lower Canada exceeded that of Upper Canada by some two hundred thousand persons. The new policy was accompanied by a vigorous pursuit of English immigration as a means of overwhelming the still significant number of French-speakers in the colony.

But, as was the case with the Proclamation of 1763, the assimilationist policies of 1840 were not entirely successful. Initially, the legislative council excluded French Canadians. However, within two years, French members were appointed, reversing a policy which had been followed since the 1835-38 rebellions. Six years later, the Governor was to write:

> The sentiment of French Canadian nationality which
> Papineau endeavours to pervert to purposes of faction,
> may yet perhaps if properly improved furnish the best
> remaining security against annexation to the States.[14]

Shortly after, the use of French language returned to the assembly, though English remained the official language.[15]

Once again, the political and economic contingencies faced by colonial policy-makers on the one hand and the fact, on the other, that the French, though in a subordinate position, held sufficient power to force compromises, served to further institutionalize the existence of the two linguistic communities in the Province of Canada. Nor can we ignore the attempt of each party to utilize national aspirations to their own advantage. English reactions to the changes in the intent of the Act of Union were less than passive. A series of related events concluded in the sacking and burning of the Parliament buildings in Montreal by a mob of some 1500 anglophones in the spring of 1849.

After 1840

The legislative union of 1840 gave way to a federal union in 1867. It is not my intent to go into the economic, political and regional interests behind the British North America Act. For our purposes, let us note that by 1867, French and English had experienced little more than a century of contact within a single colonial enterprise. The interaction between the two, though retaining a dominant-subordinate relationship, resulted in a continuing recognition and legitimation of one party by the other. The subordinate party was never completely absorbed. French and English Canada faced each other in 1867 as distinctly recognizable nationalities, tied together by class coalitions.

Confederation, like the accommodations of 1763, 1774, 1791, and 1840, was a response to a changing economic milieu and the presence of the United States, overlayed with a continuing and highly institutionalized conflict between two national communities. Certainly, the shift from mercantilism to industrial capitalism prompted shifts in the manner in which the two communities were articulated. The old alliance between French clergy and seigneur and British colonial administrator shifted to an alliance between French clergy and business elite and the English-Canadian bourgeoisie. The alliance which had permitted British imperialism to maintain a hold in North America now provided a pool of low cost labour and a market for Anglo-American capital.

Needless to say, the five constitutional acts were not sacred. The fact that five different arrangements have been worked out during the past two centuries and that the last one, Confederation, has been seriously challenged by Quebec and the Western provinces, each operating in its own interests, indicates the continuity of two unresolved conflicts — the class question and the national question. One should keep in mind that the sovereignty-association scheme proposed by the Parti Québécois bears some similarity to the Constitutional Act of 1791.

Generally, all parties in French Canada were wary of federation. The final agreement permitted both French and English adherents to the plan to derive quite different interpretations. First, the B.N.A. Act may be interpreted «simply [as] a statute of the British Parliament, distributing powers afresh among Canadian governments through the exercise of an ancient imperial sovereignty.» [16] This was seldom, if ever, the interpretation accepted by French Canada nor did it gain much support from the other provinces. The significant split was between what Frank Scott has called the «dual state» and the «compact» theories.[17] The Act was a treaty between several powers. But was it fundamentally either a «compact» between several provinces, Quebec being one among equals, or a «compact» between two nations — French and English Canada? Without complete unanimity, English Canada has generally accepted the former view, French Canada the latter. It is to this position that Quebec now turns after its brief coalition with the seven dissident provinces during the recent constitutional debates.

Confederation appeared more threatening to French Canada than the 1840 union. Though there was provincial autonomy in certain areas, no longer was Lower Canada, now Quebec, to send representatives equal in numbers to English-speaking representatives to the national parliament. Furthermore, the addition of new provinces reduced the proportion of French to English to one-third. The spectre of assimilation once again haunted French Canada. Events following 1867 denied an existence to the type of bicultural, bilingual nation visualized by the more optimistic French-Canadian supporters of Confederation, the pan-Canadian nationalists.

With few exceptions, the B.N.A. Act did not treat Quebec any differently than the other provinces.[18] The fears of Quebec during and following the Act were well grounded. A deep feeling of minority position was perhaps more prevalent following than before Confederation. The Province of Quebec, not the French-Canadian nation was technically the unit entering Confederation. Moreover, French Canadians living outside Quebec were now members of an ethnic minority rather that the francophone citizens of a union between two nations. In contrast, the English of Quebec were quite at home in a province of their state and their nation.

Only one section of the Act referred specifically to language. Section 133 provided that: (1) either French or English may be used in the proceedings of the Parliament of Canada and the Legislature of Quebec; (2) that both languages were to be used in the records and acts of both assemblies; and (3), that either may be used in all the courts of Quebec and in any court elsewhere established by federal authority. This latter point appears to be the only point at which Law 101 is at odds with the B.N.A. Act. Thus, a *minimal* protection for the French language was provided. The emphasis in relation to Quebec, given that the language in use was mainly French, was on the protection of English. The English minority gained limited language privileges in Quebec, but French minorities in the remaining provinces were left without such privileges.

To this we should add that, in spite of the numerical minority of English speakers in Quebec, Anglo-American capital dictated that the language of commerce and work would be English. This is not to say that English as a working language necessarily follows Anglo-American capital. Rather, the historical relations of French and English nationalism in Quebec and Canada, and the association of the latter with capital ensured that English would dominate. Pan-Canadian nationalism and federal bilingual policies notwithstanding, English was the dominant language in Quebec, and outside Quebec — where its dominance was hardly in question — provincial legislatures made sure that French would be curtailed, if not eliminated.

Collective Rights, Survival and Structural Change

We might now return to our statements regarding collective and individual rights. Collective rights refer to claims made in the name of some category or group of people. Individual rights refer to claims made regardless of the ascribed or achieved characteristics of a person. This all too brief and perhaps overly familiar review of French-English relations demonstrated that the French and English languages and French- and English-Canadian nationalisms served to identify and symbolize the relative strength of each category in relation to the other. In fact, the nationalisms served to shape and nurture the two categories of people in such a way that each has come close to meeting all of the criteria sociologists use to define a collectivity:

> (1) a distinctive culture; (2) tests or criteria of membership; (3) a set of constitutive norms regulating social relations both within the [category] and with outsiders; (4) an awareness of a distinct identity by both members and non-members; (5) obligations of solidarity;[...] and (6) a high capacity for continued action by the [category] on behalf of its members or itself as a unit.[19]

Lord Durham's much quoted statement, «two nations warring within the bosom of a single state», aptly described the situation. In this context, one's language was the test and identifying characteristic of membership, and the language which dominated in public and private affairs alike symbolized the dominance and very authenticity of the category itself. Language was indeed the «colour» of French-English relations.

Accordingly, any move by one or the other category to limit the use or priority of its opposite language was, and is, perceived as a threat to the opposite category, to its existence and to the identity of its members. To the extent that the Royal Proclamation of 1763, The Quebec Act of 1774, The Constitutional Act of 1791, The Act of Union of 1840 and the British North America Act referred to language, each either extended, limited or attempted to eliminate the French language. Where these policies did not succeed, provincial governments, after Confederation, sought to either limit or eliminate French. All of these acts of governments have signaled an intent to either enhance or reduce the role of the French nation in the Canadian state.

374

Over the past decade, the Province of Quebec, acting within its perogatives, has sought to limit the use — and reduce the priority — of English in the public domain through Laws 63, 22 and 101. This has reversed the relationship. To Quebec's English speakers, these laws were perceived as threats to their institutions and to their *survival as a group*, not to their survival as individuals with the usual civil rights expected in any modern democratic society. From the Government side, these laws were passed to guarantee the survival of the French-speaking group and increase its power and status relative to the English minority. Whether one examines the situation from the position of French- or English-Canadian nationalism, language policies have been, and will undoubtedly continue to be, based on a concept of a right to collective recognition and survival.

The strategy of English-speaking groups has, from time to time, called upon the values inherent in the concept of individual, or human, rights to justify their opposition to Quebec language legislation. This is understandable. The members of a dominant ethnic, racial, religious or linguistic group seldom view their own world in terms of collective survival; nor is their language, ethnicity, or whatever the identifying characteristic might be, a dominant aspect of their conception of themselves. Comfortable in their dominant position, combined with the extreme individualism found in Protestantism relative to Catholicism, Quebec English speakers have not had to contemplate their history or their survival as a collectivity. Their historical myth has placed them in th role of colonial stewards. Once the existence of their group was threatened, a threat which carried over to each member's sense of his or her own worth, it was expected that the first moves to counter the threat would be based on individual rights and their priority over collective rights. Presumably, only the opposition bases its actions on collective rights. Hence perhaps, the ambivalence in a document like that presented by the Protestant School Board of Greater Montreal to which we referred, at the beginning of the chapter.

To return to that earlier quote, parents in Quebec still have the right to choose the kind of education they wish for their children, but limitations are placed on the language of instruction, not on the «kind of education». Apart from language, parents seem to have accepted considerable limitations on the kind of education their children will experience by having long ago abdicated their individual desires to the state. Regardless of the interests of individual parents, children must attend school until they reach a certain age; they must attend certain schools in certain places; they must take certain courses of study and may not take others, and so on. Do parents really determine the kind of education their children will have, or is the education system determined in the main by the needs of capital? The fact that many parents agree with these needs is not a sufficient base upon which to build an argument for individual rights. There is much in Law 101 which is politically and economically unsound, but few, if any, regulations offend individual rights any more or any less than any other piece of legislation passed in the collective interest. Insofar as the collective interests of Quebec francophones, when assured, limit the collective interests of anglophones, the battle is best fought on the basis of collective, not individual, rights.

As our discussion has unfolded, it has been all too easy to interpret events solely in terms of French-English relations, of French and English-Canadian nationalisms, and of the way these relations are played out through language practices, customs and policies. It has been all too easy to put aside the second image. The characters in Fennario's play, though they interpreted some of their day-to-day experiences in French-English terms, experienced another reality. That reality paid little heed to language or ethnicity. A landlord is a landlord and a boss is a boss regardless of the language they speak, though it may be more pleasant to be exploited in one's own language and by one's own kind. It may well follow that changes in the relative positions of French and English in Quebec will have little effect on the political-economy of capitalism . . .

Our discussion has tended to remain at a superstructural level describing events in Quebec according to the interplay of the two nationalisms. In so doing, we may have obscured the foundation or base upon which this view of our world rests. Our historical review did reveal that the nationalisms were based on class relations, which is to say on relations of dominance and subordination tied to the development of capitalism in Canada. We noted that language policies, whether embedded in custom or law, had their roots in British colonial policy as a means of control. The use of that means ideologically defined the two categories of people and became a way of interpreting subsequent events. The ideology of nationalism took on a life of its own such that we not only interpret our lives by its logic, but we also act by its logic. We could say that the ideology of French- and English-Canadian nationalism as an element of the superstructure has gained a certain amount of autonomy from its base or foundation in class relations. This relative autonomy means that changes can be effected in the realm of language and in the relative positions of English and French *qua* linguistic or national groupings with little — if any — changes occurring in the basic structures which have supported — and continue to support — the ideology of nationalism. On the other hand, it also means that changes in the relative positions of English and French may sufficiently rend the tie between nationalism and class to bring the underlying relations of capitalism into view and create movements toward fundamental structural changes. However, I do not think that the latter course of events is likely to follow.

NOTES

(1) Camille Laurin, «French Language Charter», *Canadian Review of Sociology and Anthropology,* 15, 2 (1978):121.

(2) Protestant School Board of Greater Montreal, *Statement on Bill 101 . . .*, p. 3.

(3) *Ibid.*, p. 8.

(4) Hubert Guindon, «The Modernization of Quebec . . .», p. 244.

(5) A.R. Radcliffe-Brown, *Structure and Function in Primitive Society*, London, Cohen and West, 1952): 190.

(6) Meyer Fortes, *Time and Social Structure and Other Essays* (New York, Humanities Press Inc., 1970):3.

(7) Stanley B. Ryerson, *The Founding of Canada: Beginnings to 1815*, p. 149.

(8) Maurice Tremblay, «Orientation de la pensée sociale», J.-C. Falardeau ed., *Essais sur le Québec contemporain* (Québec, Les presses de l'Université Laval, 1953):193-194.

(9) Mason Wade, *The French Canadians 1760-1945*, p. 5; S.D. Clark, *The Developing Canadian Community* (Toronto, University of Toronto Presse, 1952):20 and Stanley B. Ryerson, *The Founding of Canada . . .*, p. 147- 164.

(10) Bernard Bernier, «The Penetration of Capitalism in Quebec Agriculture», *The Canadian Review of Sociology and Anthropology*, 13, 4(1976):425.

(11) Gilles Bourque and Nicole Laurin-Frenette, «Social Classes and Nationalist Ideologies in Quebec, 1760-1970», p. 193.

(12) Mason Wade, *The French Canadians 1760-1945*, p. 54.

(13) S.D. Clark, *Movements of Political Protest in Canada: 1640-1840* (Toronto, University of Toronto Press, 1959):44.

(14) Mason Wade, *The French Canadians 1760-1945*, p. 260.

(15) Stanley B. Ryerson, *The Founding of Canada: . . .*, p. 229.

(16) Frank R. Scott, «Areas of Conflict in the Field of Public Law and Policy», p. 84.

(17) *Ibid.*, p. 87.

(18) *Ibid.*, p. 82.

(19) Robin M. William Jr., *Strangers Next Door: Ethnic Relations in America Communities* (Englewood Cliffs (N.J.), Prentice-Hall, 1964):18.

The English and Language Legislation: A Personal History

William Tetley, Q.C.

WILLIAM TETLEY. Educated at McGill and Laval universities, William Tetley practised law for eighteen years in Montreal and represented Notre-Dame de Grâce for eight years in the Quebec National Assembly, six and a half of them as a minister in the Bourassa government. In 1976, he resigned from the National Assembly to teach law at McGill University.

For sometime now there has been an acute awareness of the extent of English-speaking out-migration from Quebec. The irony of the situation lies in the fact that the exodus is taking place precisely at that the time in Quebec's history when the English themselves are most sympathetic towards the use of French. In fact, for many years, English Quebec has taken great steps to understand, accept and adopt the French language. Unfortunately, during the same period, there has been a decrease in the use of English by the Quebec government and an acceleration in the imposition of French in business. This has caused dramatic frustration and personal bitterness on the part of many English Quebecers.

Misunderstanding Regarding the Constitution, Confederation and Linguistic Rights

A major source of misunderstanding is the British North America Act of 1867 in which English Quebecers believed their language rights were enshrined. In actual fact, the Constitution provides few language guarantees, and its failure to give protection has caused the average English-speaking Quebecer to conclude that the Constitution has been violated. English Quebecers have been also treated as a minority for the first time, which has contributed to their feelings of bitterness and bewilderment.

All these causes of anglophone frustration — the imposition of the French language, the supposed violations of the Constitution, and the slow realization that in provincial matters they are a minority — can be laid at the door of three fundamental misconceptions of the past: a) the true constitutional nature of Canada as a confederation, b) the language rights accorded French Canadians in other provinces and minorities in other countries, as opposed to English-speaking rights in Quebec, and c) the actual language safeguards under the Canadian Constitution.

English Quebecers, as a rule, had seen Canada as an almost unitary state similar to Great Britain or France with a single central government, while French Canadians accepted Canada for what it really is — a confederation with a central government having certain powers under the Constitution and provincial governments having other powers under the same Constitution. (The latter view, of course, favours French Canadian rights, although provincial rights have recently become a battle cry for certain Western provinces.)

Similarly, the English in Quebec have considered the notion of «language of choice» as a principle enshrined in the Constitution and also a right granted minorities in other provinces and the rest of the world. In fact, very few minority language rights are to be found in the Constitution of Canada or, in practice, in other provinces or in other countries. If the reader doubts the public's misconception of the law, of the Constitution and of linguistic practices in Canada, he should need only read the two-sentence CFCF petition against Law 22 signed by 600 000 Quebecers in 1975 (the petition will be discussed later).

Misunderstanding is found not solely in the public mind. Six or seven years ago, when publicly discussing the Canadian Constitution with the Hon. James Richardson (then a federal liberal cabinet minister), I soon realized that not only did he refuse to admit, but he did not in fact really appreciate that the provincial legislatures were, under the Constitution, supreme in certain fields. This supremacy is signified by the presence of the maces on the table when the House is in session — the mace being the British symbol of parliamentary supremacy. His concept of Canada was of a virtually unitary state with an all-powerful federal government.

I also remember talking to the editorial page editor of an English-language paper who was enquiring about certain rights under the Constitution — a question which was, in essence, elementary. The editor, seeing my surprise, added, «But none of us at the paper, are lawyers». The paper and its editors had nevertheless, been authoritatively advising for the past twenty years or more English Quebecers on the Constitution, the law and their rights. Indeed, such concerns figured as the most important subject of its editorials.

To rectify somewhat this confusion, it may be said, in simple terms, that education is an exclusively provincial matter in virtue of section 93 of the B.N.A. Act whereby Protestant and Catholic denominational schools were to be protected in both Quebec and Ontario. There was however, no protection for the *language* of education.

Section 93 reads, in part, as follows:

> 93 — Education
> In and for each Province the Legislature may exclusively make Laws in relation to Education, subject and according to the following Provisions:
>
> (1) Nothing in any such Law shall prejudicially affect any Right or Privilege with respect to Denominational Schools which any Class of Persons have by Law in the Province at the Union;
>
> (2) All the Powers, Privileges and Duties at the Union by Law conferred and imposed in Upper Canada on the Separate Schools and School Trustees of the Queen's Roman Catholic Subjects shall be and the same are hereby extended to the Dissentient Schools of the Queen's Protestant and Roman Catholic Subjects in Quebec.

It can also be said that, according to section 133, both French and English may be used in the Courts and Legislatures of Canada and Quebec. This is the only express language protection under the B.N.A. Act. Section 133 reads as follows:

133
Either the English or the French Language may be used by any Person in the Debates of the Houses of the Parliament of Canada and of the Houses of the Legislature of Quebec; and both those Languages shall be used in the respective Records and Journals of those Houses; and either of those Languages may be used by any Person or in any Pleading or Process in or issuing from any Court of Canada established under this Act, and in or from all or any of the Courts of Quebec.

The Acts of the Parliament of Canada and of the Legislature of Quebec shall be printed and published in both those languages.

By section 92(13), «civil rights», and by extension, culture and language, are provincial matters; but the Federal government has some power over its own activities and, hence its employees. It is salutary to consider practice regarding language and education in some other provinces.

New Brunswick joined Confederation in 1867, but failed to protect its large French-Canadian minority. Double taxation of Catholic schools (for the most part French schools) existed until recently, while the imposition of partial bilingualism in the public service constitutes an innovation. In 1969, Premier Robichaud adopted the New Brunswick Official Languages Act, but only after the adoption in Quebec of Law 22 by the Bourassa government in 1974 did the Hatfield government dare to consider putting the New Brunswick law into force. Premier Hatfield continued to take an interest in, and even publicly criticized, Law 22; but the fact of the law in Quebec actually permitted him to quietly introduce his own law, the most important provisions of which came into force only on July 1, 1977. The New Brunswick Act, however, gives the province's 30-35 per cent French minority fewer rights than the 20 per cent English-speaking minority in Quebec received under Law 22.

Manitoba joined Confederation in 1870 and by an amendment of the B.N.A. Act, immediately adopted the educational and language freedoms of sections 93 and 133 of the B.N.A. Act. In 1890, by which time the English constituted a majority in the province, Manitoba unilaterally rescinded these same provisions. Thereafter, the Manitoba Courts and Legislature were unilingually English — Catholic and French schools no longer enjoying public support. However, in 1970, Law 113 restored a legal right to French schooling in Manitoba... where there was a sufficient number of students. Recently, the law of 1890 relating to the language of the courts has been declared invalid.

Ontario, on the other hand, like New Brunswick, was never bound by section 133 and so the Courts and Legislature were unilingually English. The provisions of section 93, supposedly intended to protect Catholic schools, were tested and the Catholic schools were held to be outside the public sector and thus, unable to benefit by public taxation. Necessarily, this applied to French schools. Up to 1967, there was no publicly supported French-language high-school education in Ontario and no legal right to education in French at the elementary level. In 1968, Ontario passed a law guaranteeing education in French. As a result, French education has made progress by leaps and bounds. By 1976-77, there were 106 517 francophone students, and the contentious problem has become not whether French classes should be provided, but whether there should be separate French schools and school boards.

In Quebec, on the contrary, not only was protection granted to the English language in 1867 in the Courts and the Legislature under section 133, but Protestant schooling and, by extension, English schooling, was freely provided under section 93. Private schooling, in any language or religion, was also supported up to a level of 60 per cent or 80 per cent of the cost of equivalent public education through public taxation, provided the school complied with public standards.

This, then, was the situation in 1968 when the Catholic school board in the municipality of St. Leonard, a suburb in the north-east section of the Island of Montreal, ordered Italo-Canadian children into French schools, in the face of the parents' desire for English education for their children. It soon became clear that the school board was correct in law, but the Italo-Canadians — believing they had lost a fundamental right — organized a march to Ottawa where Prime Minister Trudeau was sympathetic, but presumably told them that education was a provincial matter.

The Protestant School Board of Greater Montreal (PSBGM) did not support the St. Leonard English Catholics because it wished to preserve the principle that a school board in Quebec could decide its own language of instruction. The PSBGM could, thus, teach in English just as the School Board of St. Leonard could decide to teach in French. Similarly, the Provincial Association of Protestant Teachers (PAPT) almost one hundred years old, gave little support to the English Catholics of St. Leonard. Rather, it was the Provincial Association of Catholic Teachers (PACT) which led the fight for the Italo-Catholics of St. Leonard. It was precisely these English-speaking Catholic teachers whose jobs would be affected if the Catholic immigrants were transferred to French schools.

It was at this time that the present author was seeking election in Notre-Dame-de-Grâce as the Liberal candidate for the seat in the National Assembly, a post vacated by Eric Kierans in April 1968. My opponent, representing the Union Nationale, was John Lynch-Staunton, a respected Montreal city councillor. The Union Nationale government wished to overcome the Liberal tradition in N.D.G. and, as the campaign was fought on educational rights, Premier Jean-Jacques Bertrand decided to pass a law protecting English education. N.D.G. was an especially fitting place for such a programme because of the large number of English Catholics.

Bertrand's method was dramatic. Lynch-Staunton and I had been guests on many occasions on hot-lines (the famous Pat Burns, now departed to Vancouver, was the host of one of them), and Bertrand himself decided to go on a CFCF hot-line as the first caller. The Union Nationale picked other callers to speak to him (the hot-line favoured their guests in those days and Jean Lesage and I were favoured the next week in the same way on the same programme). The callers, with set questions, asked about schooling, and Bertrand promised a law to provide English education to the citizens of St. Leonard and throughout the Province for those who chose it.

Subsequently, Premier Bertrand deposited Bill 85 in the National Assembly providing for freedom of choice. N.D.G. voted massively Liberal just the same. Bertrand's Bill 85 had not been popular in his own caucus or in his Cabinet and consequently, after the defeat in N.D.G., he tried to withdraw it in the Assembly. This caused an even greater uproar. Eventually, Bertrand did withdraw the bill, but in disorder.

In 1969, the Union Nationale held a formal leadership convention and Bertrand narrowly defeated Jean-Guy Cardinal. Strengthened by his victory, Bertrand kept the promise made in the N.D.G. by-election and forced Cardinal, his Education Minister, to present Bill 63 which opened the door to freedom of choice. Two members of the Union Nationale left the Party over the bill, while René Lévesque who had already left the Liberal Party, and Yves Michaud, then of the Liberals, also voted against the bill.

Law 63 not only gave freedom of choice, but it also called for some degree of French instruction in English schools. Law 63, entitled «An Act to promote the French language in Quebec», read in part as follows:

> 1. The Minister shall take the measures necessary to have the curricula, made or approved for such educational institutions, and the examination which confirm them, ensure a working knowledge of the French language to children to whom instruction is given in the English language.

> 2. To take the measures necessary to have the courses of study from the first-year level to the eleventh-year level inclusive, adopted or recognized for Catholic, Protestant or other public schools, as the case may be, given to all children domiciled in the territory under their jurisdiction if they are deemed capable of following such courses and desirous of enrolling for them. Such courses must be given in the French language.

They shall be given in the English language to any child for whom his parents or the persons acting in their stead so request at his enrolment; the curricula and examinations must ensure a working knowledge of the French language to such children and the Minister shall take the measures necessary for such purpose.

3. In co-operation with the Minister of Education, take the measures necessary so that the persons who settle in Quebec may acquire the knowledge of the French language upon arrival or even before they leave their country of origin, and may have their children instructed in educational institutions where courses are given in the French language.

In April 1970, Robert Bourassa and the Liberals were elected and Victor Goldbloom, Kevin Drummond and I joined the Cabinet as the three English-speaking ministers. From the start, we were faced with opposition to Law 63 from the French-Canadian population and, strangely, from part of the English-speaking population. One of the problems of Law 63 was that it caused, or seemed to cause, a weakening of the French school system by virtue of the fact that many French Canadians, as well as immigrants could, and did, choose English schools. A strong protest was, therefore, made against the Law both in the new Parti Québécois and in the Liberal Party, and among French Canadians in general. There was a strong feeling that it should be modified in respect to at least new Canadians who often preferred English to French schooling. At the same time, the Protestant School Board of Greater Montreal, objecting to the provision calling for some French instruction for the English of Quebec, also mounted an attack against Law 63.

Yet, the English population of Quebec did not share the fears of the PSBGM. Years before, the Protestant Home and School Associations in Westmount, Town of Mount-Royal and elsewhere, had begun extra classes in French outside school hours and at their own expense because the PSBGM opposed instruction *in* French. Later the PSBGM took over the French classes and even began immersion classes, although originally it was blindly against Law 63 and against instruction *in* French rather than *of* French. As a result the PSBGM, in the spring of 1971, decided to petition the Federal government to disallow Law 63. *The Montreal Star*, to its credit, opposed the PSBGM in an editorial.

The PSBGM opposition to Law 63 was, nevertheless, supported by the same members of the population who seemed to oppose anything connected with French, and they had the support of most of the media. A series of letters soon appeared in the letters to the editor columns of *The Gazette* and *The Montreal Star* opposing Law 63, whilst hot-lines and radio generally took up the complaints in what became an extremely tense atmosphere.

Those who were more rational on language questions — and who probably were a majority — rarely spoke up, rarely wrote letters to the editor, and rarely spoke on hot-lines on this matter, or any other. Feeling a reply was in order, I wrote to the newspapers putting forward the position that opposition to Law 63 was harmful to English-speaking interests. This brought a rain of criticism upon my head, but I replied with more letters which only brought more bitter criticism. Later, when discussing the period with Bourassa, the latter thanked me for having taken the pressure off; however, he recalled he had told me that opposing the hysteria was doomed from the start. The deputy for Ste. Anne, George Springate, joined the clamour. In the papers, letter writers against Law 63 included some of the leading lawyers and constitutional experts in Quebec, and persons inside and outside the National Assembly, all of whom called themselves defenders of English rights. Today they all have forgotten their part in the nefarious protest.

The PSBGM opposition to Law 63 is not surprising when considered from an historical perspective. The PSBGM had a long tradition of jealously protecting its own status at the expense of what may sometimes be considered the common good. For example, the right of Jews to vote for, or hold, office as Protestant school commissioners was publicly opposed by the PSBGM in court and in 1969 at a parliamentary commission in the National Assembly as well. The PSBGM was not willing to see what it considered its constitutional position eroded by any act or acquiescence on its part.

The PSBGM's basic position on education was enunciated, in an opinion dated November 29, 1969, by four leading Quebec lawyers who held that «English» school education as well as Protestant education was guaranteed under section 93 of the B.N.A. Act of 1867. They believed that the pre-Confederation law of 1861 which provided for English schooling was guaranteed by section 93 of the B.N.A. Act. Thus, English schools, as they existed in 1867, were guaranteed.

The opinion was, at best, a complicated and tenuous historical argument which was later rejected outright in Court. Even if generally accepted, it is subject to four major qualifications:

a) It only applied, by its own terms, to minority (dissentient) school boards, for the most part in metropolitan Montreal and Quebec. It did not, for instance, protect the English Catholics of St. Leonard, nor would it apply to the Protestants in Westmount who were a majority (common) board not protected by section 93. These facts were never brought to the attention of the English Catholics of St. Leonard or the Protestants of Westmount;

b) It also ran directly against the wording of section 93 of the B.N.A. Act (which spoke of Protestant and Roman Catholic) and against normal rules of statute interpretation;

c) The opinion specifically states: «It is obvious that an education system designed to protect the rights of Roman Catholics and Protestants provides little comfort for those that belong to neither denomination.» This was never brought to the attention of Jews, Greek Orthodox and others, who relied on the PSBGM position.

d) It was politically guileless as well, because it went contrary to the interpretation of legislation in respect to Catholics and French Canadians in Ontario who had been advised by the Privy Council that they did not have such rights under the same section 93, of the same B.N.A. Act, in the same Canada.

It was unfortunate that the limitations of the opinion were never made clear to the public and to Home and School Associations who had collected large sums of money to defend their «rights». Nor was it ever made clear that the opinion was based on a long, complicated, historical hypothesis as well as questionable statute interpretation. The PSBGM opinion was never supported in law outside of its limited circle, and the position was dismissed by the Chief Justice of the Superior Court on the first occasion it was raised. In effect, the Court held that *Roman Catholic* and *Protestant* schools did not mean *French* and *English* schools.

Unfortunately, the PSBGM opinion led the English-speaking public to believe that not only was English-language education an indisputable *right* for all citizens throughout Quebec, but that English-language rights existed in respect to contracts, public signs, corporate names, all business matters, and in dealings with the government. It was probably the basis for the misconceptions inherent in both the CFCF and the PSBGM petitions in favour of abolition of Law 22 addressed to the Federal government.

When I spoke on separate occasions to the chairman and the vice-chairman of the PSBGM, John Sims and Joan Dougherty, over their adamant petition against all of Law 22, they both replied with sincerity to the effect: «But we have the advice of the best lawyers.» Those lawyers, however, never made it clear publicly that their opinion was, after all, only an opinion and that, even if valid, it was limited in scope... even in respect to education.

The pre-1973 years could be likened to a false war over language. Any reasonable effort to change the *status quo* was opposed by a small but vociferous English group on one side, while a small French group on the other wanted French unilingualism. The English, in a minority position without the law on their side, acted as though they were a majority supported by law. The French, for their part, were only discovering that the law on language could be defined by the majority and were demanding increased use of French in schools, public institutions, and business. A minority of French Canadians wanted to go further and instigate French unilingualism in the school system and in Quebec life generally.

Working Within the Cabinet and Law 22

At that time, the role I saw for myself as an English- speaking minister was to promote bilingualism in Cabinet and in public, and to convince the population of its benefits. This was anathema to many English Quebecers who still did not understand the law in Quebec and Canada, or the practices in Quebec, the rest of Canada, and the rest of the world. At best, they wanted double unilingualism or «institutional bilingualism» — government public institutions and business would be bilingual so that *they* could remain unilingual English, and could be dealt with in their own language. Bilingualism, I tried to explain, was the ability and desire on the part of individuals to work and live in two languages. Herewith are three instances drawn from that tension-ridden period surrounding the implementation of Law 22 in the course of which I tried to implement my conception of bilingualism. The first touches on the question of consumer contracts. In 1971, as Minister of Financial Institutions, Companies and Cooperatives, I presented, and had adopted, what appears to have been the first law in Quebec history to promote priority of the French language but still provide protection for the English. It was article 4 of the Consumer Protection Act (Law 45) which stated that consumer contracts had to be in French but could also be in English. If a contract was bilingual and there was a contradiction between the two texts, the contract would be interpreted so that the language most favourable to the consumer would apply. Article 4 of Law 45 read:

> The contract must be legibly drawn up in French, but the consumer may require that it be drawn up in English.
>
> Every contract drawn up in French and in English shall comply with this section. In the case of a contradiction between the two texts, the interpretation most favourable to the consumer shall prevail.

Article 4 was, nevertheless, roundly criticized by the vociferous «English first» group. I had proposed such a text to the Federal government and to the other nine provinces at a Federal/Provincial conference in Ottawa of Consumer Protection ministers in 1971. The ministers, in private, were warm in their praise of it, but none adopted it.

Later, as Minister of Financial Institutions, I tried hard to convince the Stock Exchange to work not merely in English but also in French, and to switch to bilingual bylaws, instead of unilingual English ones. The Exchange unfortunately dragged its feet. Sometime later, in 1974, the Exchange celebrated its one-hundredth anniversary. Many renowned persons were invited to the week-long ceremonies, including the economists Lady Barbara Ward Jackson and Milton Friedman (later a Nobel Prize Winner), both of whom made uplifting speeches on world economic affairs. Via a communiqué, I suggested, once again, that it was time to have bilingual bylaws. It was perhaps a realistic but badly timed suggestion (it had rained on the Stock Exchange parade), and it brought considerable hostile comment in the financial pages of the papers. Eventually, however, the Exchange adopted bilingual bylaws.

In 1973, I also amended the *Companies Act*, to the effect that all new Quebec companies would be obliged to have a French name, with the option of having an additional English or a bilingual name. Companies already in existence were invited to change (without charge) their names.

I was proud of the proposal, but the proposition was met without enthusiasm by businessmen and lawyers. We sent out notices to each of over 60 000 existing Quebec companies and waived the normal government fee for a name change. How many complied? Less than twenty-five. Subsequently, I wrote a personal letter to the presidents of five-hundred top Quebec companies asking them to comply. This included paper companies which benefit enormously from Quebec's natural resources. How many volunteered? Only a handful. Finally, we conducted a survey to find out the reasons for this lack of interest. The answer was, repeatedly: «It is not in our interest». These were the people who claimed they would voluntarily accept French, but «did not want it stuffed down their throats.»

The three foregoing examples of government legislation or action in respect to language illustrate that proceeding in a piecemeal fashion might meet as much public opposition as a single, all embracing, language law. The latter course was followed, in any event, by the Bourassa government when it implemented its now famous, or infamous, Law 22.

In the 1973 general election, the Liberals were reelected. This time, they gained an overwhelming number of seats in the Assembly, but the Parti Québécois increased its popular vote from 25 per cent to 30 per cent. Language and schooling were important issues during the election campaign — the P.Q. calling for drastic measures to protect the French language and the Liberals for more realistic ones.

In May 1974, the Bourassa government presented a language law entitled Bill 22, which proved to be long overdue for the majority, but too advanced for the minority. On the night of the presentation of the Bill, I happened to meet Mr. Bourassa walking in the garden of Parliament after the 11:00 p.m. news. He was not disturbed, but in fact seemed pleased that certain French and English groups were expressing their opposition to it. He believed there were extremists in each wing and that the majority in the middle would eventually support the Bill. In this, as we now know, he was wrong. He added, sympathetically, «I know I am passing the law on the backs of you, Kevin (Drummond) and Victor (Goldbloom).» In this he was right, particularly because he allowed, and even seemed to promote, backbench public opposition to the Bill in Caucus, while we, in Cabinet, had the non-public role of bringing about softening amendments to the Bill and then seeing that its regulations and implementation were fair. All this occurred out of public view and was bound by Cabinet silence. The efforts to soften the Bill were, nevertheless, successful.

Law 22, in protecting the French language, really promoted bilingualism and gave greater protection to the English of Quebec than any French minority in Canada or any minority in most places in the world enjoys. No amount of reason, however, could convince the English press, the English letter-writers, the English teachers, or the English radio and T.V. of this fact. I distributed letters, made speeches locally and across Canada, and wrote many newspaper articles, including a weekly article in the N.D.G. newspaper, but I was swimming against the tide. Few English Quebecers seemed to want to believe the truth about Law 22 or to reach an accommodation with the French-speaking majority of Quebec. Not only was this position unpopular, it resulted in bitterness and animosity towards me. At one point, one of my friends quipped, «Who starts your car for you?».

Yet Bill 22, when deposited at first reading in May 1974, provided the following:

1. If at least ten percent of the persons administered by a municipal or school body are English-speaking and it has been its practice to draw up its official texts and documents in English, it must continue to draw up these documents in English. (s.9).

2. Every person may address the public administration in French or in English, as he may choose. (s.10).

3. Municipal and school bodies in which the majority of the persons administered are English-speaking may use French or English in their internal communication. (s.13).

4. Remarks addressed to the Chair at formal discussions held within the public administration may be made in French or in English, at the option of the persons addressing the remarks. (s.15).

5. Although corporations must have a French name, they can also have an English version of that name and carry on business under the English name. (See s.30 and the Companies Act, Chap. 271).

6. Public signs may be drawn up in both French and English or in French and another language. (s.35).

7. Advertisements appearing in English-language newspapers or periodicals may be drawn up only in English. (s.36).

8. The Minister of Education shall adopt the necessary measures to ensure that pupils receiving their instruction in English acquire a knowledge of spoken and written French. (s.44).

9. If, in the opinion of the «Régie de la Langue Française» (French Language Board) a person has suffered an injustice by the effect of any act or regulation, it may suggest amendments to the Lieutenant-Governor in Council and, if it sees fit, submit a special report to the Minister, who shall immediately lay it before the National Assembly; it may also, if it chooses, set forth the situation in its annual report. (s.93).

Amendments to Bill 22

Later, after considerable — friendly but tense — in-fighting in Cabinet, the following changes providing additional rights for English-speaking Quebecers were made:

1. Municipal and school bodies which administer for a majority English population may communicate with other governments and corporations in English (i.e., McGill University). (s.13).

2. Contracts predetermined by one party, contracts containing printed standard clauses, and printed order forms, invoices and receipts must be drawn up in English when the customer requires it. (s.33).

3. School commissions shall continue to provide instruction in the English language. This applies to all school boards presently providing education in English. (s.40) This section guarantees the right to English-language instruction as opposed to section 93 of the B.N.A. Act which guarantees Protestant education.

4. Conversely, the Minister shall ensure that pupils receiving their instruction in French acquire a knowledge of the English language. (s.44).

5. In the event of contradiction between the French and English wording of a printed or predetermined contract drawn up in both languages, the interpretation which most favours the customer prevails. (s.33).

6. English or any other language may be used by the public administration in contracts (s.17), official texts and documents when in accordance with international usage. (s.48).

7. The Ombudsman is empowered to act when there are complaints under the Official Language Act, in any matter within his jurisdiction. (s.94).

8. An amendment also removed the necessity for a firm which has or wants a permit from Quebec to have a francization certificate. (Former s.33).

9. An amendment also made it clear that the Act would not derogate contracts or practices in Quebec where international usage required otherwise, i.e., insurance contracts, shipping contracts and practices. (s.48, par.2).

In July 1974, the modified bill was deposited in the Assembly for third reading.

No amount of reasoning, however, could quieten hysterically vociferous English opponents of the Bill who refused to take counsel from anyone but themselves and their proclaimed spokesmen. They believed, in particular, that the practices of the past were rights rather than privileges. Numerous meetings were held, and on June 10, 1974, at the largest of such meetings, over five thousand persons filled Loyola College arena. Speaker after speaker, chosen from various sectors of English society including the Liberal members from Ste. Anne (Springate), Brome-Missisquoi (Glenn Brown), Mount Royal (John Ciaccia), and Huntingdon (Ken Fraser), spoke vehemently against all aspects of the bill; some going so far as to make comparisons with Nazi Germany. I was booed repeatedly by the frenzied audience, and when I stood to speak I was unable to do so. *The Gazette* and *The Montreal Star* were sympathetic to my right to speak but, notwithstanding, only *Le Devoir* published the text of my proposed speech.

The entire programme was broadcast by CJAD which also recorded the event on a tape. Reading the transcription of that tape today makes one realize how violently opposed some Quebecers were to any kind of accommodation towards the other language. Even more unfortunate, however, was the absolute silence of most moderate English-speaking Quebecers who might have turned the tide had they intervened.

Public hearings were held on Bill 22 in the summer of 1974, and various English-speaking groups appeared and pleaded for what they called «bilingualism». But what they were really advocating was «institutional» bilingualism. For example, very few of their representatives could really express themselves adequately in French. The PSBGM used the services of its director general, born and educated in France, to speak in French on its behalf at the public hearing. The Montreal Board of Trade, as well as other groups, used French-Canadian speakers. All pleaded for bilingualism without, however, appreciating the incongruity of their position.

Later the PSBGM prepared a petition to the Federal government, in protest against many of the provisions of Law 22 which the signatories saw as being unconstitutional and contrary to human rights. The petition opposed the education provisions as well as those articles of the Law providing for bilingualism in consumer affairs, bilingual signs, English advertisements in English newspapers, bilingual corporate names, the right to deal with the government in French or English, and the rights of municipalities to work in French and English.

The PSBGM and its lawyers continued to lead the general public to believe that these were rights in law and rights which, in fact, were practised in other provinces and in other countries. When I remonstrated with one of the lawyers, he replied that one has to ask for more in order to get less. He did not seem to understand the political effects of such a misleading practice on so important an issue for Quebec and Canada. The petition in question was presented on a national level, and school board leaders from Ontario, Saskatchewan and other provinces were invited to sign, although their provinces offered much less in the way of language rights. They signed, nevertheless, with apparent conviction. Today, the petition and the signatures make amusing but sad reading.

The frenzy quieted, or so it seemed . . . but a year later, in the fall of 1975, the apogee of the hysteria took place when 600 000 mostly English-speaking Quebecers, urged on by a non-stop radio campaign on CFCF, paid fifty cents each and signed a telegram petition to Ottawa and Quebec. The petition read as follows:

> We, the undersigned, Canadians in the Province of Quebec, urgently demand that you use the power vested in you by the electorate to abolish the Bill 22 and restore our fundamental rights as Canadians, to work and to educate our children in the language of our choice.

> We feel Bill 22 violates and is in direct contravention of the Federal Government's clear and emphatic official stand on bilingualism.

They, of course, ignored that there were no «fundamental rights as Canadians to work and educate our children in the language of our choice». This was not a right in law in any province, nor was such a right practised in any province. In fact, Quebec, under Law 22, guaranteed more language rights than any other province. The second paragraph of the petition shows that its authors also ignored the fact that the Federal government's language law only applied to Federal institutions and only really called for bilingualism in Quebec with a prospect of bilingualism in Ontario and New Brunswick where numbers warranted that. Finally, the call for integral bilingualism in the second paragraph contradicted the first paragraph which was really a call for institutional bilingualism.

Putting the language provisions of Law 22 into operation fell upon the shoulders of Jérôme Choquette, who, in a major Cabinet shuffle, had on August 1st 1975, been named Minister of Education. He soon found that the English language tests under Law 22, instead of being restrictive, allowed a large number of new Canadians to gain access to English education. As a result, the English school population actually began increasing, while the French school population continued to decrease. He resigned when the Cabinet would not agree to have all non-English Quebecers go to French schools whether they could pass the tests or not.

To my mind the testing of children was the most unacceptable part of Law 22 viewed as a package; on the other hand, I reconciled myself with the fact that most school boards test children in any case to determine on what conditions they will be admitted into their particular system. A «mother tongue» system as proposed by the Superior Council of Education would have required almost a personal, on-the-spot investigation of the family life, home and family history of each student. The tests, as proposed by Law 22 were not onerous. They allowed the English schools to expand, and directly concerned only a very small proportion of the children in the system.

Raymond Garneau took over the Education portfolio from Choquette for a few months, taking a hard-line position, although not as hard as Choquette. He was followed by Jean Bienvenue who was also concerned by the growth of the English system and the contraction of the French school population. Despite the fact that the English school system was growing as compared with the French system, the English-speaking uproar over Law 22 continued after 1974, impeding our work both within and outside Cabinet.

My role in Cabinet was, I believed, to see that the system was administered fairly, and I made it my practice to raise objections and suggestions on all language questions raised in Cabinet by written memos. Arguing in writing on any question not connected with one's own ministry was novel in Cabinet and did not make for the happiest relations. On the other hand, it kept the record straight. Those memos, and the replies, also make a useful record today; particularly because only one set of Cabinet minutes is kept, and those minutes only record the barest details of positive decisions taken and none of the arguments for and against a proposition.

Major debates took place in Cabinet over the language tests, their content, their difficulty, etc., and over the language regulations. At times, the memos and the replies caused a weekly confrontation between myself and Cloutier, then Choquette, then Garneau and finally Bienvenue. All four ministers, it must be said, accepted the process in good faith and spirit.

I also exchanged detailed memos with Fernand Lalonde who was in charge of the implementation of the language regulations in respect to business. In particular, after weeks of discussion, memos and debates, it was agreed and decreed in the regulations that «Québécois» meant not someone whose mother tongue was French but anyone who spoke French. This was an important decision. It will be recalled that Bill 1, the first version of the «Language Charter», contained the restrictive definition of Québécois, but it was altered when Bill 101 was adopted. The discussion by memo had the benefit of permitting an orderly debate, which most persons in Cabinet welcomed. This was especially true of Bourassa who once said, when I entered the Cabinet room late having been at Treasury Board, «Here comes the opposition. Now we can start.» He had postponed the language question until I arrived.

Epilogue: November 1976 and Law 101

On October 16, 1976, Robert Bourassa called an election. Jérôme Choquette, who had formed a new party, now supported complete freedom of choice, while the two Liberals who earlier had voted against Law 22 (Springate and Ciaccia) still felt able to support Bourassa and the Liberal language programme.

On November 15, 1976, the Parti Québécois was elected and, within a year, Bill 101, the Parti Québécois language law, was adopted. It took away most of the rights granted the English under Law 22, including bilingual signs, bilingual corporate names, the right of corporations to plead in court in English (unless all parties agree), and the right to deal with the government in English. *Bilingualism* was being replaced by *French unilingualism*.

In particular, only children whose brothers and sisters or whose parents had gone to English schools *in Quebec* would, in the future, be able to attend English schools. In 1977, an officer of the PSBGM prophesied that the English language school population of the Board would be down to five thousand by 1985. Under Law 22, the English school population had actually been increasing (if one makes an adjustment for declining school population in general).

Court actions were taken and, whereas Law 22 had been found to be constitutional, Law 101 was found to be unconstitutional in respect to the language of the Courts and of the Legislature, as protected by section 133 of the B.N.A. Act.

In 1978, Claude Ryan and Raymond Garneau faced each other over the leadership of the Quebec Liberal Party. Claude Ryan advanced «mother tongue» as the criterion for deciding which children would go to English schools. Ryan's proposition was much less generous than Law 22 and would have cut out most new Canadians. It also exchanged the test for some sort of unexplained investigation to prove what language a child had spoken in childhood. Such a method would have reduced English clientele considerably, although it would have had less effect than Law 101. Raymond Garneau, the former adamant Minister of Education, supported, surprisingly, freedom of choice; and freedom of choice was the only policy issue separating Ryan and Garneau. The two Liberal members of the National Assembly who had voted against Bill 22 (Messrs. Springate and Ciaccia), supported Mr. Ryan, the front runner, while Jérôme Choquette, who had resigned from Cabinet because of his opposition to freedom of choice, and who had proceeded to support freedom of choice in the election of November 13, 1976, joined Ryan as well.

Since Law 101, what has happened? Certainly, the English-speaking population of Quebec would seem to have accepted Law 101 better than they did Law 22. Perhaps it is a question of having lost hope; perhaps there is a changing of minds. Certainly, all of us have evolved.

Whatever the cause, I detect a change in attitude on the part of anglophones towards language rights. People who were opposed to Law 22 or who were at the Loyola meeting of June 1974 are now coming up to speak to me quite sympathetically. Some have even forgotten their hard-line position of the past. For years, my wife and I have had season tickets at a Montreal theatre company and for years, at each production, the English-speaking parking lot attendant from Côte St. Luc would berate me about how Law 22 was taking all his rights away. After Law 101, he became silent, and in 1979, when I asked him his views on Law 22, he replied, «Why, I was always for it!» Oh, yes, of course!

On the night of the defeat of November 15, 1976, Robert Bourassa was asked about his language policy and Law 22, and whether he had changed his mind. He said it all, perhaps, when he answered, «Who has not changed his mind on language over the years?» He is right: we all have.

For my own part, I particularly regret the fact that Law 22, the Quebec Liberal Party language accommodation, was rejected out of hand by the French and English of Quebec. It is difficult to predict which group will suffer most in the long run.

To my mind, Law 22 was *defensive nationalism*, properly defending a language, while Law 101 is *offensive nationalism* which attempts, at times, to promote one group in a larger society rather than a language.

The Anglophone Left in Quebec and National Self-Determination

Henry Milner

HENRY MILNER. Author of *Politics in the New Quebec*, Henry Milner is a close observer of the provincial political scene. In addition, he has been active in the Montreal Citizens Movement and the CSN, and is currently a member of the National Executive of the Parti Québécois. He teaches political science at Vanier College, and is presently researching a book on the politics of educational reform in Quebec.

The political evolution of Quebec in recent years has had a pronounced effect on its English-speaking population. This effect has sometimes been a direct and quite evident one producing concrete anglophone responses to specific developments, for example, the outbursts against Laws 22 and 101. There have also been indirect consequences for them resulting in subtle yet profound changes, changes often imperceptible at the time they were taking place.

Anglophones are defined for the purpose of this analysis simply as those residents of Quebec who operate in their daily lives more in English than in any other language. This is not a theoretical criterion but a practical one. It serves to distinguish an important element of the Quebec population whose sources of information and reference, both formal and informal, both institutional and personal, are vested in the English language. This paper looks particularly at one element within the anglophone population which, for lack of a better term, is called the Quebec anglophone left. Since we seek herein to focus mainly on political developments, the anglophone left refers to those English-speaking Quebecers who at some point were active in certain organizations or otherwise took part in political activities considered socialist, social democratic, or progressive.

The relationship is thus a three-way one: among Quebec society as a whole, the English-speaking population, and the left within this population. The changes in the role of this left within both the English population and Quebec society as a whole, as well as in the attitudes and positions of the left vis-à-vis Quebec nationalism are, not unexpectedly, examples of such subtle yet ultimately profound indirect effects.

There are two primary themes that will emerge in this essay. The first concerns the historical ambivalence of the anglophone left vis-à-vis the national project in Quebec, its sources and its present configuration. The second is the change in the place of this left in the wider English- speaking population, as interwoven with the change in the place of the English-speaking population in Quebec itself. By elaborating on these, I seek to clarify both the contributions of the anglophone left and the constraints acting on the group, raising in the end the question of the part to be played by the anglophones in the new Quebec.

Historical Antecedents

Apart from a few short-lived and isolated labour organizers and their political representatives around the turn of the century, the first lasting, organized, left presence in Quebec is a phenomenon of the 1920s and especially the 1930s centered around the activities of the Communist Party and the Cooperative Commonweath Federation (CCF). The CCF-ers presence in Quebec was almost entirely limited to the English-speaking population. Its well-known centralism and general lack of understanding for Quebec traditions and nationalist sensibilities went hand-in-hand.

> There was nothing in the CCF as a political movement that was really consistent with attitudes that prevailed in Quebec. It was a foreign element, it was opposed by the Catholic Church, it preached centralism, and it had in it English Canadians who frequently demonstrated great ignorance and prejudice where Quebec and French-Canadian rights were concerned. Throughout its sickly career in this province, the CCF spoke to Quebec with an English accent.[1]

The Communists, on the other hand, demonstrated greater sympathy for Quebec national sentiments — hesitantly coming so far as to admit the legitimacy of national self-determination for Quebec — but they too, ultimately, failed to seriously penetrate French Quebec.

> The oscillations in party policy on French Canada reflect, among other things, an endemic fear of overstepping the border line between acceptable nationalism and «bourgeois nationalism», or chauvinism. Yet this fear was much more evident in the way the Party dealt with French-Canadian than with English-Canadian nationalism, which the Party embraced frequently, and with enthusiasm. This was also reflected in the relations between French- and English-speaking members, and the fact that the Party has never (and this has continued to the present day) entrusted the leadership of the Quebec section to French Canadians. At times, French Canadians were promoted to leading positions in the Quebec section, even once to the rank of provincial leader, but on all such occasions the real power was still held by English-speaking representatives of the Party's national leadership...[2]

While both the CCF and Communist Party were rightly suspicious of the reactionary currents characteristic of much of Quebec nationalism at the time, such currents were by no means uncontested. Among francophone Quebecers, there were significant progressive elements active in the main nationalist movements, the Action libérale nationale of the 1930s and the Bloc populaire of the 1940s. The CCF had no impact on these left nationalist Quebec intellectuals, as the leading figure among them, André Laurendeau, noted in 1948:

> The CCF has always presented itself to us with an English aspect. I have known many of our young peo-

ple who normally might have been its adherents [. . .] But they found themselves in a strange climate, they were not at home [. . .] Our socialists haven't a truly independent outlook. They are ideologically linked up with labour parties in England, Australia and New Zealand. This is a plant which doesn't acclimatize itself easily in Quebec.[3]

Elsewhere,[4] Laurendeau tells of his experiences with a number of young English-speaking progressives in the late thirties and early forties, some of whom turned out to be members of the Communist Party. The young Communists first cultivated progressive nationalists like Laurendeau until the Soviet Union entered the Second World War. However, in response to international considerations, once the Soviet Union entered the War, the Party members were the first to denounce their erstwhile comrades for sabotaging the great democratic war effort. Even in the years after the War the Communists continued to repudiate «bourgeois nationalism» resulting in many scores of expulsions and resignations among important francophone members of the Party.[5]

The 1950s witness a general decline of these two, now almost entirely English-speaking, organizations in Quebec, as elsewhere in North America. The CCF was going nowhere politically all across Canada, its decline reflecting the general turning to the right throughout the continent. The Communist Party suffered from this as well as from events tied to its specific nature. The Gouzenko-Rose spy scandal discredited its activities in Canada, and Kruschev's lurid revelations of the crimes of the Stalinist regime at the twentieth Congress of the Communist Party of the Soviet Union undermined the credibility of the Party's line, not only in the public but among sympathizers and even members. Not only was the Communist Party deprived of its French-speaking contingent during this period, but its basic constituency among immigrant English-speaking Quebecers, notably the Jews, was very much weakened through resignations brought on by these events. It also suffered from the general sociological change in much of this community as post-war prosperity enabled it to move rapidly from a working class to a middle class social milieu.

The main progressive current in Quebec during the «dark» 1950s was of a left liberal and sometimes social democratic character, that of «opposition» intellectuals most commonly found writing in *Cité Libre* or *Le Devoir*, or working in the Catholic unions. While certainly influenced by progressive currents in other parts of the English-speaking world, the concrete links between them and the Quebec anglophone left were in fact extremely limited.

The 1960s mark a period of transition in the role of the English-speaking left, coinciding with important changes in Quebec as a whole. Duplessis was dead; national expression was becoming politicized and aggressive, both in its more extreme form embodied by the Rassemblement pour l'indépendance nationale

(RIN), and in the «maîtres chez nous» initiatives being taken by the Lesage Liberals. The context for left political activity was thus altered. The opposition intellectuals were in power in Quebec or close to it, in the growing quasi-state institutions, in education, the mass media and the arts, as well as in the trade unions. The moderately progressive forces that transformed Quebec in those days of the Quiet Revolution constituted a temporary and unstable coalition, one that could but fall apart once liberal reform had reached its limits as it had by the middle of the decade. It was succeeded by the «Québec dans la rue» outbursts of the late 1960s and the subsequent rise of the Parti Québécois and increase in labour militancy of the early seventies.[6] Eric Kierans is probably the anglophone most closely associated with the forces of change during the Quiet Revolution; another was Douglas Fullerton.[7] The subsequent careers of both these men — in the case of Kierans, his turning against his closest ally in the Lesage cabinet, René Lévesque, when the latter came to espouse associate status for Quebec and, in the case of Fullerton, his practically making a career in recent years of denouncing the project of the Parti Québécois — demonstrate the limitations of even the most progressive anglophones among the Liberals, when confronted with the nationalist direction being taken by their francophone counterparts. Hence, when Lévesque's group left the Liberals to become the Mouvement souveraineté-association (MSA), then joined with the Ralliement national (RN) and won over the members of the Rassemblement pour l'indépendance nationale (RIN) to form the Parti Québécois, there was no anglophone constituent element in this significant new political formation.

A more important, though also temporary, forum for anglophone left political activity during this period was the social democratic one. The CCF had been replaced by the New Democratic Party and this new Party succeeded in attracting a number of key Quebec intellectuals and trade unionists. This coincided with a moving away from rigid centralism to an official, though underplayed, recognition of Quebec's national identity. The harmony was not to last long. Divisions over the national question arose; and soon the great majority of francophone NDPers set themselves apart by founding a separate provincial party to be known as the Parti Socialiste du Québec leaving the Federal field almost entirely to the anglophone NDP leadership. The PSQ itself was, however, to be short-lived and subsequently, with the social democrats effectively eliminated from provincial politics by 1966, interest again focused on the Federal arena. During the mid-sixties minority governments in Ottawa had drawn attention to the role of the NDP, and the party thus succeeded in gaining a toehold in Quebec Federal politics. Under Robert Cliche, NDP candidates such as Denis Lazure, Charles Taylor, Laurier Lapierre, and C.G. «Giff» Gifford, as well as Cliche himself, ran credibly in Montreal area ridings.

In the end, the NDP failed to penetrate Quebec. Ultimately unable or unwilling to alienate pro-federalist supporters in English Canada, the NDP has been unable to make any progress on the national question, thus ensuring a marginal place for itself in Quebec politics. Unfortunately, not only has it failed to attract the francophone left nationalists who support the PQ but, having lost the bulk of its former anglophone electoral support to the Trudeau Liberals with their promise of stamping out separatism, the NDP has done nothing to educate its still loyal anglophone supporters in regard to Quebec's national reality. The outcome was that, by the end of the decade, English-speaking progressives in Quebec were effectively shut out of any kind of relevant political party activity at the Provincial or Federal level. Fortunately, however, other arenas do begin to open up.

The late sixties saw the emergence of a whole new range of political formations on the left.[8] These may be fitted into three basic categories, though some cross-fertilization does take place between them. The first consists of new left nationalist groupings — from the short-lived Mouvement de libération populaire (MLP) founded in 1964 by the magazine *Parti Pris*, to the 1968-69 groups: the language-oriented Ligue pour l'intégration scolaire (LIS) and the Front de libération populaire (FLP), a radical offshoot of the RIN, and, finally, to the terrorist Front de Libération du Québec (FLQ) in its various generational forms. Anglophone participation in these organizations was practically nil — the one notable exception was that of McGill lecturer Stanley Gray in the FLP. Gray and several other radicals at McGill were involved in the LIS — FLP sponsored «McGill Français» demonstration in early 1969.

The second element to emerge in the late sixties (though it is in the mid-seventies that it achieves real importance through infiltration of the trade unions and popular movements) is the handful of internationally affiliated *groupuscules*, or sects of the extreme left. From what we know, young anglophones, especially from immigrant backgrounds, continue to constitute an important segment in these Marxist-Leninist, Maoist and Trotskyist groups since, like the Communist Party before them, most began as external transplants. However, so little is known about the internal workings of these vanguardist groups, that we can only speculate on the precise role that anglophones play in them. Just as we are only now learning about the internal workings of the Communist Party to any real extent, time alone may bring the necessary insights into these groups.

The third and most interesting of these types are the *groupes populaires*. *Animation sociale* (roughly translated as community organizing) became a popular activity for many university-trained radicals, and they often found a fertile ground for mobilization in the general discontent and frustration of the population in the face of the unachieved promises of the Quiet Revolution and the willingness of many — these were after all the militant sixties — to take to the streets. Among the more important of these groups and actions in working-class districts in the Montreal area were the social animation projects in St-Henri, the Citizens' Committees of Mercier and Milton-Park, and the St-Jacques and Pointe-St-Charles community medical clinics. Projet St-Henri launched struggles in Little Burgundy against urban renewal, the location of a nearby hospital, and increased public transit fares. In Mercier, a campaign of demonstrations and hunger strikes called Opération Alarme protested student unemployment. The Milton-Park Citizens'

Committee waged a five-year campaign which delayed but failed to stop the neighbourhood's demolition to accommodate the building of Cité Concordia, a massive high-rise project. The St-Jacques and Pointe-St-Charles clinics were important scenes of political organizing and education on public health questions, confronting at different times Municipal and Provincial authorities and the pharmaceutical industry.

Anglophones played especially important roles in various community organizations in Pointe-St-Charles and in the Milton-Park Citizens' Committee. Many went on to help organize the Front d'action politique (FRAP), which united community organizers and trade unionists in what turned out to be a futile effort to oppose Jean Drapeau's Civic Party in the 1970 Montreal municipal election. The utter defeat of FRAP (in an election held under effective military occupation just after the October kidnappings) soon led to its disintegration. Active members of its anti-electoralist wing found their way, after a period of reflection, to certain of the sects, especially the new Maoist Ligue Communiste and En Lutte. Other militants returned to community organizing, many of whom, as we shall see, came to be active in setting up a more permanent municipal political opposition force in 1973-74, the Montreal Citizens Movement (MCM).

The primary breeding ground for these and other movements was the university. In the 1960s, antiwar, civil rights, and a whole series of related causes animated the universities in the West and these same currents found their way to the anglophone universities here in Quebec. For the most part, however, participation in these causes linked politicized anglophone Quebec students with students in Canada and the U.S.A. rather than with their French language counterparts. Of course, some personal links were established through the early sects that recruited and agitated around these issues. Nevertheless, the only significant political experience that concretely linked English-speaking students with Quebec developments during the mid-sixties were those revolving around the formation of the Union générale des étudiants du Québec (UGEQ). The university student left mobilized over a period of two years in 1965-66 to bring McGill into UGEQ, (and thereby withdraw from the Canadian Union of Students (CUS) the symbolism of which was lost on no one at the time). Apart from building contacts, the whole issue, and the radical as well as nationalistic content of the debates within UGEQ in those years, served to sensitize a number of anglophone student activists.

The late sixties also witnessed a change in the trade unions: the Confédération des Syndicats nationaux (CSN), in particular, going from a moderate reform organization working closely with the Liberal regime to one that is now clearly socialist in both content and direction. On the whole, as distinguished from the small number of English-speaking university graduates employed in the various trade unions, the anglophone sector within the trade unions has been undeveloped and has hardly distinguished itself in this process. In particular, the major English-speaking unions, the elementary and high school teachers in the Provincial Association of Catholic Teachers (PACT) and the Provincial Association of Protestant

Teachers (PAPT), feeling especially threatened by the changes in language legislation and economic implications for their members, have remained relatively conservative organizations especially unsympathetic to the present nationalist thrust. In recent years, however, PAPT has begun to evolve somewhat, perhaps due to its negotiating in cartel with the radical French-speaking teachers' union, the CEQ. This is, in part, true as well of the unions representing the workers in the English-speaking social affairs sector. Perhaps the most integrated are the English-speaking teachers in the colleges (CEGEPs) through their two federations, the Fédération nationale des Enseignants du Québec (Confédération des syndicats nationaux — CSN) and the Fédération des enseignants collégiaux (Centrale des enseignants du Québec).

In spite of this, the public sector common front battles of 1972, 1976 and 1979 were important events for a number of anglophone leftists, enabling them to actively participate through the union structure in important collective political actions. It remains to be seen, however, what long-term effect this activity will have. At present, the situation in the CSN and CEQ is not the most encouraging for those seeking a coming together of English and French around progressive social goals based on the sympathetic understanding of Quebec's national project and a commitment towards its realization. The trade unions' discussions and strategy on this as on other political questions have been increasingly trivialized by the rhetorical excess forced upon them. The CSN has been most affected due to the penetration of various Marxist-Leninist sects into union structures.

Like 1960, 1970 was a watershed year. It began with the Provincial election in which the Parti Québécois emerged as the real opposition, and ended with the October Crisis, the arrests and intimidation of the War Measures Act and the Montreal election which saw the rise and fall of FRAP. The combined effects of these and other events insured that, politically, the Quebec of the 1970s was fundamentally different from that of the sixties.

The Anglophone Left and the Current State of the National Question in Quebec

In terms of the evolution of the national question the present era begins in 1970. The «in the streets» period effectively comes to an end with the demise of the FLQ and the maturing of the Parti Québécois. Militancy shifts from the streets to the shop floors, picket lines, and bargaining tables. From the point of view of the anglophone community as a whole, the national question, and especially its linguistic component, became the focus if not indeed the obsession of political activities and concerns. Yet, there is little to distinguish the anglophone left in these concerns, at least until recently.

The Municipal Arena: the MCM

Nevertheless, the English-speaking left has not been idle. Probably its most important avenue of political expression has been the Montreal Citizens Movement (MCM). A brief recounting of the basic facts pertaining to the MCM's eight-year existence is in order at this point.

The MCM, which was founded in May 1974, grew out of the labour councils of Montreal, the local organizations of the Parti Québécois and the NDP, and a grouping of mainly anglophone local activists, called the Progressive Urban Movement.

The goals of the MCM were vaguely socialist and explicitly decentralist. The programme had promised reforms in public transit and cooperative housing, and stressed the creation of neighbourhood councils. In the November 1974 election, Mayor Jean Drapeau's Civic Party elected thirty-six councillors, the MCM eighteen. Further, the MCM proved somewhat stronger in English-speaking than French-speaking parts of the city.

Many party members soon became convinced that before the 1978 election the MCM would have to clarify its socialist goals and develop a socialist strategy. The period 1975-76 saw the debate escalate internally, culminating in the December 1976 congress which provided a field day for media sensation. The great show-down at the congress ended with an explicitly socialist line being adopted and its proponents taking the majority of executive positions. A backlash soon ensued with a few well-publicized resignations and denunciations by three councillors and their supporters who went on to found the middle-of-the-road Municipal Action Group (GAM).

Yet, by the summer of 1977, the MCM showed signs of extricating itself from its internal wrangling. The internal divergences, in fact, reflected problems that urban socialists in a city like Montreal cannot possibly avoid. Because of its commitment to community control, efficiency and even coherence had at times been sacrificed to decentralization. For a party of this nature to attempt to clarify its ideological position could not help but invite internal disruptions, and these later took their toll on the MCM when it next faced the voters in November 1978. MCM candidates for city council managed a mere 18,5 per cent, themselves running third in most districts and electing only Michael Fainstat in predominantly English-speaking NDG. Since 1974, the situation had changed, both in terms of Mayor Drapeau's Civic Party's ability to draw out its latent votes and, especially, forwarding the appearance of the GAM with a relatively well-known figure at its head, namely Federal Member of Parliament Serge Joyal.

Yet, the MCM has survived and is building somewhat confidently toward the November 1982 election. It was somewhat encouraged by polls taken in summer 1981 which showed the opposition to be within striking distance of the

Civic Party. The same polls indicated that, if anything, it had even strengthened its position among anglophones for whom it was actually running ahead of the Civic Party. In fact, the MCM's its image as an anglophone organization may turn out to be its most serious electoral handicap, even though it has overcome potential divisions over the national question raised by the Referendum, as it has generally managed to overcome divisions on linguistic lines.

Over one-fifth of the population of the City of Montreal speaks English at home. (Somewhere around 8 per cent speak neither English nor French.) As a proportion of its membership, anglophones have been somewhat over-represented in the MCM since its founding. Hence, with its unexpected electoral success in 1974, the MCM came to constitute the first serious public left political organization in Quebec in which anglophones played an important part. Such importance was expressed not only in the disproportionate number of anglophones who joined or voted for the MCM, but also in the fact that they always constituted between a quarter and one-half of the members of the party's executive and of active party committees.

Language has frequently been the cutting edge of the national question for anglophones. On the whole, the MCM experience provides a model in its resolution of the issue. In all city-wide meetings, French was always the working language, though anglophone members could speak in English if they wished to. Generally one found that, through time, English-speaking members grew more comfortable in the French language and came to use it regularly. In the West End districts, English has tended to be the usual working language, while disagreements over language use at MCM congresses and in the districts have been relatively infrequent.

As far as the national question is concerned, the fact that the MCM operates in the municipal arena meant that it did not have to address itself to the matter. In fact, it has very often been the strong Péquiste element in the Party that has encouraged this avoidance, judging that the real value of the MCM lies in bringing together progressive francophones and anglophones on common issues (and there is nothing more common than the kinds of day-to-day issues dealt with in municipal politics), a convergence that would probably be impossible if the national question were at issue.

While a number of francophones, identified with the MCM either as members of the executive or as former city councillors, came out in favour of the «yes» in the Referendum, the party remained neutral and took no part in the debate. Hence, while the party's actions did nothing to directly sensitize its anglophone members and supporters to Quebec's national aspirations, the MCM experience probably had a valuable indirect effect on hundreds of active members. Thus, the MCM has provided a useful political vehicle for many of the anglophone progressives who had been politicized during sixties and early seventies either in the NDP, the student organizations, or in various socially or ecologically oriented popular group activities — most of whom had been unable to find an outlet for their political energies and concerns during the 1970's.

Activities at the Provincial level

The relationship of progressive anglophones to the Parti Québécois poses the national question in unavoidable terms. Between the Party's creation in 1968, in which no anglophones appear to have participated, and November 1976, relations between the PQ and anglophones, even progressive ones, did not improve much.

As many as sixty-thousand anglophones voted for the PQ in the elections of the seventies. Of them, at least three- hundred English-speaking Quebecers did join the party during this time, but, initially, they remained isolated individuals with absolutely no weight as a group either inside the PQ or within the anglophone population. There was no one to challenge the «official» anglophone reaction to the emergence of the PQ, best symbolized by the «Brinks affair» in which a highly publicized convoy of armoured trucks carrying money and securities made its way to Ontario just prior to the 1970 election. The rebuff felt in 1970 left wounds among Péquistes and in 1973, the attitude towards anglophones was one of less than benign neglect. In 1976, token overtures were made to them, but little more. The PQ won the election essentially without the support of the anglophones.

Since coming to power, the Party has been generally correct and sometimes even good-willed towards the anglophone population. However, a major reason for its failure to develop a specific strategy vis-à-vis the anglophones has been the very absence of individual group members prepared to take their place among Quebec «souverainistes» to provide the necessary links. It remains quite clear that if any leadership is to be provided within the anglophone population to counter the rigid anti-Quebec independence posture of its elites, that leadership will have to come, at least in part, from the left.

One interesting though short-lived group that attempted to provide just such leadership was the Comité Anglophone pour un Québec Unifié (CAQU). CAQU came into existence in early 1977 and at its height comprised over sixty active members. Its action was effectively limited to the preparation and submission of a brief to the Quebec National Assembly Committee in the summer of 1977 on Bill 1 (later 101) supporting government pleas to francisize Quebec. Its brief read in part:

> The impression has been created [. . .] that the anglophones in Quebec are unified behind their «leaders» in the business world and the educational establishment in their opposition to Bill 1. This is clearly false. Our group supports a just and effective policy of francization of Quebec [. . .]

Unquestionably there exists a Quebec nation, and as such it should have the right to self-determination. We believe that the strengthening of the national language and culture is critical for breaking down barriers and thus making possible the solidarity necessary for effecting more fundamental transformations [...]

There can be little doubt that Quebec's anglophone elite has remained in a privileged position because of its economic power, reflected and reinforced by the dominance of the English language [...] Nevertheless the simple fact remains that the majority of the anglophones are not members of Quebec's economic elite. They are ordinary working people who are struggling to earn a living much like their French counterparts [...]

We feel that if the government responds with appropriate programmes to help workers adjust to the new linguistic policies, then the majority of the English working people will come in time to support and even welcome the change [...]

With the passage of Bill 101 in August 1977, CAQU disappeared from the scene. Through long and hard debate, it had painstakingly carved out a position on the language question, but it had not established the organizational structure to carry on once the debate subsided. Perhaps more important a factor in CACU's demise was its tendency to bend over backwards to eliminate any possible hint of links with the PQ and the Quebec government. Its concern with doing so was entirely unrelated to the sensitivities of its potential constituency in the anglophone community: after all, for almost all anglophones the linguistic and national projects in Quebec were intimately linked to the Parti Québécois and the performance of its government. It was instead born of a need on the part of many of its members to affirm their own and therefore CACU's standing on the Quebec left. In this respect, although specifically an anglophone phenomenon, it was symptomatic of a tendency characterizing the left in general. CAQU, the CSN and the CEQ are what might be termed «independent leftist» organizations in the sense that they attempt to steer clear both of the Marxist-Leninist groups to their left and the PQ to their right. Unfortunately, because of a style of rhetoric often borrowed from the former, it became a matter of conventional wisdom on the left to dismiss the PQ as «petit bourgeois nationaliste». As a result, concrete and serious criticism and debate, that might be engaged with the many Party members who consider themselves socialists or social democrats, is made impossible. It is hardly surprising, then, that this particular configuration of the independent left, and especially of the anglophones within it, has rendered it impossible to attain thus far any real coherence on the national question.

One possible ray of hope is to be found in the «Mouvement pour un Québec socialiste», composed of intellectuals and former labour leaders. The group's manifesto «Toward a Socialist Quebec», which was completed in the fall of 1981 after two years of discussion, was, nonetheless, disappointing. While well written, the document is almost entirely negative, attacking capitalism and its manifestations and accomplices — including the PQ — without offering any programmatic alternatives. Once again, few anglophones appear to be involved in the group. It is, nevertheless, too early to render any conclusive assessment as to the Committee's project. Another interesting and even more marginal recent phenomenon is the «Black Rock Manifesto» drawn up by playwright David Fennario and a few others and made public in November 1981. The Manifesto is a radical socialist interpretation of a Quebec English working class that is ignored and trapped between, on the one hand, their French counterparts and, on the other, the English ruling class, from whom they received preferential treatment in return «for acting as a sort of unofficial garrison troops». The group which identifies itself as «les maudits blokes» has since undertaken a bit of guerrilla theatre in a lower Westmount shopping centre. Further plans appear uncertain[9].

Postscript

While this article was substantially completed well before the Referendum, events during and after that period do not lead to a substantial change in the general assessment provided. The picture remains rather bleak. With a very partial exception of the MCM in which anglophone and francophone progressives continue to work together on real and immediate issues, activities in the other arenas have been either short-lived, marginal or co-optive. *Our Generation*, the only remaining progressive English language publication, has become even more marginal than it was in the New Left days of the mid-sixties, this by virtue of the idiosyncratic constituency of its editors and the fact that it has adopted an extreme left-wing position on Quebec independence. It now, quite simply, has ceased to speak to the immediate concerns of the anglophone population.

While outside the direct subject matter of this article, a final phenomenon is worth brief mention. This is the appearance of anglophone organizations clearly within the mainstream of the Quebec independence movement: first with the Committee of Anglophones for Sovereignty Association (CASA), and, following the Referendum, with the National Anglophone Commission within the Parti Québécois. As president of both these organizations, the author is poorly placed to assess their real significance. Nevertheless, a few words concerning their development and goals are in order.

In both cases, active membership has been limited to perhaps twenty-five activists among a total membership of three hundred. Further, while CASA, unlike the CNA, was independent of the PQ, they resemble each other ideologically.

Neither has sought to identify a specific ideological location for itself on the broad spectrum of the left, adopting in consequence a similar (fluid) terrain to that already staked out by the PQ. This had immediate consequences for the range of political involvement of the two groups, rendering them fundamentally different from the other organizations discussed thus far. Moreover, the vacuum resulting from the absence of any real discussion of the national question in the anglophone community meant that there was ample ideological and political space to occupy. Indeed, their contribution to the political education of anglophones as well as to the PQ and its national aspirations was way out of proportion to their tiny membership.

At the same time, the political spectrum within the anglophone left is far from being complete. The need for an autonomous presence is particularly acute when the population as a whole is nervous and uncertain, and turning to «guidance» from an establishment that has amply demonstrated its incapacity to operate effectively within the context of a rapidly evolving Quebec society. Yet, given the showing of rise to the occasion? It is all too difficult to outgrow bad habits: but outgrown they must be. The luxury of recourse to simplistic denunciations and automatic rejections cannot be afforded. If the mass of English-speaking Quebecers is to be provided with an alternative view of Quebec reality, it must come in good part from the left. For this to happen, anglophone leftists must liberate themselves from the strong psychological pressures generated by their status as a linguistic minority and expressed in the form of a chronic antipathy towards a national project characterized as «PQ petit bourgeois nationalism».

Hence, the fundamental challenge remains: *anglophones as leftists* have a role to play in the Quebec left as a whole, in the MCM, the trade unions, etc., while *leftists as anglophones* have a key public role to play within the wider English-speaking population.

NOTES

(1) Walter D. Young, *The Anatomy of a Party: The National CCF, 1932-1961* (Toronto, University of Toronto Press, 1969):215.

(2) Norman Penner, *The Canadian Left* (Scarborough, Ont., Prentice-Hall, 1977):123.

(3) Quoted by Young, op. cit., p. 214.

(4) Philip Strafford (editor and translator), *André Laurendeau: Witness for Quebec.*

(5) Penner, op. cit., p. 122.

(6) See Henry Milner, *Politics in the New Quebec*, especially Chapters 6-8.

(7) On Kierans, see, for example, Peter Desbarats chapters on the Lesage Cabinet in his biography of René Lévesque: *René: A Canadian in Search of a Country*, Toronto, McClelland and Stewart, 1976. Fullerton discusses his own role and political evolution at length in his *The Dangerous Delusion*, Toronto, McClelland and Stewart, 1978.

(8) Only the most sketchy description is given here of the activities of a whole range of left-wing groups in the late sixties and early seventies. For more detailed information, the reader is advised to look elsewhere, e.g., my own book, op. cit.

(9) In April 1982, a new group, somewhat reminiscent of CAQU, and calling itself «Another Voice», emerged. Composed of sixty to eighty members, the group took a public position, distinguishing the views of progressive anglophones from the essentially negative views on language in Quebec expressed publically in late 1981 by the group that was to become Alliance Quebec.

Conclusion

LOOKING TO THE FUTURE

The editors

As little as four years ago, we insisted on the lack of a debate in contemporary English-speaking Quebec on the question of its own future: we spoke of the need for a stock-taking that would allow this population to re-situate itself, refurbish its consciousness and envisage the future in a longer term perspective than it has been disposed to do in the recent past. Without a doubt, this debate and this stock-taking is now occuring. Between the time when we first undertook this book (September 1978) and the final draft (March 1982), the process we bemoaned so effusively began to take form.

In fact, a number of anglophone personalities drawn from very definite constituencies have not only taken stock of the problem and posited what they see to be the essential questions; some have proceeded to elaborate strategies for the future. One needs only mention Eric Maldoff, Henry Milner, Alex Paterson, Reed Scowen and Michael Yarowsky to cite some of the most visible. There is even, now, emerging a literary and intellectual tradition on the subject: Dominique Clift and Sheila Arnopoulos have come out with the first book-length treatment in the twentieth century; *The Montreal Review* has surfaced; the Conseil de la langue française has commissioned and published a study on the rural English; and, a sure sign that something *has* happened, the universities (our founts of institutionalized creativity) are finally acquiring an interest in the matter. . . McGill-Queen's Press publishes «Le fait anglais au Québec» in English after it has been a success in French.

A population becoming conscious of itself and subsequently assuming its destiny. . . a rather extraordinary process to behold and to participate in. Poignant as was our concern in 1978 that such was not happening, so real is our wonder and gratification in 1982 as we see it happening. . . and without the help of this book! What we propose to do in this conclusion is to resuscitate and examine the process. We begin with a caricatural but nonetheless very concrete illustration of the «problem» as we saw it to exist in post-war English-speaking Quebec. We then proceed with a distillation and review of «the essential questions» as put forward here in this book, by others who either publically addressed the issue or who, among our contributors, set down on paper their ideas at our request. Some of the more articulate of these participants in the debate have begun to elaborate «strategies for the future», and we attempt to do them justice in a section in which we will allow our own strategy a place alongside theirs.

The Problem

If pressed to distill the essence of the problem of English-speaking Quebec of the post-war period as revealed or explicitly commented on in the previous chapters of the book, we would respond in these terms: *absence from the wider institutional context which concerns us; failure to be conscious of, and articulate about, the essential issues at stake; and inability or unwillingness to assume responsibility for our particular society's future*. As late as 1974 there occurred an incident, here designated as the «Carrel estate incident», which in an inescapably concrete and surprisingly explicit way caricaturizes, we believe, the problem. An exposition of the incident is both worthwhile as real-life dramatization of the problem, as well as being consistent with the perspective permeating the book, which is to stay close to the ground of the historically specific context that we are living and writing about.

In the month of July 1974, the Quebec National Assembly passed into law private Bill 104 which modified the will of Frank Carrel, lifetime resident of Quebec, one-time publisher of the *Quebec Chronicle Telegraph* and member of the former Quebec Legislative Council. That this, apparently particular and isolated event, should have happened at all, and happened in the way it did, sums up in an eminently concrete fashion some of the issues we believe are before us. Hence, we proceed to a discussion of these issues via the appropriate examination of the «Carrel» incident.

Frank Carrel, native and resident of the City of Quebec,[1] provided in his last testament that after the death of his wife and sister (the former was indeed not yet dead in 1974) the entire revenue of his estate should be devoted to the university education of Protestant boys from the Quebec City and Gaspé Peninsula areas, as well as a certain number of Irish and Catholic boys from the Quebec City area, the last to be chosen by the rector of Laval University. These scholarships — over one hundred thousand dollars worth annually in 1940 dollars, probably a quarter of a million at the time of his wife's death — were to be made available to Queen's University which had had the foresight to award Carrel an honorary degree. Such was the expressed wish of Frank Carrel at the time he wrote his testament in 1940.

The facts of the situation — not revealed in the recorded proceedings of the parliamentary commission hearing upon which this account is based[2] — were quite simple: Queen's was unable to accept the endowment as it stood. The laws of Ontario would not permit it.[3] Queen's is a public institution in a modern liberal society which does not allow its publically supported institutions to discriminate on the basis of sex, religion, or ethnic origin. Hence, Queen's, as a public institution in Ontario, found itself in the position of not being able to award scholarships in accordance with the terms of the will which made, in addition to the sex distinction, distinctions on the basis of religion (Catholic and Protestant) and ethnic origin (English and French) which are anathema to the secularized fabric of Ontario public life.

Such was not the nature of the society which produced Frank Carrel. He was an English Protestant (Presbyterian) and he lived and wrote his will in a society in which much of the public realm was, and still is, founded on religious and ethnocultural distinctions (a confessional education system and the «historic English» of Law 101 to mention two instances). However, Ontario law could not accommodate such «anachronisms» and hence, Queen's enjoined Royal Trust to have the Quebec Legislative Assembly change Carrel's will «in the public interest». Thus, to cite the subsequent law,

> *notwithstanding* [. . .] the will of the late Frank Carrel
> [. . .] Queen's University may [. . .] apply the whole
> net annual income of the Frank Carrel estate towards
> defraying the expense of the education, at the universi-
> ty, of students *chosen irrespective of religious, ethnic
> and sex criteria imposed by the will [. . .]*[4]

This was because Queen's and Royal Trust, the executor, «trouvent cela désirable dans l'intérêt public». When asked to elaborate on «the public interest», the representative of Royal Trust enjoined, in a very revealing qualification which no one took him up on: «je ne peux en dire plus».[5]

* * *

To begin with the most immediate aspect of our caricatural episode — the changing of a man's last testament — the first issue which emerges is that there was not to be found, in the English-speaking Quebec which harboured Frank Carrel throughout his entire life, one person prepared to insist that his last wish be respected, or at least that those who wished to change it have the decency to wait until his wife had died. In fact, it was Jérôme Choquette who, through seven pages of commission proceedings, insisted vehemently — but to no avail — that Frank Carrel's will should be respected:

> Je vous dis franchement M. Stein [Royal Trust] que je
> trouve que nous sommes en train de refaire le testament
> de Cujus [Frank Carrel], alors que la nécessité de re-
> faire ce testament n'a pas été démontrée. Je ne vois
> rien, moi, vous ne nous avez apporté aucun argument
> qui démontre que le testament de Frank Carrel ne peut
> pas fonctionner tel que lui l'avait prévu. De toute
> façon, je pense que, pour apprécier cette situation, il
> faudra attendre le décès de madame veuve Frank
> Carrel.[6]

Where were Frank Carrel's English-speaking compatriots? Is there not, in English Quebec, a place for loyalty or, at a minimum, a respect for those with whom we shared the satisfaction and the ambiguities of being English in Quebec? If not, we are a society without history or a future . . . hence, it might well be better to abandon the pretence, and assimilate to the likes of Jérôme Choquette (a not unattractive prospect), or get to mainstream anglo-America (via Queen's perhaps) post haste.

Moving beyond the immediate question of the community's failure to respect the last wish of Frank Carrel, the next issue which emerges is why was the secularistic, universalistic and disembodied argument advanced by Royal Trust — which was in fact a clever legal manoeuvre in Queen's interest — allowed to prevail over Carrel's own definition of the nature of the society of which he was an active member (newspaper publisher and parliamentarian)Carrel was educated entirely in the province of Quebec and he was the representative of the Gulf region (Magdalen Islands, Gaspé, Bonaventure, Rimouski and Matane) in the Legislative Council from 1918 until his death in 1940. If his will were to be changed, it might rather have been changed in the interest of the Quebec which begat Carrel as opposed to the interest of Queen's endowment fund.

Again, it was left to French-speaking Quebecers to protest that Carrel had, after all, known what he was doing and that the distinctions he made in his will had meanings for him and Quebec:

> M. Choquette: Et depuis quand est-ce dans l'intérêt public que le législateur refuse les testaments faits par les testateurs? Au contraire, c'est contraire à l'intérêt public qu'on le fasse en général. Et puis, je vais vous dire quelque chose: des distinctions religieuses, nationales, ethniques, etc. qui ont un caractère philanthropique dans les testaments, ce n'est pas contraire à l'ordre public. On a le droit de privilégier tel groupe religieux ou tel groupe national dans un testament, à l'occasion d'une donation. Ceci est accepté et ça n'a jamais été considéré comme une infraction — on me passera le terme — à une conception non discriminatoire sur le plan juridique de la société.[7]

Earlier in the debate, in response to Royal Trust's claim that the distinction Catholic-Protestant was without significance:

> M. Desjardins: En 1940, comment le testateur faisait-il la distinction, lui, entre catholiques et protestants? [...] Oui mais cela existe encore, aujourd'hui des catholiques et des protestants.[8]

Indeed, the notion of confessionality is still sufficiently real in Quebec that the legal position of the English educational establishment in its fight against Laws 22 and 101 was based on the fact of, and the constitutional entrenchment of, Protestantism in Quebec. Rather ironically, Choquette found himself, a very short time later (as the Minister of Education responsible for the application of Law 22), assailed by the same English school establishment claiming that the rights of Protestants (the capacity to administer their own schools) were being constricted. He might well have asked where they were when no other than Queen's University maintained, *with success*, in the National Assembly that in Quebec it was not in the public interest to distinguish between Catholics and Protestants!

Incidentally, the argument that it would be impossible to find enough eligible students (a maximum of twenty a year, assuming a four-year university programme) in all of the Gulf region and the Quebec City area went unchallenged. Rather surprisingly, it was the only English-speaking MNA present who proffered this claim. It also was his major contribution to the debate — apart from the information he volunteered regarding the cost of sending *his* daughter to Queen's! Consequently, the definition of a Quebec student was transformed from that of a Gulf region or Quebec City resident to that of a person *who had been domiciled anywhere in the province of Quebec for one year prior to going to Queen's...*, a rather «liberal» conception of the significance of one's particular societal insertion.

Nevertheless, it is not enough to be conscious of what the essence of one's society is or should be: one must also be capable of contemplating its preservation. Indeed, the very notion of the public domain in our Greco-Christian tradition presumes the assumption of responsibility for the future of the society which conferred upon us our humaneness. This brings us to a further issue arising from our examination of the Carrel estate incident: what are the consequences for the future of English-speaking Quebec, not to speak of Quebec itself, of educating elsewhere a sizeable portion of its potential elite? Law 104 made us all, via the instrument of our public institutions, accomplices in this otherwise insidious process of self-decapitation of which the original dispositions of the Carrel will were a clear exemplification.

It was one thing for Frank Carrel, as a Presbyterian, to have selected the University of Presbyterian origins, namely Queen's, and to have provided financial assistance for the real beneficiaries of the will, namely Protestant boys from certain parts of the Province to go there; and quite another thing for the National Assembly to do so «in the public interest». Or, to put the matter more squarely in the context under consideration: having decided «in the public interest» to put aside most of the dispositions in Carrel's will, it would have been imperative to consider carefully whether it was equally in the public interest of English- speaking Quebec to hasten the exportation of a then already faltering elite. Might it not have been more in the public interest to send them to a Quebec university, English or French?

* * *

Yet, the three dimensions of the problem caricaturized by the Carrel estate incident — absence from the wider institutional context which concerns us, failure to be conscious of, and articulate about, the essence of what is at stake, and inability or unwillingness to assume societal responsibility — are perhaps but symptoms of a more profound malaise. There is emerging an awareness that there are even more fundamental questions which must be raised and confronted. We will attempt in the next section — as much as is possible in the words of those who have formulated them — to lay out these questions.

The Essential Questions

The questions raised here do not necessarily constitute a logical sequence, nor are they independent one of the other. Our objective here is not to present an argument, quite the contrary: it is to survey and comment on the questions which have emerged amongst the population living the events that have provoked the self-examination so essential to a reformulation of identity.

Perhaps most pertinent among the questions formulated is whether English-speaking Quebec has the desire to survive. Independently of the nature of the challenge to be confronted and the role of anglophones in the future of Quebec, «will the anglophone remain in Quebec to accept the challenge and play that role?» asks Alex Paterson in his statement *On Being at Home in Quebec*.[9]

Michael Yarowsky in addressing himself to the question of the future of the Jewish Community in Montreal recognizes the extreme pertinence of the question:

> Indeed, many of Montreal Jews ask, in view of the assault on their traditional insularity vis-à-vis French Quebec society, do they really want to «make it» in Quebec?[10]

They put the question regardless of the fact that:

> . . . in the past this community was able to «make it» so well in spite of the tremendous odds against it, the odds of prejudice, discrimination, poverty and limited education. . . [11]

A perhaps equally fundamental query is that which pertains to whom we, the anglophones of Quebec, are. A few years ago, there was much reference to the English-speaking «community» and the imperative of defending this community. Storrs McCall, in an article published in the *Montreal Star* early in 1978, alluded to this community and to what he believed to be its capacity to transform collectively shared emotions relating to home, to community and to country into a shared purpose for English-speaking Quebec. He first fixes the context:

> There are, it is true, at the moment certain features of life in our province which, if not responded to with generosity and courage could act as powerful incentives to depart.[12]

He then proceeds to point to the existence of «collective» emotion:

> Counteracting these forces are equally powerful sentiments relating to home, to community and also it has been argued, to country. These sentiments, when identified and articulated in words, can be transformed into a shared collective emotion once an appropriate vehicle for social communication and exchange is created. When this occurs, the English-speaking community in Quebec will be provided with the purpose and the confidence it now does not have.[13]

By 1979, however, most participants in the debate, including Storrs McCall and Positive Action of which he and Alex Paterson are co-chairmen, had begun questionning the existence of an English-speaking «community» or «collectivity» in Quebec. Reed Scowen, MNA, in his extensive and indeed remarkable document *Reflections on the Future of the English Language in Quebec*[14], of which the title itself is very indicative, refers to an English-speaking community in Quebec, but he takes great pains to qualify this notion. He begins by positing that «the level of group consciousness among English Quebecers, the sense of «collectivity» is low».[15] The reasons he suggests are twofold, of which the first «has to do with the ethnic diversity and mobility of the English-speaking population».[16] Consequently:

> The definition and protection of a collectivity has not been a major preoccupation for the various ethnic elements who chose to retain or adopt English, probably because the linguistic community to which it allowed access was so large, diverse and unthreatened, that by possessing it one was liberated to pursue any number of individual goals, all of which seemed realizable for the person involved, or at least for his children.[17]

Scowen then elaborates on the fragility, to say the least, of this population's sense of communality:

> From the beginning and particularly since World War II, the language and its institutions have been used by ethnic groups and by transients who had very little more in common with each other than they did with the French community.[18]

It is the language and perhaps only that which is shared:

> But the language itself, and most of the institutions using it, were accessible to Italians and Greeks, fourth generation Westmounters, sales managers transferred temporarily from Toronto to New York, young people moving from the Maritimes, Indians and Inuits, nurses from Australia, and a number of French Quebecers who chose to become acculturalized.[19]

Yet, notwithstanding, Scowen holds on to the concept of an English community, as he concludes: «They came and they went, making the English Quebec *community* the most mobile in all of Canada».[20] However, the implications of his own analysis is not lost on him:

> Given the special nature of the English society [the term «community» recedes] of Quebec, it is perhaps inevitable that a coherent version of its role will be difficult to define.[21]

In a more recent effort to delineate English Quebec, Reed Scowen begins in fact with language and goes on to speak of a community, in fact he designates it a «language community»:

> For me, the English language community is a group of people who identify with each other in terms of a common language, and common institutions which function in that language. These institutions include schools, health institutions, social services, churches, theatres and cinemas, libraries, businesses and universities and Cegeps, T.V. and radio stations. This language community, and I will emphasize this most strongly, is not an ethnic community, it includes people of many ethnic origins and it always will.[22]

Indeed, this language community comprises all those in Quebec whose social language is English and, in an answer to the question «who makes up this linguistic community», Scowen notes at least six different groups within this «mobile and highly diverse group»: the English-speaking Montreal; younger English-speaking Quebecers who are more integrated; the rural English and the immigrants who have come to Montreal and who have made English their first language etc.[23]

In fact, an earlier hesitation concerning the composition of English Quebec has been dispelled in the minds of the most visible spokesmen. Not only Scowen, but Alex Paterson and now Eric Maldoff are quite explicit, and their positions are unequivocal and identical. Maldoff puts it this way:

> The English-speaking community is a linguistic community and the first thing that the government has to recognize is the fact that the English-speaking community is not an ethnic group. Based on this conclusion, there must be an acceptance of the legitimacy of that English-speaking linguistic community.[24]

Frank Remiggi, in a piece written in reaction to an editorial by James Stewart published in the *Montreal Star* in 1979, and entitled «Will the Real Anglo Please Stand Up»,[25] is more brutal with regard to the implications arising from the socio-political diversity of anglo-Quebec. He advances the proposition that language is the only common denominator and that it is not sufficient to provide the basis for a community:

> Quite simply, the anglophone «population» of Quebec is made up of various ethnic and socio-economic «communities» which really only share their language — English. And while no one can or will, deny the importance of language as the transmitter of culture and values, language alone is not sufficient to provide a common outlook on Quebec society and politics.[26]

From this follows the interrogation:

> Why should the anglophone and allophone minorities of Quebec present and share a unified view of their social, cultural and political participation and integration in Quebec when the very composition of these minorities suggests a great heterogeneity rather than a homogeneity of views?[27]

Indeed, he warns against the consequences of a hot-house or forced consensus:

> Efforts to create this common front will only lead to greater polarization between French and English-speaking Quebecers and will damage and retard the possible integration of anglophones in Quebec society.[28]

Dominique Clift and Sheila McLeod Arnopoulos in their book entitled *Le fait anglais au Québec*,[29] attack the question from a different perspective: in addition to an exposition of the heterogeneity of English-speaking Quebec, they make of pluralism an ideological imperative for English-speaking Quebec, and by extension, for Quebec society itself. Drawing inspirations from what they believe to be the American adaptation to the race problem, Clift and McLeod Arnopoulos see a panacea in pluralism, which pluralism is the ideological postulat of the «new society» — the title of their last chapter. They forsee for Quebec:

> Only a truly pluralistic society in which discrimination and exclusiveness were no longer institutionalized, as they now are, would enable Quebec to recover the social optimism that has already been lacking for far too long.[30]

The authors' ideological penchant for an «enlightened» pluralism surfaces clearly in the following paragraph:

> What keeps French-language Quebecers at their present stage of political evolution from accepting the autonomous presence of outside cultures in their own social environment is precisely what keeps them from identifying with Canada as a country. The defensive reactions and attitudes of exclusiveness that sustained Quebec nationalism for so long can not be cast off within a single generation. It was no more than twenty five years ago, ten years before the Quiet Revolution, that the possibility of a pluralistic society in Quebec began to be anticipated and that some intellectuals active in reform movements and the Liberal Party of the time began to encourage the acceptance of religious, social and other differences. *But Quebec was significantly slow in relation to this kind of change which was beginning to materialize elsewhere in the country.*[31]

In taking such a position, the authors sweep away the premise of the two nations or charter-group concept of Canada, the demise of which would put an end to the possible claim of an English Quebec to be the guarantee of a «Charter» cultural tradition in Quebec; and equally, the claim whereby the cultural tradition of French-speaking Quebec is accorded a privileged status in Canada. Indeed, they are very explicit about this latter. Perhaps the major argument of the book is that Quebec is wrong in using one form of «exclusiveness» (the French-speaking Quebec cultural tradition) to attack another (the Canadian Anglo-Saxon tradition in Quebec). The book concludes with the following affirmation:

> The problem in the next decade will be to reconcile the objectives of all Quebecers, whatever their origins. Given the numerous differences which divide them, conflicts are inevitable. In any event, the result can

only be a pluralistic society, *with little resemblance to traditional Franco-Quebec culture*. This will be the price to pay for imposing the social and economic monopoly of the French language in Quebec. *Abandoning the culture that assured French survival* for more than two centuries is something the authors of Bill 101 did not foresee when they decided to attack the English community's economic power directly.[32]

In effect, in the light of the cultural and ethnic heterogeneity of Quebec society, Clift and McLeod Arnopoulos advocate the jettison of the «Canadian model of the thirties» of which present nationalist thinking in Quebec is but a corollary:

The cultural model French society is trying to recreate for itself in Quebec is the Canadian model of the 1930s in which it was expected that the different ethnic groups defer to the dominant culture and accept a certain ethnic stratification. . . .[33]

The authors would prefer that Quebec put aside the posture of a «defensive» society in favour of that of an «optimistic» society.

In our mind, such a «liberal» pluralism raises — unless one prefers to ignore the particularities of the historical and geo-political context as enlightened thinkers sometimes do — a disturbing question that we are far from being the first to raise. English Canada, although suffering from Anglo-Saxon exclusiveness and ethnic stratification, was indeed a distinct society in the thirties (as was, indeed, French Quebec). English Canada has since been transformed, perhaps unwittingly, into a «pluralistic» society and Quebec is being admonished to do the same, albeit in terms of a French-speaking pluralism. Were such to happen, it is questionable whether French Quebec would remain an autonomous society: the experience of English Canada is revealing in this regard.[34] Is there such a thing as English-speaking Canadian society in the post-1970 era? If Quebec were to opt for unconstrained pluralism, would it not be emulating Canada in a post-war modernism which has perhaps simply led the country into «non-identity»?

More to the point, in terms of such an «enlightened pluralism», on what grounds does one oppose the logical extrapolation which is that there is no justification in being «defensive» with regard to the most «optimistic» society of all. . . America? In fact, why should Quebec — English and French — not follow English-speaking Canada in its cultural integration into continental society? Moreover, in the present context, in what way would an English Quebec, delineated only in terms of language, be different from the continental English-language community? In other words, why should English-speaking Quebec not opt for a continentalizing pluralism?

* * *

Such a question raises the issue of the inherent good, if any, in the preservation of English Quebec (if indeed it exists). McCall, Paterson, Scowen, Yarowsky, we the editors, and, as surprising as it may be to many, Camille Laurin say there is a value in the maintenance of English-Quebec.

For Storrs McCall and Alex Paterson of Positive Action the major good — apart from the «pleasantness and cosmopolitaness of a bilingual city like Montreal» — inherent in the maintenance of English Quebec is the guarantee it provides for the preservation of Canada: the collapse of English Quebec would, they maintain, lead directly to the separation of Quebec and the dismemberment of Canada. Specifically, the argument is that Canada can only continue to exist on the basis of bilingualism, and bilingualism in the rest of Canada will not be justifiable if it does not exist in Quebec. The only ground for its existence in Quebec arises from the fact of the existence of an almost one million strong population of English speakers.

In *The History and the Activities of the Positive Action Committee*, McCall, Paterson and Brott state: «Positive Action [adherents] . . . remain firm in their belief that Quebecers must stay and fight for the sake of Canada».[35] In another statement, one finds:

> . . . We believe that there exists even more compelling
> reasons for staying. Of these, the principal one is that
> every departure erodes the fabric of Canadian unity.[36]

The good inherent in maintaining English Quebec is that of maintaining Canada; and further, there is the good involved in the diversity which arises out of the alliance of the two founding peoples:

> The most significant aspect of our people is its diversi-
> ty. Our two founding peoples, the two primary linguis-
> tic groups, have been nourished by two of the great
> cultures of the world, French and English, each with its
> own particular qualities, its own particular
> strengths. . . .[37]

Hence, the justification of English-speaking Quebec becomes that of Canada, and by extension, that of the furthering of bilingualism. The issue crystallizes itself very nicely in a telegram from Positive Action to Premier William Davis of Ontario contesting his refusal to provide for a trial in French for Gérard Filion: «Your action in Ontario does little to help *our cause at a time when the future of our country is at stake*.»[38]

In this — their plea for bilingualism in Quebec and Ontario for the sake of Canada — Positive Action follows in the footsteps of the Quebec provincial deputies, W.S. Bullock and J.T. Finnie, who, in 1915, introduced into the Quebec house a motion imploring Ontario to rescind regulation number seventeen.[39]

On the other hand, Reed Scowen's justification for the maintenance of English Quebec is to be found within Quebec itself. The English-speaking population of Quebec has, over time, built up a complex of institutions and acquired a history, argues Scowen, which has resulted in «a distinctive way of life».[40] Although he is not, upon examination, able to put his finger on anything these people have in common except the English language, he nonetheless holds to the existence of a society, the distinctiveness of which merits its preservation.

Furthermore, Scowen justifies the existence of English- speaking Quebec in terms of the contribution it has to offer to Quebec society at large. This contributioon is to be found at the level of the only characteristic which clearly defines it, the English language itself. After an exposition of the role of English as a language in Quebec, Scowen argues that the importance of knowing English in the contemporary world has not been lost on the French-speaking elite of Quebec:

> . . . the majority of the French-speaking elite appears to believe that a knowledge of English is vital, if not for all Quebecers, at least for the members of their own group.[41]

And:

> . . . there is a generally held belief that a knowledge of the English language, a link with the society of the rest of North America, is important for French-speaking Quebecers.[42]

Hence, English-speaking Quebec is, or could become, a linguistic bridge which would ensure the link with English-speaking North America:

> An English language community, because of the ease of its links with North America, is particularly well adapted to contribute to Quebec society in many key areas of modern life. The presence of companies, educational institutions and research groups which operate on a national or international basis in Quebec will

always depend on the presence of a considerable number of persons whose first or second language is English, given the high degree of mobility which the
operation of these organizations requires.[43]

One might, of course, ask whether Anglo-Quebecers are not pretentious in
assuming to themselves this «linguistic bridge» function. Is there not sufficient
evidence to show that a bilingual francophone elite can very effectively fulfill this
same function? However, irrespective of this question, it is remarkable how
essentially utilitarian and pragmatic the thinking of people like McCall, Scowen,
etc., is. None of those cited so far appear to justify the perpetuation of English-
speaking Quebec in terms of cultural values, or in terms of the irreplaceable nature
and the social value of a cultural and institutional capital built up over time. Scowen
hints, but no more, at the first, and Paterson alludes to the second. One suspects that
a late awareness of the heterogeneity of the English-speaking population — an awareness which has emerged in answer to the question «Who are we?» — has caused
them and others to draw back from an energetic expression of the merits of their
great cultural tradition. Indeed, they would become ready targets for the pluralistic
thinkers.

Paradoxically, the most visible and powerful proponent of Quebec cultural
nationalism, the present Minister of Cultural Development, indulges — within the
context of a «minorities» policy — in a glorification of the Anglo-Quebec cultural
tradition:

> The Anglo-Quebec community has cultivated certain
> values which have justifiably gained a reputation for
> the British contribution to the heritage of universal
> civilization: a sense of individual responsibility, the
> importance of the social role played by volunteer asso-
> ciation, intermediary groups and pressure groups, the
> importance of local governments to take charge of the
> responsibilities concerning the citizen in his daily
> life.[44]

How extraordinary that it should be an official representative of the majority culture
who should be one of the most explicit public apologists for the Anglo-Quebec
cultural tradition. At the same time, one cannot but reflect that Clift and Arnopoulos would see, in this official cultural policy, a confirmation of their «ethnic
stratification» thesis concerning the present Quebec national affirmation. In fairness to the author of the policy, it must be mentioned that Dr. Laurin believes in an
emergence process out of which a new culture constituted from Quebec's indigenous elements (anglo-Quebec being one) would arise: as opposed to the reification
and deification of the existing French cultural tradition.

All of the preceding leads us, the editors, to put forward a number of our own questions regarding the issue of whether English-speaking Quebec is worth preserving. First of all, if English-speaking Quebec, consisting of those whose mother tongue is English, has, in the way of a communality, nothing more than a shared language, then, as social scientists, we cannot but ask «does it exist in the first place?» Premised in the posing of such a question is the conviction that language alone is not sufficient to maintain a cultural tradition . . . it does not matter whose tradition it is. If indeed the population of which we speak holds nothing more in common than the language which it also shares with the rest of the continent and the cultural content transmitted by that language is mostly generated elsewhere, then in what way can it hope to be distinguishable from the population of the continent? If we are right in thinking that there is no such beast as language without culture, then being English without a strong local tradition means, in our context, continentalism.

Our second and subsequent question is the following: is there not to be found in the British tradition as embodied in the existence and history of substantial communities in Quebec, or perhaps (even more pertinent) as experienced by all Quebecers via their participation in political, legal and economic institutions of British origin, the elements of a cultural tradition worth acknowledging and drawing inspiration from?

However, is such a consciousness feasible amongst an English-speaking population of which approximately only half are of British ethnic origin? We are not suggesting that English-speaking Quebec should identify with the British cultural tradition — heaven help us, we would be instantly condemned as dinosaurs, «more English than the Queen», a new «ultramontanism». We wish to put into relief the dilemma: *if English-speaking Quebec in all its pluralistic richness does not acquire a cultural communality which distinguishes it from continental Anglo-American culture, not only is it probably not worth preserving, but it will probably not survive.* If one accepts this proposition and one then wishes to set out to identify what this distinct cultural communality might be, one must turn to history. Historically, like it or not, the British connection is inescapably there. Of course one could, as English-speaking Canada has done since the War, turn away, in a surge of liberalism, from our own history to the history of others . . . with the consequences we are now only too familiar with.

* * *

Even if we were to decide it was worthwhile to think in terms of the perpetuation of English Quebec, it would be of no avail if English-speaking Quebecers were unable to identify with, and subsequently participate in, the Quebec society project. *Are we capable of sufficient solidarity with Quebec to allow us to feel at home in the larger Quebec?*

Reed Scowen seems to think so:

> The sense of identification, of being at home here, and
> the sense of loss for those who leave, is a real thing
> which surpasses all ethnic divisions. [45]

The Reverend T. Miles in his *Christians in the New Quebec* expresses the belief
that within a Christian ethic such is not only possible but desirable, and that, in this
respect:

> ... we anglophone Christians have not felt the same
> concern for the francophone community as we have felt
> for other language communities on other continents.
> The Church in the future will be a fully participating
> body in Quebec, not isolated from events in the larger
> society, but sharing with this society both its witness
> and its ministry. [46]

* * *

Whatever is to happen to English-speaking Quebec, it is unlikely to be
determined by the anglophones of Quebec alone. If it is not determined by us alone,
the question which immediately suggests itself is: «Where and by whom will the
fate of English-speaking Quebec be decided?» Answers now being given to this
question are quite surprising in that responses such as those provided by Miles,
Scowen and Yarowsky would not have been even envisaged as little as five years
ago.

The Reverend T. Miles affirms that the majority in Quebec has a right to
decide its destiny and that we must, with conviction, adjust to the outcome. After
suggesting that in the English milieu little has been done...

> ... to explain or interpret to non-francophones the sim-
> ple poignant reality of a «people» seeking to survive
> with dignity and self-respect as masters of their own
> destiny. [47]

He then proceeds to:

> ... the basic question [which] seems to be whether
> Quebec has the right to choose its own destiny. A
> provincial government, democratically elected, is de-
> termined to prove it has the right and will gain the
> support of the majority of the population in the eventual
> referendum(s) on separation. So long as such decisions

are taken by the free vote of citizens, believers in the democratic process can hardly oppose the approach; however much they may disagree with the issue or the results. We all will live with the results, but this should not be a passive acceptance or fatalism.[48]

Reed Scowen, perhaps the first well-known anglophone public figure to declare that we must accept the fact that the future of English-speaking Quebec will be decided in Quebec, put it in these rather direct terms:

> The first precondition [of a solution of the issues before English-speaking Quebec] is an acceptance by English-speaking Quebecers that the future of its community will be determined primarily in Quebec, by political decisions taken here, and that these decisions will be determined in the final analysis by a consensus among the French-speaking majority.[49]

Michael Yarowsky warns us that it would be unrealistic to count on political or social forces outside Quebec:

> The reality is that there is no significant political force or social force in Quebec or within Canada which will advocate on behalf of or protect the interests of entrenched English language minority groups in Quebec which do not wish to accommodate to the new cultural realities of Quebec. This message has been delivered clearly by provincial and federal leaders in Quebec and Canada of all significant political parties. The reality is that the English-speaking population of Quebec has been told not only by the independentist leader of the Provincial opposition party, as well as by the Prime Minister, of Canada,[50] that «Quebec is to become as French as Ontario is English».[51]

But even if all the foregoing questions were to be resolved in such a way as to allow one to envisage a future for English-speaking Quebec, is such a future possible? This crucial question is often put in terms of the concepts «integration» and «assimilation»: *is integration, participation with retention of a distinct English-speaking Quebec identity, possible without assimilation?* Although «assimilation» and «integration» are widely used terms in the debate, the latter, «integration», is still without substantial content as Scowen underlines:

> On the surface, it appears that assimilation and integration are in fact the same thing one simply being a positive designation and the other negative. However,

until such time as these expressions are more fully clothed with meaning, it is impossible to tell. Can an English-speaking Quebecer be fully integrated into French Quebec society and still remain English? Perhaps a greater understanding of what was meant by integration would make it more attractive.[52]

A negative, but certainly more popular, formulation of the same question is that having to do with the capacity of perfectly bilingual English-speaking Quebecers to find jobs. Speaking to a Jewish audience, Yarowsky evoked the question on this level:

Even if we learn French perfectly, will we be able to compete for the same jobs and at the same levels with those whose names are Bélanger and Vaillancourt, even though our names may be Cohen or Goldberg?[53]

After suggesting that the question may be an impossible one to answer, Yarowsky, in the spirit of his plea that Jewish Quebec return to its history for inspiration, advances the poignant reminder that a perfect command of English «did not assure acceptance by the English-speaking community of high-level corporate positions [for Jews] in the past».[54]

Although we can readily agree with Scowen that far from enough thought has been given to the question — what form integration without assimilation might take in Quebec — we suspect that the difficulty lies in the fact that the term «integration» is itself a part of a dynamic which is in the process of being lived: hence, the difficulty one encounters in fixing the sense of the term. Nonetheless, as a result of its use in the debate, it has acquired a certain content, the essence of which we will attempt to capture in a provisional definition. . . before venturing to touch upon the dynamic we believe to be at work.

Integration refers to the possession, by the individual, of at least the capacity to participate in the institutions of the wider society. In our context, Quebec, such a capacity requires a functional command of French as well as the cultural baggage necessary to put such a strictly linguistic skill to effective use. What we have in mind here is contextual knowledge, a familiarity with the personnel and institutions of the society, and a certain historical consciousness with respect to the past of Quebec society.

As a result of the participation of such «integrated» minority culture members in the common or majority culture, there will necessarily be established a minority cultural presence which, if vigourous enough, will have an impact on the host culture. In other words, integration, if successful, is not likely to be an entirely one-way process: it will, without doubt, initiate a dynamic in which the host culture will not be entirely passive.

434

It is from this second dimension of integration — the impact on the majority culture of the cultural presence of the «integrated» culture — that there arises the possibility of a certain «convergence»; which indeed is part and parcel of the official thinking of the present government. Such a «convergence» suggests that by building upon the cultural elements already present in Quebec society (thereby including the minority cultures) and by encouraging participation of all these cultural elements in a common vehicle of collective expression — the French language and its attendant Quebec cultural forms — a developmental process is undertaken. Obviously, the success, or rather the openness and the creativeness, of such a dynamic is dependent on the effective presence of the various cultural elements as well as on a determination not to allow the atomizing drift that a rupture with history would produce... the Anglo-Celtic tradition is after all part of Quebec's history.

With respect to how the concept «integration» and the dynamic potential of an integration process which would not be solely one-way are envisaged by the official guardians of Quebec culture, the following texts are instructive. Speaking of what the base or departure point for a policy of cultural development in Quebec might be, the Minister of Cultural Development had this to say:

> Our policy must draw on sources both old and new. It reflects the reality of a people whose roots in the new world are centuries old and who have battled unfalteringly to defend their identity. It pays tribute to the contribution of the native peoples, the original inhabitants of this land, to the influence of the British and other minorities who settled among us.[55]

Given such a departure point, a cultural development policy would, it is hoped, foster a dynamic as opposed to a reification or the ossification of a closed system:

> ... To take charge of its collective means of expression while remaining a generous host to numerous cultural manifestations might well be the mode of development which will ensure the future of our culture.[56]

Within such an environment, an «integrated» (the term is used in the text[57]) English-speaking minority would be:

> ... more aware of its position as a Quebec minority, with its own cultural characteristics to define, with organic, vital relations to establish and strengthen in a society whose aspirations and objectives it shares to some extent. In short, *the anglophone cultural heritage has its own resources and its own problems*, as does

any other in the world today. *This must be considered in any development plan.*[(58)]

In more specific terms — with reference to the Jewish community in Quebec — this conception of integration is reflected upon, and elaborated on, in a particularly interesting 1978 pronouncement by the Minister of Cultural Affairs of the Government of Quebec, Denis Vaugeois.

> ... In Quebec we have no other objective than this one: to recognize the importance of the Jewish community established with us on the territory of Quebec as well as the toughness of its will to live as a homogeneous group, on the one hand, and, on the other, to invite this community to participate actively in the cultural development of the larger Quebec society which, as a whole, clearly expresses a new national pride...

> ... In today's context where Quebec society is asserting itself and expressing a new assurance, the Quebec Jewish community must assume its part of this general and lasting phenomenon. Once integrated in Quebec society and sharing the great objectives, the broad consensus, the distinctive cultural behaviour and the pride of being, the Quebec Jewish community will always necessarily have a special message for their compatriots of this country. And this particularity, which is that of another «minority» than our own on this continent, which has learned to overcome many more obstacles, we would like to hear from it and to understand it — not as a message coming from elsewhere, but as thinking which arises for us and amongst us.

> There is no question here of your committing yourselves to an irreversible process of total assimilation, quite the contrary. However, it is important that the Jewish community installed in Quebec integrate itself into this country as a community, and that it considers itself rightfully and completely at home here. And integrating oneself means accepting this land as one's own and «putting one's shoulder to the wheel» of the development of national society whose objectives and lifestyle you accept. Integrating America «à la Québécoise», with your compatriots and in this land. Your integration means also that you assume the past, the present, and the future of this country as a special way, a different way and eventually a distinct way of being.

436

Thus to integrate oneself means to participate by sharing solidarity, by keeping one's fundamental originality. For your community, as national Jewish communities, exists in so many countries.[59]

Admittedly, as students of social reality, it is difficult for us to imagine how such a dynamic could even lead to a lasting equilibrium between separate ethnic or cultural identities, on the one hand, and participation in the common collective culture on the other. In other words, we suspect that, indeed, the eventual outcome might well be assimilation, but assimilation into a Quebec culture would be quite different from what we now know... precisely because of integration.

Strategies for the Future

However, the very notion of integration assumes the maintenance of a distinct cultural community, distinct from that of the majority. Such an assumption raises the following question: *what are the conditions of minority cultural maintenance in Quebec and what are the appropriate strategies for the realization of these conditions?*

Alex Paterson and Storrs McCall of Positive Action have addressed this question. Before trying to set out their position, it is worth noting that they believe in integration; both in the participation aspect and in the maintenance of a distinct minority culture corollary:

> Positive Action... believes that the Anglophones must adapt to the new reality of Quebec. We are certain that there is no future is this province for those who refuse to speak French and that the strength of our society lies in our culture benefiting from its relationship with the others. But while we believe that English-speaking Quebecers should speak French so that they can participate fully in the life of the province, we also believe that our children should be able to learn their own language and culture.[60]

What, in the view of Positive Action are the conditions necessary that such should come to pass?

In general terms, the Committee insists on the necessity of maintaining «the bilingual and multi-cultural character of the province»[61] as well as a public ethic whereby «Quebec is for *all* Quebecers».[62]

Specifically, among other detailed proposals, the Positive Action Committee has advanced the following:

The right of every person whose mother tongue is English or French to have his children educated in the [sic] mother tongue anywhere in Canada;

The right of every person to communicate with the federal government and its agencies in English or French, anywhere in Canada;

The right of every person to health, social and cultural services, including broadcasting, in English or French, where numbers so warrant;

The right of every person charged with a criminal offence to be tried in English or French, where numbers so warrant.[63]

With regard to the strategy necessary to attain these conditions, Positive Action has been actively engaged in maintaining a strong anglophone community in Quebec, particularly by attempting to bolster the confidence and morale of those disposed to leave. In addition, as mentioned earlier, the Committee has been attempting to render Canadian bilingualism credible by supporting the rights of the French language elsewhere in Canada. Organizationally, apart from creating its own structures, the Committee has been active on two fronts inside Quebec.

The first of these consisted of taking the initiative in attempting to structure the anglophone population. Storrs McCall invoked this need in the beginning of 1978:

What I am suggesting. . . is that a certain degree of structure introduced into the Anglophone community would make it more cohesive and better able to cope with whatever pressures bear upon it.[64]

Such a structure was imperative, he believed, because:

Our community should have at least a rough idea of who it is, what people comprise it, where it is going and what it wants in life. A community ignorant of these things stands little chance of surviving a serious challenge to its existence.[65]

And it came to pass that such a structure was instituted:

We [Positive Action] sat on a committee with the task of organizing a Council of Quebec Minorities, and a

year later, in November 1978, this council was officially launched.[66]

Since, the Council of Quebec Minorities has dissolved itself to make way for
Alliance Quebec, an organization which aims to be both more militant and more
representative.

Regarding the second front, the Committee has assumed a political role in
mounting campaigns to modify government legislation. Its political presence has
found, no doubt, a more positive expression in a discreet but active participation in
the Quebec Liberal Party and the «Ryan» movement.

Reed Scowen has also addressed the question of, as he puts it:

> What are the elements of the minimal complete society,
> which will make it attractive for English-speaking
> Quebecers to stay in Quebec and for English-speaking
> people from outside Quebec to be attracted in reason-
> able numbers?[67]

Before we proceed to look at Scowen's «elements of the minimal complete
society», it should be recalled that he has three preconditions to finding a solution,
two of which are answers to questions raised in the previous section («that it [the
solution] be seen as primarily a Quebec problem »and» that the primacy of the
French language be accepted«), whereas the third deals with the «liberties» issue
(«that it be seen as a question of rights which must be worked for, rather than
liberties to be claimed»).[68] Here, then, are the elements of a solution Scowen
proposes:

> A network of accessible English language schools,
> CEGEPs and universities;
>
> A network of accessible English language hospitals,
> doctors, health and social services;
>
> The opportunity to use the English language in the
> National Assembly, the Commissions directly related
> to it and its tribunals;
>
> The possibility for English-speaking people to partici-
> pate in and take responsibility for the development and
> administration of their educational and health ser-
> vices...;
>
> The possibility of communicating with the government
> in English in all essential matters...;

Access to jobs;

The access to English language news media, entertainment and cultural institutions;

A resolution of the question of constitutional guarantees, both for their real value and their symbolic effect;

Attitudes. Overriding all of the substantive issues in the question of the attitude of the French-speaking community, the government, and the news media, to the presence of an English-speaking presence in Quebec... The feeling of «being welcome here» is probably as important as any legislation in the decision of members of the English-speaking community to come or to leave.[69]

Furthermore, in the following quote, Scowen Shows that he is convinced it is not realistic to expect everyone to be bilingual: «It seems clear that any English society in Quebec will always include a considerable number of persons who do not speak French»;[70] he insists on the need for «a definition of the position of the unilingual English person».[71]

It is likely [he advances] that investigation will reveal that one of the conditions of having an English community in Quebec will be an acceptance that a certain proportion of that community of necessity will always remain unilingual.[72]

At the level of the strategy necessary to attain these conditions, Scowen's thinking is composed of three elements. The first of these consists in an appeal to the population at large to appreciate the uniqueness and the cultural richness of a Quebec society in which two great cultures would cooperate together. Secondly, he accords a great deal of importance to the role of voluntary groups in providing leadership, in furthering the process of self- definition to which he often makes mention, and finally, in developing the essential new attitudes. He signals the efforts of three such organizations: Positive Action, Participation-Québec, and the Quebec Council of Minorities. Lastly, it is political action via existing political parties which appears to be the essential mechanism in his proposed strategy.

More recently, a more militant strategy has emerged in English Quebec, as manifested by the resurgence of the Free Choice Movement, the appearance on the scene of the Quebec For All group, and the metamorphosis of the Council of Quebec Minorities into a more mass-oriented pressure group called Alliance Quebec. This new militancy was born of a certain frustration with the failure to wrench concessions from the present government, the disappointment with the unexpected liberal defeat in 1981, the application of the unilingual sign legislation, and a rumoured educational system reform which would, if implemented, leave very few English-language school boards in Quebec. As for the strategy underlying the pursuit of the new militancy, there exists a resolve to create a province-wide organization which will be able to intervene more effectively in the political process. What we have here is a manifestation of a political involvement which is promising, in as much as it will undoubtedly result in greater anglophone involvement in the institutional life of Quebec. However, one would hope that with time this vehicle of participation in the Quebec political process will become less massively dependent on federal financing than it now is; if not, its own capacity to respond in an autonomous way to the Quebec situation may be seriously limited.

* * *

Having reviewed explicit strategies that are currently part of the debate on the future of English-speaking Quebec, we would now like to hazard our own reflections as to what an integrated anglophone minority might look like.

Like Mr. Scowen, we also would pose certain preconditions for integration. One of his — that the primacy of the French language in Quebec be accepted — would be amongst ours; however, we are less sure than he that the future of English Quebec is primarily a Quebec problem. . . the collapse of the English-Canadian tradition in Canada, be it in Quebec or elsewhere, is definitely a Canadian issue. Our second precondition would be not to lose faith with our tradition of due process and constitutional government; more specifically, the tradition of British-inspired justice and parliamentary government. Ironically, French-speaking Quebec has kept this faith, and were we — many of whom are the cultural heirs to the makers of these institutions — to break faith, it would be difficult to ask those who have adopted them to take us seriously in our demands for the rights and protection these institutions afford. Such an appeal to our sense of civilization may seem misplaced and unnecessary to many; however, it would not seem so to Lord Elgin who, as Governor General of Canada, suffered stoning *by an English mob* in Montreal in 1848 because he dared to insist on British liberties (responsible government) in Quebec.

Thirdly, in terms of preconditions, we are going to have to cultivate our sense of responsibility with respect to the public domain. A heightened sense of social responsibility is perhaps not only a prerequisite, but one of the cultural compensations of a minority culture. This matter of social responsibility — or rather the lack of it — is dramatized by the rapidly growing practice of an anglophone elite sending its children to French Catholic primary schools. What this practice reflects is a private rejection of, and a loss of faith in, the English-language school system while at the same time maintaining a public defence of that same system and of its demands. Such an inconsistent stance renders the mass of anglophones a captive clientele of a system presently incapable of preparing them to function adequately in Quebec, and hence condemned to exile or to second-class citizenship. The dilemma, of course, is that a substantial proportion of this elite depends upon the very same educational establishment of its middle-class jobs.

Proceeding now to what we see to be the conditions of the maintenance of English-speaking Quebec, these conditions are, we submit: an institutional re-vamping in the realm of education, the media and religion; the further development of an historical self-consciousness; and finally, the creation of an elite to fill the leadership vacuum which now exists in the under thirty-five age-group. Obviously, these transformations which we see as necessary are interdependent.

With respect to the institutional structure of English-speaking Quebec, the major challenge, as well as the most crucial one, is in the educational realm. Somehow the educational policy of anglophone Quebec society has to be restruc-tured in the light of long-term considerations as opposed to the present short-term reactive posture; most importantly, the challenge of preparing young people to participate in, and contribute to, Quebec society — should they wish to do so — has to be met. Otherwise, we will continue the present process of preparing young English- speaking Quebecers for out-migration or economic and social marginality in Quebec; despite temporizing arrangements which may in fact be producing a generation neither sufficiently equipped to participate in the culture of French-speaking Quebec, nor sufficiently aware of the English-speaking Canadian herit-age to be able to possess it and identify with it, leaving them vulnerable to some form of amorphous continentalism.

Incidentally, Dr. Stanley Frost's suggestion that voluntary retrenchment be considered by anglophone educational institutions is an indication of a willingness which was (as Lise Bissonnette underscores in her article in this book) remarkably absent, until recently, in the corridors of 6 000 Fielding Avenue. [73] In his «Anglo Education: Writing is on the Wall», Dr. Frost ponders:

> Will there in 10 years' time be enough English-language students to justify maintainting six or even four colleges, and two universities? . . . The time has come for McGill and Concordia, for Dawson, Vanier, John Abbott and Champlain, for the Protestant School Board of Greater Montreal, the English-Catholic sec-tor, the West Island School Board and all the English-language institutions in the province to get together and review the present state of affairs and plan, not in isolation and certainly not in competition, but in coop-eration and with hard-headed realism. [74]

There are a number of possible educational realm strategies which would merit the consideration of any Anglo-Quebec «hard-headed realist». One of these would be the possibility of arranging a school itinerary for Anglo-Quebecers that would permit them to enjoy, on the one hand, a common educational experience with francophones at one stage of their career; and on the other, to experience an authentic English cultural environment at another. Such a proposal is far from radical: it is the norm amongst the anglophone elite of child-bearing age. Another educational realm strategy worthy of consideration would be the requirement that all future personnel appointments to English-language CEGEPs and universities be of academics capable of functionning in French as well as in English — not an exorbitant demand when one considers that French is the lingua-franca of the society which is responsible for these same institutions and that in most «advanced» societies outside North America, faculty bilingualism is taken for granted. A third and final instance of such strategies, the spirit of which is to concert and change in order to save the essential, would be a voluntary limitation (at the expense of enrolments) of francophone clientele in English colleges. However, these are three suggestions among a wide range of possible strategies. The point is that unless such strategies are advanced, considered, and applied, it may soon be too late.

The media is an institutional sector of English Quebec which, until recently as least, was wasting. Very capable English-speaking journalists seem to have difficulties finding a spiritual and professional berth in the English media of Quebec. Might one of the reasons be that, whatever the structural causes (discussed by our contributors), the English media are usually one step removed from the pulse of Quebec? For instance, not a single word concerning the Carrel estate question — used by us as a caricature of the problem of English-speaking Quebec — transpired in the Montreal English-language press. In fact, the best way to attract the interest of the English media is to first provoke mention in *Le Devoir*, whereupon, having discovered a news item by reading the French press, the English media will beat a path to your door. Indeed, it is next to impossible to publish in English-speaking Quebec, whereas in French-speaking Quebec, one can take an acceptable text from manuscript to print quite easily in a matter of two months.

How long must we wait for a Quebec-based English-language review of critical comment and social and political analysis? One would imagine that three universities and five community colleges (CEGEPs) alone could sustain such a review. *The Montreal Review* was a brave attempt in that direction, but its ambitions or financial pressure — which ever came first — has forced it to succumb to the dictates of advertisement.

An institutional realm which has failed English Quebec in the post-war period more by omission than by commission is that of religion. If ever there was an institutional base whose role it is to provide spiritual consistency and strength to a community, it is the religious organizations of our Greco-Christian tradition. How responsive have they been to the socio-psychological needs of an English-speaking Quebecer beset by the uncertainties of the present timesHow much leadership have they been providing? The Ontario spokesmen of these organizations have been more present in the debate than the Quebec contingent of the same faiths. When the assertion that it is meaningless to speak of Protestantism in contemporary Quebec goes uncontested in the National Assembly — as was the case in the Carrel estate debate[75] — one feels justified in putting the question as to the effective presence of the English-speaking clergy.

Finally, with respect to the institutional structure of English Quebec, there is the perennial question of the presence of English-speaking Quebecers in the political process. English-speaking deputies, mayors, union or credit union presidents are, or have become, such rarities that they are objects of wonder. If such continues to be the case, we will have failed to make a contribution to Quebec public life, which contribution our cultural tradition has superbly equipped us for.

Even more to the point, we risk finding ourselves out in the cold as far as the political process is concerned. This was th contention of professor Léon Dion in his speech entitled: «What is the Place of Anglo-Quebecers in the Province».[76] He argued that «elite accommodation» at the level of political power between English and French- speaking Quebecers will not be possible if English-speaking Quebec confines its political participation to the Quebec Liberal Party.

Yet, there have been in recent history three notable instances of anglophone participation in the Quebec political process outside the Quebec Liberal Party. The first of these was a very significant anglophone component in the Montreal Urban Reform Movement as described by Henry Milner elsewhere in this book; the second is a now significant anglophone presence in the Parti Québécois; and finally, as we noted above, there is the political mobilization inherent in the objectives and strategy of Alliance Quebec which constitutes a definite involvement in the wider political process.

In terms of the civic responsibility inherent in being present in the political process, there is little doubt that Lord Elgin, who did so much to actualize and exemplify the best in the British tradition in this regard, would find post-war English-speaking Quebec seriously wanting.

Yet, the very allusion to James Bruce, the Scot who as the eighth earl of Elgin and Governor General of Canada became the mid-wife of responsible government in Quebec, highlights a condition which, if unchanged, precludes any significant institutional revitalization: that of a waning (if not now non-existent) historical consciousness. How many English-speaking Quebecers under forty could place the man? Those under twenty-five definitely cannot. They have, allegorically, been too occupied watching «Roots» to have seen the film version of «Two Solitudes», blissfully innocent of the fact that their having seen the former and not the latter is a demonstration of their own rootlessness. Yarowsky, in the speech referred to earlier, points to the historical character of the consciousness of the Quebec Jewish community: «What needs to be underlined here is that the Jewish community of to-day has forgotten its recent history in Quebec».[77]

When will we, for instance, rehabilitate Grosse Ile[78] where so many thousands of Irish immigrants and some of their French-speaking Quebec benefactors perishedWill the educational records (containing perhaps the only remaining documentary traces of the late nineteenth and early twentieth century life of English-speaking communities throughout Quebec) which are now lying in total oblivion in school board office basements and Quebec City warehouses be destroyed from plain neglect?

They will, and Grosse Ile will continue to be no more than a quarantine station for the occasional shipment of cattle unless we produce an indigenous elite which, we are quite convinced, could emerge only as the product of an institutional revamping and a revived historical consciousness. It is too much to expect your well-meaning CEGEP teacher from Toronto, or your sincere Anglican minister from New York or the capable plant-manager from England to do this. They have their own particular contribution, a function of their own history, to make... and they may not be around five years hence.[79]

Quebec is a small society, and the world of English-speaking Quebec is even smaller. A few score or so of young people whose imagination had been fired in the process of the reappropriation of their own and unique history in Quebec could change the face of English Quebec, and the future of Quebec... their society.

In fact, by reaffirming certain of the central values of their English-Quebec heritage such as, for instance, a very strong sense of place, a strong sense of the autonomy and responsibility of local institutions, and a social praxis informed by the conviction that only individual men and women, as opposed to institutions, can be depended upon for the creativity, initiative and morality which keeps a society vital and free, these same English Quebecers might conceivably help to deliver Quebec from the «mal français»[80] presently threatening its social fabric. How paradoxical that it might be an English value tradition that would help restore to Quebec its pre-modern vitality; and this it might do by contributing to the counter-modernization without which Quebec will be but the locale of a collection of «homeless minds».[81]

NOTES

(1) Sir Charles G.D. Roberts and Arthur Tunnel, eds. *The Canadian Who's Who 1938-39*, vol. III (Toronto, Trans-Canada Press):110.

(2) Quebec National Assembly, Journal des débats, Commissions parlementaires, deuxième version - 30ᵉ législature, Commission permanente de la Justice, Étude des projets de loi privés nos 104 à 110, le 26 juin 1974. No 108, pp. B-4147 à B-4154.

(3) This was revealed in a later exchange between Queen's University and the Protestant Committee of the Quebec Superior Council of Education.

(4) Law 104, Thirtieth Legislature, Quebec National Assembly, 1974 (emphasis ours).

(5) Commission permanente de la Justice, p. B-4150.

(6) *Ibid.*, p. B-4148.

(7) *Ibid.*, p. B-4151.

(8) *Ibid.*, p. B-4150.

(9) Alex Paterson, *On Being at Home in Quebec*, p. 1.

(10) Michael Yarowsky, *Quebec's Yewish Community...*, p. 7.

(11) *Ibid.*, p. 7.

(12) Storrs McCall, «Why Quebec Anglos Need a Voice».

(13) *Ibid.*

(14) Reed Scowen, *Reflections on the Future of the English Language in Quebec*.

(15) *Ibid.*, p. 23.

(16) *Ibid.*, p. 24.

(17) *Ibid.*, p. 23-24.

(18) *Ibid.*, p. 24.

(19) *Ibid.*, p. 25.

(20) *Ibid.*, p. 25 (emphasis ours).

(21) *Ibid.*, p. 26.

(22) Reed Scowen in a talk given before the St. James Literary Society on October 6, 1981.

(23) *Ibid.*

(24) See Eric Maldoff in *Sunday Express* (Feb. 28th 1982):4-5.

(25) See Section B of *The Montreal Star* (Sat. April 14th 1979).

(26) F. Remiggi, *Anglo-Quebecers and Socio-Political Diversity*, p. 4.

(27) *Ibid.*, p. 2.

(28) *Ibid.*, p. 7.

(29) The passages of Arnopoulos/Clift's book which are quoted in this text either do not appear in the English version or have been altered by Clift and Arnopoulos before inclusion in the English version. The reader should consequently take note that the quotes included here are translations from passages found in the French version.

(30) Dominique Clift and Sheila McLeod Arnopoulos, *Le fait anglais au Québec*, p. 224.

(31) *Ibid.*, p. 225 (emphasis ours).

(32) *Ibid.*, p. 245 (emphasis ours).

(33) *Ibid.*, p. 238.

(34) Indeed, English Canada is so pluralistic that we no longer have a tradition of national political and social commentary: it is obvious that the authors of *Le fait anglais au Québec*, one of whom is the graduate of a «Canadian» sociology department, have never read George Grant's *Lament for a Nation*, written in 1964 (or at least did not understand it).

(35) Storrs McCall et al., *The History and the Activities of the Positive Action Committee*, p. 9.

(36) *Ibid.*, pp. 17-18.

(37) From the Positive Action brief to the Task Force on Canadian Unity, delivered in January 1978 in Montreal.

(38) As reported in Storrs McCall et al., *The History and the Activities of the Positive Action Committee*, p. 5 (emphasis ours).

(39) See *Le Devoir*, Monday January 28th 1979, p. 4.

(40) Reed Scowen, *Reflections on...*, p. 20.

(41) *Ibid.*, p. 18.

(42) *Ibid.*, p. 22.

(43) *Ibid.*, pp. 36-37.

(44) Gouvernement du Québec, *A Cultural Development Policy for Quebec*, p. 63.

(45) Reed Scowen, *Reflections on...*, p. 45.

(46) Rev. T. Miles, *Christians in the New Quebec*, p. 3.

(47) *Ibid.*, p. 8.

(48) *Ibid.*, p. 10.

(49) Reed Scowen, *Reflections on...*, p. 27 (emphasis ours).

(50) Presumably the Honourable Joseph Clark (the speech was delivered June 5th 1979).

(51) Michael Yarowsky, *Quebec's Jewish Community...*, p. 8.

(52) Reed Scowen, *Reflections on...*, p. 14.

(53) Michael Yarowsky, *Quebec's Jewish Community...*, p. 14.

(54) *Ibid.*, p. 14.

(55) See Québec, le ministre d'État au Développement culturel, *A Cultural Development Policy for Quebec*, p. 1.

(56) *Ibid.*, p. 59.

(57) *Ibid.*; see p. 59: «...these groups should be integrated with a Quebec entity which is essentially francophone».

(58) *Ibid.*, p. 66 (emphasis ours).

(59) Denis Vaugeois, «The Jews and Quebec Society...», p. 8.

(60) Alex Paterson, *On Being at Home in Quebec*, p. 4.

(61) Storrs McCall et al., *The History and the Activities...*, p. 6.

(62) *Ibid.*, p. 4.

(63) Proposals made to the Task Force on Canadian Unity in January 1978.

(64) Storrs McCall, «Why Quebec Anglos Need a Voice», p. G-1.

(65) Storrs McCall et al., *The History and the Activities...*, p. 16.

(66) *Ibid.*, p. 16.

(67) Reed Scowen, *Reflections on the Future of...*, p. 38.

(68) *Ibid.*, p. 34.

(69) *Ibid.*, pp. 41-42.

(70) *Ibid.*, p. 42.

(71) *Ibid.*, p. 42.

(72) *Ibid.*, p. 42.

(73) Address of the administrative office of the PSPGM, which office also serves as a meeting place for other organizations of the anglophone educational world.

(74) Stanley Frost, «Anglo Education...».

(75) See above, in conclusion, section «The Problem».

(76) Léon Dion, *What is the Place of Anglo Quebecers...*

(77) Michael Yarowsky, *Quebec's Jewish Community...*, p. 5.

(78) Mr. David Payne, MNA, who arrived in Canada in 1971, has in fact, recommended the rehabilitation of Grosse Ile. See: *Grosse Ile, un parc national en l'honneur des Irlandais québécois*, Communiqué de Presse, March 17ᵗʰ 1982.

(79) Both the editors of the present book are themselves non-indigenous, having come to Quebec in the early sixties.

(80) This term comes from Alain Peyrefitte's book: *Le mal français* (Paris, Plon, 1976, 524 p.) in which the author examines the paralysing effect of overcentralization and irresponsible bureaucracies.

(81) The reference to «pre-modern» and to «counter- modernization» is to Peter Berger, *The Homeless Mind*, in which the author indeed cites the Case of Quebec (page 197) as an instance where the use of the term «counter-modernization» is appropriate.

Bibliography

The following is a bibliography of materials referred to by the authors in their articles and which are considered to be of general interest with regard to English Quebec.

Adams, John.
The Protestant School System in the Province of Quebec. London, Longmans, Green and Co., 1902.

A.S.O.P.E.
Aspiration scolaires et orientations professionnelles des étudiants. Quebec, Université Laval; Montreal, Université de Montréal, 1972-1980. 12 vol.

Berger, Peter, Brigitte Berger and Hansfried Kellner.
The Homeless Mind — Modernization and Consciousness. New York, Random House Inc., 1973; and Toronto, Random House of Canada Limited, 1973; New York, Vintage Books Edition, 1974.

Bernard, Paul et al.
L'évolution de la situation socio-économique des francophones et des non-francophones au Québec (1971-78). Montreal, Office de la langue française, 1979.

Berry, J., R. Kalin and D. Taylor.
Multiculturalism and Ethnic Attitudes in Canada, Ottawa, Minister of State for Muilticulturalism, 1976.

Boulet, Jac-André.
L'évolution des disparités linguistiques et revenus de travail dans la zone métropolitaine de Montréal de 1961 à 1977. Document no 127. Ottawa, Economic Council of Canada, 1979.

Bourque, Gilles and Nicole Laurin-Frenette.
«Social Classes and National Ideologies in Quebec, 1760-1970», Gary Teeple, ed., *Capitalism and the National Question in Canada* (Toronto, University of Toronto Press, 1972):185-210.

Bruce, Jean.
A Content Analysis of Thirty Canadian Newspapers (Jan. 1 to Mar. 31, 1965). Unpublished study prepared for the Royal Commission on Bilingualism and Biculturalism, Ottawa, 1966.

Bruck, M., Wallace E. Lambert and Richard G. Tucker.
«Bilingual Schooling Through the Elementary Grades: The St. Lambert Project at Grade Seven», *Language Learning*, 24(1974):183-204.

Bruck, M., Wallace E. Lambert and Richard G. Tucker.
«Cognitive Consequences of Bilingual Schooling: The St. Lambert Project Through Grade Six», *International Journal of Psycholinguistics*, (1976):13-33.

Bruck, M., J. Jakimik and Richard G. Tucker.
«Are French Immersion Programs Suitable for Working Class Children? A Follow-up Investigation», W. Engle, ed., *Child Language* (Royal Vangorcum, 1976):311-341.

Caldwell, Gary.
A Demographic Profile of the English-Speaking Population of Quebec, 1921-1971. Publication B-51, Quebec, International Center for Research on Bilingualism/Centre international de recherche sur le bilinguisme, 1974.

Caldwell, Gary.
English-speaking Quebec in the Light of its Reaction to Bill 22. Paper presented to the American Northeastern Anthropological Association, Wesleyan University, Connecticut, March 27, 1976.

Caldwell, Gary.
«L'histoire des «possédants» anglophones au Québec», *Anthropologie et sociétés*, 2, 1(1978):167-182.

Caldwell, Gary.
Out-Migration of English Mother-Tongue High-School Leavers from Quebec, 1971-1976. Lennoxville (Quebec), AQEM, 1978.

Caldwell, Gary.
Out-Migration of 1971 English Mother-Tongue High-School Leavers from Quebec 1971-1979. Lennoxville (Quebec), AQEM, 1980.

Caldwell, Gary.
Le Québec anglophone hors de la région de Montréal dans les années soixante-dix — Évolution sociodémographique. Series «Études et documents» no 4. Quebec, Conseil de la langue française, 1980.

Caldwell, Gary.
Those Who Stayed: How They Managed. Lennoxville (Quebec), AQEM, 1981.

Carter, Emmett G.
The Catholic Public Schools of Quebec. Toronto, W. J. Gage Limited, 1957.

Charbonneau, Hubert and Robert Maheu.
Les aspects démographiques de la question linguistique. Study S-3 for the Commission of Inquiry on the Position of the French Language and on Language Rights of Quebec. Quebec, Éditeur officiel du Québec, 1973.

Clarke, R.
In them Days: the Breakdown of a Traditional Fishing Economy in an English Village on the Gaspé Coast. Ph.D. Thesis (Geography), Montreal, McGill University, 1972.

Clift, Dominique and Sheila McLeod Arnopoulos.
Le fait anglais au Québec. Montreal, Libre expression, 1979. (See also: McLeod Arnopoulos).

Copp, Terry.
The Anatomy of Poverty, the Condition of the Working Class in Montreal, 1897-1929. Toronto, McClelland and Stewart, 1974.

Craig, Gerald M. (ed).
Lord Durham's Report: An Abridgement. Coll. «The Carleton Library» no 1. Toronto, McClelland and Stewart, 1963.

Cummins, J.
The Influence of Bilingualisme on Cognitive Growth. Series «Working Papers on Bilingualism» No 9. The Ontario Institute for Studies in Education, April 1976.

Cziko, G.A.
The Effects of Different French Immersion Programs on the Language and Academic Skills of Children from Various Socio-economic Backgrounds. M.A. Thesis, Montreal, McGill University, 1975.

Cziko, G.A.
«The Effects of Language Sequencing on the Development of Bilingual Reading Skills», *The Canadian Modern Language Review*, 32(1976):524-533.

Cziko, G.A. et al.
Graduates of Early Immersion: Retrospective News of Grade 11 Students and their Parents. Montreal, McGill University.

Dever, Alan R.
Economic Development and the Lower Canadian Assembly, 1828-1840. M.A. Thesis, Montreal, McGill University, 1976.

Dion, Léon.
What is the Place of Anglo-Quebecers in the Province? Speech delivered to the Canadian Club in Montreal, April 9th 1979. (Mimeo).

Frost, Stanley.
«Anglo Education: Writing is on the Wall», *The Montreal Gazette*, (Tues., Sept. 11, 1979):9.

Gagnon, M.
Attitudes à l'égard de la langue anglaise. Rapport de recherche, Faculté des sciences de l'éducation, Université de Montréal, Dec. 1972.

Gallagher, Paul.
A History of Public Education for English-Speaking Catholics in the Province of Quebec. M.Ed. Thesis, Lennoxville, Bishop's University, 1957.

Gardner, R.C. and P.C. Smythe.
«The Integrative Motive in Second-Language Acquisition», S.T. Carey, ed., *Bilingualism, Biculturalism and Education*, Edmonton, The University of Alberta, 1974.

Gosselin, André.
«L'évolution économique du Québec: 1867-1896», *L'économie québécoise* (Presses de l'université du Québec, 1969):106- 107.

Grant, George.
Lament for a Nation. The Defeat of Canadian Nationalism. Toronto/Montreal, McClelland and Stewart, 1965.

Greenlaw, J. and P. Orr.
Social Origin of Scottish Immigration to Lower Canada. Research Paper of the Montreal Business History Project/ Groupe de recherche sur l'histoire, HEC, Montreal, 1979.

Guindon, Hubert.
«The Modernization of Quebec and the Legitimacy of the Canadian State», *The Canadian Review of Sociology and Anthropology*, 15, 2(1978):227-245.

Hall, Douglas J.
«Being the Church in Quebec Today», *Perspective* (June 1978):1-2. Also printed in the June 1978 issue of *The United Church Observer*.

Hall, Douglas J.
«A Generalization on the Theological Situation of Protestantism in Quebec», *Theological Education in the 80's* (Fall, 1978):15-16, for the Division of Ministry, Education and Personnel of the United Church of Canada.

Hardin, H.
A Nation Unaware: The Canadian Economic Culture. Vancouver, Douglas, 1974.

Hughes, Everett G.
French Canada in Transition. Chicago, University of Chicago Press, 1943. Transl.: *Rencontre de deux mondes.* Montreal, Editions Lucien Pariseau, 1944.

Joy, Richard J.
Languages in Conflict. Toronto, McClelland and Stewart, 1972.

Kealey, G. (ed.).
Canada Investigates Industrialism. Toronto, Toronto University Press, 1973.

Kesteman, Jean-Pierre.
«Les travailleurs à la construction du chemin de fer dans la région de Sherbrooke (1851-53)», *Revue d'histoire de l'Amérique française*, 31, 4(March 1978):525-546.

Lacoste, Norbert.
Les caractéristiques de la population du «grand Montréal». Montreal, Les presses de l'Université de Montréal, 1958.

Lacoste, Norbert.
«Les traits nouveaux de la population du 'grand Montréal'«, *Recherches sociographiques*, 6(1965):265-282.

Lacroix, Robert and François Vaillancourt.
Les revenus et la langue au Québec (1970-1978). Series »Dossiers du Conseil de la langue française» No 8. Quebec, Éditeur officiel du Québec, 1981.

Lambert, Wallace E. and Richard G. Tucker.
Bilingual Education of Children: the St. Lambert Experiment. Rowley (Massachussetts), Newbury House, 1972.

Lambert, Wallace E., Richard G. Tucker and A. d'Anglejan.
«Cognitive and Attitudinal Consequences of Bilingual Schooling: the St. Lambert Project through Grade Five», *Journal of Educational Psychology*, 65(1973):141-159.

Lambert, Wallace E.
«The Effects of Bilingualism on the Individual: Cognitive and Sociocultural Consequences», P. A. Hornby, ed., *Bilingualism: Psychological, Social and Educational Implications* (New York, Academic Press Inc., 1977).

Lambert, Wallace E.
«Language as a Factor in Intergroup Relations», H. Giles and R. Ste Claire, eds., *Language and Social Psychology.* In press, 1978.

Laurin, Camille.
«French Language Charter», *The Canadian Review of Sociology and Anthropology/La revue canadienne de sociologie et d'anthropologie*, 15, 2(1978):115-127.

Lieberson, D.
Language and Ethnic Relations in Canada. New York, Wiley, 1970.

McCall, Storrs.
«Why Quebec Anglos Need a Voice», *The Montreal Star* (Sat., Feb. 25, 1978):G1.

McCall, Storrs, Alex Patterson and R. Brott.
The History and the Activities of the Positive Action Committee. Montreal, Positive Action Committee, 1978. (Mimeo).

McIntosh, Clark.
Devolution and Survival of the Rural English-Speaking Population in the Region North of Quebec City. B.A. Honours thesis (Geography), Montreal, McGill University, 1976.

McLeod Arnopoulos, Sheila and Dominique Clift.
The English Fact in Quebec. Montreal, McGill-Queen's University Press. 1980. This is a revised edition of the French version, *Le fait anglais au Québec*, Montreal, Libre expression, 1979.

Magnuson, Roger.
Education in the Province of Quebec. U.S. Department of Health, Education and Welfare, Office of Education, 1969.

Magnuson, Roger.
A Brief History of Quebec Education: From New France to Parti Québécois. Montreal, Harvest House, 1980.

Maheu, Robert.
La partie cachée de la mobilité linguistique. Paper presented at the Colloque de l'Association internationale des démographes de langue françaie, at Liège, Belgium in Sept. 1981. Unpublished.

Mair, Nathan H.
Quest for Quality in the Protestant Public Schools of Quebec. Quebec, Protestant Committee of the Superior Council of Education, 1980.

Mair, Nathan H.
Protestant Education in Quebec: Notes on the History of Education in the Protestant Public Schools of Quebec. Quebec, Protestant Committee of the Superior Council of Education, 1981.

Maldoff, Eric.
«The New Quiet Revolution — Fighting for the Rights of English-Speaking Minorities», Interview by Marvin Hershorn, *Sunday Express* (Feb. 28, 1982):3-7.

Mallea, John R., ed.
Quebec's Language Policies: Background and Response. Quebec, Les Presses de l'Université Laval, 1977.

Marsan, Jean-Claude.
«Montréal, de la domination au pluralisme», *Le Devoir* (4 fév. 1982).

Miles, Reverend T.
Christians in the New Quebec. Unpublished article, 1979. (Mimeo).

Millman, Thomas R.
Jacob Mountain First Lord Bishop of Quebec: a Study in Church and State 1793-1825. Toronto, University of Toronto Press, 1947.

Milner, Henry.
Politics in the New Quebec. Toronto, McClelland and Stewart, 1978.

Milner, Henry.
«Quebec Sovereignty and the Canadian Left», *Canadian Dimension*, 13, 6(March 1979):32-37.

Moir, John S.
«The Problem of Double Minority: Some Reflections on the Development of the English-Speaking Catholic Church in Canada in the Nineteenth Century», *Histoire Sociale/Social History*, 7(Apr. 1971):60.

Morton, W.L.
The Canadian Identity. 2nd edit. Toronto, University of Toronto Press, 1972 (1st edit., 1961).

Ouellet, Ferdinand.
Éléments d'histoire sociale au Bas Canada. Montreal, HMH, 1972.

Parmelee, George W.
«English Education», Adam Shortt and Arthur J. Doughty, ed., *Canada and its Provinces* (Toronto, Glasgow, Brook and Co., 1914): Vol. XVI, pp. 445-501.

Paterson, Alex.
On Being at Home in Quebec. Montreal, 1979. (Mimeo).

Pentland, H.C.
«The Development of a Capitalistic Labour Market in Canada», *Canadian Journal of Economics and Political Sciences*, 25, 4(Nov. 1959).

Percival, W.P.
Across the Years. Montreal, Gazette Printing Co., 1946.

Piédalue, Gilles.
La bourgeoisie canadienne et le problème de la réalisation du profit au Canada, 1900-1930. Ph.D. Thesis, Université de Montréal, 1976. Appendix III was published as a separate Study in *Revue d'histoire de l'Amérique française*, 30, 1(June 1976):3-34.

Porter, John.
The Vertical Mosaic: an Analysis of Social Class and Power in Canada. Toronto, University of Toronto Press, 1965.

Protestant School Board of Greater Montreal.
Statement on Bill 101 «Charter of the French Language in Quebec». (Undated).

Proulx, Jean-Pierre.
La restructuration scolaire de l'Ile de Montréal — Problématique et hypothèses de solution. Montréal, Conseil scolaire de l'île de Montréal, Sept. 1976.

Québec, le ministre d'État au Développement culturel.
«Perspectives d'ensemble: de quelle culture s'agit-il?» Volume 1 of *La politique québécoise du développement culturel*, 1978. English version: «A General View: The Culture Under Consideration» in *A Cultural Development Policy for Quebec*, 1978.

Quebec, ministère de l'Éducation.
Répertoire des organismes et des écoles. Yearly publication.

Rabushka, A. and K.A. Shepsle.
Politics in Plural Societies: a Theory of Democratic Instability. Columbus (Ohio), Merrill Company, 1972.

Remiggi, Franck.
Anglo-Quebecers and Socio-Political Diversity. Montreal, 1979. (Mimeo, unpublished). An earlier version appeared in the *Montreal Star* (April 1979).

Roberts, Sir Charles G.D. and Arthur L. Tunnell.
The Canadian Who's Who, 1938-1939. Toronto, Trans-Canada Press.

Ross, Aileen.
«The Cultural Effects of Population Change in the Eastern Townships», *Canadian Journal of Economics and Political Science*, 9, 4(1943):447-462.

Ross, Aileen.
«French and English Canadian Contacts and Institutional Change», *Canadian Journal of Economics and Political Science*, 20, 3(1954):231-295.

Rouillard, Jacques.
Les travailleurs du coton au Québec 1900-1915. Montreal, Presses de l'Université du Québec, 1974.

Ryan, William F.
The Clergy and Economic Growth in Quebec (1896-1914). Quebec, Presses de l'Université Laval, 1966.

Ryerson, Stanley B.
The Founding of Canada: Beginnings to 1815. Toronto, Progress Books, 1963.

Sancton, Andrew.
The Impact of French-English Differences on the Governmental Structures of Metropolitan Montreal. D. Phil. Thesis, Oxford University, (circa 1975).

Schachter, Susan, ed.
Working Papers on English Language Institutions in Quebec. Montreal, Alliance Quebec, March 1982.

Schmitz, Nancy.
«Éléments gaéliques dans le conte populaire canadien-français», J.C. Dupont, ed., *Mélanges en l'honneur de Luc Lacoursière. Folklore français de l'Amérique* (Montreal, Leméac, 1978):383-391.

Scott, Frank R.
«Areas of Conflict in the Field of Public Law and Policy», Mason Wade, ed., *Canadian Dualism* (Toronto, University of Toronto Press, 1960).

Scott, S.
The Relation of Divergent Thinking to Bilingualism: Cause or Effect? Report, Psychology Department, McGill University, 1973. (Mimeo).

Scowen, Reed.
Reflections on the Future of the English Language in Quebec. Montreal, May 1979. (Mimeo, unpublished paper).

Sellar, Robert.
The Tragedy of Quebec: The Expulsion of its Protestant Farmers. Huntington (Quebec), Canadian Gleaner, 1907. Other edition: Historical Reprint Series, Toronto, University of Toronto Press, 1974.

Siebert, Wilbur H.
«The Loyalist Settlements on the Gaspé Peninsula», *Transactions of the Royal Society of Canada*, Series III, Vol. VIII (March 1915):399-405.

Siegel, Arthur.
A Content Analysis: French and English Language Newspaper Coverage of the Federal Provincial Constitutional Conference, February 10-12, 1969. Unpublished Study, McGill University, 1969.

Siegel, Arthur.
Canadian Newspaper Coverage of the FLQ Crisis: a Study of the Impact of the Press on Politics. Ph.D. Thesis, McGill Univerfsity, Montreal, 1974.

Siegel, Arthur.
«The Norms and Values of the French and English Press in Canada: a Political Evaluation», W.E. Mann and Les Wheatcroft, eds., *Canada: a Sociological Profile*, 3rd edition (Toronto, Copp Clark Publishing, 1976).

Siegel, Arthur.
A Content Analysis, the Canadian Broadcasting Corporation: Similarities and Differences in French and English News. The study findings are cited in: Canada, *Report*, Committee of Inquiry C.R.T.C., 1977.

Simeon, R.E., and D. Elkins.
«Regional Political Cultures in Canada», *Canadian Journal of Political Sciences*, 7, 3(sept. 1974).

Sissons, C.B.
Church and State in Canadian Education. Toronto, The Ryerson Press, 1959.

Smith, Françoise N.
The Establishment of Religious Communities in the Eastern Townships 1797-1851. M.A. Thesis, McGill University, Montreal, 1976.

Spilka, I.V.
«Assessment of Second-Language Performance in Immersion Programs», *The Canadian Modern Language Review*, 32(1976):543-561.

«Statement Regarding Canadian Unity in the Light of Recent Political Developments in the Province of Quebec», The Executive of the General Council of the United Church of Canada, *Record of Proceedings of the Montreal and Ottawa Conference of the United Church of Canada*, 2(1976-1977): 18.

Stein, Michael B.
«Le Bill 22 et la population non-francophone au Québec: une étude de cas sur les attitudes du groupe minoritaire face à la législation de la langue», *Choix, le nationalisme québécois à la croisée des chemins* (Centre québécois de relations internationales, Université Laval, 1975):127- 159.

Stein, Michael.
«Le rôle des Québécois non-francophones dans le débat actuel entre le Québec et le Canada», *Études internationales*, 8, 3(June 1977):292-306.

Strafford, Philip (ed. and transl.).
André Laurendeau: Witness for Quebec. Toronto, MacMillan, 1973.

Taylor, Donald M. and Lise M. Simard.
Les relations intergroupes au Québec et la Loi 101: les réactions des francophones et des anglophones. Series «Langues et sociétés». Montreal, Office de la langue française, Éditeur officiel du Québec, 1981.

The Evolution of the English Education System in Quebec. Sillery (Quebec), l'Association canadienne d'éducation de la langue française, 1977.

Tucker, Richard G.
«Bilingual Education: The Linguistic Perspective», *Bilingual Education: Current Perspectives, Vol. 2*, Arlington (Virginia), Center for Applied Linguistics, 1977):1-40.

Turpin, Reginald.
«The Church in Quebec», *Report to General Synod on French- English Relations*, (The Anglican Church in Canada, August 1977):8.

Vallerand, Noel.
«Histoire des faits économiques de la vallée du Saint-Laurent: 1760-1866», *L'économie québécoise* (Presses de l'université du Québec, 1969):56-60.

Vaugeois, Denis.
«The Jews and Quebec Society: A Common Cultural Future», *Quebec at a Glance*, 9/10/11(1978):8.

Veltman, Calvin J.
«Les incidences du revenu sur les transferts linguistiques dans la région métropolitaine de Montréal», *Recherches sociographiques*, 17, 3(Sept.-Dec. 1976):323-339.

Wade, Mason.
The French Canadians 1760-1945. New York, MacMillan, 1955.

Waldron, Theodore, ed.
Letters and Journals of Lord Elgin. London, John Murray, 1972. Republished by Krauss Reprint Co., New York.

Yarowsky, Michael.
Quebec's Jewish Community: Bridging the Past and Present. Paper presented at the Annual Conference of the Jewish Communal Services held in Toronto on June 5, 1979.

LES PUBLICATIONS DE L'I.Q.R.C.

Cahiers

Collection « Culture populaire » (sous la direction de Robert Laplante).
1. Yvan Lamonde, Lucia Ferretti et Daniel Leblanc. *La culture ouvrière à Montréal (1880-1920) : bilan historiographique.* 9,00 $

Collection « Culture savante » (sous la direction de Maurice Lemire).
1. François Colbert. *Le marché québécois du théâtre.* 8,00 $

Collection « Diagnostics culturels » (sous la direction de Jean Gagné).
1. Jean-Robert Faucher, André Fournier et Gisèle Gallichan. *L'information culturelle dans les media électroniques.* 7,00 $
2. Angèle Dagenais. *Crise de croissance — Le théâtre au Québec.* 5,00 $

Collection « Documents préliminaires » (sous la direction de Pierre Anctil).
1. Danielle Nepveu. *Les représentations religieuses au Québec dans les manuels scolaires de niveau élémentaire (1950-1960).* 6,50 $
2. Jean-Pierre Dupuis, Andrée Fortin, Gabriel Gagnon, Robert Laplante et Marcel Rioux. *Les pratiques émancipatoires en milieu populaire.* 9,00 $
3. Renée Cloutier, Gabrielle Lachance, Denise Lemieux, Madeleine Préclaire et Luce Ranger-Poisson. *Femmes et culture au Québec.* 6,00 $
4. Jean Bourassa. *Le travailleur minier, la culture et le savoir ouvrier : quatre analyses de cas.* 5,25 $

Collection « Edmond de Nevers » (Sous la direction de Léo Jacques).
1. Lucie Robert. *Le manuel d'histoire de la littérature canadienne de Mgr Camille Roy.* 11,00 $

Collection « Identité et changements culturels » (sous la direction de Fernand Harvey)
1. Gary Caldwell et Eric Waddell, dir. *Les anglophones du Québec : de majoritaires à minoritaires.* 14,00 $
2. Gary Caldwell and Eric Waddell, editors. *The English of Quebec : from majority to minority status.* 14,00 $
3. Alain Vinet, Francine Dufresne et Lucie Vézina. *La condition féminine en milieu ouvrier : une enquête.* 18,50 $

Collection «**Instruments de travail**» (sous la direction de Marîse Thivierge).

    1.   David Rome, Judith Nefsky et Paule Obermeir. *Les Juifs du Québec — Bibliographie rétrospective annotée.*   13,00$

    2.   Yvan Lamonde et Pierre-François Hébert. *Le cinéma au Québec — Essai de statistique historique (1896 à nos jours).*   18,00$

    3.   Jean-Pierre Charland et Nicole Thivierge. *Bibliographie de l'enseignement professionnel au Québec (1850-1980).*   14,00$

    4.   Vivian Labrie. *Précis de transcription de documents d'archives orales.*   11,00$

    5.   Denise Lemieux et Lucie Mercier. *La recherche sur les femmes au Québec : bilan et bibliographie.*   14,25$

    6.   Sylvie Tellier. *La chronologie littéraire du Québec.*   18,50$

Hors collection

    1.   Paul Aubin. *Bibliographie de l'histoire du Québec et du Canada (1966-1975).* 2 tomes.   60,00$

Volumes

Collection «**Les régions du Québec**» (sous la direction de Fernand Harvey).

    1.   Jules Bélanger, Marc Desjardins et Yves Frenette. *Histoire de la Gaspésie.*   29,95$

Hors collection

    2.   Nicole Thivierge. *Écoles ménagères et instituts familiaux : un modèle féminin traditionnel.*   25,50$

    3.   Jean-Pierre Charland. *Histoire de l'enseignement technique et professionnel.*   25,50$

Revue

«**Questions de culture**» (sous la direction de Fernand Dumont et Gabrielle Lachance).

    1.   *Cette culture que l'on appelle savante.*   15,00$

    2.   *Migrations et communautés culturelles.*   15,00$

    3.   *Les cultures parallèles.*

Achevé d'imprimer à Montmagny
par les travailleurs des ateliers Marquis Ltée
en novembre 1982